D1563887

"For the past three decades, Greg Sterling has illuminated many aspects of Luke-Acts and helped modern readers appreciate it as an example of ancient apologetic historiography, in which a member of a societal subgroup deliberately Hellenizes its traditions so as to redefine itself within the context of the larger world in which the group now lives. All nine of the essays that comprise this new book—six revised and three new essays—usefully continue Sterling's project of helping us see how the author of Luke-Acts has shaped the past to speak to the present by defining Christian identity in ways both new and fascinating. Highly recommended."

—JOHN T. FITZGERALD
University of Notre Dame

"Combining several previously published but substantially revised essays with some new essays, Sterling has produced a tightly argued, exegetically rich monograph that further strengthens his argument for locating Luke-Acts within the tradition of apologetic historiography that had been honed in the East as an alternative to Greek traditions of history writing. Clear, methodical argumentation, command of the ancient sources, energetic engagement of recent classical and biblical scholarship, and intimate familiarity with key interpretive questions relating to Luke-Acts ensure that *Shaping the Past* will take its place alongside other field-defining works (Dibelius, Dupont et al.)."

—CARL HOLLADAY
Emory University

"Professor Sterling provides both scholars and general readers with a clear and careful case to upend the division between a 'Gospel of Luke' and 'Acts' as a founding story of how the apostles spread Christianity from Jerusalem into the cities of the Roman world. Instead both 'scrolls' belong to a single literary work, an 'apologetic history' that shows despised believers how to identify themselves as heirs to a lineage from ancient Israel to Jesus and the Church. Combining examples from comparable Jewish and Graeco-Roman historians and careful literary analyses of Luke and Acts, this book makes important contributions to both classics and biblical studies."

—PHEME PERKINS
Boston College

"Not every age produces a Mommsen or Momigliano—writers who laid new groundwork for research on ancient history. Gregory E. Sterling's monumental 1992 *Historiography and Self-Definition* is just such a work, identifying, for the first time, 'apologetic historiography' and illuminating, with respect to a range of important texts, its distinctive traits and aims. This indispensable sequel—now including treatment of Eusebius's *Ecclesiastical History*—updates and develops the thesis with fresh insights, illustrating how reconstructions of past events respond to various debates in the lives of their authors. A must-read for anyone interested in the history of the early church."

—CLARE K. ROTHSCHILD
Lewis University / Stellenbosch University

"Building on his earlier study *Historiography and Self-Definition*, Gregory Sterling develops a model for interpreting Luke-Acts as 'apologetic historiography'. By comparing Luke's work with Josephus's *Antiquities* and Eusebius's *Ecclesiastical History*, Sterling shows that they shared a concern for antiquity, but at the same time differed in the ways they presented history to their readers. Focusing on specific sections of Acts, Sterling shows that Luke wrote a continuation of the Septuagint and understood God's action in history through Jesus and the church as a period of fulfillment. This is an important study on Luke-Acts and ancient historiography by a world-leading scholar that will be read with great profit by scholars and students."

—JENS SCHRÖTER
Humboldt University

SHAPING THE PAST
TO DEFINE THE PRESENT

Luke-Acts and Apologetic Historiography

Gregory E. Sterling

WILLIAM B. EERDMANS PUBLISHING COMPANY
GRAND RAPIDS, MICHIGAN

Wm. B. Eerdmans Publishing Co.
4035 Park East Court SE, Grand Rapids, Michigan 49546
www.eerdmans.com

29 28 27 26 25 24 23   1 2 3 4 5 6 7

ISBN 978-0-8028-4873-4

Library of Congress Cataloging-in-Publication Data

A catalog record for this book is available from the Library of Congress.

For Adrian

Contents

Acknowledgments

THIS BOOK BEGAN with an invitation to deliver the Ben Gurion Deichmann Lectures at the Ben Gurion University of the Negev, Beersheba, Israel, in May of 2005. I elected to deliver four lectures on "Hellenistic Jewish and Early Christian Historiography." I chose the topic for two reasons. First, I wanted to illustrate Christianity's indebtedness to Judaism. Dr. Heinz-Horst Deichmann was a devout Christian who had taken over his father's shoe business and built it into Europe's largest shoe retailer. Sensitive to Germany's role in the Second World War, he became the largest benefactor of the Ben Gurion University—at least at that time—and was generous to multiple humanitarian causes. There was more than scholarship at stake in these lectures and I thought that the lectures should reflect that. Second, there were a number of issues that I had thought a good deal about in relationship to my first book, *Historiography and Self-Definition*, which I had completed fifteen years earlier. The lectures offered me the opportunity to pursue several of these. I am deeply grateful to Professor Roland Deines, Zipora (Zipi) Talshire (now of blessed memory), and Cana Werman, who ran the Deichmann Lectures, for the invitation to deliver these lectures and for their warm and generous hospitality during my time in Beersheba. They could not have been more gracious hosts; I still remember the dinner we had in Zipi's home.

Four lectures do not, however, a book make. In the last fifteen years, I have had a number of occasions in which to pursue additional concerns. Most notably, I was invited to deliver two other sets of lectures, which gave me the opportunity to work further on this project. Professor Jan van der Watt generously arranged for me to deliver lectures at three universities in South Africa in 2013: the University of Pretoria, Stellenbosch, and North-West University. I am deeply grateful to Jan for his exceptional hospitality and to the audiences at each university for their questions and comments. Finally, G. Scott Gleaves and Randall Bailey invited me to deliver a series of three plenary addresses at the F. Furman Kearley Conference for Biblical Scholarship at Faulkner University on Luke-Acts in June of 2016. I remember their hospitality with fondness.

In addition to these three series, I have offered a number of papers related to these chapters for various program units of the Catholic Biblical Association, the Society of Biblical Literature, and the Society of New Testament Studies. I have served as a co-chair of units devoted to Luke-Acts or Acts in two of these societies and am especially grateful to my co-chairs for their partnership and conversations, especially David Balch, Jens Schröter, and Knut Backhaus. I have also been fortunate enough to deliver lectures at other universities and seminaries including Abilene Christian University, the Lutheran School of Theology in Chicago, and Rochester Christian College (then Michigan Christian College). To all who listened patiently and asked questions or posed challenges, I am grateful.

There are many individuals who have shaped my thinking as this material coalesced. While there are too many to list, I want to express special appreciation to six who have been particularly important for this volume: Erich Gruen, my teacher who has not only been a mentor but a dear friend throughout my career; Carl R. Holladay, whose scholarship and friendship have been a *vade mecum* throughout my career; Harry Attridge, who was once my dean until we reversed roles at a different university and who has been a model of scholarship in both; John and Adela Collins, with whom—like Harry—I have had the privilege of serving on the same faculty at two universities; and John Donahue, to whom I proposed this project so many years ago and who remains an important mentor in my life. I want to express my appreciation to my colleagues at the University of Notre Dame and Yale University where I have spent my career, especially my immediate colleagues at Yale: Laura Nasrallah, Michal Beth Dinkler, and JanJan Linn, whose own work reminds me of the need for a dean to continue to work as a scholar. I do not thank these and other unnamed individuals because they agree with my views, but because they have stimulated me. The best measure of assistance is not agreement, but provocation to think.

Some of these essays have appeared in previous publications, although all have been modified. I am grateful for permission to use the following earlier materials.

"The First History of Christianity: Constructing Christian Identity from a Jewish Historiographical Tradition." *Pneumatika* 4.2 (2016): 3–22.

"Opening the Scriptures: The Legitimacy of the Jewish Diaspora and the Early Christian Mission." Pages 199–225 in *Jesus and the Heritage of Israel: Luke's Narrative Claim upon Israel's Legacy.* Edited by David P. Moessner. Harrisburg, PA: Trinity, 1999.

"Luke as a Reader of the LXX." Pages 161–79 in *Biblical Interpretation in Early Christian Gospels. Volume 3: The Gospel of Luke*. Edited by Thomas Hatina. Library of New Testament Studies 376. Edinburgh: T&T Clark, 2010.

"*Mors Philosophi:* The Death of Jesus in Luke." *Harvard Theological Review* (2001): 383–402.

"'Athletes of Virtue': An Analysis of the Summaries in Acts (2:41–47; 4:32–35; 5:12–16)." *Journal of Biblical Literature* 113 (1994): 679–96.

"'Customs That Are Not Lawful': The Social Apology of Luke-Acts." Pages 65–86 in *The New Testament in the Graeco-Roman World: Articles in Honour of Abe Malherbe*. Edited by Marius Nel, Jan G. van der Watt, Fika J. van Rensburg. Theology in Africa 4. Zurich: LIT, 2015.

Two doctoral students assisted with the transformation of earlier essays to follow a new style sheet: Brian Lee (who was a doctoral student at Notre Dame at that time) and Christopher Atkins (a doctoral student at Yale). I also want to thank Hannah Garza, a graduate student at Yale Divinity School, for compiling the indexes. All three students were immensely helpful. In addition to bringing these essays into a uniform style, I have attempted to make them intelligible to serious non-specialists by—among other things—placing Greek texts in appendixes and providing explanations and dates for ancient figures. I have also incorporated some of the relevant major works that have appeared since the dates of the original publications—although I make no claim to be comprehensive. I had to decide whether to release this work with the limits that it had or to delay it indefinitely. The case ultimately stands or falls on the ancient evidence. I hope that bringing these materials and reworking them allows the reader to follow the line of my argument in these various pieces, whether previously published or not.

Abbreviations

1 Apol.	Justin Martyr, *Apologia i*
2 Apol.	Justin Martyr, *Apologia ii*
1 Para	1 Paraleipomenon
1QS	Rule of the Community
AB	Anchor Bible
ABD	*Anchor Bible Dictionary.* Edited by David Noel Freedman. 6 vols. New York: Doubleday, 1992.
Abr.	Philo, *De Abrahamo*
ABRL	Anchor Bible Reference Library
Abst.	Porphyry, *De abstinentia*
Adv. Col.	Plutarch, *Adversus Colotem*
Aet.	Philo, *De aeternitate mundi*
Ag. Ap.	Josephus, *Against Apion*
AGJU	Arbeiten zur Geschichte des antiken Judentums und des Urchristentums
Agr.	Tacitus, *Agricola*
AJP	*American Journal of Philology*
ALGHJ	Arbeiten zur Literatur und Geschichte des hellenistischen Judentums
An.	Tertullian, *De anima*
Anab.	Arrian, *Anabasis*
AnBib	Analecta Biblica
Ann.	Tacitus, *Annales*
ANRW	*Aufstieg und Niedergang der römischen Welt: Geschichte und Kultur Roms im Spiegel der neueren Forschung. Part 2, Principat.* Edited by Hildegard Temporini and Wolfgang Haase. Berlin: de Gruyter, 1972–
Ant.	Josephus, *Jewish Antiquities*
Ant. rom.	Dionysius of Halicarnassus, *Antiquitates romanae*

Apol.	Plato, *Apologia*
Apol.	Tertullian, *Apologeticus*
Apol.	Xenophon, *Apologia Socratis*
As. Mos.	Assumption of Moses
Autol.	Theophilus, *Ad Autolycum*
AYBRL	Anchor Yale Bible Reference Library
BBB	Bonner biblische Beiträge
BCE	Before the Common Era
BETL	Bibliotheca Ephemeridum Theologicarum Lovaniensium
Bib	*Biblica*
BibInt	*Biblical Interpretation*
BJS	Brown Judaic Studies
BNP	*Brill's New Pauly: Encyclopaedia of the Ancient World.* Edited by Hubert Cancik. 22 vols. Leiden: Brill, 2002–2011
BSac	*Bibliotheca Sacra*
BTB	*Biblical Theology Bulletin*
BZ	*Biblische Zeitschrift*
BZNW	Beihefte zur Zeitschrift für die neutestamentliche Wissenschaft
ca.	circa
Cat. Min.	Plutarch, *Cato Minor*
CBQ	*Catholic Biblical Quarterly*
CBQMS	Catholic Biblical Quarterly Monograph Series
CE	Common Era
Cels.	Origen, *Contra Celsum*
Charid.	Lucian, *Charidemus*
Cher.	Philo, *De cherubim*
Christ.	Porphyry, *Contra Christianos*
CIJ	*Corpus Inscriptionum Judaicarum.* Edited by August Boeckh. 4 vols. Berlin, 1828–1877
CIL	*Corpus Inscriptionum Latinarum.* Berlin, 1862–
Claud.	Suetonius, *Divus Claudius*
Comm. Ezech.	Jerome, *Commentariorum in Ezechielem libri XVI*
Comm. Matt.	Jerome, *Commentariorum in Matthaeum libri IV*
Conj. praec.	Plutarch, *Conjugalia Praecepta*
Constant.	Seneca, *De constantia sapientis*
Contempl.	Philo, *De vita contemplativa*
Corp. herm.	Corpus hermeticum
CP	*Classical Philology*

CPJ	*Corpus Papyrorum Judaicarum*. Edited by Victor A. Tcherikover et al. 4 vols. Turnhout: Brepols, 1957–2020
CQ	*Classical Quarterly*
CRINT	Compendia Rerum Iudaicarum ad Novum Testamentum
D	Damascus Document
Decal.	Philo, *De decalogo*
Demon.	Lucian, *Demonax*
Det.	Philo, *Quod deterius potiori insidari soleat*
Dial.	Justin Martyr, *Dialogus cum Tryphone*
Diatr.	Epictetus, *Diatribai*
Diogn.	Diognetus
Div.	Cicero, *Divinatio in Caecilium*
DNP	*Der neue Pauly: Enzyklopädie der Antike*. Edited by Hubert Cancik and Helmuth Schneider. Stuttgart: Metzler, 1996–2003.
Dom.	Suetonius, *Domitianus*
DSD	*Dead Sea Discoveries*
Ebr.	Philo, *De ebrietate*
EJL	Early Judaism and Its Literature
EKKNT	Evangelisch-katholischer Kommentar zum Neuen Testament
Enarrat. Ps.	Augustine, *Enarrationes in Psalmos*
Ench.	Epictetus, *Enchiridion*
Ep.	Pliny the Younger, *Epistulae*
Ep.	Seneca, *Epistulae morales*
Epist.	Jerome, *Epistulae*
Epit.	Lactantius, *Epitome divinarum institutionum*
EPRO	Études préliminaires aux religions orientales dans l'empire romain
ET	English translation
Eth. nic.	Aristotle, *Ethica nicomachea*
ETL	*Ephemerides Theologicae Lovanienses*
Euthyphr.	Plato, *Euthyphro*
ExpTim	*Expository Times*
FGH	*Die Fragmente der griechischen Historiker*. Edited by Felix Jacoby. Leiden: Brill, 1923–2021
FJTC	Flavius Josephus: Translation and Commentary
Flacc.	Philo, *In Flaccum*
frag(s).	fragment(s)
FRLANT	Forschungen zur Religion und Literatur des Alten und Neuen Testaments
Fug.	Philo, *De fuga et inventione*
Garr.	Plutarch, *De garrulitate*

GCS	Die griechischen christlichen Schriftsteller der ersten [drei] Jahrhunderte
GLAJJ	*Greek and Latin Authors on Jews and Judaism.* 3 vols. Edited by Menahem Stern. Jerusalem: The Israel Academy of Sciences and Humanities, 1974
Gos. Eg.	III 2 Gospel of the Egyptians
Gos. Mary	BG 1 Gospel of Mary
Gos. Phil.	II 3 Gospel of Philip
Gos. Thom.	II 2 Gospel of Thomas
Gos. Truth	I 3 Gospel of Truth
GRBS	*Greek, Roman, and Byzantine Studies*
Haer.	Irenaeus, *Adversus haereses* (*Elenchos*)
HCS	Hellenistic Culture and Society
Hell.	Xenophon, *Hellenica*
Her.	Philo, *Quis rerum divinarum heres sit*
Herm. Sim.	Shepherd of Hermas, Similitude(s)
Hist.	Herodotus, *Historiae*
Hist. eccl.	Eusebius, *Historia ecclesiastica*
Hom. Act.	John Chrysostom, *Homiliae in Acta apostolorum*
HThKNT	Herders Theologischer Kommentar zum Neuen Testament
HTR	*Harvard Theological Review*
HTS	Harvard Theological Studies
HUT	Hermeneutische Untersuchungen zur Theologie
Hypoth.	Philo, *Hypothetica*
ICC	International Critical Commentary
IGR	*Inscriptiones Graecae ad res Romanas pertinentes.* 4 vols. Edited by R. Cagnat and G. LaFaye. Paris: Ernest Leroux, 1901–1927
Imit.	Dionysius of Halicarnassus, *De imitatione*
Inst.	Cassiodorus, *Institutiones divinarum et saecularium litterarum*
Inst.	Lactantius, *Divinarum institutionum libri VII*
Ios.	Philo, *De Iosepho*
JBL	*Journal of Biblical Literature*
JECS	*Journal of Early Christian Studies*
JETS	*Journal of the Evangelical Theological Society*
JJS	*Journal of Jewish Studies*
JQR	*Jewish Quarterly Review*
JRH	*Journal of Religious History*
JSHRZ	Jüdische Schriften aus hellenistisch-römischer Zeit
JSJ	*Journal for the Study of Judaism in the Persian, Hellenistic, and Roman Periods*

JSJSup	Supplements to Journal for the Study of Judaism
JSNT	*Journal for the Study of the New Testament*
JSNTSup	Journal for the Study of the New Testament Supplement Series
JSOTSup	Journal for the Study of the Old Testament Supplement Series
JSP	*Journal for the Study of Pseudopigrapha*
JTS	*Journal of Theological Studies*
J.W.	Josephus, *Jewish War*
KlT	Kleine Texte
LAB	Pseudo-Philo, *Liber Antiquitatum Biblicarum*
LCL	Loeb Classical Library
LD	Lectio Divina
Leg.	Plato, *Leges*
Legat.	Philo, *Legatio ad Gaium*
Let. Arist.	Letter of Aristeas
l., ll.	line(s)
LNTS	The Library of New Testament Studies
LXX	Septuagint
Marc.	Tertullian, *Adversus Marcionem*
Mart. Pol.	Martyrdom of Polycarp
Mem.	Xenophon, *Memorabilia*
Metam.	Apuleius, *Metamorphoses*
Migr.	Philo, *De migratione Abrahami*
Mos. 1, 2	Philo, *De vita Mosis* I, II
MS(S)	manuscript(s)
NA^{27}	*Novum Testamentum Graece*, Nestle-Aland, 27th ed.
NA^{28}	*Novum Testamentum Graece*, Nestle-Aland, 28th ed.
Nat.	Pliny the Elder, *Naturalis historia*
Nat.	Tertullian, *Ad nationes*
Nat. d.	Cicero, *De natura deorum*
Nero	Suetonius, *Nero*
n. F.	neue Folge (new series)
NHC	Nag Hammadi codices
NIGTC	New International Greek Testament Commentary
NovT	*Novum Testamentum*
NovTSup	Supplements to Novum Testamentum
NTAbh	Neutestamentliche Abhandlungen
NTS	*New Testament Studies*
OBT	Overtures to Biblical Theology
OCT	Oxford Classical Texts/Scriptorum classicorum bibliotheca oxoniensis

Oct.	Minucius Felix, *Octavius*
OGIS	*Orientis Graeci Inscriptiones Selectae*. Edited by Wilhelm Dittenberger. 2 vols. Leipzig: Hirzel, 1903–1905
Opif.	Philo, *De opificio mundi*
Or. Graec.	Tatian, *Oratio ad Graecos (Pros Hellēnas)*
PACS	Philo of Alexandria Commentary Series
Pan.	Epiphanius, *Panarion (Adversus haereses)*
Paneg.	Isocrates, *Panegyricus (Or. 4)*
Pap. London	London Papyri (see *Greek Papyri in the British Museum*. Edited by F. G. Kenyon et al. 7 vols. London: British Museum, 1893–1974)
P. Cair.	Cairo Papyri (see L. Koenen, "Papyrology in the Federal Republic of Germany and Fieldwork of the International Photographic Archive in Cairo," *Studia Papyrologica* 15 [1976]: 39–79, esp. 55–67 and 69–76)
PEQ	*Palestine Exploration Quarterly*
Peregr.	Lucian, *De morte Peregrini*
PG	Patrologia Graeca
Phaed.	Plato, *Phaedo*
Philos. orac.	Porphyry, *De philosophia ex oraculis*
Phoc.	Plutarch, *Phocion*
PL	Patrologia Latina. Edited by Jacques-Paul Migne. 217 vols. Paris, 1844–1864
Plant.	Philo, *De plantatione*
Pomp.	Dionysius of Halicarnassus, *Epistula ad Pompeium Geminum*
Praef.	Preface
Praem.	Philo, *De praemiis et poenis*
Praep. ev.	Eusebius, *Praeparatio evangelica*
Prob.	Philo, *Quod omnis probus liber sit*
Protr.	Clement of Alexandria, *Protrepticus*
PSI	*Papiri greci e latini*, Publicazioni della Società italiana per la ricerca dei papiri greci e latini in Egitto. 15 vols. Firenze: Felice le Monnier, 1912–1979
RAC	*Reallexikon für Antike und Christentum*. Edited by Theodor Klauser et al. Stuttgart: Hiersemann, 1950–
RBS	Resources for Biblical Study
Rec.	Pseudo-Clement, *Recognitiones*
Resp.	Plato, *Republic*
ResQ	*Restoration Quarterly*
RhM	*Rheinisches Museum für Philologie*
Sat.	Juvenal, *Satirae*

SBLDS	Society of Biblical Literature Dissertation Series
SBLMS	Society of Biblical Literature Monograph Series
SBLSP	Society of Biblical Literature Seminar Papers
SBLSS	Society of Biblical Literature Symposium Series
SBLTT	Society of Biblical Literature Texts and Translations
SCH	Studies in Church History
Scorp.	Tertullian, *Scorpiace*
SecCent	*Second Century*
SemeiaSt	Semeia Studies
Sert.	Plutarch, *Sertorius*
SFSHJ	South Florida Studies in the History of Judaism
SHR	Studies in the History of Religions
SNTSMS	Society for New Testament Studies Monograph Series
Sobr.	Philo, *De sobrietate*
Somn. 1, 2	Philo, *De somniis* I, II
Spec. 1, 2, 3, 4	Philo, *De specialibus legibus* I, II, III, IV
SPhiloA	*Studia Philonica Annual*
ST	*Studia Theologica*
STDJ	Studies on the Texts of the Desert of Judah
Stoic. rep.	Plutarch, *De Stoicorum repugnantiis*
StPB	Studia Post-biblica
Strom.	Clement of Alexandria, *Stromateis*
Subl.	Pseudo-Longinus, *De sublimitate*
SUNT	Studien zur Umwelt des Neuen Testaments
Test.	Testimonium/a
Thuc.	Dionysius of Halicarnassus, *De Thucydide*
Tim.	Plato, *Timaeus*
TJT	*Toronto Journal of Theology*
TQ	*Theologische Quartalschrift*
Tranq. an.	Plutarch, *De tranquillitate animi*
Tri. Trac.	I 5 Tripartite Tractate
TS	*Theological Studies*
TSAJ	Texte und Studien zum antiken Judentum
Tusc.	Cicero, *Tusculanae disputationes*
TynBul	*Tyndale Bulletin*
TZ	*Theologische Zeitschrift*
UBS[4]	*The Greek New Testament*, United Bible Societies, 4th ed.
VCSup	Vigiliae Christianae Supplements
Vita	Josephus, *Vita*

Vit. Apoll.	Philostratus, *Vita Apollonii*
Vit. Pyth.	Iamblichus, *De vita Pythagorica liber*
WBC	Word Biblical Commentary
WGRW	Writings from the Greco-Roman World
WMANT	Wissenschaftliche Monographien zum Alten und Neuen Testament
WUNT	Wissenschaftliche Untersuchungen zum Neuen Testament
ZKT	*Zeitschrift für katholische Theologie*
ZNW	*Zeitschrift für die neutestamentliche Wissenschaft und die Kunde der älteren Kirche*

OLD TESTAMENT PSEUDEPIGRAPHA

Jub.	Jubilees
T. Ash.	Testament of Asher
T. Benj.	Testament of Benjamin
T. Dan	Testament of Dan
T. Gad	Testament of Gad
T. Iss.	Testament of Issachar
T. Jud.	Testament of Judah
T. Levi	Testament of Levi
T. Naph.	Testament of Napthali
T. Reu.	Testament of Reuben
T. Zeb.	Testament of Zebulun

INTRODUCTION

HISTORIOGRAPHY AND SELF-DEFINITION appeared thirty years ago.[1] I have thought a good deal about the basic argument in the last three decades.[2] This book is a sequel that addresses a number of areas that I could not cover in *Historiography and Self-Definition*, tackles some topics that I have subsequently considered, and attempts to answer some of the challenges raised by colleagues. I have not assumed that a reader has read *Historiography and Self-Definition*, but have incorporated enough overlap in the basic argument so that this book could stand on its own. At the same time, every chapter of this book moves beyond the earlier work: it covers topics that were not treated—or cursorily treated—in the former volume. It also focuses on Josephus and Luke-Acts—primarily the latter—rather than offering a sweeping account of the historiographical tradition.

In *Historiography and Self-Definition*, I argued for the existence of an Eastern tradition of historical writing that I called apologetic historiography. The basic argument is that after Alexander the Great made his lightning-fast march east, subduing the ancient civilizations of the Near East and imposing Hellenic rulers with their culture as governing bodies over them, people in the East reacted by writing their own histories. They drew their inspiration from previous Greek ethnographic accounts of them, but insisted that they

1. Gregory E. Sterling, *Historiography and Self-Definition: Josephos, Luke-Acts and Apologetic Historiography*, NovTSup 64 (Leiden: Brill, 1992; repr., Atlanta: Society of Biblical Literature, 2006).

2. For a critical overview of how Luke-Acts has been treated as history that extends beyond this, see Clare K. Rothschild, *Luke-Acts and the Rhetoric of History: An Investigation of Early Christian Historiography*, WUNT 2.175 (Tübingen: Mohr Siebeck, 2004), 24–59. For an overview of how it has been viewed not only as a piece of historiographical writing but more broadly, see Craig Keener, *Acts: An Exegetical Commentary*, 4 vols. (Grand Rapids: Baker Academic, 2012–2015), 1:51–115 and Sean A. Adams, *The Genre of Acts and Collected Biography*, SNTSMS 156 (Cambridge: Cambridge University Press, 2013), 1–25.

tell their stories from an insider's perspective. They wrote in Greek rather than their native languages, creating hybrid accounts that paradoxically insisted on native traditions, but hellenized them so that they were intelligible within the context of the Hellenistic and Roman worlds.

I used a form of genre criticism as a means of evaluating how historiographical tradition evolved on the basis of the content, form, and function of a literary work.[3] This was not simply an exercise in literary taxonomy, but an attempt to understand how authors shaped their texts in order to create a set of expectations for readers. In order to provide continuity with *Historiography and Self-Definition*, I have retained these three evaluative components. At the same time, there has been a great deal of work on genre criticism since then.[4] Two of the major shifts that have occurred have been the abandonment of classical theories that relied heavily on formal elements and the recognition that genres are not static—they morph. One of the newer forms of genre criticism that I have found particularly helpful is prototype genre theory.[5] Drawing on the cognitive sciences, prototype theory posits a basic model that draws on our capacity to place things together in common categories, even though we recognize variations. We do not only measure or quantify constituent elements; we also measure them in relationship to the whole.[6] This allows us

---

3. I drew on the work of John J. Collins, "Introduction: Morphology of a Genre," *Semeia* 14 (1979): 1–20 and Adela Yarbro Collins, "Introduction," *Semeia* 15 (1986): 1–11.

4. For a critique of the theory in *Semeia* 14 in light of recent research, see Carol A. Newsom, "Spying out the Land: A Report from Genology," in *Bakhtin and Genre Theory in Biblical Studies*, ed. Roland Boer, SemeiaSt 63 (Atlanta: Society of Biblical Literature, 2007), 19–30. For surveys see also Carol A. Newsom, "Pairing Research Questions and Theories of Genre: A Case Study of the Hodayot," *DSD* 17 (2010): 241–59 and Michal Beth Dinkler, *Literary Theory and the New Testament*, AYBRL (New Haven: Yale University Press, 2019), 81–83 and 112–15.

5. The body of literature on this theory is now substantial. George Lakoff, *Women, Fire, and Dangerous Things: What Categories Reveal about the Mind* (Chicago: University of Chicago Press, 1987), 12–57, provides an overview of the research on categories as developed by cognitive science and scholars influenced by the new discipline. On the theory as applied to genre, I have found the following helpful: John M. Swales, *Genre Analysis: English in Academic and Research Settings* (Cambridge: Cambridge University Press, 1990), esp. 33–67; Michael Sinding, "After Definitions: Genre, Categories, and Cognitive Science," *Genre* 35 (2002): 181–220; and Tomoko Sawaki, *Analysing Structure in Academic Writing*, Postdisciplinary Studies in Discourse (London: Palgrave Macmillan, 2016), 31–67. Newsom, "Spying out the Land," 24–26, has an excellent summary of the theory. Benjamin G. Wright III, "Joining the Club: A Suggestion about Genre in Early Jewish Texts," *DSD* 17 (2010): 289–314, applies prototype theory to texts from Qumran, especially apocalyptic and sapiential texts.

6. Newsom, "Spying out the Land," 25: "The significance of this analysis of cognitive

to recognize features that have been transformed or modified through what theorists have called "conceptual integration" or "blending."[7] I have used prototype theory by creating a prototype that I call apologetic historiography. It is a result of reading a large number of ancient texts and perceiving a common pattern or schema. The best model for this is Josephus's *Jewish Antiquities*. In this book, I will routinely measure Luke-Acts against Josephus's *Jewish Antiquities* as an instantiation of the prototype—one could also use Manetho or Berrosus, but Josephus is closer to Luke-Acts chronologically and in content. I have, however, recognized that Luke blended other elements into this model and does not simply replicate it. Although not an essential component of the theory—prototype genre theory can work ahistorically—I have also asked whether the ancients had an understanding of the historiographical tradition (the prototype) or whether this is a modern construct. I ask because I have tried to work as inductively as possible, taking my *point d'appui* from ancient sources. Thus, like my earlier work, this book uses a form of genre theory to measure an historiographical tradition; however, I am using a different understanding of genre.

I used the concept of self-definition as a means of describing the function of the texts that participate in apologetic historiography. Just as literary theory has not stood still in the last three decades, so understandings of self-definition have not. Self-definition is most frequently formulated in terms of identity—a concept that has become pervasive in the humanities and social sciences—in current scholarship. In early decades of the twenty-first century there have been a number of works that have applied race theory or ethnicity or social identity theory to ancient groups.[8] I have participated in this effort and find

---

models for genre is that 'elements' alone are not what triggers recognition of a genre but rather the way in which they are related to one another in a *Gestalt* structure that serves as an idealized model."

7. Mark Turner and Gilles Fauconnier, "A Mechanism of Creativity," *Poetics Today* 20 (1999): 397–418, offer a number of examples but do not address genre. Sharon L. Armstrong, Lila R. Gleitman, and Henry Gleitman, "What Some Concepts Might Not Be," *Cognition* 12 (1983): 263–308, explain how this works with respect to the prototype (270): "There are privileged properties, manifest in most or even all exemplars of the category: these could even be necessary properties. Even so, these privileged properties are insufficient for picking out all and only the class members, and hence a family resemblance description is still required. Prototypical members have all or most privileged properties of the categories. Marginal members have only one or a few."

8. For a survey of modern scholarship on ethnic and race theories as they relate to the New Testament, see David G. Horrell, *Ethnicity and Inclusion: Religion, Race, and Whiteness in Constructions of Jewish and Christian Identities* (Grand Rapids: Eerdmans, 2020).

it intriguing.[9] At the same time, I recognize that the concept of identity as an analytical category has become so diffuse that it is challenging to use it with an agreed-upon understanding.[10] I also realize that modern understandings of ethnicity and race are quite different than the ancient grasps of *ethnos* and *genos*—"ethnicity" did not appear in English until the 1940s and there is no ancient Greek word for race, at least as we understand it. For these reasons I have opted to retain the terms self-definition and self-understanding (used interchangeably as equivalent concepts in this volume).[11] I find them less problematic for the purpose of identifying the function of historical works in an ancient historiographical tradition. I am not trying to sketch the specific Lukan view of the "group;" if I were, I would attempt to offer a more robust discussion along these lines. I am making a case that a constituent component of apologetic historiography is the creation of a self-definition for the group and that Luke-Acts participates in this tradition. Enough for analytical categories.

What about key labels? There has been a controversy in recent scholarship whether we should translate the term Ἰουδαῖος as "Jew" or "Judean."[12] I have retained the use of "Jew" largely because I am convinced that the geographical connection had become attenuated and cultural concerns had become more prominent by the first and second centuries CE. I also do not want to make the New Testament "Jew-free," a serious problem for contemporary Jewish-

---

9. Gregory E. Sterling, "Monotheism as an Identity Norm: Philo of Alexandria on Community Identity," in *A Question of Identity: Formation, Transition, Negotiation*, ed. Noah Hachem and Lilach Sagiv (Berlin: de Gruyter, 2019), 245–64. I used social identity theory or, more specifically, the social identity approach pioneered by Henri Tajfel. Tajfel defined social identity as "the individual's knowledge that he belongs to certain groups together with some emotional and value signification to him of the group membership" ("La Catégorisation Sociale," in *Introduction à la Pscyhologie Sociale*, ed. Serge Moscovici [Paris: Larousse, 1972]; cited by Michael A. Hogg and Dominic Abrams, *Social Identificaitons: A Social Psychology of Intergroup Relations and Group Processes* [London: Routledge, 1998], 7).

10. Rogers Brubaker, *Ethnicity without Groups* (Cambridge: Harvard University Press, 2004), 28–63, has argued that "identity" is overworked as an analytical category and offers three alternatives: identification and categorization; self-understanding and social location; and commonality, connectedness, and groupness.

11. Brubaker, *Ethnicity without Groups*, 44–46, offers a brief assessment of self-understanding.

12. The most important—but by no means only—advocate for the translation "Judean" is Steve Mason, "Jews, Judaeans, Judaizing, Judaism: Problems of Categorization in Ancient History," *JSJ* 38 (2007): 457–512. Mason's arguments against a cultural or religious identity are not convincing. See also Steve Mason and Philip Esler, "Judean and Christ-Follower Identities: Grounds for a Distinction," *NTS* 63 (2017): 493–515. For a different analysis of the evidence see Erich S. Gruen, *Ethnicity in the Ancient World—Did it Matter?* (Berlin: de Gruyter, 2020).

Christian relations that is in direct opposition to the argument of Luke-Acts.[13] Similarly, I have used the word "Christian" for followers of Jesus. Again, I recognize that this was a term that was first used by outsiders of the followers of Jesus and was not a self-designation. Yet, it does appear in our text twice (Acts 11:26; 26:28) and allows readers to immediately grasp that we are referring to Jesus's followers. It is important to understand that the authors whom we will consider used multiple terms for their group or individual members of their group and did not use a single designation for the people whose story they told and for whom they offered a self-definition. I will do the same. Finally, I have used the word "religion." Again, I understand that there is a difference between the contemporary understanding of religion and the ancient view.[14] The ancients did, however, have an understanding of religion and specific terms for it. For this reason, I have kept the term. In short, where there is an ancient term or concept, I have tried to maintain it and not impose modern constructions on it.

Let me now summarize the argument. This work is organized into three parts with three chapters in each part. Part 1 explores the historiographical tradition proper. When I wrote *Historiography and Self-Definition,* I wanted to extend the treatment to include Eusebius, but the work was already long enough. I have expanded my earlier discussion to include Eusebius in chapter 1 and used this as a means of introducing apologetic historiography to the reader. I will continue to use the description of the prototype that I offered in the earlier volume: *Apologetic historiography is the story of a subgroup of people in an extended prose narrative written by a member of the group who follows the group's own traditions but hellenizes them in an effort to establish the identity of the group within the setting of the larger world.* The first chapter suggests that the *Jewish Antiquities* of Josephus, Luke-Acts, and the *Ecclesiastical History* of Eusebius all tell the story of their subgroup in narratives that span the history of the subgroup by relating the story based on their own records, but in literary forms that relate them to the larger world. The chapter concentrates on the concern for antiquity since this was a point of emphasis for Josephus and of real concern for both the author of Luke-Acts and Eusebius.

The relationship of each subgroup to antiquity sets up chapter 2 that tackles the issue whether apologetic historiography is a modern construct or was a

13. On the challenge the elimination of "Jew" in the New Testament creates see Amy-Jill Levine, *The Misunderstood Jew: The Church and the Scandal of the Jewish Jesus* (New York: HarperOne, 2006), 159–66.

14. See Brent Nongbri, *Before Religion: A History of a Modern Concept* (New Haven: Yale University Press, 2013), who accentuates the difference. This was a major argument in Mason, "Jews, Judaeans, Judaizing, Judaism," 480–88.

recognizable historiographical tradition in the ancient world. In *Historiography and Self-Definition*, I took my *aphormē* or starting point from Josephus's historiographical excursus in *Against Apion*, but was not able to work through his presentation of the tradition or evaluate it. I do so in chapter 2 by working through Josephus's excursus and then evaluating it in light of the remains that we have for the tradition among Egyptian, Phoenician, and Babylonian historians. All engaged in a common polemic against Greek historians. They claimed that in contrast to the investigative methods of Greek ethnographers and historians who visited lands and asked questions (the word ἱστορέω ["inquire," "observe"] is the Greek word from which history comes), they translated their own sacred traditions and were sensitive to the quality of the Greek in which they wrote. They appear to be aware that they were writing in an Eastern tradition that was set over against Hellenic models.

This leads to the question of Luke-Acts. One of the important issues is whether the two scrolls belong together or are two treatises written by a common author or even by two different authors. Like many others, I had noted that the author of Luke omitted the temple charge against Jesus at his trial (Mark 14:58 // Luke 22:66–67) and then introduced it in the Stephen episode in Acts (Acts 6:12–14). I asked myself whether there was evidence that Luke had planned Acts at the time that he composed Luke. Chapter 3 argues that there are at least four examples of this design. This means that the two scrolls were planned as a unit. But this raises the question of why they circulated separately. There are a number of examples of multiscroll works for which ancient authors released the scrolls seriatim or at least some of them in stages. I suggest that this helps us understand differences between Luke and Acts and their transmission history. The two scrolls should therefore be viewed as a single work that tells the story of the "Way" from the time of John the Baptist through the life of Paul.

The author follows the basic conventions of apologetic historiography in telling this story. Like others in this same historiographical tradition, he created a hybrid narrative that drew on internal traditions (part 2) and hellenized them (part 3). The central issue for the former is the relationship of Luke-Acts to the LXX (the Greek Scriptures). Chapter 4 attempts to explain why Luke did not write a *Christian Antiquities* in the same way that Josephus wrote a *Jewish Antiquities*. The Jewish historian viewed the LXX as a precedent and offered the *Jewish Antiquities* as a *replacement* of the LXX for non-Jews in the larger Greco-Roman world. Luke had a different understanding of the LXX: he viewed the LXX as an unfinished work and wrote a *continuation* of it in the same way that Greek historians continued the unfinished work of their predecessors. The same criteria that permit us to recognize continuations among Greek historians are present in the relationship between the LXX and Luke-Acts. In this way, Luke-Acts spans the entire history of Israel and the Way: such a modification is a good example of "conceptual integration."

Chapters 5 and 6 ask how Luke understood the story of Israel in the LXX. There are two long speeches in Acts that retell the story of Israel. The basic argument in these chapters is that Luke did not read the LXX tabula rasa, but read it through the lens of earlier Jewish retellings. Chapter 5 wrestles with the longest speech in the work, Stephen's speech in Acts 7:2-50. There was a tradition among Hellenistic Jewish historians of arguing for the legitimacy of their diaspora locales by creating connections between Israel's ancestors and their places. We have at least three examples of this: Cleodemus Malchus, Pseudo-Eupolemus, and Artapanus. The last, in particular, is helpful since he focused on Abraham, Joseph, and Moses in Egypt (frags. 1-3), the same three figures that dominate the Stephen speech. There is solid evidence that the author of Luke-Acts knew some of the same exegetical traditions that we find in Hellenistic Jewish authors living in the diaspora. This suggests that the author knew some of this literature. It also suggests that the early Christian author used these Jewish precedents to argue that the move out of Jerusalem in 1:1-8:3 to Judea and Samaria in 8:4-12:25 was not surprising: God has always dealt with people away from the temple.

The second long retelling of the story of Israel occurs in Paul's speech in Antioch of Pisidia. The speech is carefully crafted and delineates three sections by direct addresses to the audience (Acts 13:16, 26, and 38). The first section tells the story of Israel from the ancestors through David. The scope of this retelling reflects a traditional Jewish understanding as we see in Psalm 77(78) and Pseudo-Philo's *Biblical Antiquities*. The second section of the speech associates Jesus with David by applying a series of three texts to the traditional core of the gospel: the death, burial, resurrection, and appearances of Jesus. The third section is the most Pauline formulation in Luke-Acts. Interestingly, this threefold division corresponds to the author's understanding of salvation history: the period of Israel up until John or the period of promise (Luke 16:16); the story of Jesus as related in the gospel and the story of the church culminating in Paul or the period of fulfillment. The argument is that the text is a fulfillment narrative demonstrating how God has worked through the history of the story as told. The speech thus reinforces the argument in chapter 4 that Luke-Acts is a continuation of the LXX.

Part 3 explores some of the ways that the author casts this story in terms that move it into the larger Greco-Roman world. Chapter 7 considers the way in which the author told the story of Jesus's death in Luke. Perhaps the most remarkable feature of this account is the calmness of Jesus as he confronts death. Why is Jesus so serene? There was a tradition of categorizing the story of the deaths of heroes as noble, especially those of philosophers who were unjustly executed by the state or a tyrant. Within this tradition, the death of Socrates became a model that was widely used. The chapter argues that the *exemplum Socratis* influenced the account of the death of Jesus in Luke. This is evident in the serenity of Jesus in facing death and the proclamation of his innocence (he was δίκαιος) by the centurion at the cross (Luke 23:47), the same claim made for Socrates in many sources, including a famous *chreia*. The text diffuses concerns that the founding figure of the movement was ignominiously executed by linking Jesus's death to the death of the most famous philosopher who had died nobly.

The author of Luke-Acts makes the same type of argument for the early Jerusalem community in the three summaries devoted to it in Acts (2:41–47; 4:32–35; 5:12–16). These summaries were Lukan compositions intended to describe the community and to serve as transitions for the surrounding narratives. But did the author have a model in the descriptions of the community? Chapter 8 argues that he did: the descriptions of religious and philosophical groups that were included for apologetic reasons by native authors or as groups to be admired by non-native authors. I compare the description of the Jerusalem community with the descriptions of the Egyptian priests in Chaeremon, the Essenes in Pliny, the Indian sages in Arrian and Philostratus, the naked Egyptian sages in Philostratus, and the Pythagoreans in Iamblichus. I also consider the use of the same tradition in the descriptions that we find of the Essenes in Philo and Josephus. The agreement in the topoi among these texts is striking. Luke was arguing that Christianity had its "athletes of virtue" in the same way that Philo and Josephus argued that Jews did in the persons of the Essenes.

The concern for social respectability is the theme of the final chapter, which examines pagan critiques of early Christians and their responses. Chapter 9 argues that the concerns evident in the apologetic literature of the second and third centuries CE were already present in Luke-Acts, especially overturning charges about social status, lack of respect for the established order, and rumors of obscene rituals. The text of Luke-Acts goes out of its way to deflect any hint that these charges have any validity. Why? The author was moving

Christianity out into the larger world, not as a revolutionary movement, but as a respectable and peaceful movement.

Was Luke-Acts influenced by the tradition of apologetic historiography? The words of Dionysius of Halicarnassus are apropos at this point: "You and other scholars must each judge whether I have made truthful and cogent arguments."[15]

---

15. Dionysius of Halicarnassus, *Thuc.* 2.

PART ONE

The Historiographical Tradition

Luke-Acts as Apologetic Historiography

1

Interpretatio Christiana

Constructing Christian Identity from a Jewish Historiographical Tradition

Men can do nothing without the make-believe of a beginning.

George Eliot, *Daniel Deronda*[1]

Eusebius of Caesarea (ca. 260–340 CE) opened his *Ecclesiastical History* with a long sentence setting out seven major themes that he proposed to undertake in his narrative.[2] The second sentence asks the readers to be understanding of this complex effort: "But the account asks for leniency for me from the considerate, since it is admittedly beyond our power to make our promise complete and without a gap." Eusebius felt justified in opening with such a disclaimer since "we are the first to enter into this subject as if we were attempting to take a desolate and untraveled road." The bishop maintained the journey metaphor as he appealed for divine assistance: "We pray that God will be our guide and that the power of the Lord will be our helper since nowhere can we find the merest footprint of anyone who has traveled the same road before us." The only exceptions were "those little suggestions by which some in one way and some in other ways have left us partial narratives of the times through which they have traversed."[3] The Caesarean gathered these hints together and gave them coherence in a historical narrative.[4] The process led him to conclude: "I think that it is especially necessary for me to work on this

---

1. George Eliot, *Daniel Deronda*, ed. Graham Handley (Oxford: Clarendon, 1984), 1. I selected this quotation because it opens the last novel of George Eliot (1876) in which she expressed her sympathy for the Jewish people, a sympathy that she did not share all of her life.

2. Eusebius, *Hist. eccl.* 1.1.1–2. For an analysis see below. All translations in this work—including the translations of Scripture—are my own unless otherwise noted.

3. Eusebius, *Hist. eccl.* 1.1.3.

4. Eusebius, *Hist. eccl.* 1.1.4.

subject because I am not aware of any ecclesiastical authors up till now who have made any effort concerning this kind of writing."[5]

Eusebius was not the first to claim that he was opening up a new path in historiography. Polybius (ca. 200–post 118 BCE) began his narrative by explaining that "none of our contemporaries have taken in hand to write a universal history."[6] While he had a predecessor in Ephorus (ca. 405–330 BCE),[7] the Cymian was of an earlier generation and not a contemporary.[8] Dionysius of Halicarnassus (floruit late first century BCE) made a similar claim for his *Roman Antiquities*: "Up until our own time no accurate history in Greek about the Romans has appeared, except for summary and entirely too brief epitomes."[9] He went on to mention a number of predecessors including: Hieronymus of Cardia (floruit 319–272 BCE), who wrote a history of the Successors of Alexander that extended from the death of Alexander to Pyrrhus's battles with Rome;[10] Timaeus of Tauromenium (ca. 350–260 BCE), the historian of the Greek West whose *Sicilian History* in thirty-eight books included a comprehensive treatment of Rome down to 274 BCE;[11] Polybius (ca. 200–post 118 BCE), whose forty scrolls dealt with the rise of Rome and its aftermath in his own lifetime; and several lesser known historians.[12] They had not covered the scope that Dionysius would.[13] The claim to be the first is thus something of a trope, made by an author both to point out the originality of his or her contribution and to distance it from the works of their contemporaries and predecessors.

What should we make of Eusebius's claim? On the one hand, there can be no doubt that he stands at the head of a tradition of historical writing.[14] He had

5. Eusebius, *Hist. eccl.* 1.1.5.

6. Polybius 1.4.2. See also 9.1.2–3.

7. *FGH* 70.

8. Polybius 5.33.2. Diodorus Siculus 5.1.4, thought that Ephorus wrote a universal history. On this tradition, see John Marincola, "Universal History from Ephorus to Diodorus," in *A Companion to Greek and Roman Historiography*, ed. John Marincola; 2 vols. (Oxford: Blackwell, 2007; repr., Chichester: Wiley-Blackwell, 2011), 171–79, who provides analyses of Ephorus, Theopompus, and Diodorus.

9. Dionysius, *Ant. rom.* 1.5.4.

10. *FGH* 154. See Diodorus Siculus 18–20, which depends heavily on Hieronymus.

11. *FGH* 566.

12. Dionysius, *Ant. rom.* 1.6.1–2.

13. On Dionysius's contribution see Emilio Gabba, *Dionysius and "The History of Archaic Rome*," Sather Classical Lectures 56 (Berkeley: University of California Press, 1991), esp. 1–22.

14. On this tradition see Robert A. Markus, "Church History and the Early Church Historians," SCH 11 (1975): 1–17; Brian Croke and Alanna M. Emmett, "Historiography in

a number of successors who maintained his focus on the church: Gelazius, Eusebius's second successor as bishop of Caesarea (367–395 CE);[15] Philostorgius (ca. 368–ca. 439 CE), an Arrian historian;[16] and three significant successors in the 440s: Socrates (ca. 380–450 CE),[17] Sozomen (floruit 440s CE),[18] and Theodoret (ca. 393–466 CE).[19] Cassiodorus (ca. 485–580 CE) later had the last three translated into Latin in a conflated version that is known as the *Historia ecclesiastica tripartita.* Eusebius, like Thucydides before him, can lay claim to stand at the head of a distinct historiographical tradition.

On the other hand, we may ask whether Eusebius had any predecessors. Sozomen mentioned three: Clemens, Hegesippus, and Julius Africanus.[20] The identity of Clemens is not entirely clear. It may be Clement of Rome (floruit 96 CE) who wrote a letter to the church at Corinth at the end of the first century CE,[21] but is more likely Clement of Alexandria (ca. 150–220 CE), the Middle Platonic early Christian writer who did not write a history.[22] Eusebius is our primary source for Hegesippus (second century CE) who appears to have been

---

Late Antiquity: An Overview," in *History and Historians in Late Antiquity,* ed. Brian Croke and Alanna M. Emmett (Sydney: Pergamon, 1983), 1–12; Glenn F. Chestnut, *The First Christian Histories: Eusebius, Socrates, Sozomen, Theodoret, and Evagrius,* 2nd ed. (Macon, GA: Mercer University Press, 1986); Arnaldo Momigliano, *The Classical Foundations of Modern Historiography,* Sather Classical Lectures 54 (Berkeley: University of California Press, 1990), 132–52; and Glenn F. Chestnut, "Eusebius, Augustine, Orosius, and the Later Patristic and Medieval Christian Historians," in *Eusebius, Christianity and Judaism,* ed. Harold W. Attridge and Gohei Hata (Detroit: Wayne State University Press, 1992), 687–713.

15. The standard critical edition is Gerhard Loeschcke, ed., *Gelasius Kirchengeschichte,* GCS 28 (Leipzig: Hinrichs, 1918).

16. The standard critical edition is Joseph Bidez, ed., *Philostorgius, Kirchengeschichte: Mit dem Leben des Lucian von Antiochien und den Fragmenten eines arianischen Historiographen,* 3rd ed., GCS n. F. 21 (Berlin: Akademie-Verlag, 1981).

17. The critical edition is Günther C. Hansen, ed., *Sokrates, Kirchengeschichte,* GCS n. F. 1 (Berlin: Akademie-Verlag, 1995).

18. The critical edition was prepared by Joseph Bidez, *Sozomenus, Kirchengeschichte,* 2nd ed., GCS n. F. 4 (Berlin: Akademie-Verlag, 1995).

19. See Günther C. Hansen, *Theodoret, Kirchengeschichte,* 3rd ed., GCS n. F. 5 (Berlin: Akademie-Verlag, 1996).

20. Sozomen 1.1.

21. This was suggested by Valesius in his edition of Sozomen (1659–1668). Eusebius referred to Clement of Rome a number of times in his *Hist. eccl.* 3.4.9; 3.15.1–16.1; 3.21.1; 3.38.2–4; 3.39.1; 4.22.1; 4.23.11; 5.9.2–4; 6.13.6.

22. Eusebius mentioned Clement of Alexandria repeatedly in *Hist. eccl.* and knew his writings: 2.1.3–5; 2.23.19; 3.23.2, 5–19; 4.26.4; 5.11.1–5; 5.28.4; 6.6.1; 6.11.6; 6.13.1–14.9, esp. 1–3 for his works.

an anti-Gnostic writer.[23] Julius Africanus (ca. 160–240 CE) is the well-known chronographer about whom Eusebius said, "He was not an ordinary historian."[24] While Eusebius knew and used the works of these earlier Christian writers with appreciation, there is no evidence that they served as a model for his work.

There are at least two other sources that are worth considering: Luke-Acts in the New Testament[25] and the works of Josephus, especially the *Jewish Antiquities*.[26] I am by no means the first to suggest these two authors.[27] They are major sources for Eusebius. The bishop from Caesarea cited them both at length and frequently.[28] He called Josephus "the most famous of the historians among the Hebrews"[29] and considered Luke-Acts to be part of the New Testament.[30] I am not, however, interested in them as sources as much as I am interested in them as historiographical models.

I have previously argued that the *Jewish Antiquities* of Josephus is a major representative of a historiographical tradition that I have called apologetic historiography and that this tradition served as the matrix in which the Jewish-Christian author whom we know as "Luke" wrote the first history of Chris-

23. On Hegesippus see Eusebius, *Hist. eccl.* 4.8.1–2; 4.21.1–22.1. Eusebius used him as a source in 2.23.1–9; 3.11.1; 3.16.1; 3.19.1–7; 3.20.1–2; 3.20.7; 3.32.1–8; 4.11.7; 4.8.1–2; 4.21.1–22.9.

24. Eusebius, *Hist. eccl.* 1.6.2. Eusebius used Julius Africanus as a source in 1.7.1–17; 6.31.1–3.

25. On the relationship between Acts and Eusebius see Alanna Nobbs, "Acts and Subsequent Ecclesiastical Histories," in *The Book of Acts in Its First Century Setting*, vol. 1: *Ancient Literary Setting*, ed. Bruce W. Winter and Andrew D. Clarke (Grand Rapids: Eerdmans, 1993), 153–62.

26. On the relationship between Josephus and Eusebius see Heinz Schreckenberg, *Die Flavius-Josephus-Tradition in Antike und Mittelalter*, ALGHJ 5 (Leiden: Brill, 1972), 79–88; Heinz Schreckenberg, "Josephus und die christliche Wirkungsgeschichte seines 'Bellum Judaicum,'" *ANRW* 21.2:1106–1217; Michael E. Hardwick, *Josephus as an Historical Source in Patristic Literature through Eusebius*, BJS 128 (Atlanta: Scholars Press, 1989), 75–102; Heinz Schreckenberg and Kurt Schubert, *Jewish Historiography and Iconography in Early and Medieval Christianity*, CRINT 3.2 (Minneapolis: Fortress, 1992), 63–71; and Mike Beggs, "From Kingdom to *Ethnos*: The Transformation of a Metaphor in Eusebius' *Historia Ecclesiastica*" (PhD diss., University of Notre Dame, 1999).

27. Most works that have explored the models for Eusebius mention both. Perhaps the most perceptive comments about the relationship of these two authors to Eusebius were made by Robert M. Grant, *Eusebius as Church Historian* (Oxford: Clarendon, 1980), 41.

28. For the citations of Luke-Acts, see *Biblia Patristica: Index des citations et allusions bibliques dans la littérature patristique*, vol. 4: *Eusèbe de Césarée, Cyrille de Jérusalem, Épiphane de Salamine* (Paris: Éditions du Centre National de le Recherche Scientifique, 1987), 242–57 and 278–85. For Josephus see Schreckenberg, *Die Flavius-Josephus-Tradition*, 77–88.

29. Eusebius, *Hist. eccl.* 1.5.3.

30. Eusebius, *Hist. eccl.* 3.25.1.

tianity.[31] I would like to suggest that it was this historiographical tradition, known to early Christians primarily through Jewish sources, that shaped not only Luke-Acts but Eusebius's *Ecclesiastical History* as well. We will use prototype genre criticism as a means of exploring this hypothesis. We will look at the content, form, and function of each of the three works in order to determine whether they belong to a common type that frames our expectations as readers.[32] Our survey will need to be cursory, but we can examine some of the major concerns.

Content: The History of a People

We need to begin by considering the basic content of the works of all three historians: Josephus, Luke, and Eusebius all wrote the story of a distinct people. More specifically, they wrote the story of a subgroup within the larger context of the Roman world and attempted to contextualize the subgroup within the framework of that larger world.

Background. The roots of this tradition reach back to Greek ethnography.[33] The starting point for Greek ethnography is the *Description of the Earth* that Hecataeus of Miletus (ca. 525–475 BCE) wrote as a commentary to his map of the world,[34] a map that he probably drew as a revision of the earlier map by Anaximander (ca. 610–540 BCE).[35] Hecataeus's commentary on his map de-

---

31. Sterling, *Historiography and Self-Definition*. I will use the name "Luke" throughout this work as a convention. I think that the author may have known Luke, but was not Luke. I will also use masculine pronouns on occasion since the author uses the masculine in a self-reference (Luke 1:3, παρηκολουθηκότι ["had investigated"], a masculine, singular participle in form).

32. On prototype theory of genre, see the discussion in the introduction to this volume.

33. On the development of Greek ethnography see Joseph E. Skinner, *The Invention of Greek Ethnography from Homer to Herodotus* (Oxford: Oxford University Press, 2012). On the relationship between ethnography and history see Emma Dench, "Ethnography and History," in *Companion to Greek and Roman Historiography*, 493–503.

34. *FGH* 1 frags. 36–369 and Giuseppe Nenci, *Hecataei Milesii Fragmenta* (Florence: La Nuova Italia, 1954). For a scholarly summary see Klaus Meister, *Die griechische Geschichtsschreibung: Von den Anfängen bis zum Ende des Hellenismus* (Stuttgart: W. Kohlhammer, 1990), 20–23; Klaus Meister, "Hecataeus of Miletus," *BNP* 6:35–37; and Lucio Bertelli, "Hecataeus: From Genealogy to Historiography," in *The Historian's Craft in the Age of Herodotus*, ed. Nino Luraghi (Oxford: Oxford University Press, 2001), 67–94.

35. On Anaximander's map see Agathererus 1.1; Strabo 1.1.11; and Diogenes Laertius 2.2. The texts are conveniently collected in Geoffrey S. Kirk, John E. Raven, and Malcolm Schofield, *The Presocratic Philosophers*, 2nd ed. (Cambridge: Cambridge University Press,

scribed the various lands. Based on his lead, Greek authors began to compose accounts of individual lands. The works typically used the adjectival form of the people for the title—whether the title was given by the author or by a later tradent. For example, Charon of Lampsacus (floruit fifth century BCE) wrote a *Persika* in two books;[36] Xanthus (floruit fifth century BCE) composed a *Lydiaka* on his *patria* in four volumes;[37] and Hellanicus of Lesbos (ca. 480–395 BCE) wrote a number of ethnographic works including an *Aigyptiaka*, a *Persika* in two volumes, and a *Skythika*.[38] These accounts all treated four basic concerns: the land, the history of the people, the wonders or marvels of the land, and the customs.[39] A crude way to think of these accounts would be to compare them with the accounts of different peoples in *National Geographic*, a journal that has routinely provided the English-speaking world with accounts of people who lived beyond our geographical reach. The most famous examples of ancient ethnography are the ethnographic excurses in Herodotus (e.g., book 2 on Egypt).[40]

Following the conquests of Alexander the Great, people who lived in the East began to tell their own stories, partly in response to the accounts of Greeks and partly in an effort to establish their own place in the larger world. Josephus

---

1983). The texts are nos. 98, 99, and 94, respectively. The relationship between the two maps is disputed: it could be that Hecataeus revised Anaximander's map rather than drawing his own, but *FGH* 1 test. 34, 35, and 48 suggest that he drew his own map. For a recent scholarly summary of his work see Istvan Bodnar, "Anaximander," *BNP* 1:660–61.

36. *FGH* 262 test. 1 and frags. 3, 9–10, 14. Cf. also frags. 5 and 11. For an analysis of the evidence see Lionel Pearson, *The Early Ionian Historians* (Oxford: Clarendon, 1939), 139–51; and Klaus Meister, "Charon [3]," *BNP* 3:203–4.

37. *FGH* 765 test. 1 and frags. 1–30. For an analysis of the evidence see Pearson, *Early Ionian Historians*, 109–38; and Peter Högemann, "Xanthos [3]," *DNP* 12.2:604–5.

38. *FGH* 4 frags. 53–55 and 173–76 for his *Aigyptiaka*; test. 12 and frags. 59–63, 132, 177–84 for his *Persika*; and test. 24 and frags. 64–65, 185–87, 189 for his *Skythika*. For an analysis of the evidence see Pearson, *Early Ionian Historians*, 152–235; Meister, *Die griechische Geschichtsschreibung*, 41–42; and Klaus Meister, "Hellanicus [1]," *BNP* 6:79–80.

39. So Felix Jacoby, "Über die Entwicklung der griechischen Historiographie," *Klio* 9 (1909): 89.

40. For an overview of research through most of the previous century see Charles W. Fornara, *Herodotus: An Interpretative Essay* (Oxford: Oxford University Press, 1971), 1–23. For a recent treatment see Pietro Vannicelli, "Herodotus' Egypt and the Foundations of Universal History," in *The Historian's Craft in the Age of Herodotus*, ed. N. Luraghi (Oxford: Oxford University Press, 2001), 211–40; and Alan B. Lloyd, "Egypt," in *Brill's Companion to Herodotus*, ed. Egbert J. Bakker, Irene J. F. de Jong, and Hans van Wees (Leiden: Brill, 2002), 415–35.

is the principal witness to this tradition. We will examine his claim and evaluate the evidence that supports it in chapter 2. At this point, we will work from the assumption that such an Eastern tradition of writing flourished. These writings shared a number of features in common that gave them a distinct orientation. I have called that tradition apologetic historiography. We can describe the tradition by sketching its prototype as follows: "Apologetic historiography is the story of a subgroup of people in an extended prose narrative written by a member of the group who follows the group's own traditions but Hellenizes them in an effort to establish the identity of the group within the setting of the larger world."[41] The best example of this tradition in the Roman world is the *Jewish Antiquities* of Josephus, to which we now turn.

Josephus. Josephus opened his *Antiquities* with a programmatic preface that set out the scope of the work: "I have undertaken this present work believing that it will be worthy of the attention of all Greek-speaking people. For it will cover our entire antiquities and the constitution of our government, translated from the Hebrew Scriptures."[42] While the claim that his work is a translation of the Hebrew Scriptures is more rhetoric than reality (we will discuss this in chapter 4), it is part of the historiographical tradition.[43] The scope that he promised is accurate. He went on to point out that his work covered a span of five thousand years.[44]

He summarized the contents of his magnum opus in the final book: "Here will end my *Antiquities*. After this point, I began to set out my account of the war.[45] This account includes the tradition from the original creation of humanity to the

41. Sterling, *Historiography and Self-Definition*, 17.
42. Josephus, *Ant.* 1.5.
43. On the meaning of "translate" here see Louis H. Feldman, *Judean Antiquities 1–4*, FJTC 3 (Leiden: Brill, 1999), 3–4. Josephus retold the story with freedom. The closest example of a translation among Jewish works—apart from actual translations—is 1 Esdras that translates select portions of the Scriptures: 1 Esd 1:1–55 // 2 Chr 35:1–36:21; 1 Esd 2:1–14 // Ezra 1:1–11; 1 Esd 2:15–25 // Ezra 4:6–24; 1 Esd 3:1–5:6, no basis in the biblical books; 1 Esd 5:7–70 // Ezra 2:1–4:5; 1 Esd 6:1–7:15 // Ezra 5:1–6:22; 1 Esd 8:1–9:36 // Ezra 7:1–10:44; 1 Esd 9:37–55 // Neh 7:72, 8:1–12. Pseudo-Philo, LAB is closer to Josephus in scope by retelling the story of Israel from Adam through the death of Saul, but does not claim to be a translation. It was, after all, composed in Hebrew and is an example of rewritten Bible rather than apologetic historiography.
44. Josephus, *Ant.* 1.13.
45. This is a literal translation. Josephus means that the narrative of *J.W.* began where the narrative of *Ant.* left off. He does not mean that he began to write *J.W.* after *Ant.* He wrote *J.W.* between 75–79 and completed *Ant.* in the mid-nineties CE.

twelfth year of Nero's reign."[46] Josephus proceeded to state the four basic types of material that he included: the events that befell the Jewish people in Egypt, Syria, and Palestine when they became and existed as an independent nation; their suf-ferings at the hands of the Assyrians, Babylonians, Persians, Macedonians, and Romans when they were a subject state; the line of high priests who kept the re-cords of the people for two thousand years;[47] and the record of the successive lead-ers.[48] He presented this material in "twenty books or sixty thousand lines."[49]

If we use the understanding of history that Josephus set out in *Against Apion* as a basis for thinking of the structure of the *Jewish Antiquities*, we may organize the twenty books into three major units: books 1–4 cover the period from creation to the death of Moses; books 5–11 cover the period from the death of Moses to Artaxerxes I; and books 12–20 cover the period from Artaxerxes I to Josephus's present.[50] The first two periods correspond to the material in the biblical text; the third extends beyond the sacred writings.

The *Jewish Antiquities* are thus a comprehensive account of the Jewish peo-ple based largely on their own records.[51] The first eleven books "translated" or interpreted the biblical material, while the remaining nine extended it to the point in time where the *Jewish War* began in earnest (there is an overlap between the *Jewish War* and the *Jewish Antiquities*). While the Jewish nation had suffered at the hands of the superpowers of the Ancient Near East and the more recent empires that arose in the West, it had originally existed as an in-dependent nation, complete with its own constitution that has been preserved to the present. The work thus looked back on a glorious but remote past.

46. Josephus, *Ant.* 20.259.

47. For a list of the high priests see *Ant.* 20.224–251. He does not state that they kept the records in this text, but this is surely his point as he made clear in *Ag. Ap.* 1.30–36. James C. VanderKam, *From Joshua to Caiaphas: High Priests after the Exile* (Minneapolis: Fortress; Assen: Van Gorcum, 2004), has provided a history of the high priests during the Second Temple period.

48. Josephus, *Ant.* 20.259–261.

49. Josephus, *Ant.* 20.267. The practice of counting the lines goes back to at least the fourth century, e.g., Theompompus *FGH* 115 frag. 25. The lines were counted in order to pay copyists. See Henry St. J. Thackeray, *Josephus: The Man and the Historian* (New York: Jewish Institute of Religion, 1929; repr., New York: Ktav, 1969), 73.

50. Josephus, *Ag. Ap.* 1.39–41.

51. On Josephus's vocabulary for group identity see Gruen, *Ethnicity in the Ancient World*, 166–84, who points out that Josephus used the terms γένος and ἔθνος with a wide range of connotations. It is not possible to define Israel on the basis of lineage—at least, Josephus did not present Israel in this way.

Luke-Acts. Writing at approximately the same time as Josephus, the Jewish-Christian author of Luke-Acts faced a very different situation. Unlike Josephus, whose challenge was to reshape the identity of a recognized people, this author was confronted with the difficulty of creating an identity for an unrecognized people. Christianity had begun as a revival movement within Judaism; however, the influx of Gentiles into Christianity had strained relationships with synagogues and made the status of Christians unclear in—at least—some quarters.[52] This is evident in the correspondence between Pliny, *legatus* of Bithynia-Pontus, and the emperor Trajan at the beginning of the second century. Pliny's perplexity about what to do with those accused of being Christians made it clear that he understood that they were not Jews. Rather they practiced what he called a "a perverse and unrestrained *superstitio*,"[53] a judgment that was shared by Tacitus and Suetonius who also thought that Christianity was a *superstitio*.[54]

Who were Christians? The Jewish-Christian author of Luke-Acts set out their story in two volumes. As we will see in chapter 4, the two scrolls should be understood as a single work. Luke did not write the story of Jesus and then the story of the church in two separate scrolls, but the story of Christianity in one work that required two scrolls. Like Josephus, Luke claimed that the scope of his work was comprehensive. His preface compared his account to the narratives of his predecessors (for the Greek see synopsis 1.1 in the appendix).[55]

---

52. The separation of Christianity from Judaism was a complex process. James D. G. Dunn, *The Parting of the Ways between Christianity and Judaism and Their Significance for the Character of Christianity*, 2nd ed. (London: SCMS, 2006), provided a famous discussion. However, this has been subjected to serious criticism, e.g., Jens Schröter, Benjamin A. Edsall, and Joseph Verheyden, eds., *Jews and Christians—Parting Ways in the First Two Centuries CE? Reflections on the Gains and Losses of a Model*, BZNW 253 (Berlin: de Gruyter, 2021), have challenged whether we can speak of a true parting in the first two centuries CE.

53. Pliny, *Ep.* 10.96.8. Pliny's letter to Trajan is 10.96 and Trajan's response is 10.97. On Pliny and Christians see Robert L. Wilken, *The Christians as Romans Saw Them* (New Haven: Yale University Press, 1984), 1–30.

54. Tacitus, *Ann.* 15.44 and Suetonius, *Nero* 6.16.2; cf. also Suetonius, *Divus Claudius* 5.25.4.

55. Luke 1:1–4. There is an enormous bibliography on the prologue. The single most important treatment is Loveday C. A. Alexander, *The Preface to Luke's Gospel: Literary Convention and Social Context in Luke 1.1–4 and Acts 1.1*, SNTSMS 78 (Cambridge: Cambridge University Press, 1993). For an updated analysis see Loveday C. A. Alexander, "Formal Elements and Genre: Which Greco-Roman Prologues Most Closely Parallel the Lukan Prologues?," in *Jesus and the Heritage of Israel: Luke's Narrative Claim upon Israel's Legacy*, ed. David P. Moessner (Harrisburg, PA: Trinity, 1999), 9–26.

Item	Verses 1–2, The Predecessors	Verses 3–4, The Author
Author(s)	[1]Since many	[3]it seemed good to me,
Quality Judgment	have undertaken	after I had investigated everything
Temporal Element		from the outset,
Literary Product	to set out a narrative	to write a carefully arranged account
Recipient		to you, most excellent Theophilus,
Content	about the things that have been fulfilled among us,	
Reliability Claim	[2]just as those who were eyewitnesses	[4]so that you could know the certainty
Temporal Element	from the beginning	
Transmission of Tradition	and ministers of the Word delivered to us;	of the matters about which you have received instruction.

There is a striking balance in both content and sequence between vv. 1–2 and 3–4. After a reference to writers, the author draws a contrast between the efforts of his predecessors and his own more thorough research. The distinction is reinforced in the qualifications that the author uses to describe his own "carefully arranged account" versus the simple "narrative" of his predecessors.[56] He is, however, quick to point out that the work of the predecessors is reliable since it rests on eyewitness testimony, a claim that guarantees the certainty of his own account. There is a single tradition that stretches from the eyewitnesses through the works of the predecessors to the author's own "carefully arranged account."

While the claims in the preface are standard topoi, it is clear that the author took care with the arrangement of his narrative. The scope of the narrative spanned from John the Baptist to Paul's imprisonment in Rome. Two principles governed the structure of the two scrolls. First, the author appears to

56. On the claims to reliability see David P. Moessner, "The Appeal and Power of Poetics (Luke 1:1-4): Luke's Superior Credentials (παρηκολουθηκότι), Narrative Sequence (καθεξῆς), and Firmness of Understanding (ἀσφάλεια) for the Reader," in *Jesus and the Heritage of Israel: Luke's Narrative Claim upon Israel's Legacy*, ed. David P. Moessner (Harrisburg, PA: Trinity, 1999), 84-123, and Rothschild, *Luke-Acts and the Rhetoric of History*, 67-71.

have decided on the basic contents of the two scrolls on the basis of his under-standing of history.[57] He thought that the coming of the Spirit on Jesus at his baptism marked the beginning of his ministry (Acts 10:37–38) and the coming of the Spirit on the disciples at Pentecost marked the beginning of the church (Acts 11:15). The two scrolls thus align with two stages in the development of Christianity. Second, more than any other evangelist, Luke organized his material along geographical lines.[58] The Gospel opens in Jerusalem with an infancy narrative (1:5–2:52), moves through Jesus's Galilean ministry (3:1–9:50), presents Jesus's journey to Jerusalem (9:51–19:44), and returns to Jerusalem for his final days (19:45–24:53). Acts opens with a table of contents that explains the unfolding of the narrative. Jesus said to the disciples (Acts 1:8): "You will be my witnesses in Jerusalem [1:3–8:3], in all Judea and Samaria [8:4–12:25], and unto the end of the earth [13:1–28:31]." The story thus moves from Jerusalem as the fulcrum to Rome. It explains how a movement that began exclusively among Jews in the sacred city moved out into the larger world until it came to the capital of the empire. It was in the heart of the empire that it took its place in world history.

The progression from Jerusalem to Rome forced the question of identity. Who were Christians? If the majority were now Gentiles, how should they be understood? Luke presented Christians as a people. He did this in several ways. He wrote their history. The act of writing their story was an attempt to define them as a distinct group, a group that had its own traditions and history. Further, Luke, more than any other author in the New Testament, was concerned with the names by which the movement and its people were

57. It is, of course, possible to conclude that he based the decision on pragmatic grounds (an average papyrus scroll was roughly 30 feet, about the amount of space that Luke and Acts would each occupy). The practice of dividing a work into books on the basis of contents goes back to Ephorus (ca. 405–330 BCE). See *FGH* 70 test. 11. For an analysis see Godfrey L. Barber, *The Historian Ephorus* (Cambridge: Cambridge University Press, 1935; repr., Chicago: Ares, 1993), esp. 17–48, and Klaus Meister, "Ephorus," *BNP* 4:1035–36.

58. Hans Conzelmann, *The Theology of St. Luke*, trans. Geoffrey Buswell (New York: Harper & Row, 1966), was the first to emphasize the geography of Luke. There needs to be a study of how Luke used geography as a structural device for his work. There have been some fascinating studies that use geography in studying Luke-Acts, e.g., Matthew Sleeman, *Geography and the Ascension Narrative in Acts*, SNTSMS 146 (Cambridge: Cambridge University Press, 2009), who uses the concept of "third space" to explore the geography of the text, and John M. Vonder Bruegge, *Mapping Galilee in Josephus, Luke, and John: Critical Geography and the Construction of an Ancient Space*, AGJU 93 (Leiden: Brill, 2016), esp. 91–138, who focuses on Galilee.

known.[59] His favorite term for Christianity was "the Way" (ἡ ὁδός).[60] He recognized that the "disciples" (μαθηταί), his preferred term for the followers of Jesus, were known as Christians.[61] He even called them a "people" (λαός). In the debate over the entrance of Gentiles into the community at the council held in Jerusalem, he had James say: "Simeon (Peter) has related how God first concerned himself with taking a people (λαός) from the Gentiles for his name" (Acts 15:14). James proceeded to quote the LXX version of Amos 9:11–12 that envisioned the reconstruction of the tent of David as a place where the Gentiles could seek the Lord; that is, the Gentiles on whom his name has been called. The term that Luke used for people is *laos* (λαός), from which English derives "laiety." It is the word that the author typically reserved for Israel.[62] In this text he extended his normal use by suggesting that the presence of the Spirit rather than ethnicity determined status. With this move he implied that the church stood in continuity with the people of Israel. For this reason, he could on other occasions refer to Christians as a "sect" (αἵρεσις) among the Jews.[63]

Unlike Mark, Matthew, and John, who related the story of Jesus but not of his followers, Luke told the story of both Jesus and the movement that came from him. Through the writing of the story of the movement and the effort to distinguish it, Luke attempted to give Christians "a national identity." He could not create an identity in the same way that Josephus could recreate one. After all, Christians were not a single ethnic group and lacked an ancient history. As we will see, the Christian historian found ways to negotiate these challenges.

59. The early followers of Jesus used multiple terms to refer to themselves, e.g., "brothers and sisters" (ἀδελφοί), "saints" or "holy ones" (ἅγιοι), "believers" (πιστεύοντες), and "disciples" (μαθηταί). Outsiders called them "Christians" (Χριστιανοί). Insiders referred to the movement as "the Way" (ἡ ὁδός) and their communities as an "assembly" or "church" (ἐκκλησία). On the use of terms in the NT see Paul Trebilco, *Self-Designations and Group Identity in the New Testament* (Cambridge: Cambridge University Press, 2012) and Horrell, *Ethnicity and Inclusion*, 217–48. For recent treatments of ethnicity in Acts see Eric Barreto, *Ethnic Negotiations: The Function of Race and Ethnicity in Acts 16*, WUNT 2.294 (Tübingen: Mohr Siebeck, 2010) and J. Andrew Cowan, *The Writings of Luke and the Jewish Roots of the Christian Way: An Examination of the Aims of the First Christian Historian in the Light of Ancient Politics, Ethnography, and Historiography*, LNTS 599 (London: T&T Clark, 2019). For a theological reading of Acts that takes the issues of inclusivity seriously see Willie James Jennings, *Acts*, Belief: A Theological Commentary on the Bible (Louisville: Westminster John Knox, 2017).

60. Acts 9:2; 19:9, 23; 22:4; 24:14, 22.

61. Acts 11:26; 26:28. Cf. also 1 Pet 4:16.

62. Luke 1:10, 21, 68, 77; 2:10, 32; etc.

63. Acts 24:5, 14; 28:22.

The effort to define Christians as a people did not disappear with Luke-Acts, but grew in force over time.

Eusebius. In the second century Christian authors began speaking openly of Christians as a third race (γένος).[64] *The Preaching of Peter*, a second-century collection of sermons attributed pseudonymously to Peter, divided humanity into three groups: "What relates to the Greeks and Jews is old. But we are Christians who, as a third race (τρίτον γένος), worship God in a new way."[65] Note that it is the way in which Christians worship that distinguishes them, not birth or other criteria that are normally associated with groups. Aristides, a second-century apologist who dedicated his work to the emperor Hadrian (emperor from 117–138 CE),[66] spoke of three races as he discussed the understanding of God: "For it is clear, O King, that there are three races of people (τρία γένη εἰσιν ἀνθρώπων) in this world. One of these is those among you who worship the so-called gods, another is the Jews, and still another the Christians."[67] Again, the distinction lies in liturgy. The anonymous author of the treatise directed to Diognetus opened his work by promising to answer the questions that Diognetus had raised including "why this new race (γένος) or way of life came to life now and not formerly."[68] He later wrote that "Christians are not distinguished from other people by land or language or customs. For they do not live in their own cities nor do they use some strange language nor practice an extraordinary lifestyle."[69] The normal distinguishing marks did not apply to them. Rather, Christians lived among others and followed a revealed constitution that set them apart.[70] The identification became common enough that authors outside the apologetic tradition also used it. Marcion, the member of the church

64. This is anticipated in the NT in 1 Pet 2:9, where the language is largely metaphorical. The view that Christians are a third race has spawned a great deal of literature; see Gruen, *Ethnicity in the Ancient World*, 201–14, for the paucity of the references in the first two centuries CE. On the broader importance of the concept in early Christianity and its modern relevance see Denise Buell, *Why This New Race: Ethnic Reasoning in Early Christianity* (New York: Columbia University Press, 2005).

65. Cited by Clement, *Strom.* 6.5.41.

66. The work exists in Greek, Syriac, and Armenian. The Greek and Armenian have it addressed to Hadrian; the Syriac is addressed to Antoninus Pius. The standard Greek text is Johannes Geffcken, *Zwei Griechische Apologeten*, Sammlung wissenschaftlicher Kommentare zu griechischen und römischen Schriftstellern (Leipzig: Teubner, 1907).

67. Aristides 2.2. See also 3.2; 8.1; 14.1; 15.1.

68. Diogn. 1. I have used the edition in Bart D. Ehrman, *The Apostolic Fathers*, 2 vols., LCL 24–25 (Cambridge, MA: Harvard University Press, 2003), 2:121–59.

69. Diogn. 5.1–2.

70. Diogn. 5.3–7.9.

of Smyrna who wrote an account of Polycarp's martyrdom to the church at Philomelium, spoke of the race of Christians (τὸ γένος τῶν Χριστιανῶν).[71] Similarly, the Shepherd of Hermas called Christians "the race of the just" (τὸ γένος τῶν δικαίων).[72] Among the Nag Hammadi treatises, the *Tripartite Tractate* also refers to three races, although it does not specify their identities.[73] It was apparently also used by outsiders, at least Tertuallian recognized that mobs threw the sobriquet *tertium genus* at Christians in derision.[74]

Eusebius of Caesarea was heir to these discussions. He quoted Clement of Alexandria's *On the Passover* that included a reference to "the race of the devout" (τὸ γένος τῶν εὐσεβῶν).[75] It is therefore not surprising that the bishop made the decision to tell the story of this people. He did so in ten books. There is an obvious shift in perspective from the first seven books to the last three, which has led to a debate about the number of editions of the *Ecclesiastical History* and the date of each edition.[76] The most likely explanation in my judgment is that the first seven books were published prior to the Great Persecution of 303–313 CE. Eusebius added books 8–9 after the persecution ended. He may have appended book ten a short time later and revised the entire work around 325 CE. The most significant shift for us to remember is between the first edition (books 1–7), and the second and later editions (books 8–9, 10). The two are separated by the rise of Constantine and his momentous decision to recognize Christianity. This meant that the historian would no longer have to situate Christianity as a subgroup within the larger culture: it had become part of that culture.

As we noted at the outset, Eusebius presented seven themes in his work in the first sentence.[77] The seven themes are: (1) the successors of the apostles,

71. Mart. Pol. 3.2. I have used the edition of Ehrman, *The Apostolic Fathers*, 1:355–401.
72. Herm. Sim. 9.17.5. I have used the edition of Ehrman, *The Apostolic Fathers*, 2:161–473.
73. Tri. Trac. 118–19. Cf. also 109–12. The standard edition is Harold W. Attridge, ed., *Nag Hammadi Codex I (the Jung Codex)*, 2 vols., NHS 22–23 (Leiden: Brill, 1985).
74. Tertullian, *Nat.* 1.8.1; *Scorp.* 10.10.
75. Eusebius, *Hist. eccl.* 4.26.5.
76. The most significant issue is whether there was a first edition prior to the Great Persecution. The most important representatives who favor this view are Richard Laqueur, *Eusebius als Historiker seiner Zeit* (Berlin: de Gruyter, 1929); Timothy D. Barnes, "The Editions of Eusebius' *Ecclesiastical History*," *GRBS* 21 (1980): 190–201; and Grant, *Eusebius*, 10–32. Those who favor a post-persecution origin for the first seven books include Andrew Louth, "The Date of Eusebius' *Historia Ecclesiastica*," *JTS* 41 (1990): 111–23; and Richard W. Burgess, "The Dates and Editions of Eusebius' *Chronici Canones* and *Historia Ecclesiastica*," *JTS* 48 (1997): 471–504. For an overview with full bibliography see Beggs, "From Kingdom to *Ethnos*," 53–85.
77. The specific number is a matter of interpretation. Eusebius did not enumerate them nor does the syntax of his Greek permit us to differentiate each theme with certainty.

(2) the number and nature of events in the church, (3) leaders of the church in notable provinces, (4) ambassadors of the divine word, (5) heretics, (6) the fate of the Jewish nation, and (7) persecutions and martyrs.[78] The selection of these specific themes is important: they reflect Eusebius's concern to carve out the distinct identity of Christianity. The first three deal with the internal affairs of the church. The fifth, heresy, has a Janus-like quality: it represents the threat of confusion within and the possible occasion for opposition from without by those who found the movement hopelessly confusing. The other three deal with the relationship of the church to the larger world: it sends ambassadors out just as other nations do, it is distinct from the Jewish people, and it has its own heroes who have given their lives for it. These two points of orientation suggest that Eusebius began by thinking of Christians as a subgroup in the larger world.

He made one important innovation over his predecessors in the language that he used: he called Christians a nation (ἔθνος), not just a people (λαός) like Luke, or a race (γένος) like his second-century predecessors. Eusebius acknowledged that Christians were "admittedly a new nation, although not small or weak nor founded in some corner of the earth."[79] He expressed the same thought in the panegyric on church buildings in book 10: "Who established a nation which was never heard of from time immemorial but which is now not hidden in some corner of the earth, but evident through the entire sphere under the sun."[80] In a context of persecution he could refer to "the entire nation of Christians."[81] Like Josephus and Luke, he wrote the story of a people.

FORM: APOLOGETIC CONCERNS

These authors could not, however, simply relate the story of Jews or Christians as if they were hermetically sealed units. Rather they needed to situate their subgroup within the context of the larger culture, a need that exercised some control over the form of their narratives. They made claims on behalf of the subgroup as they situated it in the larger world. One of the most important was the claim to antiquity, a claim that forced authors to think about the scope of their story. The claim to antiquity represents a view that is foreign to our way of thinking. We live in a technologically driven society that values the latest

78. Eusebius, *Hist. eccl.* 1.1.
79. Eusebius, *Hist. eccl.* 1.4.2. Cf. Acts 26:26.
80. Eusebius, *Hist. eccl.* 10.4.19.
81. Eusebius, *Hist. eccl.* 4.7.10.

invention and development. Ancient people thought that antiquity ensured value. Timaeus of Locri captured the sentiment in a phrase that he used to describe the creation of the cosmos: "The older is better than the younger."[82]

Background. This value proved to be both an embarrassment to Greeks and an opportunity for people in the East. Plato expressed the awkwardness that Greeks felt when he related Solon's visit to Egypt. In a conversation the philosopher attributed to Solon and an Egyptian priest, the Athenian legislator attempted to draw the Egyptians into a conversation about ancient history by relating the Greek stories of Phoroneus, the first human, and Deucalion, the hero of the flood. After Solon calculated the number of years between events, the Egyptian priest responded, "You Greeks are always children; there is no old Greek."[83] Josephus later threw this charge in the face of his Hellenic detractors: "One finds that everything about the Greeks is new, or dates—so to speak—to yesterday or the day before."[84] The reality of their relatively recent origins did not stop the Greeks from making claims about their antiquity as Diodorus reminds us: "Concerning the antiquity of race, not only do the Greeks lay claim [to being the oldest], but many of the barbarians as well." He explained the basis for their claims: "They claim that they are autochthonous and the first of all people to be discoverers of those things which are useful in life, and that the events which have transpired among them were considered worthy of record from the earliest period of time."[85] The claim that they *discovered* the things that are useful for human existence is part of a long exchange among different peoples who jockeyed for social prestige as the *fons* of civilization. Josephus expressed the rationale clearly when he wrote, "In point of fact, all nations attempt to trace their customs back to the most ancient time so that they will not appear to imitate others but to have instructed others on how to live lawfully."[86]

This debate played an important role in apologetic historiography (as we will see in detail in chapter 2). Jewish authors who wrote in this tradition took

---

82. Timaeus of Locri 94c (Thomas Tobin, ed., *Timaeus of Locri: On the Nature of the World and the Soul*, SBLTT 26 [Chico, CA: Scholars Press, 1985], 34). For a detailed treatment of this in the literature that we are considering see Peter Pilhofer, *Presbyteron Kreitton: Der Altersbeweis der jüdischen und christlichen Apologeten und seine Vorgeschichte*, WUNT 2.39 (Tübingen: Mohr Siebeck, 1990).

83. Plato, *Tim.* 22b. Cf. 21e-23c. Herodotus 2.143, has a similar story about Hecataeus's visit to Egypt.

84. Josephus, *Ag. Ap.* 1.7. Josephus is probably drawing on Herodotus here (see chapter 2).

85. Diodorus 1.9.3.

86. Josephus, *Ag. Ap.* 2.152.

part without reserve.[87] Demetrius, the first Jewish author who composed in Greek (late third century BCE) whose works are preserved, worked out the chronology of the LXX in an effort to demonstrate the antiquity of the Jewish people. The same concern led Artapanus (second century BCE), Eupolemus (second century BCE), and Pseudo-Eupolemus (second century BCE) to present Abraham as a *Kulturbringer* (conveyor of culture).[88] Artapanus even claimed that Moses created Egyptian religion.[89] The claims about discoveries tended to fade in later authors. However, the concern about antiquity and the implications that it held for specific peoples did not.[90]

Josephus. Josephus was open about the debate and the place of the Jewish people within it. As we have already noted, he opened his *Jewish Antiquities* with the claim that it would cover five thousand years.[91] The scope of the work extended from creation to the beginning of the Jewish War. Josephus was explicit about Jewish antiquity. He argued that Moses had been born two thousand years ago, "such an enormous span of time that their (the Greeks) poets have not dared to refer the births of the gods to it, much less human deeds or laws."[92] He concluded his magnum opus with the claim that the high priests could be traced for two thousand years, a claim that we should probably understand as a parallel to the statement that Moses was born two thousand years previously since his brother, Aaron, was the first high priest.[93] The calculation was likely traditional; at least, Philo of Alexandria also used the same two-thousand-year figure.[94] Josephus gave these figures to emphasize the antiquity of the Jewish people over against the relatively recent advent of the Western powers in the Mediterranean. He began his treatise *Against Apion* with a statement about his magnum opus: "I believe that in my writing of the *Antiquities* . . . I have made perfectly clear to any who read it that the

87. On the antiquity of the Jews in the ancient world see Louis H. Feldman, *Jew and Gentile in the Ancient World* (Princeton: Princeton University Press, 1993), 177–200.

88. Artapanus frag. 1 (Eusebius, *Praep. ev.* 9.18.1); Pseudo-Eupolemus frag. 1 (Eusebius, *Praep. ev.* 9.17.2–9).

89. Artapanus frag. 3 (Eusebius, *Praep. ev.* 9.27.1–27, esp. 4). See also Eupolemus frag. 1 (Eusebius, *Praep. ev.* 9.26.1), who presented Moses as a *Kulturbringer*.

90. For a summary of the presentation of this debate among Jewish historians see my "'The Most Ancient and Reliable Record of the Past': The Jewish Appropriation of Hellenistic Historiography," in *Companion to Greek and Roman Historiography*, 231–43.

91. Josephus, *Ant.* 1.13.

92. Josephus, *Ant.* 1.16.

93. Josephus, *Ant.* 20.261.

94. Philo, *Hypoth.* 8.6.9. This is the only place where Philo gives the two-thousand-year figure.

Jewish race is most ancient." He went on to say: "I have written this history that embraces a span of five thousand years in Greek on the basis of our sacred books."[95] In nuce, Judaism was old.

Luke-Acts. The task of arguing for antiquity was far more difficult for Luke. He was aware of the value of the old. There are at least three passages where he is directly concerned with the question of whether Christianity represents a new teaching. The first occurs in the conclusion to an exorcism from a man in the synagogue in Capernaum, the first miracle attributed to Jesus in the Synoptic tradition (for the Greek see synopsis 1.2 in the appendix).

Mark 1:27	Luke 4:36
They were all so amazed	Amazement fell on all of them
that they asked one another,	and they spoke to one another,
saying:	saying:
"What is this?	"What is this statement?
A *new* teaching with authority!	
He commands the unclean spirits	He commands the unclean spirits
	with authority and power
and they obey him!"	and they go out!"

Luke avoided Mark's statement that Jesus's teaching was new. He did so by altering Mark's response to the question, "What is this?" He dropped the first line of Mark's response "a new teaching with authority" and expanded the second by adding "authority" to Jesus's command, "with authority and power." There is no hint that Jesus's teaching is new.

The second instance occurs in the first of four banquet scenes in the Gospel (for the Greek see synopsis 1.3 in the appendix).[96] In an after-dinner exchange at a feast that Levi threw for Jesus, the itinerant rabbi is credited with the aphorism: "The old is better." In a closing statement that contrasts his teaching with that of the Pharisees, Jesus said:

Mark 2:22	Luke 5:37-39
No one puts new wine	[37]No one puts new wine
into old wine skins;	into old wine skins;
otherwise the wine will rupture	otherwise the new wine will rupture
the wine skins,	the wine skins

95. Josephus, *Ag. Ap.* 1.1.
96. Luke 5:29-39; 7:36-50; 11:37-52; 14:1-24. Cf. also 22:14-38.

and the wine will perish	and will spill
as well as the wine skins.	and the wine skins will be ruined.
Rather,	[38]Rather, it is necessary to put
new wine	new wine
goes into new wine skins.	into new wine skins.
	· [39]No one who drinks the old
	wants the new.
	For he says:
	"The old is better."

The final saying in Luke is unique in the tradition.[97] It appears to stand in opposition to what has preceded. If Judaism represents the old, how can Jesus say that "the old is better"?[98] The statement poses such difficulties with the preceding that a number of ancient scribes and modern scholars have thought that the statement was an addition to the text, although the textual evidence supports its inclusion.[99] If we accept it as part of the text, how should we understand it? Some read the final statement in continuity with the preceding statements. They understand it as an explanation of why the Pharisees rejected Jesus: their desire for the old led to a rejection of the new.[100] The problem with this interpretation is that it uses a positive value to explain the behavior of Jesus's opponents, a strange twist to say the least! Others have read the final statement in discontinuity with the preceding statements. They contend that it is Luke's radical reinterpretation of the Markan material and the popular perception: Jesus did not bring new wine, this would have destroyed the old wine

97. Compare John 2:10.

98. For a history of the interpretation of this text see Jacques Dupont, "Vin veux, vin nouveau (Lu 5,39)," *CBQ* 25 (1963): 286-304.

99. It is omitted by D and in Marcion, Irenaeus, and Eusebius. For the full evidence see *The New Testament in Greek, The Gospel according to Luke, Part One: Chapters 1-12*, ed. The American and British Committees of the International Greek New Testament Project (Oxford: Clarendon, 1984), 112. Bruce M. Metzger, *A Textual Commentary on the New Testament*, 2nd ed. (Stuttgart: Deutsche Bibelgesellschaft/United Bible Societies, 1994), 115-16, thought that it might have been omitted by Marcion, who read it as supporting the Old Testament.

100. This is a standard view in the major commentaries on Luke, e.g., I. Howard Marshall, *The Gospel of Luke: A Commentary on the Greek Text*, NIGTC (Grand Rapids: Eerdmans, 1978), 228; Joseph A. Fitzmyer, *The Gospel according to Luke*, AB 28 and 28A (Garden City, NY: Doubleday, 1981-1984), 1:597, 601-2; and John Nolland, *Luke*, WBC 35A, 35B, and 35C (Dallas: Word, 1989-1993), 1:249-50.

skins of Judaism. Rather he has preserved the old![101] This has the advantage of aligning the statement and the text with the larger aim of Luke-Acts that argues that Christianity is a continuation of the story of Israel. It suffers from the lack of a clear textual signal that it is a reversal of the preceding; only its placement at the conclusion suggests that it is the key to the entire exchange. Still others have tried to find a way to identify Jesus's teaching with both the old and the new.[102] Whatever the precise meaning, the statement indicates the evangelist's awareness of this widely held value. The text is admittedly difficult, but the next text may help us.

The third instance took place in the record of Paul's encounter with Epicurean and Stoic philosophers in Athens. Luke prefaced Paul's speech to the Areopagus with an ironic reversal. He began: "They took him and led him to the Areopagus saying: 'We want to know about this new teaching that you are offering (τίς ἡ καινὴ αὕτη ἡ ὑπὸ σοῦ λαλουμένη διδαχή). For you have introduced something strange to our ears and we want to know what it means.'"[103] Luke then added a parenthetical explanation: "All the Athenians and the nonresidents who reside there spent their time in nothing other than saying or hearing something new (τι καινότερον)."[104] The question has become who is preoccupied with the new: Paul or the Athenians? Paul went on to deliver a speech about God that argued from natural theology and even cited the Stoic-influenced poet Aratus.[105] What the Epicureans and Stoics thought was new has turned out to be old! Luke has thus turned the tables: the Athenians are preoccupied with the new; Paul preaches the old.[106] The reversal of standard expectations in this story is an argument that the same reversal might have taken place in Luke 5:37–39, which we just examined. If so, the author has consistently identified this movement with the old.

These three texts suggest that Luke was aware of the value of the old and the dilemma this value created for Christianity. He faced the same problem

101. E.g., R. S. Good, "Jesus, Protagonist of the Old in Lk 5:33–39," NovT 25 (1983): 19–36, esp. 25. Gregory J. Riley, "Influence of Thomas Christianity on Luke 12:14 and 5:39," HTR 88 (1995): 229–35, esp. 232–34, made the argument that Luke was influenced by the tradition in Gos. Thom. 47, that also recognizes the value of the old.

102. E.g., A. H. Mead, "Old and New Wine St. Luke 5:39," ExpTim 99 (1987–1988): 234–35; and Francois Bovon, Luke, 3 vols. Hermeneia (Minneapolis: Fortress, 2002–2013), 1:194.

103. Acts 17:19–20.

104. Acts 17:21.

105. Aratus, Phaenomena 5 quoted in Acts 17:28.

106. Cowan, Writings of Luke and the Jewish Roots of the Christian Way, 121–22, completely misses the point of the text by accepting the statement of the court as the Lukan conception. See pp. 120–30 for his full discussion.

that every Christian who attempted to situate Christianity in the larger world confronted. Is it possible to present Christianity as anything but a recent movement? If we put the problem in literary terms, Luke could not write a *Christian Antiquities* in the way that Josephus could write a *Jewish Antiquities*; that is, the scope of his work could not extend through time the way that Josephus's did.

While Luke had no choice but to recognize the recent development of Christianity, he attempted to mitigate the implications in several ways. He linked the birth of Jesus with the reign of Augustus.[107] The reference to the first emperor may only be a means of situating the birth of Jesus within the larger world. This was one strategy that apologetic historians used to contextualize the subgroup in the larger context of the world.[108] It is worth noting that Luke has made the birth of Jesus coincident with the birth of the Roman Empire. The coincidence may suggest a contrast between the two rulers. It is also a subtle hint that Christianity is as old as the Roman Empire.[109] Luke was not, however, content with this; he wanted to show that Christianity had older roots than the Empire. He did this by tracing Jesus's lineage back to Adam, the first human.[110] He also presented Christianity as a continuation of Israel (see chapter 4). He expressed the basic position in Paul's speech to Agrippa II. The Christian prisoner said to his judge: "Now for the hope of the promise made by God to our ancestors I stand here on trial."[111] While Christianity may be recent as a movement, there are ways in which it is possible to think of it as ancient.

In literary terms, Luke traced the full history of Christianity as he knew it and argued that it was a continuation of an earlier movement rather than something completely new.[112]

107. Luke 2:1-2.

108. Luke did this in Luke 2:1-2; 3:1-2; Acts 11:28. For the Jewish practice see Ben Z. Wacholder, "Biblical Chronology in the Hellenistic World Chronicles," *HTR* 61 (1968): 451-81.

109. Paul W. Walasky, *"And So We Came to Rome": The Political Perspective of St. Luke*, SNTSMS 49 (Cambridge: Cambridge University Press, 1983), argued that Luke-Acts was a defense of Rome to Christians. This overstates the connection.

110. Luke 3:23-38.

111. Acts 26:6.

112. Cowan, *Writings of Luke and the Jewish Roots of the Christian Way*, has devoted a monograph to the relationship of the Way to Judaism. He suggests that the motivation is theological; i.e., Luke wrote to persuade the readers that the promises have come to fulfillment in Jesus and the early church. While I agree that this is a concern of the author, Cowan—in my judgment—fails to acknowledge the social apology of the work. See, in particular, chapters 7 through 9 in this volume.

Eusebius. Eusebius was more forthright and expansive than Luke about these claims. This is not a surprise: he had the advantage of living on the other side of the apologetic literature of the second century that had addressed this issue at some length. The Caesarean laid the groundwork for his history in his chronological tables, a work to which he refers in his preface.[113] The relationship between the *Chronicle* and the *Ecclesiastical History* is not, however, straightforward.[114] For our purposes it is enough to note that when Eusebius wrote the preface to the *Ecclesiastical History*, he thought that there was a connection between the claim for the antiquity of Christianity in both works.[115]

The bishop followed his opening statements with an excursus on the antiquity of Christianity that falls into two parts: the first deals with Christ and the second with Christian teaching (1.1.7–3.2.20; 4.1–15). He began his discussion of Christ as a divine being hoping "in this way both the ancient and divine nature of the antiquity of Christians will be demonstrated to those who suppose that it is recent and outlandish, having appeared no earlier than yesterday" (1.2.1).[116] He argued that Jesus was the Logos (1.2.2–5) and then identified the Logos with the Angel of the Lord in the Pentateuch (1.2.6–13) and with Sophia in Prov 8 (1.2.14–16). His point was that the Logos was old. Eusebius then asked "why then was he not announced—as he now is—to all people in the past." His answer was that people were not ready for his appearance. He offered an interpretation of history. Unlike most ancient interpretations of history that assumed that the remote past was a golden age and the events that followed were a downhill slide, Eusebius thought that humanity began in a state of depravity and improved through culture, especially the practice of true religion. Culture was thus a *preparatio evangelica*. Christ could only appear when culture had advanced far enough, though his name, Christ, appeared in the Scriptures (1.2.17–27; 1.3.1–20).[117] The purpose of these arguments was "so

113. Eusebius, *Hist. eccl.* 1.1.6. Hereafter, references to this work will be given in parentheses in the text.

114. For details and bibliography see Beggs, "From Kingdom to *Ethnos*," 65–69.

115. On the place of Eusebius's *Chronicle* in this context see William Adler, *Time Immemorial: Archaic History and Its Sources in Christian Chronography from Julius Africanus to George Syncellus*, Dumbarton Oaks Studies 26 (Washington, DC: Dumbarton Oaks, 1989), 1–71.

116. This is a play off of the famous charge that the Greeks had only appeared recently. See Josephus, *Ag. Ap.* 1.7 and my treatment of the text in chapter 2.

117. On Eusebius's interpretation of history see the analysis of Arthur Droge, *Homer or Moses? Early Christian Interpretations of the History of Culture*, HUT 26 (Tübingen: Mohr [Siebeck], 1989), 168–93; and Arthur Droge, "The Apologetic Dimensions of the *Ecclesiastical History*," in *Eusebius, Christianity, and Judaism*, ed. Harold W. Attridge and Gohei Hata (Detroit: Wayne State University Press, 1992), 495–98.

that no one would think that our Savior and Lord, Jesus Christ, was a novelty because of the date of his residency in the flesh" (1.4.1).

The bishop contended that the same was true for Christian teaching: "Both our life and manner of conduct together with our teachings on piety were not invented by us recently but from the very creation of humanity have been lived correctly through the natural concepts of those God-beloved people in the past" (1.4.4). He had in mind the ancestors of Israel, especially Abraham, who lived the same life that Christians now live. Thus, like Justin Martyr (who argued that those who lived according to the seeds of the Logos were Christians—including Socrates!), Eusebius claimed that the ancestors of Israel were Christians, if not in name, then in fact (1.4.10).

There was one other point of origin for Eusebius. He understood Christianity to be not only as old as creation, but also as old as the Roman Empire. He went out of his way to date the birth of Jesus to the time of Augustus (1.5.1–6.11). He later cited Melito of Sardis who claimed that Christianity was born at the time of Augustus (4.26.7–8). Why such insistence on the date of Jesus's birth? It is interesting that Luke had made the same connection. There is, however, a difference: Luke never suggested that the two movements should be thought of simultaneously; Eusebius did.[118] The bishop made his point in his *Chronicle*. He began his chronological lists with multiple columns for the different nations of the world. When he came to the time of Christ, he reduced the columns to two: Rome and Christianity. Following the Great Persecution, the identification of the two became a reality. It was not simply the case that Christianity was as old as Rome, it was tied to it. Like Luke, Eusebius could not write a *Christian Antiquities*, but covered the full sweep of its story and argued that it was a continuation of a much older story.

Function: History and Identity

The effort to situate a subgroup in the larger world in these histories required the historians to provide the subgroup with an identity. Those who tell the story of the people to whom they belong by relating the full story of the people, offer a self-definition of the people. They do so by giving them a past that situates them in the present. History is as important to a people as memory is to an individual. Richard Hofstadter expressed the importance of creating a past to

---

118. This is widely recognized, e.g., Chestnut, *First Christian Histories*, 76; Momigliano, *Classical Foundations*, 139; and Droge, "Apologetic Dimensions," 498.

understand the present in these terms: "To visit a people who have no history is like going into a wilderness where there are no roads to direct the traveler."[119] What sense of identity did these historians create for their readers?

Josephus. Josephus faced a complex situation: he had multiple implied audiences for his *Jewish Antiquities*. The work was generated by the aftermath of the Jewish War. The Jewish historian realized that the war could serve as a catalyst for undermining the status of Jews in the Roman Empire. Unlike 4 Ezra, 2 Baruch, and the *Apocalypse of Abraham* that turned to apocalyptic thought or the rabbis who turned Judaism inward toward the Torah, Josephus attempted to reposition the Jewish people historically. The primary audience was Greek, an audience that he repeatedly identified.[120] The historian wanted to win respectability for his people in an era when their standing had been jeopardized. He may have had a Roman audience in mind as well. At least this would help to explain the inclusion of the *acta*[121] and the positive portrayals of Roman officials toward Jews.[122] Finally, on several occasions Josephus mentioned Jewish readers.[123] What did he hope that his Jewish readers would find in his long account? The orientation of the *Jewish Antiquities* suggests that he remained optimistic that a rapprochement between Judaism and the larger Hellenistic/Roman world was still possible. In this way, he stood in a direct line with the Hellenistic Jewish historians who preceded him and made the same case.

Luke-Acts. Luke had a simpler task in some ways and a more difficult task in other ways. On the one hand, he had a single implied audience: Christians. He did have to relate them to the larger world; however, he did not address that world directly. On the other hand, Luke had a more difficult challenge. Living at a time when Judaism and Christianity were in the process of forging distinct identities, he had to create a sense of identity for Christians as a people without the benefit of precedents. While there were earlier gospels, no one

119. Richard Hofstadter, *The Progressive Historians: Turner, Beard, Parrington* (New York: Knopf, 1968), 3, cited in Robert L. Wilken, *The Myth of Christian Beginnings* (Notre Dame: University of Notre Dame Press, 1971), 5.

120. Josephus, *Ant.* 1.4, 9b, 12; 16.174; 20.262.

121. Josephus, *Ant.* 14.145-148, 149-155, 185-195, 196-198, 199, 200-201, 202-210, 211-212, 213-216, 219-222, 225-227, 228-230, 231-232, 233, 234, 235, 236-237, 237-240, 214-243, 244-246, 247-255, 256-258, 259-261, 262-264, 306-313, 314-318, 319-322; 16.160-165, 166, 167-168, 169-170, 171, 172-173; 19.280-285, 286-291; 20.10-14.

122. For a summary see Shaye J. D. Cohen, "Respect for Judaism by Gentiles according to Josephus," *HTR* 80 (1987): 409-30.

123. Josephus, *Ant.* 1.88; 4.197.

had combined the story of Jesus with the story of his followers. In this regard, Luke-Acts is a first.

Luke understood Christianity in terms of a succession that began with Jesus, continued through the twelve apostles, and reached a crescendo in Paul, the missionary extraordinaire to the Gentiles. The succession scheme is clear enough that Charles Talbert made a case that the two-volume work was modeled on the pattern of successive biography that was prominent in philosophical schools.[124] For example, Sotion, an Alexandrian Peripatetic, wrote a thirteen-volume *Succession of the Philosophers* (Διδαχὴ τῶν φιλοσόφων). Diogenes Laertius provides a better-known example of this type of work. While the full narratives of Luke-Acts rather than the simple pattern of who studied with whom make me skeptical that Luke-Acts belongs to the biographical tradition, Talbert is correct in recognizing the use of the succession pattern. The key element in this succession was the apostles. Luke opened his two scrolls with a preface that claimed that his work rested on the eyewitness testimony of the apostles. They constituted the bridge between Jesus and the church as he knew it. This is one of the principal reasons why he underscored the history of transmission in the preface: he reminded us that his predecessor's narratives rested on the apostolic tradition ("just as those who were eyewitnesses from the beginning and ministers of the word delivered it to us") and that Theophilus had been instructed in the same tradition that he offered more fully and carefully ("so that you could know the certainty of the matters about which you

---

124. Charles H. Talbert, *Literary Patterns, Theological Themes and the Genre of Luke-Acts*, SBLMS 20 (Missoula, MT: Scholars Press, 1974); and Charles H. Talbert, *Reading Luke: A Literary and Theological Commentary on the Third Gospel* (New York: Crossroad, 1982), 2–6. For a more recent articulation of this basic case see Adams, *Genre of Acts and Collected Biography* (which, however, deals only with Acts and suggests that it is a modified collective biography similar to those of Plutarch, Philo, Suetonius, and Nepos). It should be noted that Philo's *Lives* are still commentaries. I would call them biographical commentaries. Samson Uytanlet, *Luke-Acts and Jewish Historiography: A Study on the Theology, Literature, and Ideology of Luke-Acts*, WUNT 2.366 (Tübingen: Mohr Siebeck, 2014), makes a similar case only from the perspective of the LXX. While he recognizes the parallels in Greco-Roman literature, he contends that Luke-Acts is most heavily influenced by Jewish precedents including what he calls succession narratives. He ignores a good deal of the material that will be presented in this volume. I agree that the author of Luke-Acts owes his primary understanding of *Heilsgechichte* to the LXX, but think that the author read the LXX through the lens of Hellenistic Jewish authors who were already influenced by Hellenistic concerns (see chapter 5 in particular). I also see more direct influence by Greco-Roman concerns (see chapters 7 through 9).

have received instruction"). The *traditio apostolica* was the basis for Christian self-understanding.

It was, however, not enough to define Christianity in light of itself. The historian had to define it in terms of the larger world. As we have already suggested, he thought that it should be understood in terms of continuity with Israel. He shared the same concerns that Josephus did with Rome, even if he was much further removed. While there were no *acta* to cite, Luke went out of his way to stress that Roman officials consistently found Christians innocent of crimes against Rome. Pontius Pilate declared three times that Jesus was innocent. The evangelist even counted the declarations for us, in the event that we nodded off.[125] Paul was consistently acquitted before Roman officials in Acts.[126] This effort probably explains why Acts ends with Paul in prison in Rome rather than with an account of his martyrdom. The author did not want to relate Paul's fate, even if it was at the hands of a tyrant who had fallen out of favor with many. While Luke did not address readers in this larger world, he wrote for Christians who had to relate to it.

Eusebius. Christians are also the implied audience of the first edition of Eusebius's *Ecclesiastical History*. The bishop assumed that his readers would know a great deal about the LXX and different Christian writers. He did not explain who they were or contextualize their writings. At the same time, he raised the objections that had been raised against Christianity in the larger world. In this regard he is much like Luke who wrote to help Christians think about their place in the larger world.

Like his earlier Christian counterpart, he defined Christianity in terms of the *traditio apostolica*. The very first words of the work are "the successions of the sacred apostles" (τὰς τῶν ἱερῶν ἀποστόλων διαδοχάς) (Eusebius, *Hist. eccl.* 1.1). He returned to the topic when he explained how he gave unity to the scanty accounts that preceded his: "we will attempt to make them a single body through a historical record, pleased to recover the successions, if not of all, then at least of the most distinguished apostles of our Lord in the churches that are still prominent and noteworthy" (1.1.4). Eusebius has episcopal succession principally in mind, much in the tradition of Irenaeus (ca. 130–ca. 202 CE).[127] Unlike the bishop of Lyons, the Caesarean did not focus primarily on Rome,

---

125. Luke 23:4, 14–15, 22. Cf. also 23:47, where the centurion declared him innocent.

126. Acts 18:12–17, before Gallio; 24:1–21, before Felix; 25:6–12, before Festus; and 26:1–29, before Agrippa II. For Jewish trials see 22:1–21 and 23:1–9.

127. Irenaeus, *Haer.* 3.3.1.

but emphasized the most important Eastern churches in Jerusalem, Antioch, Alexandria and Caesarea.[128]

Eusebius's stance toward the larger world changed with the shifts in the geological plates that lay beneath his world. He opened his eighth book with the observation that he had completed his account of the apostolic successions (8.1.1). He turned to the events of his own day on the far side of the Great Persecution. The world that he had known prior to the Great Persecution had changed. He could now cite the decree of Constantine and Licinius that had given Christians the right to worship God as they chose and the decrees and letters that attempted to guarantee unity among them (10.5.1–7.2). The final two columns in the *Chronicle* were becoming one. Eusebius probably envisioned government officials or their advisors as one of the audiences of the later editions.

The bishop also had to come to terms with Judaism. While he attempted to create continuity with the ancestors of Israel, he did not share Luke's larger vision of continuity. Instead, he elected to follow Josephus—although not in a way that the Jewish historian could have foreseen or appreciated. Josephus followed Polybius's interpretation of the *Achaean War* in his interpretation of the *Jewish War*. Polybius laid the blame for the destruction of his beloved Achaian League at the door of anti-Roman leaders who gained control of the league. Josephus laid the blame for the First Jewish Revolt at the door of groups of bandits who took control of events against the will of the proper leaders.[129] Eusebius accepted Josephus's general position that the Jews had themselves to blame for the destruction of their sacred city; however, he took this in a different direction. Following the lead of Origen, he thought that it was a result of the crucifixion of Jesus. He changed the relationship of the death of Jesus outside the walls of Jerusalem and the destruction of those walls from post hoc to propter hoc.[130] He continued to tell the story of the Jews through the Second Jewish Revolt and then dropped Judaism from his narrative—in spite of the fact that he lived in a city with a large and thriving Jewish community. He created distance between Christians and Jews, but a distance that has been painful for centuries and is a source of shame to many modern Christians, including me.

128. For an analysis of his lists see Grant, *Eusebius*, 45–59.

129. For details see Gregory E. Sterling, "Explaining Defeat: Polybius and Josephus on the Wars with Rome," in *Internationales Josephus-Kolloquium Aarhus 1999*, ed. J. U. Kalms, Münsteraner Judaistische Studien 6 (Münster: LIT, 2000), 135–51.

130. For a summary, see Heinz Schreckenberg, *Die christlichen Adversus-Judaeos-Texte und ihr literarisches und historisches Umfeld (1.-11. Jh.)*, Europäische Hochschulschriften 23.172 (Frankfurt am Main: Peter Lang, 1990), 262–68, esp. 266–68.

Conclusions

It is a long way from Josephus to Luke to Eusebius. We have highlighted some of the similarities without having the time to give equal attention to all of the major differences. It is evident that all three historians whom we have examined wrote stories of distinct peoples. They all attempted to relate the full story of the people about whom they wrote, a concern that led them to address the antiquity or the lack of antiquity of the people about whom they wrote. In the case of Josephus, it was possible to reflect on a long span of time and to retell a familiar story. The same was not possible for Luke and Eusebius. They had to create Christian history. This is their gift to later generations. Like Josephus, they told the full story; unlike Josephus, they attempted to connect their stories to the earlier story of a parent people. While both recognized the importance of relating their story of Christianity to Judaism, they took different approaches in their final assessments. Both hoped that the creation of a Christian history would give their fellow Christians a sense of identity in the Roman Empire.

One of the factors that they had in common was the influence of apologetic historiography, a tradition that they knew largely through Jewish channels (Luke perhaps exclusively). While there is no compelling evidence that Luke knew Josephus,[131] Eusebius undoubtedly had a copy of Josephus's writings in the library at Caesarea, probably thanks to the foresight of Origen, who brought them from Alexandria when he moved north.[132] There is a strange twist in this. Christians preserved the works of Josephus, just as they did the works of Philo of Alexandria and other Greek-speaking Jewish authors.[133] Later Christians became so attached to the works of Josephus that they considered him to be an ecclesiastical author.[134] This brings Josephus full circle. The histories of this Jewish author who cultivated and preserved the historiographical tradition that taught Christians how to create their own historical identity, took on a Christian identity.

131. There are those who argue that Luke did know Josephus. The most important recent scholar who has made this case is Steve Mason, *Josephus and the New Testament* (Peabody, MA: Hendrickson, 1992), 185–229.

132. Andrew J. Carriker, *The Library of Eusebius of Caesarea*, VCSup 67 (Leiden: Brill, 2003), 157–61.

133. On the reception of Philo see David T. Runia, *Philo in Early Christian Literature: A Survey*, CRINT 3.3 (Assen: Van Gorcum; Minneapolis: Fortress, 1993) and Gregory E. Sterling, "Philo of Alexandria," in *A Guide to Early Jewish Texts and Traditions in Christian Transmission*, ed. Alexander Kulik et al. (Oxford: Oxford University Press, 2019), 299–316.

134. Cassiodorus, *Inst.* 1.17.1. Cassiodorus was responsible for commissioning the translation of Josephus's *Ant.* and *Ag. Ap.* into Latin. For details see Schreckenberg and Schubert, *Jewish Historiography*, 76–77.

APPENDIX[135]

Luke 1:1-4, the Contrast between Luke and His Predecessors

Synopsis 1.1

Verses 1-2, The Predecessors	Verses 3-4, The Author
¹Ἐπειδήπερ πολλοὶ	³ἔδοξε κἀμοὶ
ἐπεχείρησαν	παρηκολουθηκότι
	ἄνωθεν πᾶσιν
ἀνατάξασθαι διήγησιν	ἀκριβῶς καθεξῆς
	σοι γράψαι,
	κράτιστε Θεόφιλε,
περὶ τῶν πεπληροφορημένων	
ἐν ἡμῖν πραγμάτων,	
²καθὼς παρέδοσαν ἡμῖν	⁴ἵνα ἐπιγνῷς
οἱ ἀπ᾽ ἀρχῆς αὐτόπται	
καὶ ὑπηρέται γενόμενοι τοῦ λόγου,	περὶ ὧν κατηχήθης λόγων
	τὴν ἀσφάλειαν.

Luke's Avoidance of the New

Synopsis 1.2

Mark 1:27	Luke 4:36
καὶ ἐθαμβήθησαν ἅπαντες	καὶ ἐγένετο θάμβος ἐπὶ πάντας
ὥστε συζητεῖν πρὸς ἑαυτοὺς	καὶ συνελάλουν πρὸς ἀλλήλους
λέγοντας·	λέγοντας·
τί ἐστιν τοῦτο;	τίς ὁ λόγος οὗτος
διδαχὴ *καινὴ* κατ᾽ ἐξουσίαν·	ὅτι ἐν ἐξουσίᾳ καὶ δυνάμει
καὶ τοῖς πνεύμασι τοῖς ἀκαθάρτοις	ἐπιτάσσει
ἐπιτάσσει,	τοῖς ἀκαθάρτοις πνεύμασιν
καὶ ὑπακούουσιν αὐτῷ.	καὶ ἐξέρχονται;

---

135. For the Greek text of the NT in this work I have used *Novum Testamentum Graece*, ed. Barbara and Kurt Aland, Johannes Karavidopoulos, Carlo Martini, and Bruce Metzger, 28th ed. (Stuttgart: Deutsche Bibelgesellschaft, 2012).

Synopsis 1.3

Mark 2:22
καὶ οὐδεὶς βάλλει οἶνον νέον
εἰς ἀσκοὺς παλαιούς·
εἰ δὲ μή, ῥήξει ὁ οἶνος
τοὺς ἀσκοὺς
καὶ ὁ οἶνος ἀπόλλυται
καὶ οἱ ἀσκοί·
ἀλλ᾽ οἶνον νέον
εἰς ἀσκοὺς καινούς.

Luke 5:37–39
καὶ οὐδεὶς βάλλει οἶνον νέον
εἰς ἀσκοὺς παλαιούς·
εἰ δὲ μη γε, ῥήξει ὁ οἶνος νέος
τοὺς ἀσκοὺς
καὶ αὐτὸς ἐκχυθήσεται
καὶ οἱ ἀσκοί ἀπόλυνται·
ἀλλ᾽ οἶνον νέον
εἰς ἀσκοὺς καινοὺς βλητέον.
[καὶ] οὐδεὶς πιὼν παλαιὸν
θέλων νέον·
λέγει γάρ·
ὁ παλαιὸς χηστός ἐστιν.

2

"The Reliable History of Antiquity"

The Tradition of Writing History in the East

> *Out of all these sources of almost forgotten oral history, I have tried to fashion a narrative of the conquest of the American West as the victims experienced it, using their own words whenever possible. Americans who have always looked westward when reading about this period should read this book facing eastward.*

Dee Brown, *Bury My Heart at Wounded Knee*[1]

In the polemic against Greek historiography that opens *Against Apion*, Josephus contrasted the relatively recent age of the Greeks with the hoary antiquity of the peoples of the East. During the course of his argument Josephus referred to the oldest and most famous Greek author, Homer. He said, "They say that he did not leave his poems in written form but that they were remembered (in oral form) and later composed on the basis of songs. For this reason, there are many discrepancies in the poems."[2] The historian's comment became a *locus classicus* for Friedrich August Wolf who opened the modern debate whether the Homeric poems were originally oral or written compositions with his famous *Prolegomena* in 1795.[3] While classical scholarship has made significant progress since Wolf, Josephus's observation remains a remarkable literary insight.[4]

---

1. Dee Brown, *Bury My Heart at Wounded Knee: An Indian History of the American West* (New York: Bantam, 1971), xi–xii.

2. Josephus, *Ag. Ap.* 1.12.

3. Friedrich A. Wolf, *Prolegomena ad Homerum, sive, De operum Homericorum: Prisca et genuine forma variisque mutationibus et probabilii ratione emendandi* (Halis Saxonum: E. Libraria Orphaotrophei, 1795; repr., *Prolegomena to Homer* [Princeton: Princeton University Press, 1985]), 94–95, 139.

4. Albert B. Lord, *A Singer of Tales*, Harvard Studies in Comparative Literature 24 (Cam-

This is not the only literary comment that the Jewish author made in the opening excursus of his apology.[5] The basic claim of his excursus is that there was a distinct tradition of Eastern historiography that was more reliable in recording antiquity than the Greek tradition. Josephus opened his excursus on historiography with this statement: "In the first place I am completely dumbfounded by those who think that we should pay attention to the Greeks alone and learn the truth from them about the most ancient events but not trust us or other peoples."[6] The "us," of course, are the Jews; the "other peoples" are the Egyptians, Chaldeans, and Phoenicians, who "possess a most ancient and stable tradition of the past."[7] Josephus later returned to the same contrast when he compared the Greek preoccupation with rhetoric to the Eastern concern for reliability: "Therefore with respect to eloquence or skill in articulation, we must concede to Greek authors, not however with respect to the reliable history of antiquity, especially the history of the peoples in each land."[8]

It is worth noting that this excursus is not the only place where Josephus grouped Eastern traditions against the West. In the *Jewish Antiquities* he made a similar point. Commenting on the longevity of the antediluvians, Josephus claimed: "All Greek and barbarian authors of *Antiquities* testify to my account." He then offered a list of barbarian authors and followed it with a separate list of Greek authors. Among the barbarians he included "Manetho who wrote the record of the Egyptians; Berossus who composed the Chaldean History; Mochus, Hestiaeus, and the Egyptian Hieronymus who composed Phoenician Histories."[9]

Josephus was not the only ancient author to group these writers together. Tertullian (ca. 160–ca. 240 CE), the father of Latin theology, knew the same basic tradition. The North African rhetor argued for the antiquity of the Jewish scriptures by pointing out that Moses predated Homer by five hundred years—a surprisingly accurate assessment—and that the prophets were at least

---

bridge: Harvard University Press, 1960), argued on the basis of his study of bards in Yugoslavia that the Homeric hymns were originally oral compositions sung by bards. See also Albert B. Lord, *The Singer Resumes the Tale*, ed. Mary L. Lord (Ithaca: Cornell University Press, 1995).

5. Josephus, *Ag. Ap.* 1.6–56.

6. Josephus, *Ag. Ap.* 1.6. For Greek accounts of the peoples of the East, see Robert Drews, *The Greek Accounts of Eastern History* (Washington, DC: The Center for Hellenic Studies; Cambridge: Harvard University Press, 1973).

7. Josephus, *Ag. Ap.* 1.8.

8. Josephus, *Ag. Ap.* 1.27.

9. Josephus, *Ant.* 1.107. The list of Greek authors includes Hesiod, Hecataeus, Hellanicus, Acusilaus, Ephorus, and Nicolas.

as old as the earliest Greco-Roman philosophers. He conceded that this would be difficult to prove: "The archives of the most ancient nations, the Egyptians, the Chaldeans, the Phoenicians, would have to be examined; their citizens would have to be summoned through whom the appropriate information could be furnished." He then listed the authors: "Manetho the Egyptian, Berossus the Chaldean, and Hieronimus the Phoenician king of Tyre; their successors too, Ptolemy the Mendesian, Menander of Ephesus, Demetrius Phalerus, King Juba, Apion, Thallus; and the Jew Josephus, the native champion of the ancient history of the Jews, who either approves or refutes them."[10] While Tertullian apparently knew Josephus's *Against Apion*, his statement reflects an awareness of works beyond the corpus of Josephus and the works that the Jewish historian mentioned. The latter did not mention the literary projects of Ptolemy the Mendesian, King Juba, or Thallus, although he did refer to King Juba.[11] This suggests that Tertullian had some independent knowledge of the Near Eastern authors whom Josephus mentioned.

Are these claims as worthy of our attention as Josephus's statement about the Homeric poems or are they part of a rhetorical argument that has no basis in sober literary judgements? I used the statements in *Against Apion* 1.6–56 as an ἀφορμή or starting point for the tradition that I called Apologetic Historiography in my book *Historiography and Self-Definition* and in the first chapter of this work.[12] In my monograph, I did not have the space to analyze

---

10. Tertullian, *Apol.* 19.6.

11. Josephus, *J. W.* 2.115; *Ant.* 17.349. For the literary project of Ptolemy the Mendesian see *FGH* 611; for that of King Juba see *FGH* 275. For the literary project of Thallus see *FGH* 256 and Carl R. Holladay, *Historians*, vol. 1 of *Fragments from Hellenistic Jewish Authors*, SBLTT 20 (Chico, CA: Scholars Press, 1983), 343–69.

12. Sterling, *Historiography and Self-Definition*, 9, 11. Others noted the tradition of Eastern historiography, but did not attempt to work through it in a systematic fashion to determine the criteria by which it should be assessed. E.g., Elias J. Bickerman, "Origines Gentium," *CP* 47 (1952): 73–76; Arnaldo Momigliano, *Alien Wisdom: The Limits of Hellenization* (Cambridge: Cambridge University Press, 1975), 92–93; Arnaldo Momigliano, *Classical Foundations*, 98–99; Robert A. Oden Jr., "Philo of Byblos and Hellenistic Historiography," *PEQ* 110 (1978): 115–26; John J. Collins, *Between Athens and Jerusalem: Jewish Identity in the Hellenistic Diaspora* (New York: Crossroad, 1992), 26; Charles W. Fornara, *The Nature of History in Ancient Greece and Rome*, EIDOS: Studies in Classical Kinds (Berkeley: University of California Press, 1983), 39; and Doron Mendels, "'Creative History' in the Hellenistic Near East in the Third and Second Centuries BCE: The Jewish Case," *JSP* 2 (1988), 13–20. See also John Dillery, "Greek Historians of the Near East: Clio's 'Other' Sons," in *A Companion to Greek and Roman Historiography*, 221–30 and John Dillery, *Clio's Other Sons: Berossus and Manetho, with an Afterword on Demetrius* (Ann Arbor: University of Michigan Press, 2015), esp. 55–354.

the ancient claims.[13] I would like to return to the statements of Josephus and explore the credibility of his claim in the light of the ancient evidence. Did ancients—apart from Josephus and Tertullian—recognize a distinct Eastern tradition of historiography or is this a modern construct?[14] If the genre was recognized by ancient authors, what criteria did they use to distinguish it from other forms of historical writing?

Josephus's Classification

We need to begin by setting out Josephus's outline of this tradition. As I have indicated, he made the case principally in the opening excursus of *Against Apion*. The excursus is not, however, an aside in the work, but an important point of orientation for the work as a whole. As Shaye Cohen has argued: "*Against Apion* is not just an apology; it is also an essay in historiography and historical criticism."[15] I understand it as an *explicit* statement of the claims that are made more *implicitly* in the *Jewish Antiquities*.[16] It is therefore important to examine the excursus within the whole of *Against Apion* and not as an isolated unit.[17]

13. I surveyed ancient classifications of the types of history writing in *Historiography and Self-Definition*, 3–9, but did not attempt to sketch the full contours of Apologetic Historiography on the basis of the perceptions of the indigenous authors who self-consciously wrote in the tradition.

14. Tessa Rajak, "Josephus and the 'Archaeology' of the Jews," *JJS* 33 (1982): 465–77, has compared the *Antiquities* to other *Antiquities* in a helpful essay. She argued that Josephus's *Antiquities* was Greek in form, but not in substance or intent. She did not, however, attempt to work through the native historians systematically in light of *Against Apion*.

15. Shaye J. D. Cohen, "History and Historiography in the *Against Apion* of Josephus," *History and Theory* 27 (1988): 1–11; repr. in *Essays in Jewish Historiography*, SFSHJ 15 (Atlanta: Scholars Press, 1991), 1–11.

16. Josephus makes this point in the preface (*Ag. Ap.* 1.1–5). Hereafter, references to *Ag. Ap.* will be given in parentheses in the text.

17. The most important treatment of *Against Apion* is the collection of essays edited by Louis H. Feldman and John R. Levison, *Josephus' "Contra Apionem": Studies in Its Character and Context with a Latin Concordance to the Portion Missing in Greek*, AGJU 34 (Leiden: Brill, 1996). There are four useful commentaries on the treatise that provide a number of parallels: Johann G. Müller, *Des Flavius Josephus Schrift gegen den Apion: Text und Erklärung* (Basel: Bahnmaier [C. Detloff], 1877; repr., Hildesheim: Georg Olm, 1969); Lucio Troiani, *Commento storico al "Contro Apione" di Giuseppe*, Biblioteca degli studi classici e orientali 9 (Pisa: Giardini, 1977); Aryeh Kasher, *Neged "Apyon,"* 2 vols. (Jerusalem: Merkaz Zalman, 1996); and John Barclay, *Against Apion: Translation and Commentary*, FJTC 10 (Leiden: Brill, 2007), a magisterial commentary. Christine Gerber, *Ein Bild des Judentums für Nichtjuden*

Josephus set the excursus off in a careful way by bracketing it with prefaces: the major preface in *Ag. Ap.* 1.1–5 and a secondary, resumptive preface in 1.57–59. The excursus proper falls into two major units: 1.6–27, a polemic against Greek historiography, and 1.28–56, the Eastern tradition.[18] He marked out the major conceptual units by opening and closing them with explicit references to the Eastern historiographical tradition: 1.6–9 contrasts the upstart Greeks with their elder neighbors in the East; 1.28–29 insists that the Eastern peoples were superior to their Western neighbors in keeping records; finally, 1.58–59 again refers to the superiority of the Eastern practice of keeping records. Josephus has thus carefully delineated his excursus and signaled the basic structure within it.[19]

The Jewish apologist subdivided the first half of his excursus, his critique of Greek historiography (1.6–27), into two major conceptual units. He carefully set these out by repeating the charge that the Greeks were unreliable. He made the charge three times (1.6, 15, 27). The first opens the excursus with one of his most powerful arguments: the Greeks were latecomers (1.6–14). He paraphrased Herodotus to drive his point home: "Everything in the Greek world is new and took place yesterday or the day before—as the saying goes" (1.7).[20] Herodotus was not alone in this admission; Plato also acknowledged the relatively recent age of the Greeks.[21] Josephus next accused Greek historians of inconsistency—a charge to which he could hardly plead innocent himself (1.15–27)! He cited the historiographical critiques that Greek historians leveled against one another as proof of the charge. Greek historians regularly castigated their predecessors as a means of marking out their own turf.[22] For example, Josephus wrote: "Ephorus exposed Hellanicus as a liar in most of his statements, Timaeus exposed Ephorus, later writers exposed Timaeus,

---

von Flavius Josephus: Untersuchungen zu seiner Schrift "Contra Apionem," AGJU 40 (Leiden: Brill, 1997), is also exceptionally helpful.

18. Barclay, *Against Apion,* 8–11, has a helpful overview and a summary of scholarship on the excursus.

19. Josephus carefully structured the whole of *Ag. Ap.* See Gregory E. Sterling, "The Account of the Jewish Constitution in Josephus's *"Contra Apionem"*: Afterthought or Addition?" (forthcoming).

20. Cf. Herodotus 2.53.1–3, esp. 1.

21. Plato, *Tim.* 22b–c. Thackeray thought that Josephus drew from Plato in this context, but the wording is much closer to Herodotus (*Josephus,* 10 vols.; LCL [Cambridge: Harvard University Press, 1926–1965], 1:164–65 n. a).

22. The practice began with Hecataeus of Miletus and ran through the tradition (*FGH* 1 frag. 1). For an analysis see John Marincola, *Authority and Tradition in Ancient Historiography* (Cambridge: Cambridge University Press, 1997), 217–57.

everyone exposed Herodotus" (1.15–18).[23] Josephus thought that there were two deficiencies that accounted for the inconsistencies of Hellenic accounts of ancient affairs: the Greeks failed to keep official records (1.19–22) and they were preoccupied more with rhetoric than with reliability (1.23–27).

The Greek failure to transmit trustworthy records became the basis for his sketch of the reliability of the Eastern tradition (1.28–56). The Jewish apologist maintained that, in contrast to the Greeks, the Eastern nations kept accurate records: "That the Egyptians and Babylonians devoted care to their records from the earliest ages . . . and that among those who associated with the Greeks the Phoenicians used writing both for the management of daily life and for the record of public events—I think I can let pass since everyone agrees" (1.28).[24] Just as he opened the excursus with a reference to these specific nations, so he opened his defense of Eastern historiography with a conscious nod to the East. He then argued that the Jews had kept their records carefully as well (1.30–43) and concluded with a defense of his own *Jewish War* (1.44–56).

We can summarize the structure of his excursus in this way:

1.1–5, Preface
    1.6–27, Critique of Greek Historiography
        1.6–12, Upstart Greeks
            1.6–9, Direct Contrast between the West and the East
        1.13–27, The Inconsistencies of the Greeks
        1.28–56, Apology for Eastern Historiography
        1.28–29, The Eastern Practice of Keeping Records
            1.28–29, Direct Contrast between the West and the East
        1.30–43, The Jewish Practice of Keeping Records
        1.44–56, A Defense of the *Jewish War*
1.57–59, Resumptive Preface

There is a reason why Josephus chose to mention the Egyptians, Chaldeans, and Phoenicians when he referred to Eastern nations.[25] These three groups

---

23. For Ephorus's critique of Hellanicus see *FGH* 4 frag. 116 (Strabo 8.5.5); for Timaeus's attacks on Ephorus see *FGH* 70 test. 30b (Polybius 12.23.1); for broadsides against Timaeus see Polybius book 12 and the lost work of Istros; see *FGH* 334 frag. 59; and for criticisms of Herodotus see Ctesias, *FGH* 688 test. 8; Hecataeus of Abdera, *FGH* 264 frag. 25 (Diodorus Siculus 1.69.7); Manetho, *FGH* 609 test. 7a (Josephus, *Ag. Ap.* 1.73), frag. 13 (on Manetho's critique of Herodotus, see below).

24. See also 1.28–29.

25. He mentions the Egyptians, Chaldeans, and Phoenicians in *Ag. Ap.* 1.8, 28, 70–71,

provided evidence for the antiquity of the Jews (1.69–160). The Jewish historian made his point explicit when he explained why Hieronymus of Cardia (floruit fourth through third centuries BCE) omitted the Jews in his important history of Alexander's successors or the *Diadochoi*. Josephus chalked up his silence to ill will.[26] He then countered: "Nevertheless, the records of the Egyptians, Chaldeans, and Phoenicians suffice to demonstrate our antiquity; in addition to these there are a significant number of Greek authors" (1.215).[27] Among the Egyptians the Jerusalemite mentioned Manetho (1.73–105), who "wrote his ancestral history from the sacred tablets or translated (them), as he says" (1.73). At a later point in his work Josephus attempted to answer the charges leveled against Jews in the Egyptian histories by native Egyptian authors: the alternate account in Manetho (1.227–287), Chaeremon (1.288–292), Lysimachus (1.292–303), and Apion (2.8–144). He omitted them when reciting the Egyptian evidence for Jewish antiquity since he only wanted to produce positive witnesses not hostile critics. His incorporation of them at a later point indicates their place within the tradition, even if that place is begrudgingly acknowledged. Next he turned to the Phoenician evidence (1.106–127). He claimed that the archives in a temple at Tyre contained the correspondence between Hiram and Solomon (1.106–111).[28] He offered the accounts of two Greek authors as corroborative evidence: Dius (1.112–115)[29] and Menander of Ephesus (1.116–125).[30] The final group are the Chaldeans (1.128–160). Josephus held them until the end because they were the ancestors of the Jews and therefore not as credible as witnesses (1.71). He cited one author, Berossus who followed "the most ancient records" (1.130).

The Tradition

What should we make of the historiographical tradition Josephus sketched? It would be helpful to compare the contours of the tradition that Josephus

---

215; 2.1. cf. also 1.63–64. He mentions the Egyptians and Chaldeans in 1.14; the Egyptians and Phoenicians in 1.61, 63, 70; and the Chaldeans and Phoenicians in 1.143.

26. The same issue is addressed in the Letter of Aristeas where the silence is attributed to the sacred character of the Jewish works. The explanation is attributed to Hecataeus of Abdera (=Pseudo-Hecataeus). See Let. Arist. 31.

27. He made the same point in *Ag. Ap.* 2.1.

28. For the letters see 1 Kgs 5:1–12; Eupolemus frag. 2 (Eusebius, *Praep. ev.* 9.30.1–34.18); Josephus, *Ant.* 8.50–54.

29. Cf. also Josephus, *Ant.* 8.147.

30. Cf. also Josephus, *Ant.* 8.144–146, 324; 9.283–287. For the fragments see *FGH* 783.

set out with what we know about native Eastern historians. Although our knowledge of these historians is often sketchy—sometimes we are reduced to the attribution of a work to a name—there is enough evidence to suggest that a significant number of native historians wrote the antiquities of their people.

The Egyptians. The Egyptian record is the best attested. The most important witness is Manetho, the third-century BCE priest whose three-volume *Aegyptiaca* (Αἰγυπτιακά) praised his homeland for its antiquity.[31] Manetho was joined by several other priests. Ptolemy of Mendes (second to first century BCE), wrote a three-volume history of the Egyptian kings.[32] Tatian summarized what we know: "Of the Egyptians there are accurate chronological records. The interpreter of their writings is Ptolemy, not the king, but a priest from Mendes. He set out the acts of their kings" (Test. 1a). Tatian's statement suggests that his work resembled the dynastic history of Manetho. A third priest, Chaeremon (floruit first century CE), who was an older contemporary of Josephus, composed an *Aegyptiace historia* (Αἰγυπτιακὴ ἱστορία).[33] The similarity between his account of the Jews and the alternate account in Manetho suggests that he was also concerned to magnify Egypt at the expense of other peoples. If we could be sure that his accounts of Egyptian priests and Egyptian religion belonged to his history, the case would be clearer.[34]

These priestly authors were joined by a cadre of other Egyptian writers who are largely unknown. Later tradents claim that a number of authors wrote *Aegyptiaca* (Αἰγυπτιακά). In some cases, we have a relatively good idea of the orientation of these works. For example, it is likely that Lysimachus (floruit

---

31. *FGH* 609. For a summary with bibliography see Rolf Krauss, "Manethon," *DNP* 7:804-5. To the bibliography add Sterling, *Historiography and Self-Definition*, 117-35; Ian S. Moyer, "Luculentissima fragmenta: Manetho's *Aegyptiaca* and the Limits of Hellenism," in *Egypt and the Limits of Hellenism* (Cambridge: Cambridge University Press, 2011), 84-141; and Dillery, "Greek Historians of the Near East: Clio's 'Other' Sons," 221-30, esp. 225-28; Dillery, *Clio's Other Sons: Berossus and Manetho*, 84-117, 160-82, 301-47.

32. *FGH* 611. Cf. also Menaham Stern, *Greek and Latin Authors on Jews and Judaism*, 3 vols. (Jerusalem: The Israel Academy of Sciences and Humanities, 1974), LXI.157a-b (1:379-81). Hereafter *GLAJJ*. His date is unknown, although he probably wrote prior to Apion (first century CE). We can tentatively place him between Manetho and Apion—i.e., in the last two centuries BCE.

33. *FGH* 618 test. 5, 10; frag. 1; *GLAJJ* LXIV.178 (1:417-21); Pieter W. van der Horst, *Chaeremon: Egyptian Priest and Stoic Philosopher. The Fragments Collected and Translated with Explanatory Notes*, EPRO 101 (Leiden: Brill, 1984). For a summary with bibliography see Michael Frede, "Chaeremon," *ANRW* 36.3:2067-2103 and Brad Inwood, "Chaeremon [2]," *DNP* 2:1082.

34. See Chaeremon frags. 2, 4, 5, 10.

first century BCE)[35] and Apion (floruit first century CE),[36] who shared a common anti-Jewish orientation, celebrated the antiquity and cultural superiority of Egypt. This was certainly the case for Mosmes, who claimed that the Egyptians were the oldest civilization.[37] In other cases we can only surmise that the authors shared the tendency to magnify their own history by appealing to its antiquity. Such authors include Lysias of Naucratis,[38] Asclepiades of Mendes,[39] and Thrasyllus of Mendes.[40] The same may also be true for those who composed histories vaguely entitled *On the Egyptians* (περὶ τῶν Αἰγυπτίων). These include Hermaeus and Demetrius.[41] Even if our assumptions about some of these authors or their works are inaccurate, there is enough evidence to demonstrate that priests and intellectuals in Egypt wrote histories of their *patria* that accentuated its age. The evidence also indicates that Josephus has only given us a selective sampling: he only named four of the eleven authors whom we know wrote *Egyptian Antiquities*.

The Phoenicians. The second body of evidence Josephus cited was the Phoenician. Although he does not mention any historians in *Against Apion*, he did in the *Jewish Antiquities*—as we noted in our introduction. The first he mentioned was Mochus. According to Tatian (ca. 120–ca. 180 CE), Mochus was a native historian who composed his Phoenician history in his own language. Speaking of the Phoenician evidence for antiquity, Tatian wrote: "There were three men among them: Theodotus, Hypsicrates, and Mochus. Laetus, who also composed the lives of the philosophers accurately, translated their works into Greek."[42] If Tatian is correct, we should think of Laetus as the representative of the tradition since, just as the Egyptian priests had translated their hieroglyphs into Greek, he translated a native Phoenician account into Greek. The second historian was Hestiaeus, who wrote a multivolume *Phoenicica* (φοινικικά).[43] The third was Hieronymus, whom Josephus says was an

35. *FGH* 621 frag. 1; *GLAJJ* LXII.158–62 (1:382–88). For a summary with bibliography see Gregor Damschen, "Lysimachus [6]," *DNP* 7:608.
36. *FGH* 616 test. 10, 11, 12, 15; frags. 1–6. He wrote an *Aigyptiaka* in five books. See also *GLAJJ* LXIII.163–77 (1:389–416) and Franco Montanari, "Apion," *DNP* 1:845–47.
37. *FGH* 614 test. 1.
38. *FGH* 613. He wrote an *Aigyptiaka* in at least three books.
39. *FGH* 617 frag. 1.
40. *FGH* 622 frag. 1.
41. *FGH* 620 and *FGH* 643 frag. 1, respectively.
42. *FGH* 784 test. 1. Cf. also *GLAJJ* XXIII.39 (1:128–30).
43. *FGH* 786. Our primary witness is Josephus, *Ant.* 1.107, 118.

Egyptian but Tertullian thought was a Phoenician.[44] He wrote a *Phoenician Antiquities* (ἀρχαιολογία φοινικική).

There are two additional first- or early second-century CE Phoenician historians whom Josephus did not mention. Claudius Iolaus wrote a *Phoinikika* (φοινικικά) in at least three volumes.[45] We are fortunate to have a representative portion of the work of his contemporary Philo of Byblos (ca. 70–ca. 160 CE) preserved in the *Praeparatio evangelica* of Eusebius.[46] Porphyry also mentioned "the Phoenician history . . . which Sanchuniathon composed in the Phoenician language and Philo of Byblos translated into Greek in eight books."[47] The identity and historical credibility of Sanchuniathon has been the occasion of an extended scholarly debate. The most reasonable assessment is that he was a historian in much the same way that Mochus was; that is, a native Phoenician who wrote a history of Phoenicia in his native language. Philo of Byblos played the same role for Sanchuniathon as Laetus did for Mochus. Josephus chose not to mention any of these explicitly in *Against Apion* since— presumably—they did not mention the Jews.

The Babylonians. The third tradition to which Josephus appealed is the Babylonian. The evidence for this national tradition is far more limited. The most famous native historian is Berossus (floruit 290 BCE), the older contemporary of Manetho.[48] This Babylonian priest wrote a three-volume *Babyloniaca* (βαβυλωνιακά). Like his Egyptian counterpart, he wrote for the glory of his homeland by stressing its age. Unfortunately, the only evidence that we have for native Babylonian historians after Berossus and before Josephus is a statement of the historian Agathias, who grouped Athenocles[49]

44. *FGH* 787. Our primary witness is again Josephus, *Ant.* 1.93, 107.

45. *FGH* 788 and *GLAJJ* LXXXVII.249 (1:534–35).

46. *FGH* 790. See also the edition of Harold W. Attridge and Robert A. Oden Jr., *Philo of Byblos, "The Phoenician History": Introduction, Critical Text, Translation, Notes*, CBQMS 9 (Washington, DC: Catholic Biblical Association, 1981); Albert I. Baumgarten, *"The Phoenician History" of Philo of Byblos: A Commentary*, EPRO 89 (Leiden: Brill, 1981); Albert I. Baumgarten, "Philo of Byblos," *ABD* 5:342–44; and Sotera Fornaro, "Herennios Philon," *DNP* 5:410–11.

47. *FGH* 790 test. 3. Cf. also test. 5 and frag. 1, where Eusebius indicates that the work consisted of nine volumes.

48. *FGH* 680. For a summary with bibliography see Beate Pongratz-Leisten, "Beros(s) os," *DNP* 2:579–80, to which add Sterling, *Historiography and Self-Definition*, 104–17; Dillery, "Greek Historians of the Near East: Clio's 'Other' Sons," 222–25; and Dillery, *Clio's Other Sons*, esp. 58–84, 133–60, 220–300.

49. *FGH* 682.

and Simacus[50] with Berossus. According to Agathias, they wrote the ancient histories of the Assyrians and Medes.

Other Peoples. What about the traditions of other peoples? For example, what of Xanthus's four volume *Lydiaka* (λυδιακά)?[51] Josephus has confined his comments to the traditions that dealt with the Jews. There were certainly other historians who wrote on behalf of their homelands following Alexander. Are there other considerations that might affect our judgment about the presence and viability of the larger tradition?

THE CRITERIA

Polemical Setting. Josephus used three criteria for the Eastern tradition in *Against Apion.* The first is that Eastern historiography was a deliberate counter to the Western tradition. Josephus made this explicit by juxtaposing his critique of Greek historiography (*Ag. Ap.* 1.6–27) with a defense of Eastern accounts (1.27–56). He had reason to make the contrast. Greek historians were not inclined to give any credence to accounts written by non-Greeks. Strabo captured the sentiment succinctly: "The accounts of the ancient history of the Persians, Medes, and Syrians have not won much credence as a result of the simplicity of their historians and their love of myths."[52] Josephus and other authors in the East were keenly aware of this prejudice. The Jewish historian began his excursion with a protest of this view (see above).[53] He repeated the protest when he began his critique of Greek historiography: "How unreasonable is it that the Greeks are so conceited that they believe that they alone know ancient history and pass on the truth about it accurately?" (1.15). Between his list of Eastern witnesses to the Jews' antiquity and his list of Greek authors, the Jerusalem priest wrote: "It is necessary to satisfy the desire of those who disbelieve the records of the barbarians and deem that only Greeks are worthy of belief" (1.161).[54] He made the same point in the *Jewish Antiquities* when he

50. *FGH* 683.
51. *FGH* 765.
52. Strabo 11.6.2.
53. On Josephus's attitude toward the Greeks in *Against Apion* see Christoph Schäublin, "Josephus und die Griechen," *Hermes* 110 (1982): 316–41, esp. 316–25, where Schäublin deals with the material on historiography.
54. For a similar complaint see Tacitus, *Ann.* 2.88.

introduced the Roman decrees.[55] This perspective shapes the presentation of Jewish history in the *Jewish Antiquities* and *Against Apion*.[56]

It also shaped the perspectives of other Eastern historians. Manetho criticized Herodotus's account of Egypt. His criticisms were extensive enough that some have credited him with a book against "the father of history."[57] Berossus censured Hellanicus (ca. 480–395 BCE)—and by extension Ctesias (late fifth century BCE)—for his account of Semiramis, the legendary founder of Babylon according to Greek accounts.[58] Philo of Byblos has a critique of Greek historiography that is strikingly similar to that of Josephus. He wrote: "These things were discovered by us as we attempted to understand the affairs of the Phoenicians and investigated a great deal of material, although not that of the Greeks." He excluded the Greek material because it was too inconsistent, the same charge that Josephus leveled against them. Philo went on to say that he had written a three-volume *Unbelievable History* to refute the inconsistencies of the Greeks.[59]

The open polemic against Greek historiography and historians in the major texts of Eastern authors shows that these works were written in response to Greek cultural hegemony. Peoples in the East were unhappy with the Greek representations and attempted to relate their own story as a direct counter to the versions that the Greeks had written about them. At the same time, they wrote in Greek and in a Hellenic form, a form that took its inspiration from Greek ethnography but moved into the direction of Greek historiography. One of the key figures in the transition was Hecataeus of Abdera (floruit 320–290 BCE), a Greek who transformed ethnography into a history of Egypt that celebrated Egypt as the *fons* of civilization.[60] Indigenous authors followed his lead. The tradition thus has a paradoxical relationship to Hellenism: it both promotes and protests. It promotes by casting native traditions into a Hellenic form; it protests by arguing that Greek accounts are unacceptable.

55. Josephus, *Ant.* 14.187.

56. On the relationship between the two works see Paul Spilsbury, "*Contra Apionem* and *Antiquitates Judaicae*: Points of Contact," in *Josephus' "Contra Apionem": Studies in Its Character and Context with a Latin Concordance to the Portion Missing in Greek*, ed. Louis H. Feldman and John R. Levison, AGJU34 (Leiden: Brill), 348–68.

57. *FGH* 609 test. 7; frag. 13.

58. *FGH* 680 frag. 8 (Josephus, *Ag. Ap.* 1.142).

59. *FGH* 790 frag. 1 (Eusebius, *Praep. ev.* 1.9.27–28). For the *Unbelievable History* see frags. 12–13.

60. *FGH* 264. For details and bibliography see Sterling, *Historiography and Self-Definition*, 55–91.

Sources. Native historians attempted to make their case by breaking ranks with the established method of investigation in Greek ethnography and historiography. The Greek practice consisted of visiting a foreign country and asking the inhabitants questions. The importance of reading the records of the indigenous people did not occur to most Greeks who would not have been willing to go to the trouble of learning the requisite languages. It did occur to Eastern historians who were often priests and the guardians of the records and languages of their respective peoples. They insisted—whether accurately or not—that they were drawing on their own traditions. They wrote from an insider's perspective rather than an outsider's viewpoint. More specifically, the priests and leading intellectuals among them claimed that their histories consisted of translations of their ancestral records or an earlier native historian. The claim occurs in all of the branches of the tradition: Manetho,[61] Ptolemy Mendes,[62] and probably Chaeremon make this claim among the Egyptians;[63] Laetus[64] and Philo of Byblos among the Phoenicians;[65] Berossus for the Babylonians;[66] and Josephus himself for his *Jewish Antiquities.*[67]

The method was not unique to Eastern authors. Hecataeus of Abdera claimed that unlike Herodotus who asked questions, he based his account on the Egyptian records.[68] Josephus tells us that Menander of Ephesus (floruit ca. 200 BCE) "wrote the events of each of the kings among the Greeks and barbarians, having gone to the trouble to learn the history from the native records of each" (*Ag. Ap.* 1.116). Yet even in these cases, there is a fundamental difference. Hecataeus may have consulted the Egyptian hieroglyphs but he did so through the priests who read them. Manetho, on the other hand, had no need for a native translator: he was the translator.

Why did Eastern authors insist on native traditions? Josephus again provides a clear rationale: "In fact, each people attempt to trace their events back to the earliest possible date so that they will not appear to copy others" (*Ag. Ap.* 2.152). Ancient records gave proof of antiquity. If peoples living in the East could es-

---

61. *FGH* 609 test. 7 (Josephus, *Ag. Ap.* 1.73, 104, 228). Cf. also Josephus, *Ag. Ap.* 1.287.

62. *FGH* 611 test. 1a.

63. Chaeremon is called a "sacred scribe" (ἱερογραμματεύς), which indicates his ability to handle hieroglyphs (*FGH* 618 test. 4, 6). He wrote a book on hieroglyphs that became very important in the ancient world (test. 6; frag. 12).

64. *FGH* 784 test. 1.

65. *FGH* 790 test. 3, 5; frag. 1.

66. *FGH* 680 test. 3 (Josephus, *Ag. Ap.* 1.130), 4.

67. Josephus, *Ant.* 1.5; 10.218; *Ag. Ap.* 1.54.

68. *FGH* 263 frag. 25 (Diodorus Siculus 1.69.7).

tablish that they were older than the Greeks on the basis of their records, they could overturn the Greek view that Eastern cultures were derived from Hellenic culture. The claim is thus not primarily chronological but cultural. It replaced the *interpretatio Graeca* with an *interpretatio Aegyptiaca, interpretatio Phoenicica*, or *interpretatio Babyloniaca*. The claim appears among all of the representatives of the tradition. Manetho argued that the Egyptians were the oldest people on the earth as did Mosmes.[69] The Phoenicians made similar claims. Laetus maintained that philosophy began with barbarians not Greeks.[70] Philo of Byblos boldly stated, "The oldest of the barbarians, especially the Phoenicians and Egyptians, from whom the rest of humanity has received (their traditions) thought that the greatest gods were those who had discovered something useful for daily needs or had acted in some way that helped the nations."[71] Berossus traced civilization back to a revelation vouchsafed to the Babylonians.[72] All of these claims were in direct protest to the Greek construction of human civilization.[73]

Style. Josephus offered one other criterion. He claimed that Greeks were preoccupied with style rather than substance. His charge was echoed by Philo of Byblos, who wrote that Greek history "is inconsistent and has been composed by some more for the sake of argumentation than for truth."[74] The complaint was a commonplace.[75] It also appears in the Hermetic corpus when Ascelpius forbids the translation of a series of revelations "so that these mysteries would not reach the Greeks." His concern was that "the arrogant, impotent, and elaborate talk of the Greeks would not destroy the honorable, terse, and powerful expression of the words."[76]

This charge should not be given undue weight. It may reflect the embarrassment that native historians felt when they tried to compose in a second language that was as subtle as Greek. Josephus himself worried about his style.[77] It is an easy move to argue that substance rather than style is the focus of a work when the attainment of an elevated and sophisticated style is not possible.

---

69. Manetho, *FGH* 609 frag. 4; Mosmes, *FGH* 614 test. 1. For a helpful summary of this phenomenon among the Egyptians see Reinhold Merkelbach, *Isis regina – Zeus Sarapis: Die griechisch-ägyptische Religion nach den Quellen dargestellt* (Stuttgart: Teubner, 1995), 63–64, 231–41.

70. *FGH* 784 frag. 2. Cf. also the report in Diogenes Laertius 1.1–2.

71. *FGH* 790 frag. 1.

72. *FGH* 680 frag. 1.

73. On the construction of the origins of the nations, see Bickerman, "Origines Gentium," 65–81.

74. *FGH* 790 frag. 1.

75. See also the critique of Herodian 1.1.

76. Corp. herm. 16.2.

77. E.g., Josephus, *Ant.* 20.263; *Ag. Ap.* 1.50.

JOSEPHUS'S CONSTRUCT OR HISTORIOGRAPHICAL TRADITION?

We may now return to our original question. Does this evidence suggest that there was a tradition of Eastern historiography? Josephus thought there was. Not only that, but he based a major part of his case in *Against Apion* on it. The thrust of the argument in the opening historiographical excursus in *Against Apion* is twofold. First, Josephus argued that there was an Eastern tradition that stood in contrast to the Hellenic tradition. Second, he argued that the Jews, their records, and his histories belonged to this tradition. The major argument pivoted on antiquity: Josephus did not argue that the Greeks should recognize the antiquity of the East or the written records of Eastern peoples—this was a given. Rather, he argued that the Jews and their records belonged to this honored tradition. The question that we face is whether the presence of an Eastern historiographical tradition is Josephus's construct, shaped to meet the rhetorical argumentation of *Against Apion*, or whether it was a historiographical tradition that he and others recognized. We have already noted that Tertullian was also aware of this tradition. Is there any evidence that others were as well?

Other Eastern historians appear to share the view that this was a recognized historiographical tradition. The fragmentary remains that we have canvassed suggest that Eastern authors were aware that they were writing indigenous histories in contrast to Hellenic portrayals. Their critiques of Greek authors, insistence on native sources, and evident national pride all attest to their self-consciousness. Yet we can be more specific in our questions: Were they cognizant of working within a tradition? Did they know other works that we have attributed to this tradition? Or did the common circumstances of the Hellenistic and Roman worlds in which they found themselves to be a conquered people create common but not unified perspectives? They were not continuators of one another in the same way that Xenophon, Theompompus, and the anonymous author of the *Hellenica Oxyrhynchia* took up the unfinished work of Thucydides and extended it (see chapter 4). Instead, they wrote national histories that—to some extent—competed with one another. There are a few hints that they were aware of others writing in the same tradition and were influenced by them. Syncellus thought that Manetho wrote "in imitation of Berossus" (κατὰ μίμησιν Βηρώσσου).[78] Unfortunately, it is impossible to know whether this claim was a deduction based on the general similarities between the two authors or was based on statements in the work that are no longer extant and whether the statements were known to Syncellus directly or, more

78. *FGH* 609 test. 11c. Cf. also b.

likely, indirectly from later summaries from which he drew.[79] It is certainly possible that Manetho wrote his *Aegyptiaca* as an Egyptian response to the Babylonian claims made by Berossus. This is, however, a supposition, not an established fact. The evidence within specific traditions is similar in its nature. Tertullian called Ptolemy of Mendes a "follower" (*sectator*) of Manetho.[80] The basis for this assessment is that he set out the deeds of the Egyptian kings.[81] Manetho was considered the first to organize the Egyptian dynasties, which subsequent authors followed.[82] The scant remains of Ptolemy make it impossible to know whether his work consciously followed Manetho as a model or worked indirectly from the tradition that Manetho had established. The same is true for almost all other authors who, like Manetho, wrote *Aegyptiaca* that presented native traditions via Greek conventions.[83] We can be more certain in one instance. Apion knew the work of Ptolemy of Mendes whom he cited on at least one occasion.[84] In two other places Josephus suggested that Apion knew other authors, although he does not name any from the tradition that we have sketched.[85]

If we turn to the Phoenician tradition, we should recall that Philo of Byblos claimed that his source was an ancient writer named Sanchuniathon. As we noted earlier, the credibility of this claim is part of a long debate in scholarship; however, there is a consensus that Sanchuniathon was an author and not a fiction created by Philo. If we accept the *opinio communis*, then he was, as Harold Attridge and Robert Oden describe him, "a patriotic local ethnographer of the

---

79. See the sober comments of Peter M. Fraser, *Ptolemaic Alexandria*, 3 vols. (Oxford: Clarendon, 1972), 1:505–6. Cf. also Sterling, *Historiography and Self-Definition*, 133–34.

80. Tertullian, *Apol.* 19.6 (*FGH* 611 test. 2a).

81. *FGH* 611 test. 1a, b, 2b.

82. *FGH* 609 frags. 2–3.

83. Cf. the judgment of Fraser, *Ptolemaic Alexandria*, 1:510–11: "Manethon probably made little or no impact on contemporary Alexandrian writers, who were not interested in Egyptian history or chronology . . . On the other hand there are several minor writers, mostly of the later Ptolemaic period, who, consciously or otherwise, followed the tradition of Manethon by writing about Egyptian antiquities and Egyptian religion . . . At all events such writings, unimportant though they evidently were as literature and historiography, point to the very significant fact that in the late Ptolemaic and early Imperial period, literary production followed the general trend of approximation between Greek and native."

84. On Apion see *FGH* 616 frag. 2b, c. See also *FGH* 611 frag. 1a, b, c for the evidence in the material collected for Ptolemy of Mendes.

85. Josephus, *Ag. Ap.* 2.27, 79. In the latter text he mentioned Posidonius and Apollonius Molon. On Apion's use of them for defamatory stories about the temple see the summary of Stern, *GLAJJ* LXIII.170 (1:410).

Hellenistic or Roman periods, who on the basis of ancient traditions preserved in local priestly circles, composed a harmonized and rationalistic account of Phoenician myth and legend."[86] This suggests that Philo was aware of such a tradition and consciously stood within it. Although the sum of this evidence is scanty, these hints in the fragments suggest that authors were aware of the basic orientation and conventions of the tradition and knew some of their predecessors.

It is much less clear that Greeks would have recognized the works of Eastern historians as a separate tradition. They probably thought of them as substandard attempts to write what they had written much better in ethnographies and histories. They would, however, have recognized the difference in perspective between the construct of culture that underlay the histories of Eastern historians versus their own. The Greeks subsumed the rest of the world to themselves. Native Eastern historians reversed the tables on the basis of their antiquity. They wrote to establish a new identity for themselves within a post-Alexander world created by the Greeks. What set them apart from Greek historians was not the presence of polemics—this was, as we have seen, a common practice among Greek historians—but their widespread polemic against Hellenic historians. Eastern historians believed that the Greeks had misunderstood and misrepresented them. They wanted to correct them. This did not keep them from fighting with one another for cultural superiority, but it did give them a common opponent against which they directed critiques.

CONCLUSIONS

Should we credit the Eastern historians with the creation of a distinct historiographical tradition or should we think that they simply followed a form of Hellenic historiography but gave it a distinctive perspective? Perhaps we can answer this by framing it within a larger context. The dynamics of writing a countertradition on the basis of an insider's perspective rather than an outsider's perspective did not stop in the Hellenistic and early Roman worlds. The same dynamics have recurred in numerous contexts in which a conquered people tire of the accounts of the conquerors.[87] It is certainly true of native historians of India who reacted to the official histories of their British gover-

86. Attridge and Oden, *Philo of Byblos,* 9; see 3–9 for the full discussion. Baumgarten, *"The Phoenician History,"* 42–51, esp. 51, reaches a similar conclusion.
87. It would be possible to apply postcolonial theory to this historiographical tradition.

nors.[88] The best modern example, however, may be Dee Brown's retelling of the settlement of the American West. We opened this chapter with a citation from *Bury My Heart at Wounded Knee* that focuses on the thirty-year period between 1860 and 1890 when "the culture and civilization of the American Indian was destroyed and out of that time came virtually all the great myths of the American West." The myth that was created did not incorporate the perspective of native Americans: "Only occasionally was the voice of an Indian heard . . . Yet they are not all lost, those Indian voices of the past. A few authentic accounts of American western history were recorded by Indians either in pictographs or in translated English and some managed to get published in obscure journals, pamphlets, or books of small circulation." These neglected accounts formed the basis for Brown's history.[89] He drew them together and challenged his readers to think about the American West by standing in the West looking East rather than standing in the East looking West.

This epitomizes the subgenre of *Antiquities* that I labeled Apologetic Historiography. Native historians in the East wrote to challenge Greeks to listen to the voices of the peoples that they had conquered and to read their histories by standing in the East and looking West rather than standing in the West and looking East. While a modern might quibble on formal grounds that such a shift in perspective does not constitute a distinct historiographical tradition, the ancients who had been conquered by the Greeks and modern historians of postcolonial cultures or underrepresented groups take the difference seriously. So should we.

88. Romila Thapar, *A History of India*, 2 vols. (Baltimore: Penguin Books, 1965–1966), 1:15–27, esp. 17–18, where she points out that native historians argued that the golden age long antedated the arrival of the British and were sharply critical of the British attempt to link India's glorious past with Greece.

89. Brown, *Bury My Heart at Wounded Knee*, xi–xii.

3

The First History

The Literary Relationship between Luke and Acts

The book is offered to families, and to students and lecturers in history. It is an humble attempt so to direct these, as to unembarrass the origin, and to show the relative position of the colored people in the different periods among the different nations.

James W. C. Pennington, *A Text Book of the Origin and History of the Colored People*[1]

In the preface to his *Natural History*, Pliny the Elder took aim at Greek authors who gave pretentious titles to their works and then failed to deliver. He wrote with light sarcasm, "There is a marvelous felicity to titles among Greek authors." Some of his favorite examples were *Honeycomb*, *Horn of Plenty*, and *No Holds Barred*. His personal favorite was apparently *Talks by Lamplight*, a work written by a certain Bibaculus ("drinker"). One can only imagine the quality of the talks! Pliny wrote of the lot that these are titles "on account of which a person might default on bail. But when you enter them,

---

1. James W. C. Pennington, *A Text Book of the Origin and History of the Colored People* (Hartford: L. Skinner, 1841), introduction. This is the first history of African Americans in the US—at least this is the oft-cited claim. I quote Pennington's opening statement because it indicates the function of the work. Like Dee Brown's *Bury My Heart at Wounded Knee*, this history was put together to correct misconceptions of a subgroup. Unlike Brown, Pennington did not have written accounts against which to respond, but did have specific concepts and figures in mind (e.g., Thomas Jefferson). It is an example of apologetic historiography as I have described it. Reverend Pennington was the first African American to attend Yale, although a state law prohibited his formal enrollment. Yale Divinity School has a portrait of him and a classroom named in his honor.

my heavens!, you discover virtually nothing within." Pliny preferred much more restrained titles.[2]

Ancient historians appear to have agreed with Pliny's judgment. Herodotus (floruit fifth century BCE) and Thucydides (ca. 460–ca. 400 BCE) began their histories by stating their names and the basic subject matter of their works. Their opening lines served as their titles.[3] Polybius (ca. 200–ca. 118 BCE) followed suit.[4] Later historians took other approaches. As we saw in the previous chapter, a large group of historians in the East wrote works that were known by the adjectival form of the people: *Aegyptiaca, Babyloniaca, Phoenicica.* Whether they bequeathed these titles on their works themselves or whether select readers did this for them, the titles became so associated with the works that Felix Jacoby used these titles as one means for classifying ancient historical works.[5] Others who investigated ancient material preferred to entitle their works *Antiquities* ('Ἀρχαιολογίαι). The best-known examples are Dionysius of Halicarnassus (floruit first century BCE–first century CE)[6] and Josephus.[7] Still others had more amorphous titles. Diodorus Siculus's (floruit first century BCE) universal history is known as the *Library* (βιβλιοθήκη).[8]

There were thus a number of options for entitling an ancient work, including the possibility of foregoing a formal title. This option appears to have been the option taken by those who wrote the earliest Christian narratives. The closest that a New Testament author comes to a formal title is in the earliest gospel, Mark. The second evangelist opened with a title; however, his title, "The beginning of the gospel of Jesus Christ, God's Son," is so opaque that it has generated as many questions as it has answered. The other evangelists began with various

2. Pliny, *Nat.* 24–27.

3. Herodotus, *Hist., praef.*; Thucydides 1.1. For Herodotus I have used the edition of N. G. Wilson, *Herodoti Historiae*, OCT, 2 vols. (Oxford: Clarendon, 2015). For Thucydides I have used the edition of H. Stuart Jones and J. E. Powell, *Thucydidis Historiae*, 2 vols., rev. ed. (Oxford: Oxford University Press, 1963).

4. Polybius 1.1.

5. He called them "Ethnographie." See Felix Jacoby, "Über die Entwicklung der griechischen Historiographie," *Klio* 9 (1909): 80–123 and the discussion of Fornara, *Nature of History*, 1–46.

6. Dionysius of Halicarnassus, *Ant. rom.* See 1.4.1–2, where he uses the term to describe the contents of his work.

7. Josephus uses the name as a title in *Ant.* 20.259, 267; *Vita* 430; *Ag. Ap.* 1.1, 2 (where it may be descriptive rather than titular), 54, 127; 2.136, 287. See also *Ant.* 1.93–94, 107, where he uses the term to describe the works of others. He does not distinguish between writing an *Aegyptiaca* and an *archaiologia*.

8. Pliny, *Nat.* 25.

types of prefaces, but offered no titles. The result was that it was not clear how to think of these works. Justin Martyr, writing in the middle of the second century, preferred to call them the *Memoirs of the Apostles* (ἀπομνηνεύματα τῶν ἀποστόλων),[9] although he did know that they were called *gospels* (εὐαγγέλια).[10] Marcion, Justin's contemporary in Rome, apparently understood that Luke was a gospel, at least he thought that Paul's reference to "my gospel" (τὸ εὐαγγέλιόν μου) in his letter to the Romans referred to Luke.[11] Some of the earliest papyri that have the gospels call them such.[12] The Nag Hammadi manuscripts move in the same direction. Like Mark, the author of the Gospel of Truth opens with a line that has served as the title.[13] Other texts have scribal colophons attached to the end that denote the work as a gospel, such as the Gospel of Thomas, the Gospel of Philip, the Gospel of the Egyptians, and the Gospel of Mary.[14] It is thus clear that by the end of the second century, the first four books of the New Testament and similar works were being called gospels.[15]

The same situation is true for the other early Christian narrative of the first century, the work that we have come to know as the Acts of the Apostles. Like the Gospels, it came to have a name in the second century. While there were variations, it was associated with the *acts* (πράξεις) literature that was biographical in orientation.[16]

There was one very unfortunate result of the lack of titles. It led to the separate circulation of the two related works: the Third Gospel and the work that we have come to know as the Acts of the Apostles. From the second through the nineteenth centuries, the two were viewed as separate works by a common author.[17] At the end of the nineteenth century and the beginning of the twen-

9. Justin Martyr, *1 Apol.* 66.3; 67.3–4; *Dial.* 100.4; 101.3; 102.5; 103.6, 8; 104.1; 105.1, 5, 6; 106.1, 3, 4; 107.1.

10. Justin Martyr, *1 Apol.* 66.3; *Dial.* 10.2; 100.1.

11. On Marcion's view see Tertullian, *Marc.* 4.2.

12. E.g., P[75], the oldest manuscript of the Gospel, has *The Gospel according to Luke* (εὐαγγέλιον κατὰ Λοῦκαν) as the title.

13. Gos. Truth, I 3 (NHC I 16.31–33; cf. also I 17.1–4; I 18.11–19).

14. Gos. Thom. II 2 (NHC II 51.28–29); Gos. Phil. II 3 (NHC II 86.19–20); Gos. Eg. III 2 (NHC III 69.6); Gos. Mary BG 1 1:7, 19.3–5 (Papyrus Berolinensis 8502, I).

15. Helmut Koester, *Ancient Christian Gospels: Their History and Development* (Philadelphia: Trinity, 1990), 1–48, provides an important survey of all of the relevant evidence.

16. E.g., the *Canon Muratorianus* called it the "Acts of all the Apostles" (*Acta omnium apostolorum* [34–35]). The so-called anti-Marcionite prologue has *Acts of the Apostles* (Πράξεις ἀποστόλων and *Acta apostolorum*).

17. There have only been a handful of scholars who have questioned the common authorship. The most important are Albert C. Clark, *The Acts of the Apostles* (Oxford: Claren-

tieth century a number of scholars began to argue for their unity, a view that led Henry Cadbury to champion the hyphenated name Luke-Acts.[18] While Cadbury was not the first to assign this name, he was the most influential.[19] The hyphenated name stuck and became the *opinio communis*. There have, however, been dissenters. Mikeal Parsons and Richard Pervo wrote a small book challenging the consensus. They recognized the relationship between the two works, but argued against the assumption that they should be conceived as a single work. We might characterize their position by speaking of Luke and Acts rather than Luke, Acts or Luke-Acts.[20] There are a significant number of scholars who hold this view today.[21] The debate is thus hardly over. A major conference in Leuven held in 1998 explored the issue again.[22] It remains a point of debate.[23]

What is at stake? There are several important consequences of this debate for our understanding of the New Testament and early Christianity. If Luke is separate from Acts, then the two probably belong to different genres. In this case we should speak of Luke as a *bios* and Acts as a historical monograph or collective biography. This would mean that the first history of Christianity was a history of the church from its birth in Jerusalem to the imprisonment

---

don, 1933), 393–408; Aubrey W. Argyle, "The Greek of Luke and Acts," *NTS* 20 (1973–1974): 441–45; and Patricia Walters, *The Assumed Authorial Unity of Luke and Acts: A Reassessment of the Evidence*, SNTSMS 145 (Cambridge: Cambridge University Press, 2009), who has analyzed the style of seams and summaries in Luke and in Acts and argued on the basis of the differences that the works come from different hands. While she has demonstrated some stylistic differences, I find it difficult to dismiss the larger stylistic, thematic, and narrative unity. I also think that more attention should be paid to deliberate stylistic strategies (see the discussion in chapter 4).

18. Henry J. Cadbury, *The Making of Luke-Acts* (New York: Macmillan, 1927; repr., London: SPCK, 1961), 1–11, esp. 11.

19. See Benjamin W. Bacon, *An Introduction to the New Testament* (London: Macmillan, 1907), 211–29, for an earlier example.

20. Mikeal C. Parsons and Richard I. Pervo, *Rethinking the Unity of Luke and Acts* (Minneapolis: Fortress, 1993).

21. E.g., Nolland, *Luke*, 1:xxxiii: "To say that we have part one and part two of a single work would, however, be an exaggeration and would do less than justice to the evident differences between the works."

22. Joseph Verheyden, ed., *The Unity of Luke-Acts*, BETL 142 (Leuven: Leuven University Press, 1999).

23. A more recent collection of essays devoted to this is Andrew F. Gregory and C. Kavin Rowe, *Rethinking the Unity and Reception of Luke and Acts* (Columbia: University of South Carolina Press, 2010). Knut Backhaus, *Das Lukanische Doppelwerk: Zur literarischen Basis frühchristlicher Geschichtsdeutung*, BZNW 240 (Berlin: de Gruyter, 2022), has just published an important work that unfortunately appeared after this manuscript was complete.

of Paul in Rome. If, on the other hand, the two represent independent scrolls of a single work, then we have a history of Christianity beginning with Jesus as the founder and continuing through the apostles to Paul.[24] This raises the question of the nature of such a history. What type of history relates the story of a people in an attempt to define their place within the larger world? The most likely genre is the Eastern tradition that Josephus set out in *Against Apion* and that I have called apologetic historiography.[25]

The consequences of thinking of Luke-Acts in this tradition are greater for our understanding of Luke than they are for our perception of Acts. Luke is no longer a work about Jesus of Nazareth, but the first half of a story about a movement that began with him. It also means that unlike Matthew, Mark, and John, the third evangelist could keep the story of the church more distinct than the other evangelists. It was not necessary for him to relate a statement about the founding of the church as Matthew did[26] or to share the coming of the Spirit as John did.[27] He could delay them until their appropriate point in Acts.

It is this point that may help us to solve the issue of the nature of the relationship between the two scrolls. I would like to explore the possibility that the author demonstrates an awareness of the planned contents of Acts at the time that he wrote the Gospel of Luke. We cannot do this by looking at ways in which Acts takes up or echoes Luke, a phenomenon that every student of Acts knows. This only shows that Acts knew and modeled itself on Luke. Rather, we must explore whether a preplanned second scroll affected the writing of the first scroll. In order to do this, we will need to examine whether the evangelist altered pre-existing source material in such a way that it appears that he is setting the readers up for Acts.[28] Statements that the author freely composed

24. On the role of Jesus as founder see David L. Balch, "ΜΕΤΑΒΟΛΗ ΠΟΛΙΤΕΙΩΝ Jesus as Founder of the Church in Luke-Acts: Form and Function," in *Contextualizing Acts: Lukan Narrative and Greco-Roman Discourse*, ed. Todd Penner and Caroline Vander Stichele, SBLSS 20 (Atlanta: Society of Biblical Literature, 2003), 139–88; repr. in *Contested Ethnicities and Images: Studies in Luke-Acts*, WUNT 345 (Tübingen: Mohr Siebeck, 2015), 196–239.

25. Sterling, *Historiography and Self-Definition*, 311–89.

26. Compare Matt 16:13–20, esp. vv. 18–19, and Luke 9:18–21, esp. v. 20. Luke relates the founding of the church in Acts 2:1–47.

27. John 20:21–23. This parallels the coming of the Spirit in Acts 2:1–4.

28. I am aware of three earlier attempts to follow this line of investigation: Charles K. Barrett, "The Third Gospel as a Preface to Acts," in *The Four Gospels: Festschrift. Frans Neirynck*, ed. F. van Segbroek et al.; 3 vols.; BETL 100 (Leuven: Leuven University Press, 1992), 2:1451–66; I. Howard Marshall, "Acts and the 'Former Treatise,'" in *Ancient Literary Setting*, ed. Bruce W. Winter and Andrew D. Clarke; vol. 1 of *The Book of Acts in Its First Century Setting*, ed. Bruce W. Winter (Grand Rapids: Eerdmans, 1993), 174–75; and Joseph Verhey-

are not adequate. For example, the Third Gospel ends with Jesus's summary of the fulfillment of Scripture: "Then he opened their minds to understand the Scriptures and said to them: 'Therefore it is written that the Messiah must suffer, be raised from the dead on the third day, and that repentance for the forgiveness of sins should be preached in his name to all peoples.'" He went on: "Beginning from Jerusalem you are witnesses of these things. I am sending you the promise of my Father. You stay in the city until you are clothed with power from on high" (Luke 24:44–49). The fact that the Messiah has already died and been raised, but that repentance for the forgiveness of sins in his name has not been proclaimed, makes it clear that the reader has been set up. However, we are not sure whether we have been set up to read a second volume in which the preaching occurs or whether we are being challenged to make this proclamation. This is the Lukan formulation of the Great Commission. Matthew has a different formulation of the same commission without a sequel (Matt 28:18–20). The commission functions as a challenge in Matthew and could function in the same way in Luke. This leads us back to the issue of sources. If it appears that Luke altered his sources to set up Acts then we can be reasonably sure that he had Acts planned when he wrote the Third Gospel. Fortunately, we have a source that provides a reasonable test case, Mark. Did Luke edit Mark with Acts in mind? I would like to explore four places where this is possible.

THE INCLUSION OF THE GENTILES

The first is the extended citation of Isa 40 in Luke 3. The opening lines of Deutero-Isaiah were of immense importance to both early Christians and the covenanters at Qumran. The text appears multiple times in the scrolls and in all four Gospels of the NT.[29] Luke knew the relevance of the text through Mark. The second evangelist opened his gospel with a composite citation of the LXX of Exod 23:20, Mal 3:1, and Isa 40:3 (see synopsis 3.1 in the appendix). The three texts are linked by the presence of the word "way," a common technique known as *gezerah shawah*. The connection may have been drawn by Semitic-speaking

---

den, "The Unity of Luke-Acts," (paper presented at the Annual Meeting of the Society for New Testament Studies, Pretoria, South Africa, August 2017). I am grateful to Jos Verheyden for reading this chapter and commenting on it.

29. E.g., 1QS 8:12–16; 9:17–20. Evidence in the Gospels: Mark 1:2–3 // Matt 3:3 // Luke 3:4; and John 1:23.

Christians prior to Mark on the basis of דֶּרֶךְ ("way") and then translated into Greek or could have been connected directly from the LXX on the basis of the presence of ὁδός ("way").[30] However the texts came to Mark, he introduced them with the statement "as it is written in Isaiah the prophet."

Luke made two major alterations to Mark (see synopsis 3.2 in the appendix). The first is an omission. The third evangelist dropped the citations from Exod 23:20 and Mal 3:1. There may be several reasons for this omission. If, as seems likely, the third evangelist knew that the citations did not come from Isaiah, he might have excised them to avoid the difficulty that their inclusion created in a citation attributed to Isaiah. He made similar corrections to Mark in other cases.[31] He certainly could have kept the other two texts but used a different introductory formula as he did when he later cited Exod 23:20 and Mal 3:1 in Luke 7:27. This is, however, a Q text rather than the Markan text. It may be that he omitted them in the early text because he planned to use a Q form of the same texts in his discussion of John the Baptist's fate (see synopsis 3.3 in the appendix).[32] Luke generally avoided doublets. Unlike Matthew, who often preserved the Q and Markan versions of the same material, Luke preferred to select one and omit the other. He may have simply decided to wait for the Q version and to omit the Markan version here.

The second alteration is unique to Luke: he continued the citation of Isa 40 from verse three down through verse five (see synopses 3.2 and 3.4 in the appendix). The continuation was apparently made to bring the citation down to the final clause, "and all flesh will see the salvation of God." Luke is the only evangelist to make this extension. What led him to make the extension? It is well known that the third evangelist preferred to speak of the effects of the Christ-event in salvific language. While all of the evangelists use the verb "to save" (σώζειν), only Luke among the Synoptic Gospels uses the terms "savior" (σωτήρ),[33] "salvation" (σωτηρία),[34] and "salvation" (σωτήριον).[35] It is, in fact, the last term that forms an echo with the immediate context. The aged Sim-

---

30. For an overview of the possibilities see Joel Marcus, *Mark 1–8*, AB 27 (New York: Doubleday, 2000), 143–45. Marcus does not allow for the second option.

31. He quietly dropped the incorrect reference to Abiathar in Mark 2:26 in Luke 6:4. Ahimelech, Abiathar's father, was the priest. See 1 Sam 21:1–6 for the story.

32. Luke 7:27 // Matt 11:10. For Q see James M. Robinson, Paul Hoffmann, and John S. Kloppenborg, eds., *The Critical Edition of Q*, Hermeneia (Minneapolis: Fortress, 2000).

33. Luke 1:47 (God); 2:11; Acts 5:31; 13:23.

34. Luke 1:69, 71, 77; 19:9; Acts 4:12; 7:25; 13:26, 47; 16:17; 27:34.

35. Luke 2:30; 3:6; Acts 28:28.

eon had taken the child Jesus into his arms and blessed God saying: "My eyes have seen your salvation (σωτήριον)" (Luke 2:30). The statement from Isaiah echoes this. There is, however, an element that must be recognized. In the Isaiah citation it is not just a pious Israelite who sees the salvation of God as it is in Luke 2:30, but "all flesh." Luke picked up this element at the end of Acts when he used the phrase, "salvation of God" or "your salvation," for a third and final time.[36] At the conclusion of his speech to the Jewish community in Rome Paul said: "Let this be known to you that this salvation of God has been sent to the Gentiles. They also will hear."[37] Is this an echo of Luke 3 or did Luke 3 set up Acts 28? I suggest that the latter is more likely. It is the more probable explanation because the Gospel of Luke does not include a mission to the Gentiles; this mission is narrated in Acts. The inclusion of the Gentiles at this early stage of Luke suggests that the evangelist had planned to write the story of the mission to the Gentiles. Why didn't he narrate it in the gospel?

THE DELAY OF THE GENTILE MISSION

We have already noted that the other evangelists collapsed the period of the church into the period of Jesus, but that Luke made an attempt to keep them separate, at least in some ways. This means that Mark had to include the mission to the Gentiles within his story of Jesus. He did this through a series of journeys to non-Jewish territories in which Jesus evangelized the Gentiles. Mark used the Sea of Galilee as both the real and the symbolic barrier between the Jewish and Gentile worlds. He set out four journeys in which Jesus crossed the Sea of Galilee "to the other side": three sea voyages and one overland journey. For ease of reference, I have set the journeys out in a chart.

Reference in Mark	Destination	Episode
First journey		
4:35–41	To the other side	First boat scene
5:1–20	To the other side of the Sea	Exorcism of Legion
	To the land of the	
	Gerasenes	

36. These are the only three texts in the New Testament that use σωτήριον in connection with Isa 40:5. As Heinz Schürmann remarked: the association is "offensichtlich eine apostolische Beweisstelle für die Heilsberufung der Heiden" (*Das Lukasevangelium*, HThKNT 3 [Freiburg: Herder, 1969], 160n104).

37. Acts 28:28. On the intertextual significance of the three passages see Dietrich Rusam, *Das Alte Testament bei Lukas*, BZNW 112 (Berlin: de Gruyter, 2003), 160–61.

5:21	To the other side of the Sea	
Second journey		
6:45–52	To the other side	Second boat scene
	To Bethsaida	
6:53	To Genesaret	
Third journey		
7:24–30	To Tyre	Healing of Syrophoeni-cian woman's daughter
7:31–37	Through Sidon	Healing of deaf and mute man
	To the Sea of Galilee	
8:1–9		Feeding of four thousand
8:10	To Dalmanoutha	
Fourth journey		
8:13–21	To the other side	Third boat scene
8:22–26	To Bethsaida	Healing of blind man
8:27–9:1	Caesarea Philippi	Peter's confession First passion prediction
9:2–13	High mountain	Transfiguration
9:14–29		Healing of epileptic
9:30	Through Galilee	

The first voyage is brief and resulted in Jesus's exorcism of the demons from Legion (4:35–5:21), just as his first miracle among Jews had been an exorcism (1:21–28). The second is truncated: Jesus set out for the other side, but appears to have disembarked back on the Jewish side (6:45–53). The third is a land voyage. It is the most extensive journey of the four and took Jesus to Phoenicia (7:24–8:10). The journey is set up by Jesus's dispute with the Pharisees over hand washing, a dispute that culminated in a declaration that kosher regulations were no longer valid (7:1–23). It can hardly be an accident that Mark set this text immediately before Jesus went to Phoenicia and interacted with Gentiles directly. While he was on this journey in Mark he fed four thousand Gentiles, just as he had fed five thousand Jews on an earlier occasion (8:1–19 and 6:32–44). The final sea voyage took Jesus across the Sea from whence he journeyed north by land and then returned (8:13–9:30). The point of these journeys is to justify the presence of Gentiles in the Markan community by postulating a mission to them by Jesus.

How did Luke handle Mark's first journey? While he retold it (Mark 4:35–5:21 // Luke 8:22–40), he altered the geographical markers to make it clear that

Jesus stayed in the vicinity of the lake. Luke modified the first notice of the journey, but did not change the basic reference to the journey (see synopsis 3.5 in the appendix). He was not, however, content with Mark's notice of disembarkation (see synopsis 3.6 in the appendix).[38] The third evangelist went out of his way to let us know that the country of the Gerasenes is in the vicinity of the lake. He did so by adding a qualifying phrase, "and they sailed to the land of the Gerasenes, *which is opposite Galilee.*" The relative clause (in italics) shows that the evangelist wanted to incorporate the incident, but did not want to let it go without explaining that it was still within the basic orb of Jesus's Galilean movements. It appears that the author knew that this was outside of Galilee but emphasized that it was beside the lake as a way to minimize its significance.[39] His concern is evident at the conclusion of the episode as well. Luke replaced Mark's notice that the man began to announce what Jesus had done throughout the Decapolis with a statement that mentioned only his own city. In the place of Mark's description, "He left and began to announce in the Decapolis all that Jesus had done for him and all were amazed" (Mark 5:20), Luke wrote, "He left announcing to the entire city what Jesus had done for him" (Luke 8:39) (see synopsis 3.7 in the appendix). He has thus restricted the geographical scope of the Markan pericope both at the beginning and at the end.

Luke's concern becomes clearer in his handling of the final three Markan journeys: he dropped all three. The omission of these three journeys constitutes what is often called "Luke's Big Omission." Why did the third evangelist omit Mark 6:45–8:26? He has used Mark as the basic structure for his gospel and preserved the bulk of Mark. When he has departed from the order in Mark, there are obvious reasons for his transpositions. Why drop such a major section? There have been a number of guesses and it may well be that there were multiple reasons. Some have suggested that the third evangelist knew a truncated version of Mark; however, this appears to be the counsel of despair.[40] Similarly, the

---

38. There is a famous text critical problem in all of the canonical gospels about the specific locale. I have followed NA²⁷, NA²⁸, and UBS⁴ in reading Γερασηνῶν for Luke 8:26. For details see Metzger, *A Textual Commentary on the New Testament*, 18–19 (Matt 8:28, where the Greek editions cited read Γαδαρηνῶν), 72 (Mark 5:1, where the Greek editions cited read Γερασηνῶν), and 121 (Luke 8:26).

39. The comments of Conzelmann on this text are still worth reading, *Theology of St. Luke*, 49–50.

40. Burnett H. Streeter, *The Four Gospels: A Study in Origins, Treating of the Manuscript Tradition, Sources, Authorship and Dates* (London: Macmillan, 1956), 172–79, thought that he had a defective copy of Mark. Koester, *Ancient Christian Gospels*, 284–86, argued that Mark went through a series of editions and used this as proof of one stage in his reconstruction of Mark's formation.

suggestion that Luke had to abbreviate Mark to allow for the inclusion of other material is less than convincing.[41] It raises the question: why omit this material and include other material? A better explanation is that the third evangelist did not approve of the doublets that occur in this section of Mark.[42] I have set out the material in a chart for the sake of clarity. The chart has the Markan stories (including the first or second story of the doublet in italics and in smaller font in the row below), the Q parallels where relevant (the references in Luke are listed first and then those in Matthew), and the Lukan parallels.

Episode	Mark	Q (Luke // Matthew)	Luke
Second boat scene	6:45–52		
First boat scene	*4:35–41*		*8:22–25*
Dispute over hand washing	7:1–23	11:39–41 // 23:25–26	
Healing of Syrophoenician woman's daughter	7:24–30		
Healing of deaf and mute man	7:31–37		
Feeding of four thousand	8:1–10		
Feeding of five thousand	*6:32–44*		*9:10–17*
Demand for a sign	8:11–13	11:29–32 // 12:38–42	
Third boat scene	8:14–21		
First boat scene	*4:35–41*		
Second boat scene	*6:45–52*		
Healing of blind man	8:22–26		
Healing of blind man	*10:46–52*		*18:35–43*

The chart demonstrates the presence of four Markan doublets: the second boat scene, the feeding of the four thousand, the third boat scene, and the healing of the blind. Luke has narrated all of these; however, he has only given one of the two or three Markan stories: the first boat scene (but not the second or third), the feeding of the five thousand (but not the feeding of the four thousand), and the second healing of the blind (but not the first). While

---

41. Schürmann, *Das Lukasevangelium*, 1:526–27.

42. On the issue of doublets see Heinz Schürmann, "Die Dubletten im Lukasevangelium: Ein Beitrag zur Verdeutlichung des lukanischen Redaktionsverfahrens," *ZKT* 75 (1953): 338–45 and Heinz Schürmann, "Die Dublettenvermeidungen im Lukasevangelium: Ein Beitrag zur Verdeutlichung des lukanischen Redaktionsverfahrens," *ZKT* 76 (1954): 83–93. They are both reprinted in Heinz Schürmann, *Traditionsgeschichtliche Untersuchungen zu den synoptischen Evangelien: Beiträge* (Düsseldorf: Patmos, 1968), 272–78 and 279–89.

Luke can have duplicates, he typically does not like to repeat whole stories in the way that Mark did.[43]

Yet this only explains some of the material. Luke has omitted a good deal of material that does not involve doublets: the dispute over hand washing, the healing of the Syrophoenician woman's daughter, and the healing of a deaf and mute man. There must be something more at stake than the mere doubling of a story or Luke could have omitted the doublets and found ways to incorporate the remainder of the material. There is a hint of the main reason when the evangelist rejoined the Markan narrative with Peter's confession (see synopsis 3.8 in the appendix). The third evangelist dropped the geographical reference to Caesarea Philippi that was so important to Mark, who traced Jesus's journey south from there to Jerusalem. In Luke the confession took place in Galilee rather than Caesarea Philippi. This suggests to me that one of the major reasons why Luke omitted Mark 6:45–8:26 was his desire to keep Jesus in Galilee.[44] The only episode that Mark related in Galilee in this material was the dispute over hand washing, the dispute that justified the Gentile mission for Mark. Luke's equivalent to this material is the conversion of Cornelius in Acts 10:1–11:18. The broad lines of similarity between the two accounts are important: they both deal with the abolition of kosher laws. In both Mark and Acts, this is the argument for the inclusion of the Gentiles. I suggest that Luke omitted Mark 6:45–8:26 because he knew that he would deal with the Gentile mission in Acts.[45] It would have been out of place in his gospel and ruined the point that he wanted to make in his second scroll.[46]

43. I am only contrasting the narrative techniques of Mark and Luke in this comparison. The presence of doublets has played a significant role in the debate over the Synoptic problem. I accept the two-source hypothesis, but I am primarily interested in Luke's redaction of Mark in this case. For a recent summary and evaluation of the larger issue see Wolfgang Grünstäudl, "Luke's Doublets and the Synoptic Problem," *NTS* 68 (2022): 13–25.

44. On the geographical perspective in Luke see Ernst Lohmeyer, *Galiläa und Jerusalem bei Lukas*, FRLANT n. F. 34 (Göttingen: Vandenhoeck & Ruprecht, 1936), 41–46; repr. in *Das Lukas-Evangelium: Die redaktions- und kompositionsgeschichtliche Forschung*, ed. G. Braumann, Wege der Forschung 280 (Darmstadt: Wissenschaftliche Buchgesellschaft, 1974), 7–12; Chester C. McCown, "The Geography of Luke's Central Section," *JBL* 57 (1938): 51–66; Chester C. McCown, "Gospel Geography: Fiction, Fact, and Truth," *JBL* 60 (1941): 1–25, esp. 14–18; Conzelmann, *Theology of St. Luke*, 18–94, esp. 52–55; Fitzmyer, *Gospel according to Luke*, 1:164–71; and Vonder Bruegge, *Mapping Galilee in Josephus, Luke, and John*, 91–138, esp. 98–101.

45. He did not eliminate all of Jesus's contacts with non-Jews. For example, in 7:1–10, Jesus healed the centurion's daughter in Capernaum (a city of Galilee). However, Luke makes it unambiguously clear that the centurion has close ties to the Jewish community: the Jewish elders are his embassy and they attest his importance to the community. This is considerably different than the story of the healing of the Syro-Phoenician woman's daughter in Mark 7:24–30.

46. Luke's concern to keep Jesus within a restricted geographical frame may have also

THE TRIALS OF THE DISCIPLES

The third place where Luke may have redacted Mark with Acts in mind is the apocalyptic discourse in Mark 13. Luke wanted to indicate to the readers that the disciples should expect to experience the same trials that Jesus had. He recast the Markan warning about their future to bring it more into line with what he would narrate about the disciples in Acts (see synopsis 3.9 in the appendix).

He began by repeating the language that he had used about Jesus in Luke 20:19, "they will cast their hands on you" (21:12). He collapsed the next two clauses into a single clause but expanded it. Mark's "they will deliver you to councils and you will be beaten before synagogues" (Mark 13:9) has become "they will persecute you (διώξουσιν) and deliver you (παραδιδόντες) to synagogues and prisons" (Luke 21:12). Luke has thus doubled the first verbal unit. The reference to "they will persecute you (διώξουσιν)" may echo Luke 11:49, where it referred to the treatment of Wisdom's emissaries. However, it is more likely that it anticipates the series of persecutions that will be narrated in Acts. The same combination of verbs is placed on the lips of Paul to describe his persecution of early Christians: "I persecuted (ἐδίωξα) this way to the point of death, beating and delivering over (παραδιδούς) into prisons both men and women" (Acts 22:4). Just as in Luke, "delivering over" results in imprisonments. Another important change is the omission of "councils" (συνεδρία) (Mark 13:9 // Luke 21:12). Why omit this? The evangelist knew the word and used it fifteen of the twenty-two times that it appears in the New Testament. However, he only used it in the singular; he never used the plural.[47] He probably dropped Mark's plural because it did not square with his understanding of what would happen. He might have kept the singular; however, this would have only applied to some of the disciples in Jerusalem and not to disciples more broadly.[48] He therefore chose to drop it. He probably added "prisons" to set up the numerous imprisonment accounts in Acts.[49] Finally, he reversed the order of "governors and kings" (Mark 13:9) to "kings and governors" (Luke 21:12). Why? He may have preferred to begin with the more elevated position and then move to a more limited role in the same way

---

influenced his decision to drop the phrase "across the Jordan" to describe his route to Jerusalem (Mark 10:1 // Luke 9:51).

47. Luke 22:66; Acts 4:15; 5:21, 27, 34, 41; 6:12, 15; 22:30; 23:1, 6, 14, 20, 28; 24:20.

48. Peter and John (Acts 4:15), the apostles (Acts 5:21, 27, 34, 41), Stephen (Acts 6:12, 15), and Paul (Acts 22:30; 23:1, 6, 15, 20, 28; 24:20).

49. The apostles in Jerusalem (Acts 5:19, 22, 25), Paul's persecutions (Acts 8:3; 22:4; 26:10), Herod Agrippa I's persecution (Acts 12:4, 5, 6, 17), and the arrest of Paul and Silas in Philippi (Acts 16:23, 24, 27, 37, 40).

that the author of 1 Peter did.[50] However, Luke only used "governor" to denote Roman governors.[51] It is likely that he reversed the order to bring the sequence into line with the series of trials in Acts where Herod Agrippa I dealt with the Christians prior to the Roman governors Felix and Festus.[52]

These shifts indicate that the author has recast Mark with Acts in mind. The statement in Luke would not have given an ancient reader/auditor who knew Acts any pause. The two texts would have flowed together well. The same could not be said if a reader moved from Mark 13 to Acts.

THE TEMPLE CHARGE

These redactions are subtle. There is at least one instance relating to trial scenes that is not. There are a series of well-known literary and historical difficulties with the trial scenes of Jesus in the Gospels. For example, Mark, followed by Matthew, has two trials before the Sanhedrin: one at night in which Jesus was interrogated (Mark 14:53-72 // Matt 26:57-75), and the other early the next morning where the council decided to deliver him to the Romans (Mark 15:1 // Matt 27:1-2). Luke has Jesus go to the house of the high priest at night, but there is no indication that an interrogation took place (Luke 22:54-65). The interrogation occurred the next morning before the Sanhedrin (22:66-23:1). The Fourth Gospel has a nocturnal interrogation by Annas (John 18:13-23) and an early morning meeting at the house of Caiaphas, although there is no indication that there was a trial at this second meeting (18:24-28). The evangelists scatter the denials of Peter throughout these two events, although in different places. All the accounts agree that after the second meeting, Jesus was taken to the Praetorium. The discrepancies among the accounts have generated extended debates over the historicity of the accounts. Fortunately, we do not need to enter the historical debate.

It is enough for our purposes to note how Luke handled the basic issues. First, he has transferred the interrogation from night (Mark 14:53-64, esp. 53-55) to the next morning (Luke 22:66-71, esp. 66). He filled the first scene in Mark (Mark 14:53-54) with the three denials of Peter (Luke 22:54-62). Sec-

50. 1 Pet 2:14. So Marshall, *Luke*, 767.
51. Luke 20:20; Acts 23:24, 26, 33; 24:1, 10; 26:30.
52. Herod Agrippa I (Acts 12:1); Felix (Acts 23:24, 26, 33; 24:1, 10); and Festus (Acts 26:30). However, it should be noted that Herod Agrippa II comes after Felix and simultaneously with Festus (Acts 25:23-26:32). It would have been awkward to have written "kings, governors, and kings." The initial reference to kings covered both and maintained the sequence.

ond, he has elided a significant section of the Markan interrogation scene (Mark 14:55–61; see synopsis 3.10 in the appendix). There are two major issues in Mark: the charge that Jesus spoke against the temple (Mark 14:58) and Jesus's claim to be the Messiah (Mark 14:60–62). Luke omitted the former and kept the latter. He omitted the former not only here but in the crucifixion scene when it appears again in Mark as the crowds hurled abuses at Jesus (Mark 15:29 // Luke 23:35; see synopsis 3.11 in the appendix). Why did the third evangelist consistently omit the temple charge? The charge itself may rest on a firm historical basis—a basis that made the charge problematic for early Christians. All of the other evangelists found ways to handle it. For example, Mark developed a contrast between the "human made" (χειροποίητον) temple that Jesus threatened to destroy and the temple that was "not human made" (ἀχειροποίητον) that he would build (Mark 14:58). Did Luke find this insufficient? It is important to note that the charge does appear in Luke's writings; however, it is not in the Gospel of Luke but in Acts, where it occurs in the trial of Stephen.[53] There is a long-standing scholarly tradition that Luke has combined two separate traditions about Stephen's trial: a lynching account (Acts 6:9–11; 7:54–58a) and an official trial (Acts 6:12–14; 7:58b–60). Although this source critical analysis is not free from difficulties, it points out that the "official trial" is in 6:12–14. It is here that we find both the presentation of false witnesses and the temple charge that were part of Mark's trial of Jesus (Mark 14:55–59; see synopsis 3.12 in the appendix). Why place the Markan material about Jesus's trial here? Stephen will deliver a speech that argues that God has not been restricted to Jerusalem or to the area surrounding the temple (see chapter 5 below). God has always dealt with people away from the temple as the lives of Abraham, Joseph, and Moses demonstrate. I suggest that Luke held the temple charge until Acts because he knew that he would deal with the temple at length in this context.[54] This suggests that the evangelist had preplanned the writing of Acts—at least some of the basic contents—prior to or during the writing of the gospel.

---

53. There is a great deal of literature on the Stephen material. For a survey see Todd Penner, *In Praise of Christian Origins: Stephen and the Hellenists in Lukan Apologetic Historiography*, Emory Studies in Early Christianity 10 (New York: T&T Clark, 2004), 1–103, esp. 83; and Michal Beth Dinkler, "The Politics of Stephen's Storytelling: Narrative Rhetoric and Reflexivity in Acts 7:2–53," *ZNW* 111 (2020): 33–64, with a bibliography on works that have used a rhetorical approach (46–53). In contrast she argues that the speech tells a narrative about Israel.

54. It is worth pointing out that Luke has also repeated the statement about the Son of Man at the end of Stephen's speech (Mark 14:62 // Luke 22:69; see Acts 7:56). The statement sets in motion the final events in each scene.

Conclusions

There are thus a number of texts that suggest that Luke edited Mark with Acts in mind. If this is the case, then we must think of Luke-Acts as a single work in two parts. Someone will still object: Why is it that the two scrolls circulated separately in the manuscript tradition? If they were originally a single work, how did they come to be separated?

The objection is not as telling as it might first appear. It assumes that the two scrolls must have been written and released together. This may not be an accurate assumption. Just as today some multivolume works appear together while others appear in sequence, so in antiquity some works appeared together while others came out in sequence. Let me offer three examples of the latter. There is some evidence that Polybius released a number of his books in succession rather than in major units. Maurice Holleaux pointed out that the allusion to the earthquake in Rhodes in 227 BCE that Polybius mentioned in book 5 would have been far better situated in book 4 where he discussed Rhodes.[55] He suggested that it was added to book 5 because book 4 had already been released.[56] This suggests that Polybius released at least his first five books—or some of them—sequentially rather than collectively.

Dionysius of Halicarnassus is more explicit. In the seventh book of his *Roman Antiquities* he informed the reader that he would fulfill the promise that he made at the end of his first book to demonstrate that the founders of Rome were Greeks. He said: "For I promised at the end of the first scroll, which I composed and published (συνταξάμενος ἐξέδωκα) about their origin, the demonstration by many certain proofs, supplying customs, laws, and ancient ways of living which they guard to the present time just as they received them from their ancestors."[57] Dionysius assumed that his readers had access to the first scroll as he wrote the seventh. There can be no doubt that he released some of the books of the *Roman Antiquities* sequentially rather than holding them until he had completed the work.

---

55. See Polybius 5.88–90 and 4.47–56.

56. Maurice Holleaux, *Études d'épigraphie et d'histoire grecques*, ed. L. Robert, 6 vols. (Paris: Adrien-Maisonneuve, 1938–68), 1:445–62. Frank W. Walbank, *Polybius*, The Sather Classical Lectures 42 (Berkeley: University of California Press, 1972), 20–21, accepted this suggestion. See also Frank W. Walbank, *A Historical Commentary on Polybius*, 3 vols. (Oxford: Oxford University Press, 1956–79), 1:293–95.

57. Dionysius of Halicarnassus, *Ant. rom.* 7.70.2. For "the end of the first scroll," see *Ant. rom.* 1.90.2.

The third example is Jewish. Philo of Alexandria wrote a two-scroll account of Moses (*De vita Mosis*). The Alexandrian structured the work carefully, noting the basic components in his prefaces and marking them with transition statements. Interestingly, the plan that appears at the conclusion of book 1 does not square with the plan in the preface of book 2.[58] As the Jewish commentator came to the conclusion of his first scroll, he summarized his treatment of Moses as king and promised to address his roles as high priest and legislator. When we come to the preface of the second scroll, we find that Philo both altered and expanded his plan by including the role of prophet and reversing the sequence of Moses's role as legislator and high priest—the order that he, in fact, used in book 2.[59] The best explanation for these shifts is that some time has elapsed between the time when Philo composed book 1 and when he began book 2, a time in which he altered his plan. These statements make it clear that some authors released their scrolls as they completed them rather than waiting until they could release the entire work. This helps to explain the famous difference between the time of Jesus's resurrection and ascension in Luke versus Acts.

It is also the case that multiple scrolls of a single work sometimes circulated separately. So, for example, there are a number of two-volume works of Philo of Alexandria for which we only have one volume. We have only one of two volumes of *On Sobriety* and only one of two of *On the Eternity of the World*.[60] The second scrolls have been lost in both cases. Several works that were companion pieces to other treatises have also been lost: *On the Essenes*, a lost companion scroll to *On the Contemplative Life* that treated the Therapeutae,[61] and *That Every Bad Person Is a Slave*, a lost companion volume to *That Every Good Person Is Free*.[62] These examples demonstrate that scrolls often took a life of their own, even when they were designed to be read as a two-scroll work or companion scrolls. It should therefore hardly be the occasion for surprise that a two-scroll work in the New Testament came to circulate separately, especially since the first scroll was quickly associated with other similar scrolls including one of its major sources.

---

58. Compare Philo, *Mos.* 1.334 and 2.1–7.

59. For details see Gregory E. Sterling, "A Human *Sui Generis*: The Structure and Composition of Philo's *De vita Moysis*," *JJS* (forthcoming).

60. For *On Sobriety*, see Philo, *Sobr.* 1; Eusebius, *Hist. eccl.* 2.18.2. For *On the Eternity of the World*, see Philo, *Aet.* 150.

61. See Philo, *Contempl.* 1.

62. Philo, *Prob.* 1.

This could have been avoided had the author not shared Pliny's reticence to give his work a name. The primary preface and the secondary preface of the two scrolls should have been enough. Unfortunately, they were not. While it would be presumptuous for us to create a name for the two scrolls at this point in time, it is fair to say that they constitute the first history of Christianity. What kind of history was this? We will attempt to answer this in the next two parts of this book.

APPENDIX[63]

The Inclusion of the Gentiles

Synopsis 3.1

Exod 23:20; Mal 3:1; Isa 40:3	Mark 1:2–3
	[2]καθὼς γέγραπται
Exod 23:20	ἐν τῷ Ἠσαΐᾳ τῷ προφήτῃ·
καὶ ἰδοὺ ἐγὼ ἀποστέλλω	ἰδοὺ ἀποστέλλω
τὸν ἄγγελόν μου	τὸν ἄγγελόν μου
πρὸ προσώπου σου,	πρὸ προσώπου σου,
ἵνα φυλάξῃ σε ἐν τῇ ὁδῷ,	ὃς κατασκευάσει τὴν ὁδόν σου·
ὅπως εἰσαγάγῃ σε εἰς τῇ γῆν,	
ἣν ἡτοίμασά σοι.	
Mal 3:1	
ἰδοὺ ἐγὼ ἐξαποστέλλω	ἰδοὺ ἀποστέλλω
τὸν ἄγγελόν μου	τὸν ἄγγελον μου
καὶ ἐπιβλέψεται ὁδὸν	
πρὸ προσώπου μου, ...	πρὸ προσώπου σου,
	ὃς κατασκευάσει τὴν ὁδόν σου
Isa 40:3	
φωνὴ βοῶντος ἐν τῇ ἐρήμῳ	φωνὴ βοῶντος ἐν τῇ ἐρήμῳ·
Ἐτοιμάσατε τὴν ὁδὸν κυρίου,	ἑτοιμάσατε τὴν ὁδὸν κυρίου,
εὐθείας ποιεῖτε τὰς τρίβους	εὐθείας ποιεῖτε τὰς τρίβους
τοῦ θεοῦ ἡμῶν.	αὐτοῦ,

63. I have used text from the Göttingen edition of the LXX: *Septuaginta: Vetus Testamentum Graecum, Volume II, I: Exodus*, ed. J. W. Weavers (Göttingen: Vandenhoeck & Ruprecht, 1991); *Septuaginta: Vetus Testamentum Graecum, Volume XIII: Duodecim of prophetae*, 3rd ed., ed. J. Ziegler (Göttingen: Vandenhoeck & Ruprecht, 1984); and *Septuaginta: Vetus Testamentum Graecum, Volume XIV: Isaias*, 3rd ed., ed. J. Ziegler (Göttingen: Vandenhoeck & Ruprecht, 1983).

Synopsis 3.2

Mark 1:2–3
²καθὼς γέγραπται
ἐν τῷ Ἠσαΐᾳ
τῷ προφήτῃ·
ἰδοὺ ἀποστέλλω τὸν ἄγγελόν μου
πρὸ προσώπου σου,
ὃς κατασκευάσει τὴν ὁδόν σου
φωνὴ βοῶντος ἐν τῇ ἐρήμῳ·
ἑτοιμάσατε τὴν ὁδὸν κυρίου,
εὐθείας ποιεῖτε τὰς τρίβους αὐτοῦ,

Luke 3:4–6
⁴ὡς γέγραπται
ἐν βίβλῳ λόγων Ἠσαΐου
τοῦ προφήτου·

φωνὴ βοῶντος ἐν τῇ ἐρήμῳ·
ἑτοιμάσατε τὴν ὁδὸν κυρίου,
εὐθείας ποιεῖτε τὰς τρίβους αὐτοῦ·
⁵πᾶσα φάραγξ πληρωθήσεται
καὶ πᾶν ὄρος
καὶ βουνὸς ταπεινωθήσεται,
καὶ ἔσται τὰ σκολιὰ εἰς εὐθεῖαν
καὶ αἱ τραχεῖαι εἰς ὁδοὺς λείας·
⁶καὶ ὄψεται πᾶσα σὰρξ
τὸ σωτήριον τοῦ θεοῦ.

Synopsis 3.3

Matt 11:10
οὗτος ἐστιν περὶ οὗ γέγραπται·
ἰδοὺ ἐγὼ ἀποστέλλω
τὸν ἄγγελόν μου
πρὸ προσώπου σου,
ὃς κατασκευάσει τὴν ὁδόν σου
ἔμπροσθέν σου.

Luke 7:27
οὗτος ἐστιν περὶ οὗ γέγραπται·
ἰδοὺ ἀποστέλλω
τὸν ἄγγελόν μου
πρὸ προσώπου σου,
ὃς κατασκευάσει τὴν ὁδόν σου
ἔμπροσθέν σου.

Synopsis 3.4

Isa 40:3–5

³φωνὴ βοῶντος ἐν τῇ ἐρήμῳ
Ἑτοιμάσατε τὴν ὁδὸν κυρίου,
εὐθείας ποιεῖτε τὰς τρίβους
τοῦ θεοῦ ἡμῶν·
⁴πᾶσα φάραγξ πληρωθήσεται

Luke 3:4–6
⁴ὡς γέγραπται
ἐν βίβλῳ λόγων Ἠσαΐου τοῦ προφήτου·
φωνὴ βοῶντος ἐν τῇ ἐρήμῳ·
ἑτοιμάσατε τὴν ὁδὸν κυρίου,
εὐθείας ποιεῖτε τὰς τρίβους
αὐτοῦ·
⁵πᾶσα φάραγξ πληρωθήσεται

καὶ πᾶν ὄρος
καὶ βουνὸς ταπεινωθήσεται,
καὶ ἔσται πάντα τὰ σκολιὰ
εἰς εὐθεῖαν
καὶ ἡ τραχεῖα εἰς πεδία·
⁵καὶ ὀφθήσεται ἡ δόξα κυρίου,
καὶ ὄψεται πᾶσα σὰρξ
τὸ σωτήριον τοῦ θεοῦ·
ὅτι κύριος ἐλάλησεν.

καὶ πᾶν ὄρος
καὶ βουνὸς ταπεινωθήσεται,
καὶ ἔσται τὰ σκολιὰ
εἰς εὐθείαν
καὶ αἱ τραχεῖαι εἰς ὁδοὺς λείας·

⁶καὶ ὄψεται πᾶσα σὰρξ
τὸ σωτήριον τοῦ θεοῦ.

The Delay of the Gentile Mission

Synopsis 3.5

Mark 4:35–36
³⁵καὶ λέγει αὐτοῖς
ἐν ἐκείνῃ τῇ ἡμέρᾳ
ὀψίας γενομένης·
διέλθωμεν εἰς τὸ πέραν.
³⁶καὶ ἀφέντες τὸν ὄχλον
παραλαμβάνουσιν αὐτὸν
ὡς ἦν ἐν τῷ πλοίῳ,

καὶ ἄλλα πλοῖα ἦν μετ᾽ αὐτοῦ.

Luke 8:22
Ἐγένετο δὲ
ἐν μιᾷ τῶν ἡμερῶν

καὶ αὐτὸς ἐνέβη
εἰς πλοῖον
καὶ οἱ μαθηταὶ αὐτοῦ

καὶ εἶπεν πρὸς αὐτούς·
διέλθωμεν εἰς τὸ πέραν τῆς λίμνης,
καὶ ἀνήχθησαν.

Synopsis 3.6

Mark 5:1
Καὶ ἦλθον εἰς
τὸ πέραν τῆς θαλάσσης
εἰς τὴν χώραν τῶν Γερασηνῶν.

Luke 8:26
Καὶ κατέπλευσαν

εἰς τὴν χώραν τῶν Γερασηνῶν,
ἥτις ἐστὶν ἀντιπέρα τῆς Γαλιλαίας.

Synopsis 3.7

Mark 5:18–20
¹⁸Καὶ ἐμβαίνοντος αὐτοῦ
εἰς τὸ πλοῖον

παρεκάλει αὐτὸν
ὁ δαιμονισθεὶς

ἵνα μετ᾽ αὐτοῦ ᾖ.
¹⁹καὶ οὐκ ἀφῆκεν αὐτόν,
ἀλλὰ λέγει αὐτῷ·
ὕπαγε εἰς τὸν οἶκόν σου
πρὸς τοὺς σοὺς
καὶ ἀπάγγειλον αὐτοῖς
ὅσα ὁ κύριός σοι πεποίηκεν
καὶ ἠλέησέν σε.
²⁰καὶ ἀπῆλθεν
καὶ ἤρξατο κηρύσσειν
ἐν τῇ Δεκαπόλει
ὅσα ἐποίησεν αὐτῷ ὁ Ἰησοῦς,
καὶ πάντες ἐθαύμαζον.

Luke 8:37c–39
³⁷ . . . αὐτὸς δὲ ἐμβὰς
εἰς πλοῖον
ὑπέστρεψεν.
³⁸ἐδεῖτο δὲ αὐτοῦ
ὁ ἀνὴρ ἀφ᾽ οὗ ἐξεληλύθει
τὰ δαιμόνια
εἶναι σὺν αὐτῷ·
ἀπέλυσεν δὲ αὐτὸν
λέγων·
³⁹ὑπόστρεφε εἰς τὸν οἶκόν σου

καὶ διηγοῦ
ὅσα σοι ἐποίησεν ὁ θεός

καὶ ἀπῆλθεν καθ᾽ ὅλην τὴν πόλιν
κηρύσσων

ὅσα ἐποίησεν αὐτῷ ὁ Ἰησοῦς.

Synopsis 3.8

Mark 8:27
Καὶ ἐξῆλθεν ὁ Ἰησοῦς
καὶ οἱ μαθηταὶ αὐτοῦ
εἰς τὰς κώμας
Καισαρείας τῆς Φιλίππου·
καὶ ἐν τῇ ὁδῷ

ἐπηρώτα τοὺς μαθητὰς αὐτοῦ
λέγων αὐτοῖς·
τίνα με λέγουσιν
οἱ ἄνθρωποι εἶναι;

Luke 9:18

Καὶ ἐγένετο ἐν τῷ εἶναι
αὐτὸν προσευχόμενον κατὰ μόνας
συνῆσαν αὐτῷ οἱ μαθηταί,
καὶ ἐπηρώτησεν αὐτοὺς
λέγων·
τίνα με λέγουσιν
οἱ ὄχλοι εἶναι;

The Trials of the Disciples

Synopsis 3.9

Mark 13:9	Luke 21:12
βλέπετε δὲ ὑμεῖς ἑαυτούς·	Πρὸ δὲ τούτων πάντων
	ἐπιβαλοῦσιν ἐφ᾽ ὑμᾶς
	τὰς χεῖρας αὐτῶν
	καὶ διώξουσιν,
παραδώσουσιν ὑμᾶς	παραδιδόντες
εἰς συνέδρια	
καὶ εἰς συναγωγὰς δαρήσεσθε	εἰς τὰς συναγωγὰς
	καὶ φυλακάς,
καὶ ἐπὶ ἡγεμόνων	ἀπαγομένους ἐπὶ βασιλεῖς
καὶ βασιλέων σταθήσεσθε	καὶ ἡγεμόνας
ἕνεκεν ἐμοῦ εἰς μαρτύριον αὐτοῖς.	ἕνεκεν τοῦ ὀνόματός μου·

The Temple Charge

Synopsis 3.10

Mark 14:55–64	Luke 22:66–71
	⁶⁶Καὶ ὡς ἐγένετο ἡμέρα,
	συνήχθη τὸ πρεσβυτέριον τοῦ λαοῦ,
⁵⁵Οἱ δὲ ἀρχιερεῖς	ἀρχιερεῖς τε καὶ γραμματεῖς,
	καὶ ἀπήγαγον αὐτὸν
καὶ ὅλον τὸ συνέδριον	εἰς τὸ συνέδριον αὐτῶν
ἐζήτουν κατὰ τοῦ Ἰησοῦ μαρτυρίαν	
εἰς τὸ θανατῶσαι αὐτόν,	
καὶ οὐχ ηὕρισκον·	
⁵⁶πολλοὶ γὰρ ἐψευδομαρτύρουν	
κατ᾽ αὐτοῦ,	
καὶ ἴσαι αἱ μαρτυρίαι οὐκ ἦσαν,	
⁵⁷καί τινες ἀναστάντες	
ἐψευδομαρτύρουν κατ᾽ αὐτοῦ	
λέγοντες	
⁵⁸ὅτι ἡμεῖς ἠκούσαμεν αὐτοῦ	
λέγοντος	
ὅτι ἐγὼ καταλύσω	

τὸν ναὸν τοῦτον τὸν χειροποίητον
καὶ διὰ τριῶν ἡμερῶν
ἄλλον ἀχειροποίητον οἰκοδομήσω.
⁵⁹καὶ οὐδὲ οὕτως ἴση ἦν
ἡ μαρτυρία αὐτῶν.
⁶⁰Καὶ ἀναστὰς ὁ ἀρχιερεὺς
εἰς μέσον
ἐπηρώτησεν τὸν Ἰησοῦν λέγων·
οὐκ ἀποκρίνῃ οὐδὲν
τί οὗτοί σου καταμαρτυροῦσιν;
⁶¹ὁ δὲ ἐσιώπα
καὶ οὐκ ἀπεκρίνατο οὐδέν.
πάλιν ὁ ἀρχιερεὺς
ἐπηρώτα αὐτὸν
καὶ λέγει αὐτῷ·
σὺ εἶ ὁ χριστὸς
ὁ υἱὸς τοῦ εὐλογητοῦ;

⁶²ὁ δὲ Ἰησοῦς εἶπεν·

ἐγώ εἰμι,
καὶ ὄψεσθε τὸν υἱὸν τοῦ ἀνθρώπου
ἐκ δεξιῶν καθήμενον
τῆς δυνάμεως
καὶ ἐρχόμενον
μετὰ τῶν νεφλῶν τοῦ οὐρανοῦ.

⁶³ὁ δὲ ἀρχιερεὺς
διαρρήξας τοὺς χιτῶνας αὐτοῦ
λέγει·
τί ἔτι χρείαν ἔχομεν μαρτύρων;

⁶⁷λέγοντες·
εἰ σὺ εἶ ὁ χριτός,

εἰπὸν ἡμῖν.
εἶπεν δὲ αὐτοῖς·
ἐὰν ὑμῖν εἴπω,
οὐ μὴ πιστεύητε·
⁶⁸ἐὰν δὲ ἐρωτήσω,
οὐ μὴ ἀπορκριθῆτε.
⁶⁹ἀπὸ τοῦ νῦν δὲ ἔσται

ὁ υἱὸς τοῦ ἀνθρώπου
καθήμενος ἐκ δεξιῶν
τῆς δυνάμεως τοῦ θεοῦ.

⁷⁰εἶπαν δὲ πάντες·
σὺ οὖν εἶ ὁ υἱὸς τοῦ θεοῦ;
ὁ δὲ πρὸς αὐτοὺς ἔφη·
ὑμεῖς λέγετε
ὅτι ἐγώ εἰμι.
⁷¹οἱ δὲ

εἶπαν·
τί ἔτι ἔχομεν μαρτυρίας χρείαν;

⁶⁴ἠκούσατε τῆς βασφημίας·

τί ὑμῖν φαίνεται;
οἱ δὲ πάντες κατέκριναν αὐτὸν
ἔνοχον εἶναι θανάτου.

αὐτοὶ γὰρ ἠκούσαμεν
ἀπὸ τοῦ στόματος αὐτοῦ.

Synopsis 3.11

Mark 15:29
Καὶ οἱ παρατοπευόμενοι
ἐβλασφήμουν αὐτὸν
κινοῦντες τὰς κεφαλὰς αὐτῶν
καὶ λέγοντες·
οὐὰ ὁ καταλύων τὸν ναὸν
καὶ οἰκοδομῶν ἐν τρισὶν ἡμέραις.

Luke 23:35
Καὶ εἱστήκει ὁ λαὸς θεωρῶν.

Synopsis 3.12

Mark 14:55-59

Acts 6:12-14
¹²συνεκίνησάν τε τὸν λαὸν
καὶ τοὺς πρεσβυτέρους
καὶ τοὺς γραμματεῖς
καὶ ἐπιστάντες
συνήρπασαν αὐτὸν

⁵⁵Οἱ δὲ ἀρχιερεῖς
καὶ ὅλον τὸ συνέδριον
ἐζήτουν κατὰ τοῦ Ἰησοῦ μαρτυρίαν
εἰς τὸ θανατῶσαι αὐτόν,
καὶ οὐχ ηὕρισκον·
⁵⁶πολλοὶ γὰρ ἐψευδομαρτύρουν
κατ᾽ αὐτοῦ,
καὶ ἴσαι αἱ μαρτυρίαι οὐκ ἦσαν,
⁵⁷καί τινες ἀναστάντες
ἐψευδομαρτύρουν κατ᾽ αὐτοῦ
λέγοντες

καὶ ἤγαγον εἰς τὸ συνέδριον,

¹³ἔστησάν τε
μάρτυρας ψευδεῖς
λέγοντας·
ὁ ἄνθρωπος οὗτος οὐ παύεται
λαλῶν ῥήματα
κατὰ τοῦ τοποῦ τοῦ ἁγίου [τούτου]
καὶ τοῦ νόμου·

⁵⁸ὅτι ἡμεῖς ἠκούσαμεν αὐτοῦ
λέγοντος
ὅτι ἐγὼ
καταλύσω
τὸν ναὸν τοῦτον τὸν χειροποίητον
καὶ διὰ τριῶν ἡμερῶν
ἄλλον ἀχειροποίητον οἰκοδομήσω.

⁵⁹καὶ οὐδὲ οὕτως ἴση ἦν
ἡ μαρτυρία αὐτῶν.

¹⁴ἀκηκόαμεν γὰρ αὐτοῦ
λέγοντος
ὅτι Ἰησοῦς ὁ Ναζωραῖος οὗτος
καταλύσει
τὸν τόπον τοῦτον

καὶ ἀλλάξει τὰ ἔθη
ἅ παρέδωκεν ἡμῖν Μωϋσῆς.

PART TWO

The Connection to the Past

The Story of Israel in Luke-Acts

4

Imitatio Septuaginta

The LXX as a Historiographical Model

A large part of art consists of imitation.

Quintillian 10.2.1

In a candid observation about the subject matter of rhetorical speeches, Isocrates, one of Athens's most significant orators, said, "Since discourses have such a nature that it is possible to set out the same events in many different ways . . . it is not necessary to avoid the topics about which others have previously spoken, rather it is necessary to try to speak better than they."[1] He went on to comment specifically about past events: "For past deeds have been left as common to us all. But to make use of those at the appropriate time, to conceive of what is proper in each circumstance, and to set them out in well-chosen words is the peculiar property of the wise."[2] Later generations fully embraced Isocrates's advice: *mimesis* (μίμησις) or *imitatio* was a staple of classical education.[3]

Historians followed the convention in two different ways. Some followed the line of debate initiated by Plato and Aristotle and commented on the role of imitation as a reflection of reality. In this case the historian was measured by the degree to which he or she created verisimilitude of characters and events

1. Isocrates, *Paneg.* 7–8.
2. Isocrates, *Paneg.* 9.
3. Some of the most important treatments of it that have come down to us from antiquity are Dionysius of Halicarnassus, *Imit.* (there is only the Greek edition of Hermann Usener, ed., *Dionysii Halicarnassensis quae fertur Ars rhetorica* (Leipzig: Teubner, 1895), 2:197–217; Pseudo-Longinus, *Subl.* 13.1–14.3; and Quintillian 10.1–2. For a scholarly treatment see Donald A. Russell, "De Imitatione," in *Creative Imitation and Latin Literature*, ed. David West and Anthony Woodman (Cambridge: Cambridge University Press, 1979), 1–16.

for the hearers.[4] Others understood mimesis more prosaically and spoke of the *exemplaria* or models that they should imitate.[5] So Dionysius of Halicarnassus could define mimesis as "the activity that has thoroughly learned its model through investigations."[6] He thought that "it was necessary to read the ancient historians so that we may not only be supplied with the material for a theme from them but the particular styles."[7] According to Quintillian, the two preferred models were Herodotus and Thucydides.[8]

We can safely assume that Jewish and Christian authors were educated in the same system. It should hardly be a surprise to learn that Josephus's *Jewish Antiquities* was modeled on the *Roman Antiquities* of Dionysius in name, size (each had twenty scrolls), and some specific content.[9] This was not, however, the work that Josephus held out as a precedent for his own work. He thought that the LXX served as a precedent. This is an intriguing position for him to take. We have argued that Josephus wrote his *Jewish Antiquities* in the Eastern historiographical tradition that I have called apologetic historiography. As we noted in chapter 2, one of the dominant characteristics of this tradition is that indigenous authors claimed that they were translating their sacred records: Berossus, Manetho, Philo of Byblos, and Josephus himself all made this claim.[10] In the case of the first three, it is probable that they were the first to translate their sacred records into Greek. This was not, however, true for Josephus, who had to recognize an earlier translation.

This raises the question of the role that the LXX played in the writing of historians who worked within the tradition of apologetic historiography. I would like to take two examples, one Jewish and one Christian, to explore how the LXX functioned within this specific tradition. I am not interested in the place of the LXX as a source for the authors who wrote in the tradition: it

---

4. For a treatment of imitation along these lines see Vivienne Gray, "Mimesis in Greek Historical Writing," *AJP* 108 (1987): 467–86.

5. For a summary of the options along this line see Marincola, *Authority and Tradition in Ancient Historiography*, 12–19, esp. 13–15. He lists five types of imitation: verbal, dialect or style, types of incidents, arrangements of material, and the disposition of the historian. See also Rothschild, *Luke-Acts and the Rhetoric of History*, 86–93.

6. Dionysius, *Imit.* 3.

7. Dionysius, *Imit.* 6.

8. Quintillian 10.1.73–75. Cf. 10.1.101–104 for his list of potential Latin models.

9. For details see my *Historiography and Self-Definition*, 284–90.

10. Berossus, *FGH* 680 frag. 1 (cf. also test. 3 and 4); Manetho, *FGH* 609 test. 7a (Josephus, *Ag. Ap.* 1.73); Philo of Byblos, *FGH* 790 test. 3 and frag. 1; and Josephus, *Ant.* 1.5; 10.218; *Ag. Ap.* 1.1.

was a primary source. I am rather interested in how they conceived of it as a model worthy of imitation.

A PRECEDENT

We will begin with Josephus. The Jewish historian commented on the LXX in three texts. The first is in the proem of his magnum opus. He wondered whether there were any precedents for Jews to transmit their traditions to Greeks and whether there were Greeks who were eager to learn them. He answered affirmatively: "I found then that Ptolemy II, a king who was especially interested in education and in the collection of books, was particularly eager to translate our law and the constitution in it into Greek." Fortunately, Ptolemy had a willing Jewish counterpart: "Eleazar, who in virtue was second to none of our high priests, did not hesitate to grant this benefaction to the previously mentioned king, although he could have forbade it except it is not our custom to keep anything good a secret." The historian continued: "I then thought that it was appropriate for me to imitate the magnanimity of the high priest and to assume that even now there are many lovers of learning similar to the king." This led him to offer a rationale for his own translation: Ptolemy had only received the law, Josephus promised to provide his readers with a "translation" that covered a five-thousand-year span.[11] Thus Josephus would provide the material that the LXX did not.

It is worth asking why Josephus offered the LXX as a precedent? Perhaps he did not think that he could ignore it. It may have been too well known in literary circles in Rome. At least Caecelius of Calacte (first century BCE), a Jewish scholar who helped to lead the Atticistic movement, and the circles of Pseudo-Longinus knew the LXX at the turn of the era.[12] Josephus may have thought that he needed to make some account of the famous translation that was used in Jewish synagogues in the Greek-speaking diaspora. Like most historians who noted a predecessor, he was critical. The translation only included the law; it was therefore incomplete.[13] The criticism is both correct and incorrect. On the one hand, it is true that the Old Greek probably began with a translation

11. Josephus, *Ant.* 1.10–13.

12. For details see Gregory E. Sterling "Recherché or Representative? What Is the Relationship between Philo's Treatises and Greek-Speaking Judaism?," *SPhiloA* 11 (1999): 23–26.

13. See Jerome, *Comm. Ezech.* 2.5 (Ezek 5:12): "Yet Aristeas and Josephus and the whole Jewish school assert that only the five books of Moses were translated by the Seventy."

of the Torah in the early part of the third century BCE. Aristobulus,[14] Pseudo-Aristeas,[15] and Philo of Alexandria[16]—the three Jewish accounts preceding Josephus—all attribute the translation of the Torah to Ptolemy II Philadelphus. On the other hand, the LXX had expanded since then, a fact that Josephus knew all too well. After all, he used some of the translations as a basis for his own "translation." He simply reported the tradition of the origins of the LXX as a basis for a criticism of its scope as a way to open the door to his own work.

The second text is his retelling of the account of the LXX at the appropriate point in his narrative. He reached this point in the twelfth scroll in the midst of recounting the *acta* that different rulers had passed on behalf of the Jewish people. The rulers included Ptolemy I Soter (367/366–262 BCE),[17] Ptolemy II Philadelphus (308–246 BCE),[18] the Seleucids,[19] and the Romans.[20] He elected to rephrase the Letter of Aristeas's account of the LXX to illustrate the benefactions of Ptolemy II.[21] He is quite open about his source. He elected to omit the majority of details about the symposium that Pseudo-Aristeas narrated. Instead, Josephus said that "the one who wishes to know the details of the questions that were asked at the symposium can learn them by reading the book of Aristeas that was written as a result of this event."[22] He followed the account in the Letter of Aristeas closely as the following chart summarizing the contents of the two narratives demonstrates.

Event	Let. Arist.	Josephus, *Ant.* 12
Introduction	1–8	11
Demetrius's request for translation	9–11	12–16
Aristeas's petition	12–17	17–23

14. Aristobulus frag. 3.2 (Eusebius, *Praep. ev.* 13.12.2). I have used the edition of Carl R. Holladay, *Aristobulus*, vol. 3 of *Fragments from Hellenistic Jewish Authors*, SBLTT 39 (Atlanta: Society of Biblical Literature, 1995).

15. Let. Arist. 3, 309.

16. Philo, *Mos.* 2.25–44, esp. 26, 27, 31, 34, 36, 37, 43, 44.

17. Josephus, *Ant.* 12.8–9.

18. Josephus, *Ant.* 12.11–118.

19. Josephus, *Ant.* 12.119–120, esp. 119.

20. Josephus, *Ant.* 12.121–128: 121–124, Vespasian and Titus; 125–128, Marcus Agrippa.

21. For a thorough analysis of the relationship between Josephus and the Letter of Aristeas see Andre Pelletier, *Flavius Josèphe, adaptateur de la Lettre d'Aristée: Une réaction atticisante contre la Koinè* (Limoges: A. Bontemps, 1962).

22. Josephus, *Ant.* 12.100. See also his comment on the omission of the names of the translators in Let. Arist. 47–50 in *Ant.* 12.57. Hereafter, references to this work will be given in parentheses within the text.

Ptolemy's release of Jewish captives	18–27	24–33
Ptolemy's decree ordering translation	28–32	34–39
Preparation of gifts	33–34	40–42
Onias		43–44
Letters between Ptolemy and Eleazar	35–46	45–56
Names of translators	47–51a	57
Return to gifts	51b–55	58–59
Description of table	56–72	60–77
Description of bowls	73–82	78–84
Description of Jerusalem	83–120	
Arrival of delegation in Jerusalem	120–127	
Jewish laws	128–171	
Reception in Alexandria	172–181	85–93
Preparations for symposium	182–186	94–98
Symposium	187–292	99–100
Menedemus	(201)	101
Conclusion	293–294	102
Defense of inclusion of symposium	295–300	
The translation	301–307	103–107a
Acceptance by Jewish community	308–311	107b–109
Acceptance by Ptolemy	312–316	110–113
Gifts for translators	317–321	114–118
Epilogue	322	

The agreement in the order of events makes Josephus's debt to the Letter of Aristeas transparent.[23] The historian follows his source with surprising closeness at times; for example, like the Letter of Aristeas, Josephus introduced Ptolemy's gifts for the Jewish high priest and authorities, suspended discussion of them until the correspondence between Ptolemy and Eleazar was recorded, and then described the gifts. The accounts even agree in wording.[24] This makes it possible to ask how Josephus redacted the text. Can we learn anything about his assessment of the LXX?

There are three places in his retelling of the Letter of Aristeas where Josephus weakened the claims for the LXX made in the Letter of Aristeas. The first occurs in the description of the work of the translators (see synopsis 4.1

23. For omissions and additions see Pelletier, *Flavius Josèphe*, 199–206.
24. For details see Pelletier, *Flavius Josèphe*, 207–49. He provides a synopsis (in Greek) on pp. 307–27 and a concordance on pp. 329–50.

in the appendix). The Letter of Aristeas claimed that the translators produced a fully harmonized translation: "They set to work, making each detail harmonize by means of comparisons among themselves" (§302). Josephus noted that they worked hard at making an accurate translation, but did not claim that when the translators presented their work that it fully agreed: "They set out working as devotedly and as painstakingly as possible to make the translation accurate" (*Ant.* 12.104). Josephus thus moved in the opposite direction from Philo of Alexandria (ca. 20 BCE–50 CE) who described the process in these words: "Inspired, they were translating [ἐπροφήτευον] not some one thing and another something else, but all used the same terms and words as if an invisible prompter were speaking to each."[25] This represents the expected trajectory of latter tradents making stronger claims as time marched on. Why did Josephus move in the opposite direction than the Alexandrian interpreter?

The second place occurs when Josephus reported the acceptance of the translation by the Jewish community (see synopsis 4.2 in the appendix). The Letter of Aristeas claims that the seventy-two translators completed their task in seventy-two days "as if by some purpose" (οἱονεῖ κατὰ πρόφησίν τινα). Josephus was content to note the time period without any hint of divine providence: "The law was transcribed and the work of translation had reached its completion in seventy-two days" (*Ant.* 12.107).

The final text is the most revealing. It appears in the section of the narrative that records the Jewish community's acceptance of the translation (see synopsis 4.3 in the appendix). The Letter of Aristeas assigned three adverbs to the translation of the LXX: it was translated well, piously, and accurately in every respect. Josephus kept the first of these and dropped the last two.[26] He weakened Pseudo-Aristeas's emphatic "so that no revision occur" and wrote "so that it might not be altered."[27] This was not a simple rephrasing. The Jewish historian made his view clear at the end of the assessment. The Letter of Aristeas invoked the famous curse against any who would tamper with the text, a curse that clearly wants to preserve the text as it stood: "They ordered that there should be a curse, as it is their custom, if anyone should revise it, by adding or paraphrasing anything at all of what was written or making a deletion." Josephus virtually reversed this by stating that "if someone sees something superfluous that had been written in the law or something missing,

---

25. Philo, *Mos.* 2.37.
26. Let. Arist. 310 // Josephus, *Ant.* 12.108.
27. Let. Arist. 310 // Josephus, *Ant.* 12.108.

he should examine it again, make it known, and correct it."[28] The historian has opened the door for revision! Josephus's motives are even more transparent if we consider the three times that he employed the curse formula in the *Jewish Antiquities*. In all three instances, it applied to his own translation.[29] What the Letter of Aristeas claimed for the LXX, Josephus claimed for his *Jewish Antiquities*!

These three texts represent the strongest claims that the Letter of Aristeas made for the LXX. Some have thought that the author was defending the Old Greek against charges that it was inaccurate and should be set aside for a revised translation.[30] Others have suggested that Pseudo-Aristeas was defending the LXX against a rival translation at Leontopolis.[31] Whatever claims it made, it is clear that Josephus did not accept them. Why? I suggest that he altered Pseudo-Aristeas in order to make room for his own work.[32] He had invoked the LXX as a precedent at the outset of the *Jewish Antiquities*. He needed both to honor the LXX and to make room for his own "translation."

The third and final place where the Jewish historian commented on the LXX is in a list of benefactions bestowed on Jews by Alexander the Great and his Ptolemaic successors in *Against Apion*.[33] While Ptolemy Philadelphus freed Jewish captives and often gave sums of money, his greatest benefaction was the LXX. Josephus appears to have drawn from either his own retelling of the Letter of Aristeas or, possibly, directly from the Letter of Aristeas. This account simply affirms the efforts of the king to ensure the accuracy of the translation by appointing his most trusted lieutenants to oversee the project.

What can we make of Josephus's posture toward the LXX? It is clear that he regarded it as a precedent for his own "translation." While we may demur with his claim that the *Jewish Antiquities* are a translation in the same way that the LXX is, we should at least acknowledge his rhetorical posture. The more

28. Let. Arist. 311 // Josephus, *Ant.* 12.109.

29. Josephus, *Ant.* 1.17; 10.218; 20.261. Cf. also *Ag. Ap.* 1.42, where he applied it to Scripture. This is based on Deut 4:2; 12:32.

30. See the criticisms against translations in Sir *Praef.* 15–26. For a defense of this view see Albertus F. J. Klijn, "The Letter of Aristeas and the Greek Translation of the Pentateuch in Egypt," *NTS* 11.2 (1965): 154–58.

31. Sidney Jellicoe, "The Occasion and Purpose of the Letter of Aristeas: A Re-Examination," *NTS* 12 (1965–1966): 144–50.

32. So also see Pelletier, *Flavius Josèphe*, 189.

33. Josephus, *Ag. Ap.* 2.42–47: §§42–43, Alexander; §44, Ptolemy I; and §§45–47, Ptolemy II.

difficult question is what we should make of his criticisms of it. It is safe to say that his criticisms and removal of claims to its finality were intended to make room for his own work. In particular, he recognized that the scope of the LXX was more restricted than his own work. But how did he see his magnum opus in relation to the LXX? Did his work *replace* the LXX in any way? It is hard to imagine that Josephus thought that the *Jewish Antiquities* would replace the LXX in Jewish synagogues. It is, however, conceivable that he hoped that the majority of his implied audience, Gentiles, would listen to his work as an authoritative translation of Jewish sacred traditions, a hope that was less likely to occur with the LXX with its barbarous Greek. The relationship was thus complex: he needed both to affirm the LXX and to present it in a way that did not exclude his own "translation." He did this by presenting it not as a timeless work, but as a precedent.

An Unfinished Work

Josephus was not the only Jewish author to note the incompleteness of the LXX. The Jewish-Christian author who composed Luke-Acts also thought that the LXX was incomplete in the form in which it circulated. It may relate the story of Israel's past, but not of the present. For that reason, Luke elected to write a continuation of the LXX. Unlike Josephus, who rewrote the entire story of Israel, this Christian author elected to continue the story without re-writing the earlier scrolls. This is a good example of "conceptual integration" or "blending" (see the introduction) in the historiographical tradition. The author did not, however, do this de novo: there were precedents for this undertaking in the historians who attempted to continue the work of their predecessors.

This precedent began in earnest when Thucydides died without completing his history. The Athenian made it clear that he planned to continue his work to 404 BCE; however, the story stops in mid-narrative in the winter of 411 BCE.[34] A number of writers elected to begin where Thucydides left off. We know of at least four: Xenophon (ca. 430–355/354 BCE),[35] the Oxyrhynchus historian (flo-

---

34. Thucydides 5.26.1; 8.109.2.

35. Xenophon, *Hell.* 1.1.1–2.3.10. A number of ancient authors claimed that Xenophon continued Thucydides, e.g., Diodorus 13.42.5; Diogenes Laertius 2.57, who claims that he published Thucydides's history; Marcellinus, *Vita* 45 (in H. Stuart Jones and J. E. Powell, eds., *Thucydidis Historiae*, 2 vols., OCT [Oxford: Clarendon, 1900–1901, rev. 1942], 1:xi–xx). For Xenophon, I have used the edition of Edgar C. Marchant, *Xenophontis opera omnia*, 5 vols., OCT (Oxford: Clarendon, 1900–1920).

ruit fourth century BCE),[36] Theopompus (floruit fourth century BCE),[37] and Cratippus of Athens (floruit fourth century BCE).[38] This became a precedent for later historians who elected to continue the work of their predecessors. Ephorus (ca. 405–330 BCE)[39] was continued by Diyllus (early third century BCE)[40] who was continued by Psaon of Plataea (late third century BCE).[41] A more famous example from the Hellenistic period is the sequence that began with Timaeus of Tauromenium (ca. 350–260 BCE)[42] and Aratus of Sicyon (271–213 BCE),[43] who were continued by Polybius (ca. 200–ca. 118 BCE), who was further continued by Poseidonius (ca. 135–ca. 51 BCE)[44] and Strabo (ca. 64 BCE–post 21 CE).[45] Other examples could be cited, but these illustrate the widespread presence of the practice.[46]

I would like to explore whether this tradition might help us understand the relationship between Luke-Acts and the LXX. We will use the criteria that have led both ancient and modern authors to posit continuations among historians.

The Beginning Point. The first and most important criterion is the beginning point of the successor. Most of the continuators began where their predecessor left off. Diodorus stated simply: "Xenophon and Theopompus began at the point that Thucydides left off."[47] Diodorus had good reasons for his judgment. Xenophon began his *Hellenica* with the battle of Cynossema, the battle at which Thucydides's narrative broke off. While there are rough spots in the

36. *FGH* 66 and Paul R. McKechnie and Stephen J. Kern, eds., *Hellenica Oxyrhynchia* (Warminster, Wiltshire: Aris & Phillips, 1989).

37. *FGH* 115 frags. 5–23. See also Gordon S. Shrimpton, *Theopompus the Historian* (Montreal: McGill-Queen's University Press, 1991), 29–57 and 217–19, who provides a discussion and translation. Theopompus wrote a *Hellenika* in 12 books (test. 1, 13, 14). A number of ancient authors claimed that he continued Thucydides, e.g., Polybius 8.11.3 (test. 19); Diodorus 13.42.5 (test. 13); 14.87.7 (test. 14); Marcellinus, *Vita* 45 (test. 15); Dio Chrysostom 18.10 (test. 45).

38. *FGH* 64. Dionysius, *Thuc.* 16 (=test. 1 and frag. 1), claimed that he continued Thucydides.

39. *FGH* 70.

40. *FGH* 73 test. 2.

41. *FGH* 78 test. 1.

42. *FGH* 566. See Polybius 12.

43. *FGH* 231. See Polybius 2.37–71.

44. *FGH* 87.

45. *FGH* 91 test. 2.

46. For details see Luciano Canfora, "Il ciclo storico," *Belfagor* 26 (1971): 653–70 and Marincola, *Authority and Tradition in Ancient Historiography*, 237–57 and appendixes VI and VII that provide charts of Greek and Roman continuators (pp. 289–90 and 291–92, respectively).

47. Diodorus 13.42.5.

transition, Xenophon self-consciously chose to begin at the approximate point where his Athenian predecessor left off.[48] He made his continuation clear by beginning not only sans preface, but in medias res. His opening words were "after these things" (μετὰ ταῦτα), a phrase that presupposes the implied reader's knowledge of events narrated elsewhere.[49] He apparently hoped that a subsequent historian would pick up his narrative just as he had picked up Thucydides. The final words of the *Hellenica* are: "The events after these events will perhaps be of concern to another" (τὰ δὲ μετὰ ταῦτα ἴσως ἄλλῳ μελήσει).[50]

The other continuators also began where Thucydides left off. Unfortunately, we do not have complete texts for them, only fragments. However, the general picture is clear. As Diodorus suggested, Theopompus appears to have begun at the same place as Xenophon, with the battle of Cynossema.[51] The Cairo and Florence fragments of the *Hellenica Oxyrhynchia* begin with events in 409 BCE: the Cairo fragments describe the expedition against Ephesus under the leadership of Thrasyllus[52] while the Florence fragments relate the battle in Megara.[53] Cratippus also began his account in 411 BCE, at least according to Plutarch's summary.[54]

This evidence suffices to demonstrate the pattern. This pattern appears to create a problem for the suggestion that Luke-Acts is a continuation of the LXX since it begins with events set in the late first century BCE. There are, however, some factors that need to be considered. Unlike the narrative of Thucydides that had an unambiguous terminal point, it is not clear whether there was a terminal point for the LXX at the end of the first century CE or how the author of Luke-Acts conceived of the boundaries of the LXX. The LXX was not

48. For treatments of the problems see Malcolm McLaren, "A Supposed Lacuna at the Beginning of Xenophon's *Hellenica*," *AJP* 100 (1979): 228–38, and the helpful comments of Antony Andrewes in Arnold W. Gomme, Antony Andrewes, and Kenneth J. Dover, eds., *A Historical Commentary on Thucydides*, 5 vols. (Oxford: Clarendon, 1945–1981), 5:439–40.

49. Xenophon, *Hell.* 1.1.1.

50. Xenophon, *Hell.* 7.5.27.

51. *FGH* 115 frag. 5. Shrimpton, *Theopompus the Historian*, 37–38, has made the case that Theopompus provided some recapitulation of Thucydides; e.g., Theopompus described the battle of Cynossema as "the second battle of Cynossema" (frag. 5). Thucydides has narrated the first in 8.104. Did Theopompus rehearse this earlier battle or did he assume that the implied reader knew Thucydides's account?

52. *P. Cair.* 26 6 SR 3049 and 27 1 frag. 1 and frag. 1+3 (McKechnie and Kern, 30–34). See also Diodorus Siculus 13.64.5 and Xenophon, *Hell.* 1.21–18, esp. 6–13.

53. *PSI* 1304 (McKechnie and Kern, 36–38). Cf. Diodorus Siculus 13.65.1–2. Xenophon does not narrate this battle.

54. *FGH* 64 test. 2.

a single entity in the first century CE, but a collection of scrolls without clearly defined boundaries. While there may have been an Old Greek translation of the Torah in the third century BCE, the translation and composition of other texts took place in different locales from the third century BCE to the first century CE. In nuce, the contents of the Greek Bible for Second Temple Jews and early Christians were not firmly fixed.[55]

The author of Luke-Acts provides a hint at the scope of the Greek Bible as he knew it at the end of the gospel. He has Jesus say to the disciples in Luke 24:44: "It is necessary for everything written about me in the law of Moses, the prophets, and the Psalms to be fulfilled." Many have read this and understood it to refer to the threefold division of Scripture that became normative in Judaism: Torah (תרה), Prophets (נבים), and Writings (כתובים). However, this assumes several things. First, it assumes that Psalms=Writings, pars pro toto. This is a problematic assumption since there is not another example of such a usage in this period.[56] It is more likely that the evangelist has the Psalter proper in mind since it plays such a large role in the fulfillment of Scripture argument in Luke-Acts. Second, it is also not clear that we should assume that the author intends this as a table of contents to the complete Greek Bible. It emphasizes the comprehensive scope of the fulfillment motif, but this does not require a definition of the Greek Bible. It only needs to suggest that the fulfillment motif is expansive. This means that we probably do not know what termini the author of Acts would have put on the Greek Bible.

If the final boundary of the Greek Bible was not fixed and the author does not indicate how he understood its terminus, where should he begin? He began where his Christian predecessors had with John the Baptist. This is the starting point for Q and for Mark.[57] The decision was, however, more than a matter of following precedent. The author understood John to be the transition point from the period of Israel to the period of the kingdom proclaimed by Jesus. He wrote: "The law and the prophets continue until John. From that point on the kingdom of God is announced and everyone is urged to enter into it" (Luke 16:16). While there has been a great deal of debate about whether John was

55. For a summary see Gilles Dorival, Marguerit Harl, and Olivier Munnich, *La Bible grecque des Septante: du judaïsme hellénistique au christianisme ancien*, Initiations au christianisme ancien (Paris: Éditions du C.N.R.S., 1988) and Martin Hengel and Roland Deines, *The Septuagint as Christian Scripture: Its Prehistory and the Problem of Its Canon* (Edinburgh: T&T Clark, 2002).

56. See the treatment of Rusam, *Das Alte Testament bei Lukas*, 259-62.

57. The Q material in Matthew and Luke begins with the Baptist (Matt 3:7-10 // Luke 3:7-9 and Matt 3:11-12 // Luke 3:16-17) as does Mark 1:2-13.

included or excluded in the law and the prophets, he is clearly at the transition. The evangelist elected to begin with John because he served as a bridge from the law and the prophets to Jesus.[58] While this is not a specific point in a text of the LXX, it reflects the author's understanding of the turning point in history.

The Style. A second criterion that is sometimes invoked for continuators is style. There is at least one famous example of an author who has a style that is similar to his predecessor. As we noted above, it was not unusual for historians to imitate the style of a predecessor. Dionysius of Halicarnassus recommended that historians imitate Herodotus, Thucydides, Xenophon, Philistus, and Theopompus.[59] He thought that Xenophon imitated the style of Herodotus.[60] He was by no means the last to do so: Dionysius himself was heavily influenced by the style of Herodotus in his *Roman Antiquities.*[61] The question is whether successors imitated the style of their predecessors as a sign of continuation.

Since the first part of the nineteenth century, scholars have recognized that Xenophon's *Hellenica* consists of two major parts: 1.1.1–2.3.10, which completes the account of the war that Thucydides had envisioned down to 404 BCE, and 2.3.11–7.5.27, which continues the war down to the second battle of Mantinea in 362 BCE.[62] The two parts are linguistically distinct. There are a number of stylistic features that characterize the two parts. For example, the first part is known to be thin on particles. A search on the Thesaurus Linguae Graecae confirms this. The following table sets out the use of the common particle μήν, a word that strengthens an assertion and is often combined with another term. An English equivalent is something like "certainly," "truly." It appears seventy-five times in the *Hellenica.*

Particle	1.1.1–2.3.10	2.3.11–2.4.43	3	4	5	6	7
μήν	0	1	3	2	0	2	4
ἀλλὰ μήν	0	1	1	0	2	1	1
γε μήν	0	2	5	6	8	11	8

58. For a balanced assessment of John in Luke see Joseph A. Fitzmyer, *Luke the Theologian: Aspects of His Teaching* (New York: Paulist, 1989), 86–116.

59. Dionysius, *Pomp.* 3.

60. Dionysius, *Pomp.* 4.

61. Sven Ek, *Herodotismen in der Archäologie des Dionys von Halikarnass: Ein Beitrag zur Beleuchtung des beginnenden Klassizismus* (Lund: Gleerupska Univ.-bokhandeln, 1942); and Stephen Usher, "The Style of Dionysius of Halicarnassus in the 'Antiquitates Romanae,'" *ANRW* 30.1:817–38.

62. The first to point this out was Barthold G. Niebuhr, "Über Xenophons *Hellenika*," *RhM* 1 (1828): 194–98.

| καὶ μήν | 0 | 0 | 2 | 3 | 0 | 3 | 9 |
| Totals | 0 | 4 | 11 | 11 | 10 | 17 | 22 |

There are several striking features of this chart. First, it moves progressively from no usage in the opening part of the *Hellenica* to the greatest usage in the final, seventh book. Second, Xenophon's use of the particle is relatively reserved. Third, it confirms that Xenophon's style is different in the opening section. The same pattern holds for other particles. Consider, for example, δή, that is a temporal particle ("now," "then") but can also indicate emphasis ("in fact") or simply to mark a transition.

Particle	1.1.1–2.3.10	2.3.11–2.4.43	3	4	5	6	7
δή	9	10	23	56	50	37	46

The sparse appearance of δή in 1.1.1–2.3.10 is striking in comparison to its frequency in the second part of the *Hellenica*. This phenomenon could be duplicated with other particles and expressions, but there is no need to belabor the point: the linguistic data are not in dispute.[63] There is a consensus that the style shifts from 1.1.1–2.3.10 to 2.3.11–7.5.27.[64]

The issue is how to explain the shift in Xenophon's style from the opening section to the later parts of the work. There have been several explanations. The most plausible understandings are that the style either reflects the early period of Xenophon's writing before he developed his own voice,[65] or that he deliberately imitated Thucydides's style,[66] or that he was heavily influenced by

63. E.g., Herbert Richards, "The Hellenica of Xenophon," *The Classical Review* 15 (1901): 197–203 and P. Defosse, "A propos du début insolite des 'Helléniques,'" *Revue Belge* 46 (1968): 1–24.

64. E.g., William P. Henry, *Greek Historical Writing: A Historiographical Essay Based on Xenophon's* Hellenica (Chicago: Argonaut, 1967), 35: "Everyone agrees that the style of i–ii.3.10, at least in certain of its features, differs conspicuously from that of the rest of the *Hellenica*, but there is little concurrence about what interpretation we should place on this disparity." Cf. also Christopher Tuplin, *The Failings of Empire: A Reading of Xenophon* Hellenica 2.3.11–7.5.27, Historia 76 (Stuttgart: Franz Steiner, 1993), 11. Hans Baden, "Untersuchungen zur Einheit der *Hellenika* Xenophons" (diss. Hamburg, 1966), argued against the consensus (I have not seen this work).

65. So, for example, Henry, *Greek Historical Writing*, esp. 35–38 and Vivienne Gray, *The Character of Xenophon's "Hellenica"* (Baltimore: Johns Hopkins University Press, 1989), 1–2.

66. So, for example, Edgar C. Marchant and George E. Underhill, *Xenophon's* Hellenica, 2 vols. (Oxford: Clarendon, 1900–1906; repr., Salem, NH: Ayer, 1984), 2:xi–xviii.

Thucydides without attempting to imitate him.[67] If we compare the use of the same particles in Thucydides, we find the following.

Particle	1	2	3	4	5	6	7	8
δή	31	29	16	22	23	25	25	24
μήν	4	2	1	3	3	3	1	3

This brief chart makes it clear that Thucydides rarely used μήν, a particle that Xenophon avoided in the first part of his *Hellenica*, but used rather freely in the second part. Both also used δή sparingly. Thucydides used it an average of twenty-five times per book, while Xenophon averaged forty-one times in his last five books and only nine times in 1.1.1–2.3.10, a frequency much more in line with Thucydides, especially when we remember that Thucydides's books are roughly twice as long as Xenophon's.[68] Whether phenomena such as these reflect a conscious decision on Xenophon's part to imitate Thucydides or reflect only a style that he learned from his Athenian predecessor is difficult to determine. It is safe to say that the style of the first part of Xenophon's *Hellenica* is closer to Thucydides than the second part.[69]

This shift in style is worth noting when we remember the styles of Luke-Acts. Luke opens with the most classical sentence in the New Testament, which is immediately followed by the infancy narrative that is easily one of the most Semitized sections of the Greek New Testament. Luke appears to reach his own voice in the body of the Gospel and the first half of Acts, although there is noticeable Semitic influence in the first half of Acts. He returns to a more elevated style toward the end of Acts. The shift in styles between the full period of the preface and the Semitized infancy narrative is so abrupt that it has been the occasion for a good deal of speculation.

As was the case with Xenophon, the linguistic data are not in question.[70] It is universally acknowledged that the Greek of the infancy narrative is colored

67. Andrewes, *Historical Commentary on Thucydides*, 5:437–44, esp. 444.

68. By my count the average length of a book in the OCT edition of Thucydides is seventy-five pages, while the average length of a book in Xenophon's *Hellenica* is thirty-six pages.

69. On this whole question see Marta Sordi, "I caratteri dell'opera storiografica di Senofonte nelle *Elleniche*," *Athenaeum* 28 (1950): 3–53 and 29 (1951): 273–348, who argues that Thucydides's influence extends beyond 2.3.10.

70. For overviews of the language of Luke-Acts, including, the infancy narrative, see Cadbury, *Making of Luke-Acts*, 213–38; Joachim Jeremias, *Die Sprache des Lukasevangeliums: Redaktion und Tradition im Nicht-Markusstoff des dritten Evangeliums* (Göttingen: Vandenhoeck & Ruprecht, 1980), 15–103; James H. Moulton, Wilbert F. Howard, and Nigel Turner, *A Grammar of New Testament Greek*, 4 vols. (Edinburgh: T&T Clark, 1906–1976), 4:45–65; and Fitzmyer, *Luke*, 1:107–27.

by heavy Semitic influence.[71] There are fewer hypotactic constructions in this section of Luke-Acts than any other section.[72] Even a selection of papyri yields higher hypotactic constructions.[73] The author prefers the connective καί to δέ in a 5:1 ratio, a ratio matched only by Mark and exceeded only by the Apocalypse in the New Testament. By contrast, a selection from Josephus's *Jewish Antiquities* yields a ratio of 0.3:1.[74] Again, there are no "on the one hand . . . on the other" (μέν . . . δέ) constructions in the infancy narrative, although they appear in the remainder of Luke-Acts.

The question is how do we explain the Semitized character of these chapters? There is a long-standing debate over whether the Semitized character reflects sources that the author adopted or a deliberate style that he cultivated.[75] Several facts lead me to the latter alternative. The infancy narrative has the earmarks of Lukan composition (with the possible exception of the canticles). Further, many of the same Semitized constructions appear in the body of Luke-Acts. The difference is one of relative frequency rather than presence or absence. Finally, Luke may well have drawn from some traditions or sources in the infancy narrative; however, Luke typically rewrites his sources sufficiently to make it all but impossible to recover them unless they are extant or there is another witness. It is hard to see why he would not rewrite traditions in the infancy narrative as well. For these reasons I prefer to think that Luke composed the infancy narrative in a style that deliberately imitated the LXX.

The issue then becomes why he imitated the style of the LXX. One possibility is that he wanted to create local color through the style of the narrative. When the narrative was set in Palestine, he gave the narrative a more Semitized character.[76] This is a reasonable suggestion; however, it does not explain why

---

71. For recent treatments see Fearghus Ó Fearghail, "The Imitation of the Septuagint in Luke's Infancy Narrative," *Proceedings of the Irish Biblical Association* 2 (1989): 57–78 and Rusam, *Das Alte Testament bei Lukas*, 40–89. Both deal more with allusions than with linguistic features.

72. A hypotactic construction involves the use of subordinate clauses rather than coordinate clauses that are linked by connectives or conjunctions such as "and." Northwest Semitic languages like Hebrew and Aramaic use coordinate constructions, while Greek thrives in hypotactic constructions; e.g., Eph 1:3–14 and 15–23 are each one sentence in Greek.

73. Moulton, Howard, and Turner, *Grammar of New Testament Greek*, 4:50–51.

74. Moulton, Howard, and Turner, *Grammar of New Testament Greek*, 4:57–58.

75. For the older literature see John Gresham Machen, *The Virgin Birth of Christ* (New York: Harper & Row, 1930; repr., Grand Rapids: Baker, 1965), 102–18. For a summary of literature see Raymond E. Brown, *The Birth of the Messiah: A Commentary on the Infancy Narrative in the Gospels of Matthew and Luke*, rev. ed. (New York: Doubleday, 1993), 245–46, 253–55.

76. Moulton, Howard, and Turner, *Grammar of New Testament Greek*, 2:7–8, who are followed by Cadbury, *Making of Luke-Acts*, 221–24.

the style is concentrated so heavily in Luke 1–2. Why would the evangelist drop this coloring when the scene moves to Galilee? Was it restricted to Jerusalem? If so, why didn't he bring it back when Jesus arrived in Jerusalem? It is more reasonable to conclude that Luke was imitating the LXX in order to show that he wanted to continue the story of Israel.[77] He wrote in the style of the LXX in the early chapters of his first scroll in order to create a seamless transition from the LXX to his own history. It is worth remembering that both Xenophon and Luke opened their works with styles that are reminiscent of the works that they continued. The styles lasted as long as they provided an overlap with their predecessor and then moved in the direction of their own voice. While we may never be able to claim more than a hypothesis for this suggestion, the similarities in stylistic strategy between Xenophon's *Hellenica* and Luke's Gospel suggest that they imitated literary style as a mark of continuation.

CONCLUSIONS

There are other factors that should also be weighed in a full-scale analysis of Luke's relationship to the LXX, most notably the fulfillment motif. We have not considered it here because it does not play a role in the continuation tradition among historians. It is, however, a significant factor for Luke-Acts that must be included in a comprehensive investigation (see chapter 6).[78]

Why would Luke want to continue the LXX? The most pressing reason is that he wanted to forge a link between Israel of the LXX and Christianity in Luke-Acts. Christianity was a movement in search of an identity. Luke attempted to give it one by claiming that Christians were the people of God. As we have already noted, the author even used the same term (λαός) for Christians that the LXX had applied to Israel.[79] The *laos* of the LXX were now Christians. Christianity was not a new movement but an old movement. To borrow a Pauline metaphor, a branch had been grafted onto the tree; as part of the tree, it could claim ancestry back to the roots of the tree.

This may also help us understand why Luke did not rewrite the LXX as Josephus did. We have noted that apologetic historians "translated" their ancestral traditions; Luke did not. While this means that Luke-Acts is different

---

77. So Ó Fearghail, "Imitation of the Septuagint," 58–78, esp. 70–73 and Rusam, *Das Alte Testament bei Lukas*, 40. Eckhard Plümacher, *Lukas als hellenistischer Schriftsteller: Studien zur Apostelgeschichte*, SUNT 9 (Göttingen: Vandenhoeck & Ruprecht, 1972), 38–72, posits imitation of the LXX for the early chapters of Acts and the missionary speeches.

78. For a thorough treatment see Rusam, *Das Alte Testament bei Lukas*, 150–431.

79. Luke 1:17; Acts 15:14; 18:10.

than other apologetic historians, I do not think that it removes him from the tradition: I would call this "conceptual integration" or "blending." Instead of rewriting the Scriptures, Luke elected *to continue* them. Josephus could present his "translation" as a *replacement* of the LXX for interested pagans. At least two factors prevented Luke from doing the same. First, Luke wrote to a Christian audience. He could not rewrite the LXX in a *Christian Antiquities* and present it as a replacement "translation." The audience already accepted the LXX as Scripture. Second, the LXX was in Greek. It is doubtful that Luke or his implied audience knew Hebrew or Aramaic. It would make no sense to rewrite a Greek source and present it as a translation. Josephus did this, but could also claim to have consulted the Hebrew scriptures. While his claim is clearly a fiction at times, it was not entirely fictional. For these reasons, Luke elected not to offer a new "translation," but to extend the established one.

Did he understand his writing to be Scripture? There is no concrete evidence that he did. He made the same claims for it that other historians made for their works, but did not claim that it was Scripture. At the same time, it is worth stating the obvious: his work became Scripture for Christians whether he thought of it as such or not. Further, his basic premise that Christianity was the continuation of Israel historically and that his work was a continuation of the LXX historiographically became the basis for the formation of the Christian Bible in two testaments. The second-century apologists echoed the same position: Christianity was not new; it was a continuation. Based on this conviction, Christians insisted on keeping the LXX as Scripture, even as they, like Luke, added to it.

Appendix[80]

The Letter of Aristeas and Josephus on the LXX

Synopsis 4.1

Letter of Aristeas 302	**Josephus, *Ant.* 12.104**
οἱ δὲ ἐπετέλουν	οἱ δ᾽ ὡς ἔνι μάλιστα
	φιλτίμως καὶ φιλοπόνως

---

80. For the Letter of Aristeas, I have used the text in L. Michael White and G. Anthony Keddie, *Jewish Fictional Letters from Hellenistic Egypt: The Epistle of Aristeas and Related Literature/Texts and Translations with Notes and Introductions*, WGRW 37 (Atlanta: SBL Press, 2018). For Josephus, I have used the text printed in *Josephus*, ed. Henry St. J. Thackeray, Ralph Marcus, and Louis Feldman, 10 vols., LCL (Cambridge: Harvard University Press, 1926–1965).

ἕκαστα σύμφωνα ποιοῦτες   ἀκριβῆ τὴν ἑρμηνείαν ποιούμενοι . . .
πρὸς ἑαυτοὺς ταῖς ἀντιβολαῖς·
τὸ δὲ ἐκ τῆς συμφωνίας γινόμενον
πρεπόντως
ἀναγραφῆς οὕτως ἐτύγχανε
παρὰ τοῦ Δημητίρου.

Synopsis 4.2

Letter of Aristeas 307   **Josephus, Ant. 12.107a**
συνέτυχε δὲ οὕτως

                                     μεταγραφέντος δὲ τοῦ νόμου
                                     καὶ τοῦ κατὰ τὴν ἑρμηνείαν
                                     ἔργου τέλος
ἐν ἡμέραις ἑβδομήκοντα δυσὶ   ἐν ἡμέραις ἑβδομήκοντα καὶ δυσὶν
τελειωθῆναι τὰ τῆς μεταγραφῆς,   λαβόντος . . .
οἱονεὶ κατὰ πρόθεσίν τινα
τοῦ τοιούτου γεγενημένου.

Synopsis 4.3

Letter of Aristeas 308–311   **Josephus, Ant. 12.107b–109**
[308]τελείωσιν δὲ ὅτε ἔλαβεν
συναγαγὼν ὁ Δημήτιος   [107b]συναγωγὼν ὁ Δημήτριος
τὸ πλῆθος τῶν Ἰουδαίων   τοὺς Ἰουδαίους ἅπαντας
εἰς τὸν τόπον,   εἰς τὸν τόπον
οὗ καὶ τὰ τῆς ἑρμηνείας ἐτελέσθη, ἔνθα καὶ μετεβλήθησαν οἱ νόμοι,
παρανέγνω πᾶσι,   παρόντων καὶ τῶν ἑρμηνέων
παρόντων καὶ τῶν διερμηνευσάντων,   ἀνέγνω τούτους,
οἵτινες μεγάλης ἀποδοχῆς   [108]τὸ δὲ πλῆθος ἀπεδέξατο μὲν
καὶ παρὰ τοῦ πλήθους ἔτυχον   καὶ τοὺς διασαφήσαντα
                                   πρεσβυτέρους τὸν νόμον,
ὡς ἂν μεγάλων ἀγαθῶν
παραίτιοι γεγονότες.
[309]ὡσαύτως δὲ καὶ τὸν Δημήτριον   ἐπήνεσαν δὲ καὶ τὸν Δημήτριον
ἀποδεξάμενοι   τῆς ἐπινοίας
                                   ὡς μεγάλων ἀγαθῶν
                                   αὐτοῖς εὑρετὴν γεγενημένον,
παρεκάλεσαν μεταδοῦναι   παρεκάλεσάν τε δοῦναι

τοῖς ἡγουμένοις αὐτῶν,
μεταγράψαντα τὸν πάντα νόμον.
³¹⁰καθὼς δὲ ἀνεγνώσθη τὰ τεύχη,
στάντες οἱ ἱερεῖς
καὶ τῶν ἑρμηνέων οἱ πρεσβύτεροι
καὶ τῶν
ἀπὸ τοῦ πολιτεύματος
οἵ τε ἡγούμενοι τοῦ πλήθους
εἶπον,
ἐπεὶ καλῶς καὶ ὁσίως
διηρμήνευται
καὶ κατὰ πᾶν ἠκριβωμένως,
καλῶς ἔχον ἐστίν,
ἵνα διαμείνῃ ταῦθ᾽ οὕτως ἔχοντα,
καὶ μὴ γένηται μηδεμία διασκευή.
³¹¹πάντων δ᾽ ἐπιφωνησάντων
τοῖς εἰρημένοις,
ἐκέλευσαν διαράσασθαι,
καθὼς ἔθος αὐτοῖς ἐστιν,
εἴ τις διασκευάσει
προστιθεὶς

ἢ μεταφέρων
τι τὸ σύνολον τῶν γεγραμμένων
ἢ ποιούμενος ἀφαίρεσιν,

καλῶς τοῦτο πράσσοντες,
ἵνα διὰ παντὸς ἀένναα
καὶ μένοντα φυλάσσηται.

καὶ τοῖς ἡγουμένοις αὐτῶν

ἀναγνῶναι τὸν νόμον,
ἠξίωσάν τε πάντες ὅ τε ἱερεὺς
καὶ τῶν ἑρμηνέων οἱ πρεσβύτεροι
καὶ τοῦ
πολιτεύματος
οἱ προεστηκότες,

ἐπεὶ καλῶς
τὰ τῆς ἑρμηνείας ἀπήρτισται,

καὶ διαμεῖναι ταῦθ᾽, ὡς ἔχει
καὶ μὴ μετακινεῖν αὐτά.
¹⁰⁹ἁπάντων δ᾽ ἐπαινεσάντων
τὴν γνώμην
ἐκέλευσαν,

εἴ τις
ἢ περισσόν τι προσγεγραμμένον
ὁρᾷ τῷ νόμῳ

ἢ λεῖπον,
πάλιν ἐπισκοποῦντα τοῦτο
καὶ ποιοῦντα φανερὸν διορθοῦν,
σωφρόνως τοῦτο πράττοντες,
ἵνα τὸ κριθὲν ἅπαξ ἔχειν καλῶς
εἰς ἀεὶ διαμένῃ.

5

"Opening the Scriptures"

The Legitimation of the Jewish Diaspora and the Early Christian Mission

> *For one land does not hold the Jews since they are so numerous. For which reason they reside in many of the most desirable lands of Europe and Asia— both on islands and on the mainlands. Although they consider the sacred city in which the holy temple of the Most High God stands to be their mother city, each holds that the lands they have inherited from their parents, grandparents, great grandparents, and earlier ancestors are their home countries in which they were born and raised.*
>
> Philo, *Against Flaccus* 45–46

In his response to Christianity's first intellectual pagan critic who challenged Christianity's social contributions, Origen argued that the gospel produces sages. As an example, he cited a text from Acts: "Stephen, who undoubtedly took [this information] from old writings which have not become accessible to most, testifies to the great learning of Moses in the Acts of the Apostles. For he says: 'and Moses was educated in all of the wisdom of the Egyptians.'"[1] While the apologist is primarily concerned with Moses, his comments on Stephen are fascinating. What writings did Origen think Stephen had read? Is he remembering the descriptions of Moses's Egyptian education in Greek-speaking Jewish authors?[2] The possibility raises an important but overlooked body of material for understanding the longest and most difficult speech in Acts.

---

1. Origen, *Cels.* 3.46. I have used the text in Paul Koetschau, ed., *Origenes Werke,* vol. 1: *Die Schrift vom Martyrium, Buch I-IV Gegen Celsus,* GCS 2 (Leipzig: Hinrichs, 1899).

2. Ezekiel, *Exagoge* 36–38; Philo, *Mos.* 1.20–24; Josephus, *Ant.* 2.236. Cf. also Artapanus frag. 3 (Eusebius, *Praep. ev.* 9.27.4). Charles K. Barrett, *A Critical and Exegetical Commentary*

In what has become a classic essay on the speeches in Acts, Martin Dibelius put his finger on one of the key difficulties posed by the Stephen speech: "The irrelevance of most of this speech has for long been the real problem of exegesis. . . . From 7.2–34 the point of the speech is not obvious at all; we are simply given an account of the history of Israel."[3] How does the story of Abraham, Joseph, and the detailed biographical material on Moses relate to the charges of 6:11, 13–14? One of the standard responses to textual incongruities such as this is to attribute the material to a source that the author has taken over but failed to contextualize fully. In the last half of the twentieth century, scholars attempted to find the basis for the speech in a wide range of traditions that share common exegetical or thematic concerns. These include the Essenes,[4]

---

on the Acts of the Apostles, 2 vols., ICC (Edinburgh: T&T Clark, 1994–1998), 1:356, considers this a possibility.

3. Martin Dibelius, *Studies in the Acts of the Apostles* (New York: Scribner's Sons, 1956), 167. Cf. the similar complaint of Kirsopp Lake and Henry Cadbury in Frederick J. Foakes Jackson and Kirsopp Lake, *The Beginnings of Christianity: The Acts of the Apostles*, 5 vols. (London: Macmillan, 1920–1933; repr., Grand Rapids: Baker, 1979), 4:69 and Hans Conzelmann, *Acts of the Apostles*, trans. James Limburg, A. Thomas Kraabel, and Donald H. Juel, Hermeneia (Philadelphia: Fortress, 1987), 57. More recently, Janusz Kucicki, *The Function of the Speeches in the Acts of the Apostles: A Key to Interpretation of Luke's Use of Speeches in Acts*, BibInt 158 (Leiden: Brill, 2018), 87–101, esp. 98, simply wrote: "Of all the speeches in Acts this presents the greatest difficulty in determining its function." For a survey of scholarship on the speeches in Acts see Osvaldo Padilla, *The Speeches of Outsiders in Acts: Poetic, Theology and Historiography*, SNTSMS 144 (Cambridge: Cambridge University Press, 2008), 16–41.

4. E.g., Oscar Cullmann, "The Significance of the Qumran Texts for Research into the Beginnings of Christianity," *JBL* 74 (1955): 213–26, esp. 220–24 and Albertus F. J. Klijn, "Stephen's Speech–Acts vii 2–53," *NTS* 4.1 (1957): 25–31. For a critique see Herbert Braun, *Qumran und das Neue Testament*, 2 vols. (Tübingen: Mohr Siebeck, 1966), 2:157–58, 181–83. Cf. also Helmer Ringgren, "Luke's Use of the Old Testament," *HTR* 79 (1986): 227–35, esp. 234–35, who appeals to CD 2.14–6.11 as a parallel use of the OT.

the Nasaraioi,[5] the Samaritans,[6] a sectarian Jewish-Christian sect,[7] Hellenistic Jewish homilies,[8] or a Christian version of a Hellenistic Jewish homily that has undergone a Deuteronomistic revision.[9] The fundamental difficulty with

5. Marcel Simon, *St. Stephen and the Hellenists in the Primitive Church* (London: Longemans, Green and Co., 1958), 78–97, esp. 90–94.

6. E.g., Abram Spiro in Johannes Munck, *The Acts of the Apostles*, rev. by William F. Albright and C. S. Mann, AB 31 (Garden City: Doubleday, 1967), 284–300; Martin H. Scharlemann, *Stephen: A Singular Saint*, AnBib 34 (Rome: Pontifical Biblical Institute, 1968), 34–56; Robin Scroggs, "The Earliest Hellenistic Christianity," in *Religions in Antiquity: Essays in Memory of Erwin Ramsdell Goodenough*, ed. Jacob Neusner, SHR 14 (Leiden: Brill, 1968), 176–206, who argues that the speech arose in the Hellenistic Christian mission to the Samaritans; Lloyd Gaston, *No Stone on Another: Studies in the Significance of the Fall of Jerusalem in the Synoptic Gospels*, NovTSup 23 (Leiden: Brill, 1970), 155–61; Charles H. H. Scobie, "The Origins and Development of Samaritan Christianity," *NTS* 19 (1973): 390–414; Charles H. H. Scobie, "The Use of Source Material in the Speeches of Acts iii and vii," *NTS* 25 (1978–1979): 399–421, who thought the sermon was the product of a Christian mission to Samaria; Oscar Cullmann, *The Johannine Circle*, trans. John Bowden (Philadelphia: Westminster, 1975), 39–53, who argued for the origins in heterodox Judaism that served as the nexus for both Acts 7 and the Gospel of John. Major critiques include: Reinhard Plummer, "The Samaritan Pentateuch and the New Testament," *NTS* 22 (1976): 441–43, who answers Scobie; Earl Richard, "Acts vii: An Investigation of the Samaritan Evidence," *CBQ* 39 (1977): 190–208; Gerhard Schneider, *Die Apostelgeschichte*, 2 vols., HThKNT 5.1–2 (Freiburg: Herder, 1980–1982), 1:448–52; and Wayne Litke, "Acts 7:3 and Samaritan Chronology," *NTS* 42 (1996): 156–60.

7. Terence L. Donaldson, "Moses Typology and the Sectarian Nature of Early Christian Anti-Judaism: A Study in Acts 7," *JSNT* 12 (1981): 27–52; repr. in *New Testament Backgrounds: A Sheffield Reader*, ed. Craig A. Evans and Stanley Porter (Sheffield: Sheffield Academic Press, 1997), 230–52.

8. Dibelius, *Studies in the Acts of the Apostles*, 169; Ernst Haenchen, *The Acts of the Apostles: A Commentary*, trans. Bernard Noble and Gerald Shinn; rev. Robert McL. Wilson (Philadelphia: Westminster, 1971), 288–89; Charles K. Barrett, "Old Testament History according to Stephen and Paul," in *Studien zum Text und zur Ethik des Neuen Testaments: Festschrift zum 80. Geburtstag von Heinrich Greeven*, ed. Wolfgang Schrage, BZNW 47 (Berlin: de Gruyter, 1986), 66; Barrett, *Acts of the Apostles*, 1:338. John W. Bowker, "Speeches in Acts. A Study in Proem and Yellammedenu Form," *NTS* 14 (1967): 96–111, esp. 107, argues that Acts 7 is an example of a proem homily.

9. Odil H. Steck, *Israel und das gewaltsame Geschick der Propheten: Untersuchungen zur Überlieferung des deuteronomistischen Geschichtsbildes im Alten Testament, Spätjudentum und Urchristentum*, WMANT 23 (Neukirchen-Vluyn: Neukirchener Verlag, 1967), 265–29, esp. 267; Ulrich Wilckens, *Die Missionsreden der Apostelgeschichte: Form- und traditionsgeschichtliche Untersuchungen*, 3rd ed., WMANT 5 (Neukirchen-Vluyn: Neukirchener Verlag, 1974), 208, 213–20; Gerhard Schneider, "Stephanus, die Hellenisten und Samaria," in *Les Actes des Apôtres: Traditions, redaction, théologie*, ed. Jacob Kremer, BETL 48 (Leuven: University Press, 1979), 215–40, esp. 224–37; Gerhard Schneider, *Die Apostelgeschichte*, 1:448. Edvin Larsson, "Temple Criticism and the Jewish Heritage: Some Reflections on Acts 6–7,"

all source criticism in Acts is that the author has so completely rewritten all preexisting material that it is impossible to separate source from redaction on stylistic grounds. It is therefore predictable that a good number of other scholars have contended that the speech is a Lukan composition.[10] This has led them to attempt to find the unity of the speech and explain how it functions within the context. Responses range from accentuating the motif of Israel's rejection of God's representatives,[11] to a positive emphasis on the Jewishness of Stephen,[12] and even to a tragic portrayal that demonstrates how the optimistic promises to Israel have failed to find fulfillment as a result of Israel's own opposition.[13]

I share the view that the speech is a Lukan composition; however, I think that the author may have had models for the writing of the speech. By models I do not mean that the author incorporated a preexisting source; rather, I mean that the author knew narratives that retold the story of Israel in ways analogous to what we have in the speech. I will argue that these earlier retellings shaped the way that the author read and understood the LXX. Just as we do not read Scripture in a vacuum today, neither did the author of Luke-Acts learn the LXX tabula rasa. The models I have in mind are the Hellenistic Jewish historians.

There are at least two reasons why on a priori grounds these neglected texts deserve to be considered. First, there is an *opinio communis* that the author of Acts was either a Hellenistic Jew or a God-fearer who had been attached to a Jewish synagogue. It is at least reasonable to examine texts that we know were

---

NTS 39 (1993): 379–95, esp. 384–85, argues for a pre-Lukan Christianized version of a Hellenistic Jewish homily, but does not posit Deuteronomistic influence.

10. E.g., Johannes Bihler, *Die Stephanusgeschichte in Zusammenhang der Apostelgeschichte*, Münchener Theologische Studien 1.16 (Munich: Max Hueber, 1963), 86; John Kilgallen, *The Stephen Speech: A Literary and Redactional Study of Acts 7,2–53*, AnBib 67 (Rome: Biblical Institute Press, 1976), 121–63, esp. 121, 163; Earl Richard, *Acts 6:1–8:4: The Author's Method of Composition*, SBLDS 41 (Missoula, MT: Scholars Press, 1978), whose work has been significant for the formation of my own judgment; Maurita Sabbe, "The Son of Man Saying in Acts 7,56," in *Les Actes des Apôtres*, 245–49; Craig C. Hill, *Hellenists and Hebrews: Reappraising Divisions within the Earliest Church* (Minneapolis: Fortress, 1992), 67–101; and Simon Légasse, *Stephanos: Histoire et discours d'Étienne dans les Actes des Apôtres*, LD 147 (Paris: Cerf, 1992), 149–77.

11. John J. Kilgallen, "The Function of Stephen's Speech (Acts 7, 2–53)," *Bib* 70 (1989): 173–93, who does make a serious attempt to explain the relevance of Abraham (p. 180), Joseph (p. 181), and—less persuasively—the expansive section on Moses (p. 176); and Earl Richard, "The Polemical Character of the Joseph Episode in Acts 7," *JBL* 98 (1979): 255–67.

12. E.g., Dennis D. Sylva, "The Meaning and Function of Acts 7.46–50," *JBL* 106 (1987): 269n2.

13. Robert C. Tannehill, "Israel in Luke-Acts: A Tragic Story," *JBL* 104 (1985): 79–81, who points to a number of reversals in the text (7:4 vs. 43; 7:7 vs. 42; 7:8 vs. 51).

associated with the Greek diaspora. Second, a minimalist interpretation of Acts 6–7 associates Stephen with the Hellenists; a maximalist reading identifies him as one of the Hellenists.[14] If the author wanted to maintain a degree of verisimilitude, Stephen should speak like a Greek-speaking Jew. It is therefore quite reasonable to look in the direction of Hellenistic Jewish authors to see if we can determine how their retellings of the LXX might have served as a model for the Stephen speech.[15]

The Legitimation of the Jewish Diaspora

Jews in the diaspora faced some issues that their compatriots in Judea and Jerusalem did not. One of the most significant was the establishment of their identity in a place removed from the temple. What did lifelong separation from the center of Judaism mean for their identity as Jews? For most the issue was not an either/or decision (i.e., either Jerusalem was or was not the center of Jewish life), but a both/and (i.e., Jerusalem was the center of Judaism and yet residence in the diaspora did not diminish Jewish identity). This was not an issue that a diaspora Jew who reflected on Jewish identity could dodge. It is worth pointing out that both of the major literary representatives of Greek-speaking Judaism addressed it. Philo confronted it while the temple was standing. His response was to present the Jews scattered throughout the empire as a single nation, united on the grounds of religion: Jerusalem with the temple was the mother city ("metropolis"); the diaspora consisted of colonies. He wrote of the former: "She is—as I have said—my native city, the mother city not of one country, Judea, but of a great many others as a result of the colonies which she has sent out at different times. . . ."[16] Josephus, writing after the destruction of the temple, faced a slightly different issue: how important was the land for Jew-

14. On the identity of the Hellenists as Greek-speaking Jews from the diaspora see Martin Hengel, *Between Jesus and Paul: Studies in the Earliest History of Christianity*, trans. John Bowden (Philadelphia: Fortress, 1987), 4–11.

15. There have been some attempts to take these authors into account, most notably Richard Pervo, *Profit with Delight: The Literary Genre of the Acts of the Apostles* (Philadelphia: Fortress, 1987), 115–21; and my *Historiography and Self-Definition*, 363–65. Marion Soards, *The Speeches in Acts: Their Content, Context, and Concerns* (Louisville: Westminster John Knox, 1994), 157–60, points to the importance of the material, but does not develop it.

16. Philo, *Legat.* 281. For an exposition of Philo's views see Henry A. Wolfson, *Philo: Foundations of Religious Philosophy in Judaism, Christianity, and Islam*, 2 vols. (Cambridge: Harvard University Press, 1947), 2:241–48, 396–426; Hans-J. Klauck, "Die heilige Stadt: Jerusalem bei Philo und Lukas," *KAIROS* 28 (1986): 129–51. This view did not mean that Philo

ish identity? His response was to downplay the significance of land theology in his retelling of Israel.[17] Both writers insisted on full Jewish identity for those living in the diaspora. There were other ways in which the same case could be made.[18] The most important for our purposes was the attempt to legitimize life in the diaspora by making connections between Israel's early heroes and locales in the diaspora.[19]

Cleodemus Malchus. The first example of this is a fragment attributed to a Cleodemus, the prophet surnamed Malchus, whom the polymath and ethnographer Alexander Polyhistor (ca. 105–ca. 35 BCE) cited, from whom Josephus in turn quoted in his *Antiquities* (1.239–41), from whom in turn Eusebius extracted the material in his *Praeparatio evangelica* (9.20.2–4).[20] The fact that Polyhistor cited it provides our only firm evidence for dating: it was prior to ca. 50 BCE. While some have disputed the Jewish identity of the author, the appeal to Abraham makes more sense for a Jewish or Samaritan author than for any other. Since the fragment claims to deal with the Jews, I prefer to think of a Jewish author.[21]

The fragment relates an ethnographic genealogy of Abraham's descendants through Keturah. According to Cleodemus, Abraham and Keturah had three sons who each became the founder of an important locale: Sures of Assyria,

---

was not a proud resident of Alexandria; he was. See David T. Runia, "Polis and Megapolis: Philo and the Founding of Alexandria," *Mnemosyne* 42 (1989): 398–412.

17. Betsy Halpern-Amaru, "Land Theology in Josephus' *Jewish Antiquities*," *JQR* 71 (1980): 201–29; Betsy Halpern-Amaru, *Rewriting the Bible: Land and Covenant in Post-Biblical Jewish Literature* (Valley Forge, PA: Trinity, 1994), 95–115, 165–69.

18. Some authors spiritualized the sacrifices, e.g., Philo. Cf. Valentin Nikiprowetzky, "La spiritualisation des sacrifices et le culte sacrificiel au Temple de Jérusalem chez Philon d'Alexandrie," *Semitica* 17 (1967): 97–116; repr. in *Études philoniennes*, Patrimoines Judaïsme (Paris: Cerf, 1996), 79–96.

19. Nikolaus Walter, *Fragmente jüdisch-hellenistischer Historiker*, 2nd ed. JSHRZ 1.2 (Gütersloh: Gerd Mohn, 1980), 117, has also recognized the practice. Bezalel Bar-Kochva, *Pseudo-Hecataeus: Legitimizing the Jewish Diaspora*, HCS 21 (Berkeley: University of California Press, 1996), 232–48, has argued that Pseudo-Hecataeus made a similar case by appealing to the migration of Jews to Egypt under the leadership of Hezekias the priest. I have not included Pseudo-Hecataeus since the appeal is not to an ancient hero.

20. For these fragments I have used the edition of Holladay, *Fragments from Hellenistic Jewish Authors*, 1:245–59. For significant discussions see Walter, *Fragmente jüdisch-hellenisticher Historiker*, 115–20; Robert Doran, "The Jewish Hellenistic Historians before Josephus," *ANRW* 20.1:255–57; and Erich Gruen, *Heritage and Hellenism: The Reinvention of Jewish Tradition*, HCS 30 (Berkeley: University of California Press, 1998), 151–53.

21. Frag. 1 (Josephus, *Ant.* 1.240); frag. 2 (Eusebius, *Praep. ev.* 9.20.3). For the arguments with bibliography see Holladay, *Fragments from Hellenistic Jewish Authors*, 1:245–46, 248–49.

Iapheras of Africa, and Iaphras of the city of Ephra (presumably a city in Africa).[22] The two African colonists, Iapheras and Iaphras, fought with Heracles against Libya and Antaeus, the Libyan giant.[23] The alliance between Jews and Greeks was sealed when Heracles married the daughter of Iaphras from which union came the later kings of Libya. The Greek mythological hero is thus connected to Abraham.

Why interweave Greek mythology and biblical figures in order to make Abraham the ancestor of the Assyrians and Carthaginians? While the fragment is too brief to permit firm conclusions, we can draw some reasonable conclusions about the geographical interests. The fragment has a distinct geographical focus: it associates Abraham with Libya. Three pieces of evidence support this conclusion. First, Libya is the central geographical location in the fragment. We might wonder whether the larger text was just as concerned with Assyria since it is also mentioned, but I am skeptical that it was. The reference to Assyria is due to the genealogical connection between Sures and Assouris.[24] The reference was too obvious to ignore; however, the text that we have only mentions it in passing. The fulcrum of the fragment is Libya. Second, the fragment probably comes from Polyhistor's *Libyca* rather than his *Concerning the Jews* since Josephus failed to name it and Eusebius, who consistently lifted material from Polyhistor, cited Josephus rather than the Roman when he quoted it.[25] This suggests that the work that Alexander Polyhistor cited dealt principally with Libya; otherwise, he would have most likely cited it in his

22. There are a number of problems with the orthography of the names and their identifications. The names of the three sons vary in Josephus and Eusebius: Iepheras, Sures, and Iaphras (Josephus, *Ant.* 1.241 [frag. 1A]); Apher, Assouri, and Aphran (Eusebius, *Praep. ev.* 9.20.3 [frag. 1B]). According to Gen 25:1–4, Abraham and Keturah had six sons: Zemran, Ieksan, Madan, Madiam, Iesbok, and Soue (LXX). The second son, Ieksan, had three sons including a son named Daidan, who in turn begat five sons including Assouriim. The fourth son, Madiam, had five sons including Gaipha and Apher. Josephus, *Ant.* 1.238–41, has a slightly different genealogy. He informs us that the sixth son, Soue (=Souos in Josephus) had two sons including Dadanes, who in turn had three sons including Assouris. The three sons named in Cleodemus Malchus appear to be Soue (the sixth son in the LXX), Gaipha (Abraham's grandson through Madiam, the fourth son, in the LXX), and Apher (Abraham's grandson through Madiam, the fourth son, in the LXX).

23. Cf. Diodorus Siculus 1.21.4; 1.24.1; 4.17.4–5; Plutarch, *Sert.* 9.4–5, for the tradition. For a discussion see Holladay, *Fragments of Hellenistic Jewish Authors*, 1:258–59n15.

24. The relationship of Abraham to the Assyrians varies in the tradition: in the LXX, Assouriim is Abraham's grandson through Daidan (Gen 25:3); in Josephus, Assouris is Abraham's great-grandson through Souos and Dadanes (*Ant.* 1.238); in Eusebius, Assouri is Abraham's son through Keturah (*Praep. ev.* 9.20.3).

25. So also Walter, *Fragmente jüdisch-hellenistischer Historiker*, 115; Holladay, *Fragments*

work *Concerning the Jews* as he did other Jewish works. Third, Josephus introduced the fragment in this way: "It is reported that this Heophren (=Iapheras) campaigned against Libya and occupied it. His grandsons took up residence in it and named it Africa after his name."[26] The historian corroborates his interpretation by citing the fragment: he understood that the fragment related the *origo* of Jews in Libya.

The limited evidence that we have suggests that the work dealt with the Jewish community in Libya. Why? Was it to enlarge the figure of Abraham as a *Kulturbringer* by associating him with yet another locale, even if through his descendants?[27] While I think that this must play some role in the work since it is a ubiquitous feature of such works, it is worth pointing out that Abraham and his descendants are not credited with any specific cultural contributions in this fragment. This leads me to ask whether we should nuance our reading of this fragment to accentuate what the text does affirm, namely the founding of the Jewish community in Libya—perhaps Carthage in particular—through the migration of Abraham's descendants.[28] If this was turned *ad extra*, it must have functioned apologetically: the Jews were not newcomers to the city but ancient residents whose associations reach back as far as the fabled Hellenistic founding myths. If it was addressed *ad intra*, it must have been an attempt to build self-identity: the Jewish community had a right to be there since the community was founded by a direct descendant of Abraham. In either case, it appears to offer legitimation for the Jewish community in Libya by associating their origins with an ancestor.

Pseudo-Eupolemus. The second example consists of the first and third fragments, which Eusebius cited from Polyhistor's work (*Praep. ev.* 9.17.1–9; 9.18.2).[29] Polyhistor attributes the first to Eupolemus and the third to some anonymous

---

from *Hellenistic Jewish Authors*, 1:245; and Doran, "Jewish Hellenistic Historians before Josephus," 256. For the *Libyca* see *FGH* 273 frags. 32–47.

26. Josephus, *Ant.* 1.239.

27. For a provocative statement supporting this perspective see Gruen, *Heritage and Hellenism*, 152–53.

28. So also Walter, *Fragmente jüdisch-hellenistischer Historiker*, 116. Holladay, *Fragments from Hellenistic Jewish Authors*, 1:246, lists both Samaria and Carthage as possible locales for the author, although he appears to incline to the latter. Doran, "Jewish Hellenistic Historians before Josephus," 256, prefers Carthage.

29. For the text see Holladay, *Fragments from Hellenistic Jewish Authors*, 1:157–87. Cf. also Walter, *Fragmente jüdisch-hellenistischer Historiker*, 137–43; Doran, "Jewish Hellenistic Historians before Josephus," 270–74; Sterling, *Historiography and Self-Definition*, 187–206; Gruen, *Heritage and Hellenism*, 146–50; and Gregory E. Sterling, "Pseudo-Eupolemus," in *Outside the Bible*, ed. Louis Feldman, James Kugel, and Lawrence H. Schiffman, 3 vols.

writings in spite of the similarity between the two. The agreements demonstrate that the two belong together, although the specific relationship is a point of debate.[30] Fortunately for our purposes we need only posit that they attest a work composed sometime prior to Polyhistor, probably in the early second century BCE.[31] It is certain that they do not come from Eupolemus since they have an explicit orientation away from Jerusalem and toward Samaria. The author is therefore anonymous and, as we will see, probably a Samaritan.

These fragments concentrate on Abraham who is cast in the role of a *Kulturbringer*, a common depiction of an ancient ancestor in apologetic historiography. Drawing on only frag. 1, we may summarize the material as follows. Abraham was born in the tenth generation after the tower of Babel in Camerine (=Ur). After he learned astrology, God instructed him to migrate to Phoenicia, where he enlightened the inhabitants by teaching them astrology. Following a rout of the Armenians who had invaded Phoenicia, Abraham was honored by Melchizedek on Mount Gerizim. He then made his way to Egypt, where after recovering his wife from a lustful but innocently ignorant Pharaoh, he offered the Egyptian priests instruction in astrology. The fragment ends with a genealogy that situates the Phoenicians and Egyptians in the biblical material.

The fragments have a distinct double-edged geographical orientation. On the one hand, there is a pronounced bias in favor of Samaria. The first hint appears in the consistent use of "Phoenicia" for Canaan. This appears to reflect the Samaritans' proximity to and ties with the Phoenicians.[32] The hint becomes an open claim when we are told that Abraham was entertained "by the city at the temple Argarizin which is interpreted 'mountain of the Most High.'"[33] Given the polemical nature of the rival claims for temple sites, it is difficult to overlook the Samaritan insistence on Gerizim as the sacred site. This is reinforced by the implicit identification of Argarizin with Salem (versus Salem=Jerusalem) when the fragment states that Melchizedek honored Abraham (at Argarizin).[34] While the identification of Salem varied in the tra-

---

(Lincoln: University of Nebraska Press; Philadelphia: Jewish Publication Society of America, 2013), 705–13, esp. 705–6.

30. For details see my *Historiography and Self-Definition*, 191–93 and "Pseudo-Eupolemus."

31. Sterling, *Historiography and Self-Definition*, 190–91.

32. So Walter, *Fragmente jüdisch-hellenistischer Historiker*, 138 and Holladay, *Fragments from Hellenistic Jewish Authors*, 1:181n13. For the tie see Josephus, *Ant.* 11.344 and 12.260. The Samaritans claimed to be Sidonians.

33. Frag. 1 (Eusebius, *Praep. ev.* 9.17.5).

34. Frag. 1 (Eusebius, *Praep. ev.* 9.17.6).

dition—a fact that made its identity problematic—the specific identification of it with Mount Gerizim is an explicit Samaritan claim. I find it difficult to think that anyone other than a Samaritan (or perhaps, a proto-Samaritan) would make such an identification.[35] Finally, the fragment rearranges the order of the biblical text by placing the story of Gen 14:1–24 (Eusebius, *Praep. ev.* 9.17.4–6) before that of Gen 12:10–20 (*Praep. ev.* 9.17.6–8). This has the effect of giving priority to Phoenicia over Egypt. On the other hand, this priority points to the negative polemic in the fragment. The critique becomes explicit in the concluding genealogy when Canaan is presented as the father of the Phoenicians and of Mizraim who is the father of the Egyptians. The Egyptians are thus one step behind the Phoenicians in culture and one generation behind in age.

Why make this case? The polemical nature of the geographical data suggests that there is a political aspect to the argument: the Seleucids are favored over the Ptolemies. The fragments also make cultural claims: some think that Pseudo-Eupolemus used pagan material as confirmation of the biblical tradition, others suggest that he demythologized the pagan material polemically, and still others argue that he accentuated the superiority of the Jews.[36] There is another dimension to the fragments as well, the geographical aspect. Like Cleodemus Malchus, this work addresses the issue of the *origo* of a specific people: Abraham came to Phoenicia (not Canaan or Judea); and more specifically, to the temple at Mount Gerizim. What can this be but an argument for the legitimation of the Samaritan community who wanted to anchor their roots in the story of their ancestors? While the evidence is very limited, this is—at least in my judgment—the best way to read what we have.

Artapanus. The third example is the most extensive and most significant. We have three fragments from Artapanus, all preserved by Polyhistor.[37] In this instance we may have more of an idea of the scope of the full work since the fragments are internally linked by means of transitional genealogical introductions and end with a summary statement.[38] Like the fragments from Cleode-

35. Contra Gruen, *Heritage and Hellenism*, 147–48.

36. For a summary with bibliography see Gruen, *Heritage and Hellenism*, 149–50.

37. Holladay, *Fragments from Hellenistic Jewish Authors*, 1:189–243; Walter, *Fragmente jüdisch-hellenistischer Historiker*, 121–36; Nikolaus Walter, "Jüdisch-hellenistische Literatur vor Philo von Alexandrien (unter Ausschluß der Historiker)," *ANRW* 20.1:98–99; Doran, "Jewish Hellenistic Historians before Josephus," 257–63; Sterling, *Historiography and Self-Definition*, 167–86; and Gruen, *Heritage and Hellenism*, 150–51 (frag. 1), 87–89 (frag. 2), 155–60 (frag. 3).

38. Frag. 2 (Eusebius, *Praep. ev.* 9.23.1) and frag. 3 (Eusebius, *Praep. ev.* 9.27.1–3, esp. 1). For the concluding summary see frag. 3 (Eusebius, *Praep. ev.* 9.27.37).

mus Malchus and Pseudo-Eupolemus, we can only date this work between the two known termini: the LXX and Polyhistor. Since the focus of the fragments is unambiguously on Egypt, the author was probably an Egyptian Jew.

The first fragment is a brief recapitulation of the career of Abraham in Egypt. Like Pseudo-Eupolemus, Artapanus claims that Abraham taught the Egyptians astrology. The second fragment celebrates the career of Joseph who, since he cannot be a *Kulturbringer* in the sense that he brought culture from one civilization to another, is cast as an "inventor" or "discoverer." The greatest panegyric, however, is reserved for Moses in fragment three. The Jewish legislator is presented as the "discoverer" of many features of Egyptian civilization. The fragment is extensive enough that we could call it a short "romance." Artapanus draws not only on the biblical text, but more significantly on the traditions of heroes of other civilizations whose careers are paralleled and exceeded by Moses.

As was true in the other two examples we have noted, the geographical focus is unambiguous. In this instance it is on Egypt. This is evident in a number of ways. Artapanus has selected the careers of the three Hebrew ancestors who were active in Egypt. In the case of Abraham, Artapanus has made his orientation quite clear by only discussing—if Polyhistor has not misled us by his condensation—Abraham's activities in Egypt. This is reinforced by the fact that the Moses fragment appears to end with the crossing of the Red Sea, marking the departure from Egypt as the terminus of the story. The only statements that follow this final scene are a brief note about the manna during the forty years in the wilderness and a description of Moses based on Deut 34:7. Since this text marks the end of the Torah, it probably had a similar function for Artapanus.[39] Within these limits, Artapanus has expanded the biblical material to underscore the Jewish presence in Egypt. In the case of Abraham, he has done so in two ways: he claims that Abraham spent twenty years in Egypt and that some of his retinue remained in Egypt when he returned to Syria. The latter is a clear apologetic claim attempting to extend the Jewish residence in Egypt to the earliest possible period. Philo of Alexandria makes a similar claim in one of his apologetic treatises.[40] It is another example of the *origo* motif. In the cases of Joseph and Moses, Artapanus expanded the biblical narrative by making them the founders of all that is worthwhile in Egyptian civilization, even Egyptian religion!

---

39. Cf. Walter, *Fragmente jüdisch-hellenistischer Historiker*, 122–23.
40. Philo, *Hypoth.* 8.6.1 (Eusebius, *Praep. ev.* 8.6.1), where he refers to Jacob.

There is a consensus that Artapanus wrote *ad maiorem Iudaeorum gloriam*. While it is possible that he wrote in order to rebut defamatory presentations such as those of Manetho, I think it more probable that he wrote for a Jewish audience—at least there is no evidence that pagans read Jewish works in this period. But why would he write such a story for the Jewish community? Artapanus offered a history of the Jews in Egypt as a means of providing Egyptian Jews with a sense of identity. Jews living in Egypt had an illustrious past, a past that was in no way inferior to that of other nations. He demonstrated this by incorporating the traditions of other national heroes. The combination of Jewish and foreign traditions showed how Jews could integrate into the larger society without forfeiting their own identity. In this way he legitimated the Egyptian diaspora.

Summary. These three Greek-speaking Jews/Samaritans of the diaspora share a number of perspectives and techniques. They all used the biblical stories about their ancestors as a basis for creative stories about the origins of their respective communities. Why? Each lays claim to the cultural superiority of the Jewish people as a means of developing a healthy identity. Their efforts are evident in the incorporation and subordination of non-Jewish traditions within the ancestral stories. At the same time, they did not make these claims globally, but within specific geographical limits. The use of the *origo* motif and the focus on specific locales suggests that each of these authors wanted to legitimate their own community's existences. They did this by anchoring their past in the lives of their most illustrious heroes. The specific focus did not negate the legitimation of other Jewish communities, but validated their own. The community had a legitimate right to exist in a foreign land where they were not cultural inferiors, but equals or superiors to the people around them.

THE LEGITIMATION OF THE EARLY CHRISTIAN MISSION IN ACTS 7

Do these texts illumine the Stephen speech? Or to frame the question more specifically: How does the understanding of ancient Jewish history in these Hellenistic Jewish historians explicate the understanding of Jewish history in Acts 7? Before we attempt to answer the question, we need to explore the possibility that the author of Acts knew Hellenistic Jewish interpretative traditions. While this will not determine whether the author used the tradition we have sketched, it will assist us in weighing the probability of such a use.

Hellenistic Jewish Exegetical Traditions in the Stephen Speech. The Stephen speech is a learned recitation of select sections of the LXX. The language of the LXX permeates the speech in the form of direct citations, paraphrases, and allusions (see the appendix). More importantly, the speech departs from the LXX in eight places where it agrees with exegetical traditions attested in Hellenistic Jewish literature. The argument that follows is not that the author of Acts knew these specific works, but that the author of Acts and these Hellenistic Jews knew and used similar exegetical traditions when they retold the LXX. Here are eight examples, although not all of these are of equal weight.

1. Acts suggests that God appeared to Abram in Mesopotamia: "He appeared to our ancestor Abram" (Acts 7:2). The LXX does not support this; rather, Gen 12:1 reads: "and the Lord said to Abram." The phrase in Acts comes from Gen 12:7, when Abram was already in Canaan. The author may have paraphrased Gen 12:1 with a phrase that he considered synonymous or confused the two incidents. However, it is worth noting that Philo of Alexandria makes the same move: he cites Gen 12:7 in association with the initial call of Abram rather than the later event.[41] This could be a coincidental exegetical agreement; however, there are other agreements in the same context.

2. It is well known that the author of Acts telescoped the call of Abram by locating it in Ur (Acts 7:2) rather than in Haran where the LXX places it (Gen 11:27–12:3). This was a fairly well-known tradition in Hellenistic Jewish authors: Pseudo-Eupolemus, Philo, and Josephus all attest it.[42] Since there is nothing in the biblical text that requires the rearrangement, it is likely that the tradition was the lens by which many Jews read or heard the text, including the author of Acts.

3. There is a third agreement in connection with the call of Abraham. Acts tells us that Abraham left Haran after the death of Terah (Acts 7:4). This, however, stands in tension with the chronological information in the LXX. According to the latter, Terah was 70 when Abram was born (Gen 11:26). Abram was 75 when he set out for Canaan (Gen 12:4), making Terah 145. Since Terah died in Haran at 205 years of age (Gen 11:32), he lived 60 years after Abram left. Those who have argued for the Samaritan origin of the speech have been quick to point out that the Samaritan Pentateuch says that Terah died at 145 years of age, or when Abram left Haran. This might well be a Palestinian text tradition. There is, however, another possibility. Philo makes the same argu-

---

41. Philo, *Abr.* 77.

42. Pseudo-Eupolemus frag. 1 (Eusebius, *Praep. ev.* 9.17.3–4); Philo, *Abr.* 60–88, esp. 72; Josephus, *Ant.* 1.154. Philo speaks of two migrations in *Abr.* For details see Ellen Birnbaum and John Dillon, *Philo of Alexandria "On the Life of Abraham": Introduction, Translation, and Commentary*, PACS 6 (Leiden: Brill, 2021), 213, 228–29.

ment: "It is likely that no one who is well read in the sacred laws is ignorant of the fact that Abraham first left the land of Chaldea, then resided in Haran, and after his father died, he also transferred from that country. . . ."[43] It may be that both Philo and the author of Acts either made a simple narrative assumption without doing the arithmetic made possible by the hints in the text.[44] Or, that they drew on a common tradition that had already made this assumption.

4. The Joseph material contains some phenomena similar to what we found in the Abraham traditions. As with Abraham's call, the author of Acts collapses the story of Joseph's entry into Egypt by dropping all mention of the Ishmaelites/Midianites and simply affirming that the brothers sold Joseph into Egypt (Acts 7:9). The Jewish historian/chronographer Demetrius condenses the story in the same way.[45] This could either be an example of a common attempt to compress a much larger story or a common report of a tradition that had already condensed the text.

5. Acts claims that God gave Joseph not only grace but wisdom (Acts 7:10), a quality never ascribed to Joseph in the LXX. Philo and Josephus likewise emphasize Joseph's wisdom.[46] The ubiquity of such a virtue in the Hellenistic world is sufficient to explain its appearance in all three authors.

6. The agreements in the Moses material are more significant. Acts alters the birth story of Moses in two ways: it omits any reference to the Egyptian midwives and uses the language of exposure (ἐκτίθημι) to describe the fate of Jewish children and Moses (Acts 7:19, 21). The same alterations appear in Ezekiel the Tragedian and Philo who also omit any reference to the midwives and use the language of exposure (ὑπεκτίθημι [Ezekiel] and ἐκτίθημι, ἔκκειμαι [Philo]).[47] There seems to have been a tradition among Hellenistic Jews in Egypt that recast the birth story of Moses to reflect the well-known practice of exposure.

7. The most obvious instance of dependence is the education of Moses. Like Ezekiel the Tragedian, Philo, and Josephus, Acts emphasizes Moses's Egyptian education (Acts 7:22).[48] This runs counter to some of the Semitic presentations of Moses that emphasize his Hebrew education.[49] Since Origen knew Philo's

---

43. Philo, *Migr.* 177.

44. So Barrett, "Old Testament History according to Stephen and Paul," 61, and Litke, "Acts 7:3 and Samaritan Chronology," 159.

45. Demetrius frag. 2 (Eusebius, *Praep. ev.* 9.21.11).

46. Philo, *Ios.* 106; Josephus, *Ant.* 2.87.

47. Ezekiel, *Exagoge* 12-13, 16; Philo, *Mos.* 1.8, 10, 11, 14.

48. Ezekiel, *Exagoge* 36-38; Philo, *Mos.* 1.20-24; 2.1; Josephus, *Ant.* 2.236. Cf. also Artapanus frag. 3 (Eusebius, *Praep. ev.* 9.27.4)

49. E.g., Jub. 47:9.

works and through Philo's library may have known Ezekiel, he could have had such writings in mind when he made his comments on Acts 7.[50]

8. The author of Acts uses a well-known schema to describe Moses's early years: "was born . . . was nurtured . . . was educated" (ἐγεννήθη . . . ἀνετράφη . . . ἐπαιδεύθη) (Acts 7:20–22), a schema he will use again in connection with Paul (Acts 22:3). This is a standard encomiastic pattern that is widely attested.[51] It is, however, worth noting that Philo uses the same pattern in regard to Moses. He summarized the first treatise on his *Life of Moses* in the preface to the second treatise with these words: "The former treatise dealt with the birth (γένεσις) of Moses and his upbringing (τροφή), also with his education (παιδεία) and office as ruler. . . ."[52] It is likely that Hellenistic Jews commonly used standard encomiastic patterns to present their ancestral heroes.

These eight cases show that the author of Acts may have known Hellenistic Jewish traditions about the call of Abraham and the Egyptian career of Moses. The Joseph material is too inconclusive to be persuasive. While these examples neither exhaust the possible traditions the author knew, they at least point to the presence of a common body of exegetical traditions in Greek-speaking Jewish circles.[53]

The Legitimation of the Diaspora. But does the author know and use traditions that make claims of legitimation for locales outside Jerusalem and Judea? There is one clear example of an exegetical tradition and one intriguing possibility of a pattern that made such a claim. The speech relates the death and burial of not only Jacob, but also of his sons: "And Jacob went down into Egypt and died, he and our fathers. They were brought to Shechem and placed in the tomb that Abraham bought for a sum of silver from the sons of Hamor in Shechem" (Acts 7:15–16).[54] This narrative stands in tension with the LXX in several details. According to the LXX, Jacob was buried near Hebron (Gen 49:29–32; 50:13) not in Shechem. Jacob, not Abraham, purchased land in Shechem from the sons of Hamor (Gen 33:18–20); Abraham purchased a burial plot near Hebron from Ephron (23:1–20). Why the confusion in Acts?

---

50. Origen, *Cels.* 3.46. Cf. the opening paragraph in this chapter.

51. For details see Willem C. van Unnik, *Tarsus or Jerusalem: The City of Paul's Youth* (London: Epworth, 1962), 18–27.

52. Philo, *Mos.* 2.1.

53. Another noteworthy pattern is the parallel between Acts 7:36 and the *Assumption of Moses* 3.11.

54. The most helpful analysis of this material is still Joachim Jeremias, *Heiligengräber in Jesu Umwelt (Mt. 23,29; Lk. 11,47): Eine Untersuchung zur Volksreligion der Zeit Jesu* (Göttingen: Vandenhoeck & Ruprecht, 1958), 36–38.

According to the LXX, Joseph was buried in Shechem in the plot of land Jacob purchased from the sons of Hamor (Josh 24:32). Perhaps the author of Acts confused burial traditions.[55] While this is possible, it is important to note that there is a well-known tradition that situates the burial of Joseph's brothers in Hebron.[56] Josephus even claims that the tomb could be seen in his day.[57] The claim that they were buried in Shechem may therefore be a rival claim. Those who have argued for a Samaritan background to the speech have understandably pointed to the importance of Shechem for the Samaritans. This is a reasonable appeal even though we do not know of a Samaritan text that makes this identification; however, it is another matter to claim that the larger speech has an underlying Samaritan source.[58] This draws too much from too little. What we can say is that Acts 7:15–16 is the earliest evidence for the tradition attested in later texts that locates the tomb of Jacob's sons in Shechem.[59] The tradition probably had its origins among the Samaritans who used it as a counter to the Judean tradition that the twelve were buried in Hebron.[60] The competitive traditions of the Judeans and Samaritans demonstrate that each vied to legitimate their sacred site through the geographical details of the sacred story.

There is one other possibility, although it is more tenuous. It is worth noting that the rehearsal of Israel's early history in Acts 7 selects the same material and same balance of material as we find in Artapanus. That is to say that the three fragments of Artapanus that deal with Abraham (frag. 1), Joseph (frag. 2), and Moses (frag. 3) are paralleled here by the careers of Abraham (Acts 7:2–8), Joseph (Acts 7:9–19), and Moses (Acts 7:20–43). Just as Abraham and Joseph are preliminary to the main presentation of Moses in Artapanus, so the account in Acts 7 expands the Moses traditions beyond the more cursory retellings of the earlier figures. The result is that both authors focus on Egypt, although Acts is

---

55. So Barrett, *Acts of the Apostles*, 1:351.

56. E.g., Jub. 46:9–10; T. Reu. 7:1–2; T. Levi 19.5; T. Jud. 26.4; T. Iss. 7.8; T. Zeb. 10.7; T. Dan 7.2; T. Naph. 7.1–3; T. Gad 8.3; T. Ash. 8.1–2; T. Benj. 12.1–4; Josephus, *J. W.* 4.530–532; *Ant.* 2.199.

57. Josephus, *J. W.* 4.532.

58. Scobie, "Use of Source Material in the Speeches of Acts iii and vii," 409, goes so far as to claim that Shechem as the site of the true sanctuary "gives the historical section of Acts 7 a remarkable and hitherto unnoticed underlying unity." This unity was unnoticed because it does not exist.

59. For the latter Christian tradition see Jerome, *Epist.* 57.10; Syncellus, p. 284 (Dindorf).

60. One of the most sane assessments of this material is F. Scott Spencer, *The Portrait of Philip in Acts: A Study of Roles and Relations*, JSNTSup 67 (Sheffield: Sheffield Academic, 1992), 70–81.

far less exclusive than Artapanus. As I have already indicated, I do not want to imply that the author of Acts knew Artapanus—although I do consider this a possibility on larger grounds—but that the author of Acts knew retellings of Israel that concentrated on the history of the Jews in Egypt.[61]

The Legitimation of the Early Christian Mission. Why would the author incorporate both a tradition arguing for the legitimacy of Shechem as a sacred site and a history of the Jews in Egypt that probably argued for the legitimacy of Egyptian Judaism? I suggest that the author wanted to argue for the legitimacy of the Christian mission beyond Jerusalem and drew from the histories of Hellenistic Jews who had already made similar geographical arguments. The author of Acts differs from the traditions we have examined in at least one important aspect: the Hellenistic Jewish authors legitimated specific communities; the author of Acts legitimated a mission that transcended the temple and Jerusalem. What they share in common is that they all contend for legitimation by making connections between Israel's ancestral heroes and geographical locales beyond the immediate vicinity of the temple and homeland. For all of these texts it is not a matter of either the temple/Jerusalem or the diaspora, but of both the temple/Jerusalem and the diaspora. The use of the same strategy to make this both/and case argues for the dependence of Acts on the established Jewish diaspora tradition.

Acts does this by emphasizing God's dealings with Israel away from the temple.[62] We see this in a number of ways. There is a greater preoccupation with the concept of land (γῆ) here than anywhere else in Luke-Acts: nine of the

---

61. This is quite different than the old Alexandrian source theory. Cf. Benjamin W. Bacon, "Stephen's Speech: Its Argument and Doctrinal Relationship," in *Biblical and Semitic Studies: Critical and Historical Essays by the Members of the Semitic and Biblical Faculty of Yale University* (New York: Scribner's Sons, 1901), 213–76; Wilhelm Soltau, "Die Herkunft der Reden in der Apostelgeschichte," *ZNW* 4 (1903): 144–46; and Leslie W. Barnard, "Saint Stephen and Early Alexandrian Christianity," *NTS* 7 (1960–1961): 31–45, who argues for the influence of Acts 7 on the Epistle of Barnabas.

62. This has been noted by a number of scholars, e.g., Gaston, *No Stone on Another*, 156–57; William D. Davies, *The Gospel and the Land: Early Christianity and Jewish Territorial Doctrine* (Berkeley: University of California Press, 1974; repr., Sheffield: JSOT Press, 1994), 267–74, esp. 269–72; Schneider, "Stephanus, die Hellenisten und Samaria," 234; Frederick F. Bruce, "Stephen's Apologia," in *Scripture: Meaning and Method; Essays Presented to Anthony Tyrell Hanson for His Seventieth Birthday* (Pickering: Hull University Press, 1987), 40; Klaus Haacker, "Die Stellung des Stephanus in der Geschichte des Urchristentums," *ANRW* 26.2:1535–40; and Donaldson, "Moses Typology and the Sectarian Nature of Early Christian Anti-Judaism," 236. Contra Larsson, "Temple-Criticism and the Jewish Heritage," 385–88, 392–94.

fifty-seven uses of the term in the two volumes are clustered here. Nor are the references restricted to Israel (7:3, 4): they refer to Chaldea (7:3, 4), Egypt (7:6, 36, 40) and Midian (7:29, 33). Events are situated in the following locales:

Locale	Coverage in text of Acts
Mesopotamia	7:2–3
Haran	7:4a–c
This land	7:4d–5, 7d–e, 11b–12a, 14, 45–50
Egypt	7:6, 9–11a, 12b–13, 15, 17–28, 35–36c
Shechem	7:16
Midian	7:29–34
Wilderness	7:36d–44

More importantly, the Stephen speech emphasizes God's dealings with Israel's heroes away from the temple and surrounding area. If we restrict our survey to the explicit statements, we find the following: God appeared to Abraham in Mesopotamia (7:2); God did not give Abraham a single foot of ground in the homeland (7:5), making Abraham the first Jew without a homeland; God was with Joseph in Egypt (7:9); and God appeared to Moses in the form of the angel in Midian (7:30, 35). Even more telling is the treatment of "place" (τόπος). The term appears in both the charges leveled against Stephen and in the speech proper. In the accusations against Stephen, it denotes the temple (6:13, 14). In the speech proper it surfaces three times. The first is the promise to Abraham that combines Gen 15:13–14 with Exod 3:12. The author alters the citation of the latter by replacing "mountain" with "place," thus changing the reference from Mount Horeb to the temple (Acts 7:7). This appears to run counter to the tendenz we have noted of locating activities outside the land.[63] It does fit quite nicely with the broader assessment of the temple in Luke-Acts as a sacred place. However, the next time a reference to Sinai occurs, the Stephen speech permits Horeb to stand as the "place" (Exod 3:5). God said to Moses: "Loose the sandals from your feet, for the place (τόπος) where you are standing is sacred land (γῆ ἁγία)" (Acts 7:33). This recalls the language of the charge that Stephen spoke "against this holy place (κατὰ τοῦ τόπου τοῦ ἁγίου [τούτου])" (Acts 6:13). The implication is that there is more than one

---

63. Allan J. McNicol, "Rebuilding the House of David: The Function of the Benedictus in Luke-Acts," *ResQ* 40 (1998): 35–37, makes the intriguing suggestion that the place refers to the Jerusalem church. I am not sure that we should assign an eschatological meaning to the biblical citations in this context.

holy place.[64] This is confirmed by the third use of the term at the end of the sermon in the Isaiah citation: "Heaven is my throne, the earth is the footstool of my feet. What house will you build for me, says the Lord? Or what is the place (τόπος) of my rest?" (Acts 7:49) God cannot be confined to a single holy place: the temple is holy, but so is Mount Sinai.

The Stephen speech was not the first to make such arguments. The Hellenistic Jewish historians had been making similar arguments for several centuries. The author of Acts used these retellings as models to argue a new case (i.e., the Christian mission). For his Jewish predecessors the heroes of ancient Israel demonstrated God's dealings outside the land where the temple would one day stand. For the author of Acts they served as a means of legitimating a mission beyond territory where the temple once stood. It therefore makes perfectly good sense to retell the story of Israel's earliest heroes when confronting the issue of expansion beyond the temple and its environs.

The Legitimation of the Early Christian Mission in Luke-Acts

This is not the first time in Luke-Acts that the author has used this hermeneutical strategy. In the inaugural sermon of Jesus in Luke 4:16–30, Jesus appealed to Elijah and Elisha as a warrant for his activities in Capernaum since true to the aphorism "no prophet is acceptable in his own hometown," the residents of Nazareth rejected him (Luke 4:23–27). Most interpreters also understand the references to point beyond the immediate context to anticipate the later Gentile mission.[65] In both cases, Jesus's mission in Capernaum and the Gentile mission, the appeal is to ancient geography: Elijah journeyed to the widow of Zarephath in Sidon and Elisha healed Naaman who came from Syria. Just as in Acts 7, the appeal is to ancient figures—here appropriately prophets. Whether the prophet moved beyond the borders of Israel or a foreigner came to Israel from the outside, the point is the same: the mission of Christianity cannot be restricted geographically.

64. Contra Larsson, "Temple Criticism and the Jewish Heritage," 388.
65. Larrimore C. Crockett, "Luke 4:25–27 and Jewish-Gentile Relations in Luke-Acts," *JBL* 88 (1969): 177–83, argued that the text also anticipated Jewish-Gentile relations. While these are logically presupposed by the Gentile mission, the point of the text is the extension of the prophetic mission beyond Israel.

The author of Luke-Acts was careful, however, where he situated the mission in the story. It stands on the cusp between Jewish Christianity and Gentile Christianity. We should therefore read the speech of Stephen as a suprahistorical speech—that is, a speech that is designed to justify not Stephen as an individual martyr, but Stephen as a representative of the early Christian mission. Or to put it in the specific terms of the Acts narrative, the speech is an attempt to legitimate the early Christian mission in the four major narratives that directly follow it in the transitional section of Acts (8:4–12:25).[66] Taking the geographical comments in Acts 1:8 as a rough guide to the structure of the work, the narrative falls into three major units: 2:1–8:3, Jerusalem; 8:4–12:25, Judea and Samaria; 13:1–28:31, the ends of the earth. The section on Judea and Samaria is set off in several ways. First, Acts 8:1 echoes 1:8 as a means of signaling the transition from Jerusalem to Judea and Samaria. Lest we forget the geographical orientation of the work, we are reminded of it again in 9:31. Second, the unit is marked by a framing device: just as the section on Jerusalem ended in persecution including the death of a significant martyr (Stephen), so the Judean-Samaritan section comes to a terminus with the death of James and an attempt on Peter's life.

There is, however, a difference between the way the two martyr stories function: the Stephen story serves as a closing marker and sets up the next four narratives; the James story only serves as a closing marker. This is clear from the intertextual connections between the Stephen story and the four major narrative strands that flow from it. The first is connected in the person of Philip (Acts 8:4–40) who was one of the seven (6:5). The second is connected through the person of Saul (9:1–30) who was an accomplice to Stephen's violent death (7:58; 8:1, 3). The connection is made explicitly in the text. When the narrative relating Saul's Damascus experience begins, it recalls the events surrounding Stephen's death ("Saul was still breathing out threat and murder against the

---

66. Cf. also Dibelius, *Studies in the Acts of the Apostles*, 169–70 for the function of Acts 7; and 138, 140, 169, where he deals with the broader phenomenon; Klijn, "Stephen's Speech," 26, who argues that it reflects a mission within the orb of Judaism, not the later Gentile mission; Haenchen, *Acts of the Apostles*, 289; Davies, *Gospel and the Land*, 272, who understands it to address the relationship between Christianity and Judaism; Donaldson, "Moses Typology and the Sectarian Nature of Early Christian Anti-Judaism," 234, who thinks that it introduces and defends the mission to the Samaritans and diaspora Judaism; Bruce, "Stephen's Apologia," 40, who calls it a manifesto of Hellenistic Christianity; and Barrett, *Acts of the Apostles*, 1:340, who thinks that it addresses the relationship between Christianity and Judaism.

disciples of the Lord" [9:1]). When Saul returned to Jerusalem, he debated Stephen's former opponents in the synagogue (9:29; cf. 6:9–10). Lest any doubt remain, the author has Paul make the connection between Stephen's death and his call explicit in a later speech (22:20–21). The third narrative strand (9:32–11:18) recounts the activities of Peter, who began an itinerant mission (διέρχομαι in 9:32 as in 8:4). Eventually a report of his activities found its way back to those who had remained in Judea (11:1; cf. 8:1). The fourth narrative strand (11:19–30) has an explicit transition statement that connects the activities of the missionaries with Stephen's death (11:19). In this way we understand that all of the succeeding narratives are grounded in the Stephen episode. How? I suggest that the speech constitutes the argument for the legitimation of the actions in these narratives. It may even be that the reference to Shechem anticipates the Samaritan mission and the Egyptian orientation anticipates the Ethiopian eunuch. Whether such specific associations are present or not, the general orientation is clear.

If this is correct, then it also has implications for two other issues relating to the speech: the place of the temple and the "anti-Judaism" of the speech. Does the Stephen speech sound a more critical note than the remainder of Luke-Acts vis-à-vis the temple? The traditional answer has been yes.[67] In recent years several have challenged this view, arguing that the speech makes the case that the Christian mission transcends the temple, but does not reject it.[68] If I am correct about the use of the Abraham, Joseph, and Moses traditions, then the speech is not intended to reject the temple but to qualify it by arguing that just as Judaism could extend beyond the temple, so could Christianity. This in turn means that the geographical aspect of the speech—including the comments on the temple—is not anti-Jewish. It is, rather, Judaism extended geographically and ethnically.

Conclusions

The Stephen speech permits us an opportunity to peer behind the Christianity of the author of Acts into the world of Judaism that nourished him. Probably

---

67. For contemporary examples of this view see Bruce, "Stephen's Apologia," 40, 48 and Barrett, *Acts of the Apostles*, 1:373–76.

68. E.g., Sylva, "Meaning and Function of Acts 7:46–50," 261–75; Francis D. Weinert, "Luke, Stephen, and the Temple in Luke-Acts," *BTB* 17 (1987): 88–90; and Kucicki, *Function of the Speeches in the Acts of the Apostles*, 98–101.

a diaspora Jew, the author learned to understand the LXX through earlier retellings—whether histories or homilies—which created a perspective by which
he read the scriptures. One of these lenses was the legitimacy of life under
God outside the land of Israel. The strategy this took was the association of an
ancestral hero with the geographical area in which the diaspora community
resided. I have suggested that the author knew of at least Samaritan and Egyptian Jewish models for such an understanding, although I am suspicious on a
priori grounds that he knew more. This hermeneutic offered a biblical warrant
for the early Christian mission beyond Jerusalem. Rather than puzzling over
the relevance of Acts 7:2–34, we should realize that it has been placed in the
narrative at the critical point. It demonstrates that the mission was in harmony
with God's dealings with the ancestors: they offer a warrant for a geographically unlimited mission. It also reminds us that the two-volume work we call
Luke-Acts was carefully planned and written, and that the author was aware
of the tradition that I have called apologetic historiography. While the author's
awareness of the tradition does not prove that he wrote within it, it strengthens
the possibility that he made use of it when retelling the story of Israel.[69]

Appendix

Exegetical Traditions in Acts 7:2–50[70]

Acts 7:2–50	LXX Base Citation, Paraphrase/ Allusion	Hellenistic Jewish Exegetical Traditions
[2]ὁ θεὸς τῆς δόξης	Ps 28:3	
ὤφθη τῷ πατρὶ ἡμῶν Ἀβραάμ	Gen 12:7	Philo, *Abr.* 77

69. I argued that Pseudo-Eupolemus and Artapanus were part of the tradition in Sterling, *Historiography and Self-Definition*, 187–206 and 167–86, respectively. While I did not
treat Cleodemus Malchus, I would place him in the same historiographical tradition.

70. When there is a clear citation of the LXX I have set the text of Acts 7:2–50 in bold
font. When the speech paraphrases the LXX, I have italicized the text. Otherwise, I have
noted the appropriate references in the LXX and in Hellenistic Jewish authors. I have only
listed Hellenistic Jewish authors when the speech of Acts and the Hellenistic Jewish au-
thor(s) jointly depart from the LXX.

Acts 7:2–50	LXX Base	Hellenistic Jewish Exegetical Traditions
ὄντι ἐν τῇ Μεσοποταμίᾳ		Ps.-Eupolemus frag. 1 (Eusebius, *Praep. ev.* 9.17.3–4)
πρὶν ἢ κατοικῆσαι αὐτὸν ἐν Χαρρὰν		Philo, *Abr.* 72; Josephus, *Ant.* 1.154
³καὶ εἶπεν πρὸς αὐτόν· ἔξελθε ἐκ τῆς γῆς σου καὶ ἐκ τῆς συγγενείας σου, καὶ δεῦρο εἰς τὴν γῆν ἥν ἄν σοι δείξω.	Gen 12:1	
⁴τότε ἐξελθὼν ἐκ γῆς Χαλδαίων κατῴκησεν ἐν Χαρράν.	Gen 11:31	
κἀκεῖθεν μετὰ τὸ ἀποθανεῖν		
τὸν πατέρα αὐτοῦ	Gen 11:32	Philo, *Migr.* 177
μεῴκισεν αὐτὸν	Gen 12:5	
εἰς τὴν γῆν ταύτην εἰς ἥν ὑμεῖς νῦν κατοικεῖτε,		
⁵καὶ οὐκ ἔδωκεν αὐτῷ κληρονομίαν ἐν αὐτῇ οὐδὲ βῆμα ποδὸς	Deut 2:5	
καὶ ἐπηγγείλατο δοῦναι αὐτῶ εἰς κατάσχεσιν αὐτὴν	Gen 17:8	
καὶ τῷ σπέρματι αὐτοῦ μετ᾽ αὐτῶν,	Gen 48:4	
οὐκ ὄντος αὐτῷ τέκνου.	Gen 15:2; cf. 11:30	
⁶ἐλάλησεν δὲ οὕτως ὁ θεὸς ὅτι ἔσται τὸ σπέρμα αὐτοῦ πάροικον ἐν γῇ ἀλλοτρίᾳ καὶ δουλώσουσιν αὐτὸ καὶ κακώσουσιν ἔτη τετρακόσια·	Gen 15:13–14 cf. Exod 2:22	
⁷καὶ τὸ ἔθνος ᾧ ἐὰν δουλεύσουσιν κρινῶ ἐγώ, ὁ θεὸς εἶπεν, καὶ μετὰ ταῦτα ἐξελεύσονται	Gen 15:14	
καὶ λατρεύσουσίν μοι ἐν τῷ τόπῳ τούτῳ.	Exod 3:12	

Acts 7:2–50	LXX Base	Hellenistic Jewish Exegetical Traditions
[8]καὶ ἔδωκεν αὐτῷ διαθήκην περιτομῆς· καὶ οὕτως ἐγέννησεν τὸν Ἰσαὰκ	Gen 17:10–11	
καὶ περιέτεμεν αὐτὸν τῇ ἡμέρᾳ τῇ ὀγδόῃ,	Gen 21:1–4	
καὶ Ἰσαὰκ τὸν Ἰακώβ,	Gen 25:24–26	
καὶ Ἰακὼβ τοὺς δώδεκα πατριάρχας.	Gen 29:31–30:24	
[9]*καὶ οἱ πατριάρχαι ζηλώσαντες*	*Gen 37:11*	
τὸν Ἰωσὴφ ἀπέδοντο εἰς Αἴγυπτον.	Gen 37:25–28, 36	Demetrius frag. 2 (Eusebius, *Praep. ev.* 9.21.11)
καὶ ἦν ὁ θεὸς μετ᾿ αὐτοῦ	*Gen 39:2, 3, 21, 23*	
[10]καὶ ἐξείλατο αὐτὸν	Gen 39:1–41:46	
ἐκ πασῶν τῶν θλίψεων αὐτοῦ *καὶ ἔδωκεν αὐτῷ χάριν*	*Gen 39:21*	
καὶ σοφίαν		Philo, *Ios.* 106; Josephus, *Ant.* 2.87
ἐναντίον Φαραὼ βασιλέως Αἰγύπτου καὶ κατέστησεν αὐτὸν ἡγούμενον ἐπ᾿ Αἴγυπτον	*Gen 41:43*	
καὶ [ἐφ᾿] ὅλον τὸν οἶκον αὐτοῦ.	Gen 45:8; Ps 104:21	
[11]ἦλθεν δὲ λιμὸς ἐφ᾿ ὅλην τὴν Αἴγυπτον	Gen 41:53–57	
καὶ Χανάαν	Gen 42:5	
καὶ θλῖψις μεγάλη,	Gen 41:57	
καὶ οὐχ ηὕρισκον χορτάσματα οἱ πατέρες ἡμῶν.		
[12]*ἀκούσας δὲ Ἰακὼβ*	*Gen 42:1*	
ὄντα σιτία ἐν Αἴγυπτον *ἐξαπέστειλεν*	Gen 42:1–28	
τοὺς πατέρας ἡμῶν πρῶτον.		
[13]καὶ ἐν τῷ δευτέρῳ	Gen 43:1–44:34	

131

Acts 7:2–50	LXX Base	Hellenistic Jewish Exegetical Traditions
ἀνεγνωρίσθη Ἰωσὴφ	Gen 45:1	
τοῖς ἀδελφοῖς αὐτοῦ		
καὶ φανερὸν ἐγένετο τῷ Φαραὼ	Gen 45:16	
τὸ γένος τοῦ Ἰωσήφ.		
¹⁴ἀποστείλας δὲ Ἰωσὴφ	Gen 45:27	
μετεκαλέσατο Ἰακὼβ	Gen 45:9–13, 21–24, 27	
τὸν πατέρα αὐτοῦ		
καὶ πᾶσαν τὴ συγγένειαν		
ἐν ψυχαῖς ἑβδομήκοντα πέντε.	Gen 46:27; Exod 1:5	
¹⁵καὶ κατέβη Ἰακὼβ εἰς Αἴγυπτον	Gen 46:3; Deut 26:5 Gen 46:1–7	
καὶ ἐτελεύτησεν αὐτὸς	Gen 49:33	
καὶ οἱ πατέρες ἡμῶν,	Gen 50:26; Exod 1:6	
¹⁶καὶ μετετέθησαν εἰς Συχὲμ	Josh 24:32	
καὶ ἐτέθησαν ἐν τῷ μνήματι	Gen 49:29–32	
ᾧ ὠνήσατο Ἀβραὰμ	Gen 50:13;	
τιμῆς ἀργυρίου	23:16–20; 33:19	
παρὰ τῶν υἱῶν Ἐμμὼρ ἐν Συχέμ.		
¹⁷καθὼς δὲ ἤγγιζεν ὁ χρόνος		
τῆς ἐπαγγελίας		
ἧς ὡμολόγησεν ὁ θεὸς τῷ Ἀβραάμ,	Cf. Exod 2:24	
ηὔξησεν ὁ λαὸς	Exod 1:7; cf. Gen 47:27	
καὶ ἐπληθύνθη ἐν Αἰγύπτῳ		
¹⁸ἄχρι οὗ ἀνέστη βασιλὺς ἕτερος [ἐφ᾽ Αἴγυπτον]	Exod 1:8	
ὃς οὐκ ᾔδει τὸν Ἰωσήφ.		
¹⁹οὗτος κατασοφισάμενος		
τὸ γένος ἡμῶν		
ἐκάκωσεν τοὺς πατέρας [ἡμῶν]	Exod 1:9–22	

Acts 7:2–50	LXX Base	Hellenistic Jewish Exegetical Traditions
τοῦ ποιεῖν τὰ βρέφη ἔκθετα αὐτῶν		Ezekiel, *Exagoge* 12–13, 16; Philo, *Mos.* 1.8, 10, 11, 14
εἰς τὸ μὴ ζωογονεῖσθαι. ²⁰ἐν ᾧ καιρῷ ἐγεννήθη Μωϋσῆς καὶ ἦν ἀστεῖος τῷ θεῷ· ὃς ἀνετράφη μῆνας τρεῖς ἐν τῷ οἴκῳ τοῦ πατρός,	Exod 2:2	
²¹ἐκτεθέντος δὲ αὐτοῦ	Cf. Exod 2:3	Ezekiel, *Exagoge* 16; Philo, *Mos.* 1.10, 11, 14
ἀνείλατο αὐτὸν ἡ θυγάτηρ φαραὼ	Exod 2:5	
καὶ ἀνεθρέψατο αὐτὸν ἑαυτῇ εἰς υἱόν.	Exod 2:10	
²²καὶ ἐπαιδεύθη Μωϋσῆς		Ezekiel, *Exagoge* 36–38; Philo, *Mos.* 1.20–24 Josephus, *Ant.* 2.236; Cf. Artapanus, frag. 3 (Eusebius, *Praep. ev.* 9.27.4)
ἐν πάσῃ σοφίᾳ Αἰγυπτίων,⁷¹ ἦν δὲ δυνατὸς ἐν λόγοις καὶ ἔργοις αὐτοῦ. ²³ὡς δὲ ἐπληροῦτο αὐτῷ τεσσερακονταετὴς χρόνος, ἀνέβη ἐπὶ τὴν καρδίαν αὐτοῦ ἐπισκέψασθαι **τοὺς ἀδελφοὺς αὐτοῦ τοὺς υἱοὺς Ἰσραήλ.**	Exod 2:11	
²⁴καὶ ἰδών τινα ἀδικούμενον ἠμύνατο καὶ ἐποίησεν ἐκδίκησιν τῷ καταπονουμένῳ πατάξας τὸν Αἰγύπτιον. ²⁵ἐνόμιζεν δὲ συνιέναι τοὺς ἀδελφοὺς [αὐτοῦ]	Exod 2:11–12	

71. On the sequence of ἐγεννήθη . . . ἀνετράφη . . . ἐπαιδεύθη in vv. 20–22 see Philo, *Mos.* 2.1.

THE CONNECTION TO THE PAST

Acts 7:2–50	LXX Base	Hellenistic Jewish Exegetical Traditions
ὅτι ὁ θεὸς διὰ χειρὸς αὐτοῦ δίδωσιν σωτηρίαν αὐτοῖς· οἱ δὲ οὐ συνῆκαν. ²⁶τῇ τε ἐπιούσῃ ἡμέρᾳ ὤφθη αὐτοῖς μαχομένοις καὶ συνήλλασσεν αὐτοὺς εἰς εἰρήνην εἰπών· ἄνδρες, ἀδελφοί ἐστε· ἱνατί ἀδικεῖτε ἀλλήλους; ²⁷ὁ δὲ ἀδικῶν τὸν πλησίον		
	Exod 2:13–14	
ἀπώσατο αὐτὸν εἰπών· τίς σε κατέστησεν	Exod 2:14	
ἄρχοντα καὶ δικαστὴν ἐφ᾽ ἡμῶν; ²⁸μὴ ἀνελεῖν με σὺ θέλεις ὃν τρόπον ἀνεῖλες ἐχθὲς τὸν Αἰγύπτιον; ²⁹ἔφυγεν δὲ Μωϋσῆς	Exod 2:15	
ἐν τῷ λόγῳ τούτῳ καὶ ἐγένετο πάροικος ἐν γῇ Μαδιάμ, οὗ ἐγέννησεν υἱοὺς δύο.	Exod 2:21–22	
³⁰καὶ πληρωθέντων ἐτῶν τεσσεράκοντα ὤφθη αὐτῷ	Exod 3:2	
ἐν τῇ ἐρήμῳ τοῦ ὄρους Σιννᾶ ἄγγελος ἐν φλογὶ πυρὸς βάτου. ³¹ὁ δὲ Μωϋσῆς ἰδὼν	Exod 3:2–4	
ἐθαύμαζεν τὸ ὅραμα, προσερχομένου δὲ αὐτοῦ κατανοῆσαι ἐγένετο φωνὴ κυρίου· ³²ἐγὼ ὁ θεὸς τῶν πατέρων σου,	Exod 3:15, 16	
ὁ θεὸς Ἀβραὰμ καὶ Ἰσαὰκ καὶ Ἰακώβ. ἔντρομος δὲ γενόμενος Μωϋσῆς	Exod 3:6	
οὐκ ἐτόλμα κατανοῆσαι. ³³εἶπεν δὲ αὐτῷ ὁ κύριος·	Exod 3:5	

134

Acts 7:2–50	LXX Base	Hellenistic Jewish Exegetical Traditions
λῦσον τὸ ὑπόδημα		
τῶν ποδῶν σου,		
ὁ γὰρ τόπος ἐφ᾽ ᾧ ἕστηκας		
γῆ ἁγία ἐστίν.		
³⁴ἰδὼν εἶδον τὴν κάκωσιν	Exod 3:7	
τοῦ λαοῦ μου τοῦ ἐν Αἰγύπτῳ		
καὶ τοῦ στεναγμοῦ αὐτῶν ἤκουσα,	Exod 3:7	
καὶ κατέβην ἐξελέσθαι αὐτούς·	Exod 3:8	
καὶ νῦν δεῦρο ἀποστείλω σε	Exod 3:10	
εἰς Αἴγυπτον.		
³⁵τοῦτον τὸν Μωϋσῆν		
ὃν ἠρνήσαντο εἰπόντες·		
τίς σε κατέστησεν	Exod 2:14	
ἄρχοντα καὶ δικαστήν;		
τοῦτον ὁ θεὸς		
καὶ ἄρχοντα		
καὶ λυτρωτὴν ἀπέσταλκεν		
σὺν χειρὶ ἀγγέλου		
τοῦ ὀφθέντος αὐτῷ ἐν τῇ βάτῳ.	Exod 3:2	
³⁶οὗτος ἐξήγαγεν αὐτοὺς	Exod 3:10–12	
ποιήσας τέρατα καὶ σημεῖα	Exod 7:3; Deut 34:11	
ἐν γῇ Αἰγύπτῳ		As. Mos. 3:11[72]
καὶ ἐν ἐρυθρᾷ θαλάσσῃ	Exod 14:15–31	
καὶ ἐν τῇ ἐρήμῳ		
ἔτη τερρεράκοντα.	Num 14:33	
³⁷οὗτός ἐστιν ὁ Μωϋσῆς		
ὁ εἴπας τοῖς υἱοῖς Ἰσραήλ·		
προφήτην ὑμῖν ἀναστήσει ὁ θεὸς	Deut 18:15	
ἐκ τῶν ἀδελφῶν ὑμῶν ὡς ἐμέ.		
³⁸οὗτός ἐστιν ὁ γενόμενος		
ἐν τῇ ἐκκλησίᾳ ἐν τῇ ἐρήμῳ		
μετὰ τοῦ ἀγγέλου		
τοῦ λαλοῦντος αὐτῷ		
ἐν τῇ ὄρει Σινᾶ		

72. See the sequence ἐν γῇ Αἰγύπτῳ . . . ἐν ἐρυθρᾷ θαλάσσῃ . . . ἐν τῇ ἐρήμῳ.

Acts 7:2–50	LXX Base	Hellenistic Jewish Exegetical Traditions
καὶ τῶν πατέρων ἡμῶν,		
ὃς ἐδέξατο λόγια ζῶντα		
δοῦναι ἡμῖν,		
³⁹ᾧ οὐκ ἠθέλησαν		
ὑπήκοοι γενέσθαι		
οἱ πατέρες ἡμῶν,		
ἀλλὰ ἀπώσαντο καὶ ἐστράφησαν	Num 14:3	
ἐν ταῖς καρδίαις ἀὴτῶν		
εἰς Αἴγυπτον		
⁴⁰εἰπόντες τῷ Ἀαρών·		
ποιήσον ἡμῖν θεοὺς	Exod 32:1	
οἳ προπορεύσονται ἡμῶν·		
ὁ γὰρ Μωϋσῆς οὗτος,		
ὃς ἐξήγαγεν ἡμᾶς		
ἐκ γῆς Αἰγύπτου,		
οὐκ οἴδαμεν τί ἐγένετο αὐτῷ.		
⁴¹καὶ ἐμοσχοποίησαν		
ἐν ταῖς ἡμέραις ἐκείναις		
καὶ ἀνήγαγον θυσίαν τῷ εἰδώλῳ	Exod 32:4, 8	
καὶ εὐφραίνοντο		
ἐν τοῖς ἔργοις τῶν χειρῶν αὐτῶν.		
⁴²ἔστρεψεν δὲ ὁ θεὸς		
καὶ παρέδωκεν αὐτοὺς λατρεύειν	Deut 17:3	
τῇ στρατιᾷ τοῦ οὐρανοῦ		
καθὼς γέγραπται		
ἐν βίβλῳ τῶν προφητῶν·		
μὴ σφάγια καὶ θυσίας	Amos 5:25–27	
προσηνέγκατέ μοι		
ἔτη τεσσεράκοντα ἐν τῇ ἐρήμῳ,		
οἶκος Ἰσραήλ;		
⁴³καὶ ἀνελάβετε τὴν σκηνὴν		
τοῦ Μόλοχ		
καὶ τὸ ἄστρον τοῦ θεοῦ ὑμῶν		
Ῥαιφάν,		
τοὺς τύπους		
οὓς ἐποιήσατε προσκυνεῖν		
αὐτοῖς,		

Acts 7:2–50	LXX Base	Hellenistic Jewish Exegetical Traditions
καὶ μετοικιῶ ὑμᾶς ἐπέκεινα Βαβυλῶνος.		
⁴⁴ἡ σκηνὴ τοῦ μαρτυρίου ἦν	Exod 27:21	
τοῖς πατράσιν ἡμῶν ἐν τῷ ἐρήμῳ		
καθὼς διετάξατο ὁ λαλῶν		
τῷ Μωϋσῇ		
ποιῆσαι αὐτὴν		
κατὰ τὸν τύπον ὃν ἑωράκει·	Exod 25:40	
⁴⁵ἣν καὶ εἰσήγαγον διαδεξάμενοι		
οἱ πατέρες ἡμῶν μετὰ Ἰησοῦ	Josh 3:14; 18:1	
ἐν τῇ κατασχέσει τῶν ἐθνῶν,		
ὧν ἐξῶσεν ὁ θεὸς	Deut 7:1, 22	
ἀπὸ προσώπου		
τῶν πατέρων ἡμῶν		
ἕως τῶν ἡμερῶν Δαυίδ,		
⁴⁶ὃς εὗρεν χάριν		
ἐνώπιον τοῦ θεοῦ		
καὶ ἠτήσατο εὑρεῖν σκήωμα	Ps 131:5	
τῷ οἴκῳ Ἰακώβ.	cf. 2 Kgdms 7:2	
⁴⁷Σολομὼν δὲ οἰκοδόμησεν αὐτῷ οἶκον.	3 Kgdms 6:2; 1 Para 22:6	
⁴⁸ἀλλ᾽ οὐχ ὁ ὕψιστος	3 Kgdms 8:2; Isa 57:14	Philo, *Cher.* 99–100; Josephus, *Ant.* 8.108
ἐν χειροποιήτοις κατοικεῖ,		
καθὼς ὁ προφήτης λέγει·		
⁴⁹ὁ οὐρανός μοι θρόνος,	Isa 66:1–2	
ἡ δὲ γῆ ὑποπόδιον		
τῶν ποδῶν μου·		
ποῖον οἶκον οἰκοδομήσετέ μοι,		
λέγει κύριος,		
ἢ τίς τόπος		
τῆς καταπαύσεώς μου;		
⁵⁰οὐχὶ ἡ χείρ μου ἐποίησεν		
ταῦτα πάνα . . .		

6

"Do You Understand What You Are Reading?"

The Understanding of the LXX in Luke-Acts

> . . . No exegesis is without presuppositions, inasmuch as the exegete is not a
> tabula rasa, but on the contrary, approaches the text with specific questions
> or with a specific way of raising questions and thus has a certain idea of the
> subject matter with which the text is concerned.

RUDOLF BULTMANN, "Is Exegesis without Presuppositions Possible?"[1]

IN A WELL-KNOWN SCENE, the author of Acts had Philip the evangelist approach an Ethiopian official who had been to Jerusalem and was headed home.
The Ethiopian was reading the Scriptures in his chariot. With a famous word-
play Philip asked: "Do you understand what you are reading?" (ἆρά γε γινώ-
σκεις ἃ ἀναγινώσκεις;). The Ethiopian rejoined: "How can I unless someone
guides me?" (Acts 8:26–40, esp. 30–31). The exchange sets up the author's
explanation of the LXX. The question might, however, be pushed one step back
and posed to the author. Who guided the author as he read the LXX? Did the
author know any retellings of the LXX that shaped the way that he read and
understood the story of Israel?

There are two major speeches in Acts that offer retellings of the story of
Israel in the LXX: the speech of Stephen before the Sanhedrin (7:2–53) and the
speech of Paul to a synagogue audience at Antioch of Pisidia (13:16–41). We
explored the former in the previous chapter and argued that the author drew
on a tradition of Hellenistic Jewish historiography that contended for the legitimation of communities in the diaspora, especially in Egypt. It appears likely

---

1. Rudolf Bultmann, "Ist voraussetzungslose Exegese möglich?" *TZ* 13 (1957): 409–17,
esp. 409; repr. in ET as "Is Exegesis without Presuppositions Possible?," in Rudolf Bultmann,
Existence and Faith: Shorter Writings of Rudolf Bultmann, ed. and trans. Schubert M. Ogden
(Cleveland: World Publishing Books, 1960), 289–96, 314–15, citation from p. 289.

that the author knew the historiographical tradition attested in the works of Cleodemus Malchus, Pseudo-Eupolemus, and Artapanus—and perhaps knew the works of some of these. I would like to raise the same question for the second major retelling of the story of Israel in Acts. Are there any indications that the Christian author knew earlier Jewish retellings of the LXX that shaped his selection of material? If so, does this material help us understand the function of the material in the speech attributed to Paul?

THE SPEECH

The speech is situated at the outset of the Pauline mission (Acts 13–28).[2] Paul and Barnabas made their way into the hinterland of Asia, to the city of Antioch. In keeping with his practice, Paul went to the synagogue.[3] Following the reading of the law and the prophets, the rulers of the synagogue invited them to address the audience.[4] Paul accepted the invitation and used the law and the prophets as a basis for his "word of exhortation" (λόγος παρακλήσεως) (Acts 13:15).[5] In this way, Luke made a direct connection between the setting and the sermon, just as he did when Jesus spoke at the synagogue service in Nazareth (Luke 4:16–30).

As most interpreters have recognized, the sermon falls into three movements marked off by explicit addresses to the audience that consist of both a direct reference to the composition of the audience and a call to listen.[6]

---

2. There are several full-length studies of the speech. These include Marcel Dumais, *Le langage de l'évangélisation: L'Announce missionaire en milieu juif (Acts 13, 16–41)*, Coll. 'Theologie. Recherches' 16 (Tournai: Desclé; Montreal: Belarmin, 1976); C. A. Joachim Pillai, *Early Missionary Preaching: A Study of Luke's Report in Acts 13* (Hicksville, NY: Exposition, 1979); C. A. Joachim Pillai, *Apostolic Interpretation of History: A Commentary on Acts 13:16–41* (Hicksville, NY: Exposition, 1980); Matthäus F.-J. Buss, *Die Missionspredigt des Apostels Paulus im pisidischen Antiochien: Analyse von Apg 13,16–41 im Hinblick auf die literarische und thematische Einheit der Paulusrede* (Stuttgart: Katholisches Bibelwerk, 1980). There are also some important shorter works including David A. DeSilva, "Paul's Sermon in Antioch of Pisidia," *BSac* 154 (1994): 32–49; Soards, *Speeches in Acts*, 79–88; and Kucicki, *Function of the Speeches in the Acts of the Apostles*, 119–28, 316–17.

3. E.g., Acts 14:1–7, Iconium; 17:1–9, Thessalonica; 17:10–14, Berea; 17:16–17, Athens; 18:1–10, Corinth; and 18:19–31 and 19:8–10, Ephesus. Cf. 26:11 for a summary statement.

4. For an attempt to reconstruct the synagogue service of this period see Paul Billerbeck, "Ein Synagogen-gottesdienst in Jesu Tagen?" *ZNW* 55 (1964): 143–61.

5. This is the same expression that the author of Hebrews used to describe the letter (Heb 13:22). Luke identifies the speech with "the word of salvation" (ὁ λόγος τῆς σωτηρίας) in v. 26.

6. DeSilva, "Paul's Sermon in Antioch of Pisidia," 34–35, offers a summary of the different bases that result in various outlines: the audience (as I have suggested), topical or

Acts 13:16
Fellow Israelites and God-fearers,
listen.

Acts 13:26
Brothers, members of Abraham's family, and God-fearers among you,
the word of this salvation was sent to you.

Acts 13:38
Let this be known to you,
brothers.

The three parts of the sermon (vv. 16–25, 26–37, 38–41) each have a thematic unity.

The Story of Israel. The first section is a rehearsal of the story of Israel (13:16–25).
The Ancestors
[17]The God of this people Israel chose (ἐξελέξατο) our ancestors,
advanced (ὕψωσεν) the people in their residence in the land of Egypt,
and with a raised arm led (ἐξήγαγεν) them out of it.

The Wilderness
[18]For forty years' time[7] he cared (ἐτροφοφόρησεν)[8] for them in the wilderness.

---

thematic analyses, and temporal analyses. Some noteworthy alternatives are four divisions; e.g., Huub van de Sandt, "The Quotations in Acts 13,32–52 as a Reflection of Luke's LXX Interpretation," *Bib* 75 (1994): 26–58, esp. 26, where he divided the speech into vv. 17–25, 26–31, 32–37, and 38–41; and Wilckens, *Die Missionsreden der Apostelgeschichte*, 54, who thought that there were six divisions: vv. 15–23, 24–25, 26–31, 32–37, 38–39, 40–41. Richard Pervo, *Acts: A Commentary*, Hermeneia (Minneapolis: Fortress, 2009), 335, has the same structure as I have offered here.

7. Exod 16:35; Num 14:33–34; 32:13; 33:38; Deut 1:3; 2:7; 8:4; 29:4.

8. There is a textual problem: the manuscript evidence is divided between ἐτροποφόρησεν ("he put up with" or "he bore") and ἐτροφοφόρησεν ("he nourished" or "he cared for"). The text is drawing from Deut 1:31, where the same split occurs in the MSS. The issue is determining which one the author is more likely to have used. Unlike the speech in Acts 7 where the rebellion of the people is emphasized, the emphasis here is on God's actions. I therefore prefer to read ἐτροφοφόρησεν. For a helpful discussion see Metzger, *Textual Commentary*, 357. Others who follow this reasoning include Barrett, *Acts of the Apostles*, 1:632 and Pervo, *Acts*, 335–36. Haenchen, *Acts of the Apostles*, 408; Schneider, *Die Apostelgeschichte*, 2:125; and

The Inheritance of the Land
[19]After he had destroyed (καθελών) seven nations in the land of Canaan,
he gave them their land as an inheritance (κατεκληρονόμησεν)
[20]for four hundred and fifty years.[9]

The Judges
Afterward he gave (ἔδωκεν) them judges up until Samuel the prophet.

Saul
[21]Then they asked (ᾐτήσαντο) for a king
and God gave (ἔδωκεν) them Saul, the son of Kish,
a man from the tribe of Benjamin, for forty years.[10]

David
[22]When he had removed (μεταστήσας) him,
he raised up (ἤγειρεν) David as their king,
to whom he said (εἶπεν) in a solemn statement (μαρτυρήσας):
"I have found (εὖρον) David, the son of Jesse, a man after my heart,
who will do (ποιήσει) all my will."
[23]From the seed of this person, God, by promise,
brought (ἤγαγεν) a savior to Israel, Jesus.

John the Baptist
[24]Before his entrance,
John proclaimed (προκηρύξαντος) a baptism of repentance
to all the people Israel.
[25]As John was completing (ἐπλήρου) his course, he said (ἔλεγεν):
"What do you suppose (ὑπονοεῖτε) that I am (εἶναι)?
I am not (οὐκ εἰμί) he.

Joseph A. Fitzmyer, *The Acts of the Apostles*, AB 31 (New York: Doubleday, 1998), 510–11, consider ἐτροφοφόρησεν a harmonization with Deut 1:31 and prefer ἐτροποφόρησεν.

9. This is not a biblical figure. For a good summary of how the figure was reached see Barrett, *Acts of the Apostles*, 1:633–34. Cf. also E. H. Merrill, "Paul's Use of 'About 450 Years' in Acts 13:20," *BSac* 138 (1981): 246–57.

10. This is a traditional number. See also Josephus, *Ant.* 6.378, where he gives eighteen years and twenty-two for a total of forty, a figure that differs with the number he gives in *Ant.* 10.143. For details see Christopher T. Begg, *Flavius Josephus, Judean Antiquities 5–7*, FJTC 4 (Leiden: Brill, 2005), 204.

> Look, there is one coming (ἔρχεται) after me
> whose sandals I am not (οὐκ εἰμί) worthy to untie (λῦσαι)."

There are several aspects of this retelling of the story of Israel that we should note. Just as the author carefully marked out the major units of the speech through the repetition of the audience, so he marked off seven moments in the story of Israel through various temporal markers. I have underscored the temporal phrases above to call attention to them. It is worth noting that two of these are not biblical but traditional, as indicated in the notes. The temporal phrases serve not only to summarize a much longer story, but also to indicate the subunits of the rehearsal.[11] The opening section on the ancestors lacks a temporal marker and does not need one since it is the initial subunit. The conclusion of this subunit is set off by the temporal phrase that opens the second subunit. The treatment of David lacks a temporal marker other than the opening aorist participle. The omission of a temporal phrase calls attention to the figure of David.

The language of the text is also important to note. The retelling is saturated with the language of the LXX, although it does not cite it verbatim beyond the use of selected words and phrases (see the appendix).[12] The most important linguistic feature is the verbs for which I have provided the Greek as a means of calling attention to them. There are sixteen verbal forms in vv. 17–23: God is the subject of all verbal forms except the people's request for a king (13:21) and God's expression of confidence that David will do all his will (13:22). This means that God is the subject of the story of Israel. The exceptions deal with David, a move that calls attention to him in the history of Israel. As we will see, this is not an accident; David will play an important role in the second section of the speech as well. The centrality of God's actions is broken when

11. The numbers may have other functions as well. Gerhard Delling, "Israels Geschichte und Jesusgeschehen nach Acta," in *Neues Testament und Geschichte: Historisches Geschehen und Deutung im Neuen Testament: Oscar Cullmann zum 70 Geburtstag*, ed. Heinrich Baltensweiler and Bo Reicke (Zurich: Theologischer Verlag; Tübingen: Mohr Siebeck, 1972), 191 suggested that the numbers connected the abbreviated events and demonstrated the length of time until the coming of the Messiah.

12. There have been a number of studies that have addressed the specific references in detail. Some of the more important include: Delling, "Israels Geschichte und Jesusgeschehen nach Acta," 187–97; Pillai, *Early Missionary Preaching*, 40–41; and Frederick F. Bruce, "Paul's Use of the Old Testament in Acts," in *Tradition and Interpretation in the New Testament: Essays in Honor of E. Earle Ellis*, ed. Gerald F. Hawthorne and Otto Betz (Tübingen: Mohr Siebeck; Grand Rapids: Eerdmans, 1987), 71–79, esp. 71–73.

we come to John who is the immediate precursor to Jesus (vv. 24–25). We will return to this when we consider the function of the speech in Acts. The subject of the verbs may also help us to understand why the story is so spare in offering details about the heroes of Israel. The speech only mentions four figures by name: Samuel, Saul, David, and John. The omission of the names of the ancestors and Moses calls attention to the establishment of the monarchy. Samuel was, after all, the prophet who anointed the first two kings of Israel. Yet even here, the emphasis is on God, who controls history and has guided it to the entrance of Jesus.

The scope of the retelling of Israel's past is striking. The author has elected to tell the story from Genesis through 1 Samuel. Why this selection of events? The first reaction that we might register is that the speech led up to David in order to set up the gospel in the second part that makes an explicit argument that Jesus fulfilled the promise made to David. While this is unquestionably correct, it does not exhaust the possibilities. Several have suggested that the retelling depends on a traditional retelling of Israel.[13] We can do better yet. There are several examples of works that retell the story of Israel with the same scope as the speech in Acts 13. The first and most obvious is Ps 77(78).[14] The structure of this psalm and its nature have been widely discussed.[15] It is not necessary for us to enter into these discussions other than to note that the psalm extends from the exodus to David, or as Beat Weber cleverly wrote: "from Zoan to Zion" (*"von Zoan nach Zion"*).[16] The psalm treats the same basic material as the speech in Acts 13:

vv. 1–8, an introduction

vv. 9–53, the exodus and wilderness

vv. 54–55, possession of the land

13. E.g., Otto Glombitza, "Akta xiii.15–41: Analyse einer lukanischen Predigt vor Juden: Ein Beitrag zum Problem der Reden in Akta," *NTS* 5 (1958–1959): 306–17, esp. 308–10; Wilckens, *Die Missionsreden der Apostelgeschichte*, 50; and Delling, "Israels Geschichte und Jesusgeschehen nach Acta," 190.

14. Soards, *Speeches in Acts*, 82, also noted the similarity.

15. Some of the major studies include Anthony F. Campbell, "Psalm 78," *CBQ* 41 (1979): 51–79; Richard J. Clifford, "In Zion and David a New Beginning: An Interpretation of Psalm 78," in *Traditions in Transformation*, ed. Baruch Halpern and Jon D. Levinson (Winona Lake, IN: Eisenbrauns, 1981), 121–41; E. L. Gruenstein, "Mixing Memory and Design: Reading Psalm 78," *Proof* 10 (1990): 197–208, esp. 197–200, where he provides an overview of interpretations; and Beat Weber, "Psalm 78: Geschichte mit Geschichte deuten," *TZ* 56 (2000): 193–214.

16. Weber, "Psalm 78," 213.

vv. 56–66, judges
vv. 67–72, Zion and David

The culmination in David could have served multiple functions depending on the *Sitz im Leben* of the psalm.[17] Unfortunately, the possibilities extend from the lifetime of David to the Second Temple period. Whether we understand the psalm as arguing for the Davidic dynasty during the king's life or one of his descendants or as anticipating a future Davidic king, the psalm looked to Zion and David as the final point in the story of Israel.

There is another work that retells the story of Israel up to the time of David, the *Biblical Antiquities* (*Liber antiquitatem biblicarum*) of Pseudo-Philo.[18] The first-century Jewish author relates the story of Israel by drawing on the following biblical traditions:

1–19, the Pentateuch
20–24, Joshua
25–48, Judges
49–65, 1 Samuel

The work ends somewhat abruptly with the death of Saul and anticipation of the reign of David. The suddenness of the final scene has led many to argue that the ending has been lost, a distinct possibility.[19] However, there are some good reasons for arguing that the book originally ended at this point.[20] The narrative celebrates the righteous ruler. The character of some of the stories about David's rise to or exercise of power (e.g., the episode with Bathsheba and Uriah) would have required the author to recast the stories appreciably or to offer a selective retelling of David's life. If the work is complete, then it is most likely that the author elected to anticipate the ideal ruler without having

17. For an overview of the positions with a bibliography see John Goldingay, *Psalms*, vol. 2: *Psalms 42–89* (Grand Rapids: Baker Academic, 2007), 481.

18. Eckart Reinmuth, *Pseudo-Philo und Lukas: Studien zum Liber Antiquitatum Biblicarum und seiner Bedeutung für die Interpretation des lukanischen Doppelwerks*, WUNT 74 (Tübingen: Mohr Siebeck, 1994), has provided a detailed comparison between the two works but did not address the similarity of the scope of their treatments of Israel.

19. Some of the major representatives of this view include Montague R. James, *The Biblical Antiquities of Philo*, Translations of Early Documents Series 1: Palestinian Jewish Texts (Pre-Rabbinic) (London: SPCK, 1917; repr., New York: Ktav, 1971), 60-65, 73.

20. E.g., Louis Feldman, "Prolegomena," in James, *Biblical Antiquities of Philo*, LXXVII, who questions whether it is unfinished; Frederick J. Murphy, *Pseudo-Philo: Rewriting the Bible* (New York: Oxford University Press, 1993), 16-18; and Howard Jacobson, *A Commentary on Pseudo-Philo's* Liber Antiquitatum Biblicarum, 2 vols. (Leiden: Brill, 1996), 1:253-54.

to retell the actual life of David.[21] If so, it is another witness to a retelling of the story of Israel culminating in the figure of David.

These texts demonstrate that Luke's retelling of Israel's story from the ancestors through David is not uniquely Christian. The broad level of agreement in scope among Ps 77(78), Pseudo-Philo, and the speech in Acts 13 suggests that the author was working with an established pattern of retelling Israel's story. While there are no examples of Hellenistic Jewish historians who shared the same scope, it is entirely possible that there were other treatments that have been lost. Whether such speculation is valid or not, the pattern is clear. It was possible to retell the story of Israel and bring the culmination to David. Like his Jewish predecessors, Luke elected to bring the retelling of Israel's story to a culmination in David in order to draw attention to the connection between David and his later descendent.[22] This helps us understand the break in the pattern of verbs that calls attention to David only in Israel's history.

The Gospel as the Fulfillment of Scripture. The second part of the speech proclaims the gospel and connects it back to the story of Israel. The section has two distinct subsections: the first proclaims the gospel and the second argues that the gospel is anchored in the Scriptures of Israel. We will look at each briefly, starting in Acts 13:27.

The Gospel

Death
[27]For the residents of Jerusalem and their rulers were ignorant of this one
and—although the voices of the prophets are read every Sabbath—
fulfilled them by condemning him.
[28]Although they found no cause of death in him,
they asked Pilate to have him executed.

Burial
[29]When they completed everything written about him,
they took him down from the tree and laid him in a tomb.[23]

---

21. So Murphy, *Pseudo-Philo*, 16–18.

22. There are a number of studies on the connection, e.g., Lars Hartman, "David's Son: Apropa Acta 13, 16–41," *Svensk Exegetisk Arsbok* 28–29 (1963–1964): 117–34, and Walter C. Kaiser Jr., "The Promise to David in Psalm 16 and Its Application in Acts 2:25–33 and 13:32–37," *JETS* 23 (1990): 219–29, a rather tendentious reading of Ps 16.

23. The Western text of vv. 27–29 is significantly different. For a discussion see Barrett, *Acts of the Apostles*, 1:642–43.

145

Resurrection
[30]But God raised him from the dead.

Appearances
[31]For many days he appeared
to those who had gone up with him from Galilee to Jerusalem,
who are his witnesses to the people.

Many interpreters have noted the striking similarity between this section of the speech and the gospel as Paul laid it out in 1 Cor 15:3–8:

[3]For I delivered to you in the first place what I also received,

Death
that Christ died on behalf of our sins according to the Scriptures,

Burial
[4]that he was buried,

Resurrection
that he was raised on the third day according to the Scriptures,

Appearances
[5]and that he appeared to Cephas, then to the twelve,
[6]then he appeared to more than five hundred brothers at one time—
of whom most are still with us, although some have died—
[7]then he appeared to James,
then to all of the apostles,
[8]and last of all—as if to one born out of time—he also appeared to me.

The similarities are striking. Both emphasize that the death of Jesus fulfilled Scripture, mention the burial *en passant*, argue that Jesus was raised in fulfillment of Scripture—although Luke does not mention that it was on the third day—and refer to the witnesses. In keeping with his understanding of witnesses, Luke does not include a reference to the risen Lord's appearance to Paul.[24] There can be little doubt that Luke drew on a traditional understanding of the gospel for this section of the speech.

24. See Acts 1:21–22 for the requirement to be with Jesus from the time of John the Baptist to the resurrection.

The following subunit (Acts 13:32–37) expands on the claim that Jesus fulfilled the Scriptures in his death and resurrection. Luke drew from three major texts to develop his argument: Ps 2:7; Isa 55:3; and Ps 15(16):10.[25]

The Fulfillment of Scripture

Psalm 2:7
[32]We also announce the good news to you
about the promise made to our ancestors,
[33]that God has fulfilled this for us, their descendants,
by raising Jesus, as it is written in the second Psalm:
You are my son,
Today I begot you.

Isaiah 55:3
[34]With respect to the fact that he raised him from the dead
no longer to return to corruption, he said:
I will give you the holy trusts of David. (τὰ ὅσια Δαυὶδ τὰ πιστά).

Psalm 16:10
[35]Since in another place he said:
You will not allow your Holy One (τὸν ὅσιόν σου) *to see corruption.*
[36]For after David served the will of God in his own generation
he died, was added to his ancestors, and *saw corruption.*
[37]But God raised Jesus; he did *not see corruption.*

There are some obvious links among these texts, especially between "the holy trusts of David" (τὰ ὅσια Δαυὶδ τὰ πιστά) of Isa 55:3 and "your holy one" (τὸν ὅσιόν σου) of Ps 16:10. It is possible that Luke drew from an early Chris-

25. There is a significant body of studies on the use of citations from the LXX in Acts including Jacques Dupont, "L'interprétation des psaumes dans les Actes des Apôtres," in *Le Psautier: Ses origenes. Ses problèmes littéraires. Son influence*, Orientalia et biblica lovaniensia 4 (Louvain: Publications universitaires, 1962), 357–88, who deals with seven citations from the Psalter in Acts; Martin Rese, "Die Funktion der alttestamentlichen Zitate und Anspielungen in den Reden der Apostelgeschichte," in *Les Actes des Apôtres: Traditions, rédaction, théologie*, ed. Jacob Kremer, BETL 48 (Leuven: Leuven University Press, 1979), 61–79, esp. 62–72, where he provides an overview of scholarship, and p. 72, where he offers a fivefold analysis of the functions of the citations; van de Sandt, "Quotations in Acts 13,32–52," 26–58; and J. Schmitt, "Kerygma pascal et lecture scripturaire dans l'instruction d'Antioche (Act. 13,22–37)," in *Les Actes des Apôtres*, 155–67, who argued that 2 Sam 7:11–14 was the key underlying text.

tian testimonium for the collection of these texts, although these texts are not brought together elsewhere in the New Testament.[26] Whether Luke drew them from a single source or simply knew them as significant royal Messianic texts, the point for our purposes is the same: they demonstrated the connection between David and the Messiah.

A Pauline Conclusion. The third and final unit (Acts 13:38–40) has a distinctive Pauline ring. Like the preceding section, it has two subunits: the first extends an offer of salvation while the second warns against rejection.

The Offer of Salvation
[38]Let this be known to you brothers,
that through him the forgiveness of sins is announced to you;
from everything that you are not able to be justified by the law of Moses,
[39]the one who believes in him is justified.

The Warning
[40]Pay attention that what was said in the prophets not befall you:
[41]Look you scoffers;
marvel and vanish,
because I am working a work in your days,
a work that you will not believe
even if someone explains it to you.

The offer of salvation is the most Pauline formulation in Luke or Acts, and it is the only time that faith and justification are linked in Acts.[27] The asso-

---

26. On early Christian testimonia see Charles H. Dodd, *According to the Scriptures* (London: Collins, 1952), and Barnabas Lindars, *New Testament Apologetic: The Doctrinal Significance of the Old Testament Quotations* (Philadelphia: Westminster, 1961). The existence of *testimonia* has been confirmed by the discovery of 4Q175 that cites or retells Num 24:15–17; Deut 5:28–29; 18:18–19; 33:8–11; Josh 6:26. On this text see Joseph A. Fitzmyer, "'4QTestimonia' and the New Testament," *TS* 18 (1957): 513–37, who counters Dodd's view that *testimonia* were a Christian creation by correctly pointing to 4QTestimonia, and George J. Brooke, *Exegesis at Qumran: 4QFlorilegium in Its Jewish Context*, JSOTSup 29 (Sheffield: JSOT Press, 1985), 309–19.

27. Philipp Vielhauer, "On the 'Paulinism' of Acts," in *Studies in Luke-Acts*, ed. Leander E. Keck and Louis Martyn (Philadelphia: Fortress, 1966), 33–50, esp. 41–43, argued against Luke's knowledge of Paul. He suggested that Luke equated forgiveness of sins and justification, making justification a negative; that justification is associated with Jesus's resurrection rather than his death; and that this justification is only partial. For a response see Barrett, *Acts of the Apostles*, 1:651, who concluded: "Vielhauer then is not wholly right; but he is on the whole right."

ciation of "the forgiveness of sins" with justification is Deutero-Pauline. Paul never used the phrase "forgiveness of sins" (ἄφεσις ἁμαρτιῶν); a phrase that is a Lukan favorite.[28] The closest that the Apostle comes to this formulation is in Romans 3:25, when he speaks of "the glossing over of previously committed sins" (πάρεσις τῶν προγεγονότων ἁμαρτημάτων). A Pauline disciple may have picked up on this when he equated redemption with "the forgiveness of sins" ("in whom we have redemption, the forgiveness of sins" [ἐν ᾧ ἔχομεν τὴ ἀπολύτρωσιν, τὴν ἄφεσιν τῶν ἁμαρτιῶν]).[29] Whether the author of Colossians and the later author of Ephesians drew their inspiration from Romans or not, they did speak of "the forgiveness of sins." Luke associates the phrase with the Pauline justification by faith. The specific formulation has led some to suggest that Luke believed that the law provided justification from many things and where it fell short, faith provided the remedy.[30] This, however, puts too fine a point on the formulation.[31] It is more likely that Luke simply used a Pauline formulation alongside one with which he was comfortable, "forgiveness of sins," to represent the Pauline mission.

The presence of the Pauline mission is also evident from the warning.[32] Luke altered the citation of Hab 1:5 in one significant way (see the appendix). Habakkuk has: "Because I am working a work in your days, which you will not believe if someone explains it." Luke added an additional use of the noun "work": "Because I am working a work in your days, *a work* which you will by no means believe even if someone explains it to you." The work that Luke has in mind is the mission to the Gentiles. The subsequent narrative of the next Sabbath makes this unambiguously clear when the Jews rejected the offer of salvation and Paul and Barnabas turned to the Gentiles (Acts 13:44–47). God had begun to work a work in their days.

---

28. The phrase appears twelve times in the NT: once in Mark (Mark 1:4); once in Matthew (Matt 26:28), once in Colossians (Col 1:14), once in Ephesians (Eph 1:7), and eight times in Luke-Acts (Luke 1:77; 3:3; 24:47; Acts 2:38; 5:31; 10:43; 13:38; 26:18).

29. Col 1:14, which is echoed in Eph 1:7.

30. So Adolf von Harnack followed by Vielhauer, "On the 'Paulinism' of Acts," 42.

31. So also Haenchen, *Acts of the Apostles*, 412n4 and Fitzmyer, *Acts of the Apostles*, 518–19.

32. It is worth quoting the words of Haenchen, *Acts of the Apostles*, 416–17: "The speech ends with an Old Testament warning that rumbles with the menace of an earth-tremor and drives home the responsibility of the Jews should they reject the message, God has an unexpected and surprising work in store. What is meant is not said. But the reader knows it is the mission to the Gentiles."

The Function of the Speech

Why did Luke situate this speech at the outset of Paul's mission in Acts? There have been a number of responses to this question. Some have defended the historicity of the speech as a close approximation to the speech that Paul delivered.[33] This is problematic on several grounds: it presumes that the author had access to a reliable source for the speech and fails to recognize that the speech does not represent the thought of Paul as we know it from his letters. Martin Dibelius argued that the missionary speeches shared a common outline and represented the preaching of Luke's day: "This is how the gospel is preached and ought to be preached!"[34] More recently some have suggested that the sermon fits the pattern of preaching in Jewish synagogues; however, these reconstructions rest on multiple hypotheses.[35]

There is another possibility. Dibelius also recognized that the speeches shared a common function with speeches in Hellenistic historiography: they cast light on the surrounding narrative. He wrote: "At vital points in the history of the community Luke has inserted speeches which do not necessarily fit the occasion but which have an obvious function in the book as a whole." Dibelius gave Acts 13 as a specific example: it defends "the rightness of the mission to the Gentiles."[36] A number of subsequent scholars have argued that the speeches are authorial compositions intended to illuminate the narrative.[37]

I am convinced that the final view is correct. Most recognize that the author provided a table of contents for Acts at the outset of the narrative when he had Jesus say to the disciples: "You will receive power when the Holy Spirit comes on you and you will be my witnesses in Jerusalem, in all Judea and Samaria, and to the ends of the earth" (Acts 1:8). As we have previously noted, the three major geographical divisions correspond to the three major sections of Acts:

---

33. E.g., Pillai, *Early Missionary Preaching*, 67–71, 77–111, esp. 111.

34. Martin Dibelius, "The Speeches in Acts and Ancient Historiography," in *Studies in the Acts of the Apostles*, 165.

35. Bowker, "Speeches in Acts," who is followed by Barrett, *Acts of the Apostles*, 1:624. Bowker suggested that the seder was Deut 4:25–26, the haftarah was 2 Sam 7:6–16, and the proem was 1 Sam 13:14. For earlier efforts to situate the speech within a Jewish framework see the summary by Schneider, *Die Apostelgeschichte*, 2:130.

36. Dibelius, "Speeches in Acts and Ancient Historiography," 175.

37. Wilckens, *Die Missionsreden der Apostelgeschichte*, 55, 71, acknowledged the agreement of the speech with standard preaching, but emphasized the connection the author made between the speech and the narrative.

1:1–8:3, Jerusalem; 8:4–12:25, Judea and Samaria; 13:1–28:31, the ends of the earth. It is not an accident that the two speeches that retell the story of Israel are situated at the critical turning points of the narrative.[38] I earlier argued that Stephen's speech set up narrative about Judea and Samaria by arguing that God had always dealt with the people outside of Jerusalem and the temple. In the same way, Luke has placed the speech of Paul in a position to defend the Gentile mission. The question is how.

We need to return to the structure of the speech. Why did the author divide the speech as he did? The first part relates the story of Israel up to John the Baptist. The span thus covers the story of Israel from the ancestors through John. This aligns with Luke's broader understanding of history. The evangelist viewed John as the transition point from the period of Israel to the period of Jesus and the Church. He attributed the following logion to Jesus: "The law and the prophets were until John, from that point on the kingdom of God is announced and everyone enters it by force" (Luke 16:16). Later he had Peter introduce the gospel to Cornelius and his house with a reference to John: "you know the message that went throughout Judea, beginning in Galilee after the baptism that John preached" (Acts 10:37). Both texts suggest that John was the terminus for the time of Israel. It is for this reason that Luke situated him within the story of Israel in the speech.[39]

There has been a debate in scholarship whether Luke thought of history in two or three periods. Hans Conzelmann thought that there were three distinct periods: Israel, Jesus, and the Church.[40] Many contemporary scholars think that there are two periods, promise and fulfillment, although fulfillment is frequently subdivided into Jesus and the Church. This subdivision is clearly marked in the double work by the coming of the Spirit: the Spirit descended

38. A number of scholars have pointed out that the speech is located at a critical juncture: Wilckens, *Die Missionsreden der Apostelgeschichte*, 52; Pillai, *Early Christian Missionary Preaching*, 50–52, esp. 50; and DeSilva, "Paul's Sermon in Antioch of Pisidia," 32, 41.

39. Schneider, *Die Apostelgeschichte*, 2:134, correctly wrote: "er gehört in die Zeit *vor* Jesus, tritt vor der εἴσοδος Jesu auf. Die Sätze über den Täufer (VV 24.25) haben parenthetischen Charakter; v 26 knüpft an V 23 an. Johannes der Täufer gehört in die Zeit der Propheten. Was er laut V 25 über Jesus sagt, is noch Ankünkigung (ἔρχεται μετ' ἐμοῦ)." See also Pervo, *Acts*, 336n52. See also our discussion in chapter 4.

40. Conzelmann, *Theology of St. Luke*, 12–15, 149–51. He was followed by Fitzmyer, *Gospel according to Luke*, 1:179–92, esp. 181–87.

on Jesus at the outset of his ministry[41] and on the disciples on Pentecost.[42] The explanations of these events mark new epochs in Luke's understanding of *Heilsgeschichte*: the opening of Jesus's proclamation of the kingdom and the beginning of the church. The author called both "beginnings." In his preface he referred to "those who from the beginning were eyewitnesses and ministers of the message" (Luke 1:2). This means those who accompanied Jesus from the outset of his ministry. Similarly, when Peter defended his offer of salvation to Cornelius before the Jerusalem church, he mentioned the decisive event: "As I began to speak, the Holy Spirit fell on them just as it had on us at the beginning" (Acts 11:15). There are thus two beginnings: one that began with Jesus and one with the church. In an earlier work, I suggested that Luke's view of *Heilsgeschichte* matched the literary works with which he was working.[43] If we think of the promise and fulfillment, the scheme looks like this:

	Period	**Literary work**
Promise	Israel	LXX
Fulfillment	Jesus	Luke
	Church	Acts

The fascinating aspect of this analysis is that the speech of Paul in Antioch of Pisidia matches this understanding of history.

	Period	**Speech at Antioch of Pisidia**
Promise	Israel	Acts 13:17–25
Fulfillment	Jesus	Acts 13:26–37
	Church	Acts 13:38–41

The sermon is thus a brief sketch of Luke's understanding of *Heilsgeschichte* and is structured to reflect that grasp.

Why place his understanding of *Heilsgeschichte* at this juncture? There are some striking similarities between this text and the inaugural sermon of Jesus in Nazareth: both take place in a synagogue, both present the protagonist as the

---

41. Luke 3:21–22, the baptism, followed by the explanation in 4:16–21, the sermon in the synagogue in Nazareth. The latter includes the citation of Isa 61:1.

42. Acts 2:1–4, the descent, followed by the explanation in 2:17–21 that includes the citation of Joel 3:1–5 (LXX).

43. Sterling, *Historiography and Self-Definition*, 361–62.

homilist for the day, both open the preaching ministry of each protagonist, and both warn against rejection.[44] Just as Luke 4:16–30 is widely recognized as a set piece for the gospel, we should recognize that Acts 13:16–41 is a critical speech for the last part of Acts. The outset of the Pauline mission raised the entire issue of the inclusion of the Gentiles into the Church. Luke's sermon argues that God worked through Israel to bring the savior and that the Pauline mission extends the offer of salvation to all. The Gentile mission is thus part of *Heilsgeschichte*: it is no accident; it is part and parcel of God's plan for history.

CONCLUSIONS

The final clause of the speech in Acts 13:41, "a work that you will not believe even if someone explains it to you," is a way of reminding us of the function of the speech: it explains God's work. It does so by laying out an understanding of *Heilsgeschichte* that moves from Israel to Jesus to the Pauline mission. The story of Israel anticipated a Davidic Messiah. Jesus is that Messiah as his resurrection in fulfillment of the Scriptures demonstrates. It was on the basis of the resurrection that Luke had Paul offer salvation, a salvation that justified the believer in a way that the law could not. In this way not only does Jesus stand in continuity with Israel, but so does Paul.

The final clause of the speech also reminds us of the author's preoccupation with understanding the LXX. One of the functions of the risen Christ was to "interpret" the Scriptures" (Luke 24:25–27, esp. 26) or "to open the minds" of the disciples so that they could understand them (Luke 24:44–49, esp. 45). The disciples carried on this function in Acts, especially in the speeches. It is in the speeches that the author cited the LXX and explained the citations in terms of the story of Jesus.

On two pivotal occasions, Luke offered sweeping rehearsals of the story of Israel in the LXX. At first glance it might appear that he has used distinctly Christian perspectives in order to compose these rehearsals; however, we have shown that he had Jewish models for his understanding of the story of Israel. In this way the speeches encapsulate the author's understanding of *Heilsgeschichte*: Christianity grew out of and was the extension of Judaism. It

44. Daniel Marguerat, *The First Christian Historian: Writing the Acts of the Apostles*, SNTSMS 131 (Cambridge: Cambridge University Press, 2002), 136–41, compares the two under the heading of a prophetic model of rupture.

was not set over against Judaism, but was the continuation of it. While this is a variation in the tradition of apologetic historiography—a "conceptual integration"—it is the type of blending that had to be made.

APPENDIX

The LXX in Paul's Speech at Antioch of Pisidia[45]

Acts 13:16b–41	Possible LXX base
[16b]ἄνδρες Ἰσραηλῖται	
καὶ οἱ φοβούμενοι τὸν θεόν,	
ἀκούσατε.	
[17]ὁ θεὸς τοῦ λαοῦ τούτου Ἰσραὴλ	Deut 4:37 διὰ τὸ ἀγαπῆσαι αὐτὸν
ἐξελέξατο τοὺς πατέρας ἡμῶν	τοὺς πατέρας σου
	καὶ ἐξελέξατο τὸ σπέρμα αὐτῶν
καὶ τὸν λαὸν ὕψωσεν	μετ᾽ αὐτοὺς ὑμᾶς
ἐν τῇ παροικίᾳ ἐν γῇ Αἰγύπτου	καὶ ἐξήγαγέν σε αὐτὸς
καὶ μετὰ βραχίονος ὑψηλοῦ	ἐν τῇ ἰσχύι αὐτοῦ τῇ μεγάλῃ
ἐξήγαγεν αὐτοὺς ἐξ αὐτῆς,	ἐξ Αἰγύπτου ...
	Deut 1:31 καὶ ἐν τῇ ἐρήμῳ ταύτῃ,
	ἣν εἴδετε,
[18]καὶ ὡς τεσσερακονταετῆ χρόνον	
ἐτροφοφόρησεν αὐτοὺς	ὡς ἐτροφοφόρησέν σε
	ὁ θεός σου,
	ὡς εἴ τις τροφοφορήσει ἄνθρωπος
	τὸν υἱὸν αὐτοῦ,
ἐν τῇ ἐρήμῳ	κατὰ πᾶσαν τὴν ὁδόν,
	ἣν ἐπορεύθητε,
	ἕως ἤλθετε εἰς τὸν τόπον τοῦτον.
	Deut 7:1 ἐὰν δὲ εἰσαγάγῃ σε
	κύριος ὁ θεός σου
	εἰς τὴν γῆν,

45. The LXX texts listed in the synopsis are not exhaustive. In some cases, the expression in Acts is paralleled in a number of LXX texts. The point of the synopsis is not to be exhaustive, but illustrative as a means of indicating the pervasive influence of the LXX. For the LXX I have followed the text in *Septuaginta*, 2 vols., ed. Alfred Rahlfs (Stuttgart: Württembergische Bibelanstalt, 1935).

εἰς ἣν εἰσπορεύῃ ἐκεῖ κληρονομῆσαι,
[19]καὶ καθελὼν ἔθνη ἑπτὰ   καὶ ἐξαρεῖ ἔθνη μεγάλα
     ἀπὸ προσώπου σου
     τὸν Χετταῖον καὶ Γεργεσαῖον
ἐν γῇ Χανάαν   καὶ Αμορραῖον καὶ Χανναῖον
     καὶ Φερεζαῖον καὶ Ευαῖον
     καὶ Ιεβουσαῖον,
     ἑπτὰ ἔθνη πολλὰ
     καὶ ἰσχυρότερα ὑμῶν.
κατεκληρονόμησεν τὴν γῆν αὐτῶν
[20]ὡς ἔτεσιν τετρακοσίοις
καὶ πεντήκοντα.
καὶ μετὰ ταῦτα
ἔδωκεν κριτὰς   Judg 2:16 καὶ ἤγειρεν κύριος κριτάς
ἕως Σαμουὴλ [τοῦ] προφήτου.

     1 Kgdms 8:10 καὶ εἶπεν Σαμουὴλ
     πᾶν τὸ ῥῆμα κυρίου πρὸς τὸν λαὸν
[21]κἀκεῖθεν ᾐτήσαντο βασιλέα   τοὺς αἰτοῦντας παρ᾽ αὐτοῦ βασιλέα
     1 Kgdms 10:21 καὶ προσάγει σκῆπτρον
     Βενιαμιν εἰς φυλάς,
     καὶ κατακληροῦται φυλὴ Ματταρι·
     καὶ προσάγουσιν
     τὴν φυλὴν Ματταρι
     εἰς ἄνδρας,
καὶ ἔδωκεν αὐτοῖς ὁ θεὸς   καὶ κατακληροῦται
τὸν Σαοὺλ υἱὸν Κίς,   Σαουλ υἱὸς Κις.
ἄνδρα ἐκ φυλῆς Βενιαμίν,
ἔτη τεσσεράκοντα,

     1 Kgdms 15:23 ὅτι ἐξουδένωσας
     τὸ ῥῆμα κυρίου,
[22]καὶ μεταστήσας αὐτὸν   καὶ ἐξουδενώσει σε
     κύριος μὴ εἶναι βασιλέα ἐπὶ Ισραηλ.
ἤγειρεν τὸν Δαυὶδ αὐτοῖς
εἰς βασιλέα ᾧ καὶ εἶπεν μαρτυρήσας·
εὗρον Δαυὶδ τὸν τοῦ Ἰεσσαί,   Ps 88:21 εὗρον Δαυιδ τὸν δοῦλόν μου
     1 Kgdms 13:14 καὶ νῦν ἡ βασιλεία σου
     οὐ στήσεται,
     καὶ ζητήσει κύριος
ἄνδρα κατὰ τὴν καρδίαν μου,   ἄνθρωπον κατὰ τὴν καρδίαν αὐτοῦ

ὃς ποιήσει πάντα τὰ θελήματά μου.
²³τούτου ὁ θεὸς

ἀπὸ τοῦ σπέρματος κατ᾽ ἐπαγγελίαν

Isa 44:28 ὁ λέγων Κύρῳ φρονεῖν,
καὶ πάντα τὰ θελήματά μου ποιήσει
Ps 88:4–5 ὤμοσα Δαυιδ τῷ δούλῳ μου
ἕως τοῦ αἰῶνος ἑτοιμάσω
τὸ σπέρμα σου
καὶ οἰκοδομήσω εἰς γενεὰν
καὶ γενεὰν
τὸν θρόνον σου. διάψαλμα.

ἤγαγεν τῷ Ἰσραὴλ σωτῆρα Ἰησοῦν,
²⁴προκηρύξαντος Ἰωάννου
πρὸ προσώπου τῆς εἰσόδου αὐτοῦ
βάπτισμα μετανοίας
παντὶ τῷ λαῷ Ἰσραήλ.
²⁵ὡς δὲ ἐπλήρου Ἰωάννης
τὸν δρόμον, ἔλεγεν·
τί ἐμὲ ὑπονοεῖτε εἶναι;
οὐκ εἰμὶ ἐγώ·
ἀλλ᾽ ἰδοὺ ἔρχεται μετ᾽ ἐμὲ
οὗ οὐκ εἰμὶ ἄξιος
τὸ ὑπόδημα τῶν ποδῶν λῦσαι.
²⁶Ἄνδρες ἀδελφοί,
υἱοὶ γένους Ἀβραὰμ
καὶ οἱ ἐν ὑμῖν φοβούμενοι τὸν θεόν,
ἡμῖν ὁ λόγος τῆς σωτηρίας ταύτης
ἐξαπεστάλη.

Ps 106:20 ἀπέστειλεν τὸν λόγον αὐτοῦ
καὶ ἰάσατο αὐτοὺς
καὶ ἐρρύσατο αὐτοὺς
ἐκ τῶν διαφθορῶν αὐτῶν.

²⁷οἱ γὰρ κατοικοῦντες ἐν Ἰερουσαλὴν
καὶ οἱ ἄρχοντες αὐτῶν
τοῦτον ἀγνοήσαντες
καὶ τὰς φωνὰς τῶν προφητῶν
τὰς κατὰ πᾶν σάββατον
ἀναγινωσκομένας
κρίναντες ἐπλήρωσαν,
²⁸καὶ μηδεμίαν αἰτίαν θανάτου
εὑρόντες ᾐτήσαντο Πιλᾶτον
ἀναιρεθῆναι αὐτόν.
²⁹ὡς δὲ ἐτέλεσαν πάντα
τὰ περὶ αὐτοῦ γεγραμμένα,

καθελόντες ἀπὸ τοῦ ξύλου
ἔθηκαν εἰς μνημεῖον.
[30]ὁ δὲ θεὸς ἤγειρεν
αὐὸν ἐκ νεκρῶν,
[31]ὃς ὤφθη ἐπὶ ἡμέρας πλείους
τοῖς συναναβᾶσιν αὐτῷ
ἀπὸ τῆς Γαλιλαίας
εἰς Ἰερουσαλήμ,
οἵτινες [νῦν] εἰσιν μάρτυρες αὐτοῦ
πρὸς τὸν λαόν.
[32]καὶ ἡμεῖς ὑμᾶς εὐαγγελιζόμεθα
τὴν πρὸς τοὺς πατέρας
ἐπαγγελίαν γενομένην,
[33]ὅτι ταύτην ὁ θεὸς ἐκπεπλήρωκεν
τοῖς τέκνοις [αὐτῶν] ἡμῖν
ἀναστήσας Ἰησοῦν
ὡς καὶ ἐν τῷ ψαλμῷ
γέγραπται τῷ δευτέρῳ·
υἱός μου εἶ σύ,   Ps 2:7 υἱός μου εἶ σύ,
ἐγὼ σήμερον γεγέννηκά σε.   ἐγὼ σήμερον γεγέννηκά σε.
[34]ὅτι δὲ ἀνέστησεν αὐτὸν
ἐκ τῶν νεκρῶν
μηκέτι μέλλοντα ὑποστρέφειν
εἰς διαφθοράν,
οὕτως εἴρηκεν
ὅτι δώσω ὑμῖν   Isa 55:3 καὶ διαθήσομαι ὑμῖν
                                                         διαθήκν αἰώνιον,
τὰ ὅσια Δαυὶδ τὰ πιστά.   τὰ ὅσια Δαυὶδ τὰ πιστά.
[35]διότι καὶ ἐν ἑτέρῳ λέγει·
οὐ δώσεις τὸν ὅσιόν σου   Ps 15:10 οὐδὲ δώσεις τὸν ὅσιόν σου
ἰδεῖν διαφθοράν.   ἰδεῖν διαφθοράν.
[36]Δαυὶδ μὲν γὰρ
ἰδίᾳ γενεᾷ ὑπηρετήσας
τῇ τοῦτ θεοῦ βουλῇ
ἐκοιμήθη καὶ προσετέθη   3 Kgdms 2:10 καὶ ἐκοιμήθη Δαυιδ
πρὸς τοὺς πατέρας αὐτοῦ   μετὰ τῶν πατέρων αὐτοῦ
καὶ εἶδεν διαφθοράν·   καὶ ἐτάφη ἐν πόλει Δαυιδ.
[37]ὃν δὲ ὁ θεὸς ἤγειρεν,
οὐκ εἶδεν διαφθοράν.

157

³⁸γνωστὸν οὖν ἔστω ὑμῖν,
ἄνδρες ἀδελφοί,
ὅτι διὰ τούτου ὑμῖν
ἄφεσις ἁμαρτιῶν καταγγέλλεται,
[καὶ] ἀπὸ πάντων ὧν οὐκ ἠδυνήθητε
ἐν νόμῳ Μωϋσέως δικαιωθῆναι,
³⁹ἐν τούτῳ
πᾶς ὁ πιστεύων δικαοῦται.
⁴⁰βλέπετε οὖν μὴ ἐπέλθῃ
τὸ εἰρημένον ἐν τοῖς προφήταις·
⁴¹ἴδετε, οἱ καταφροννηταί,

καὶ θαυμάσατε
καὶ ἀφανίσθητε,
ὅτι ἔργον ἐργάζομαι ἐγὼ
ἐν ταῖς ἡμέραις ὑμῶν,
ἔργον ὃ οὐ μὴ πιστεύσητε
ἐάν τις ἐκδιηγῆται ὑμῖν.

Hab 1:5 ἴδετε, οἱ καταφρονηταί,
καὶ ἐπιβλέψατε
καὶ θαυμάσατε θαυμάσια
καὶ ἀφανίσθητε,
διότι ἔργον ἐγὼ ἐργάζομαι
ἐν ταῖς ἡμέραις ὑμῶν,
ὃ οὐ μὴ πιστεύσητε
ἐάν τις ἐκδιηγῆται.

PART THREE

Looking to the Future

The Greco-Roman World in Luke-Acts

7

Mors philosophi

The Death of Jesus in Luke

> *Let it be, Crito, let us act in this way since God is guiding us in this way.*

SOCRATES IN PLATO, *Crito* 54e[1]

THE DEATH OF JESUS OF NAZARETH by crucifixion was the source of numerous difficulties for early proponents of Christianity. Paul's statement to the Corinthians, "We preach Christ crucified, to the Jews a cause of offense and to the Gentiles foolishness" (1 Cor 1:23), was not hyperbolic rhetoric, but a sober assessment of the difficulty of proclaiming a condemned criminal to be the "the Lord of glory" (1 Cor 2:8). The fundamental problem is obvious: a crucified Lord struck most ancients as an oxymoron.[2] The Gospels did little to overcome the problem from a pagan perspective; in some cases they even exacerbated it. For example, Celsus, the learned and perceptive second-century critic of Christianity, found that the manner in which the evangelists described Jesus as he faced death undermined Christian claims for him. He wrote: "Why does he howl (ποτνιᾶται), lament (ὀδύρεται), and pray to escape the fear of destruction, expressing himself in a manner like this: 'O Father, if it be possible, let this cup pass'?" Origen countered by pointing out that Celsus had doctored the texts by adding to the biblical text and omitting the all-important qualifying clause that demonstrates Jesus's voluntary obedience to the Father, "nevertheless, not as I will, but as you will."[3] However, he found

---

1. This is the final line in Plato's *Crito*. Crito, a wealthy friend, has failed to persuade Socrates to escape; Socrates has chosen to remain and to face death.

2. Early Christian authors were keenly aware of the negative associations of the cross, e.g., Justin Martyr, *1 Apol.* 13.4; Origen, *Cels.* 6.10; Lactantius, *Inst.* 4.26 and *Epit.* 50–51.

3. Neither ποτνίαομαι nor ὀδύρομαι appear in the Gospels. Celsus is paraphrasing

it difficult to offer much more of a rebuttal and was forced to conclude: "But these matters, which require extended discussion by the wisdom of God, and which may reasonably be considered by those whom Paul calls 'perfect' . . . we, for the present, pass by. . . ."[4]

The basis for the dilemma that Celsus and Origen perceived stemmed from the noble death tradition: it was not acceptable for a hero—much less a figure accorded divine honors—to demonstrate anxiety in the face of death.[5] It is reasonably well known that one of the strategies that early Christian apologists used to deflect criticisms like those of Celsus was to compare Jesus and early Christian martyrs with Socrates.[6] I, however, suggest that the use of the traditions about Socrates as an apologetic strategy took place well before Celsus trained his pene-

---

Mark 14:33–34 // Matt 26:37–38. Cf. Heb 5:7–10, for the strongest statement about Jesus's suffering in Gethsemane.

4. Origen, *Cels.* 2.24. I have used the edition of Koetschau, *Origenes Werke 1.*

5. Early Christian authors were sensitive to the tension between the noble death and the accounts of Jesus's death in the Gospels. They found different ways of handling the tension, e.g., Jerome, *Comm. Matt.* 4.26.37 (PL 26.197) and Augustine, *Enarrat. Ps.* 21.3–4 (PL 36.172–73). One of the most interesting legacies of this discussion is the debate between John Colet (1467–1519 CE), who denied that Christ feared death, and Erasmus of Rotterdam (1466–1536 CE), who argued that he did. Their exchanges incorporate a great deal of the early Christian material. The initial discussion took place at Oxford in October 1499. Erasmus later published his *Disputatiuncula de taedio, pavore, tristicia Iesu* as a summary of the debate. For details and an English translation see Michael J. Heath, "A Short Debate Concerning the Distress, Alarm, and Sorrow of Jesus," in *Collected Works of Erasmus* (Toronto: University of Toronto Press, 1998), 70:1–67.

6. For the use of the Socratic tradition in the Early Church see Adolf von Harnack, "Sokrates und die alte Kirche," *Reden und Aufsätze*, 7 vols. (Gießen: A. Töpelmann, 1903), 1.1:29–48; Joannes M. Pfättisch, "Christus und Sokrates bei Justin," *TQ* 90 (1908): 503–23; Ernst Benz, "Christus und Sokrates in der alten Kirche (Ein Beitrag zum altkirchlichen Verständnis des Märtyrers und des Martyriums)," *ZNW* 43 (1951): 195–244; Erich Fascher, "Sokrates und Christus: Eine Studie 'zur aktuellen Aufgabe der Religionsphänomenologie' dem Andenken Heinrich Fricks († 31.12.52)," *ZNW* 45 (1954): 1–41; Theofried Baumeister, "Anytos und Meletos können mich zwar töten, schaden jedoch können sie mir nicht," in *Platonismus und Christentum: Festschrift für H. Dörrie*, ed. Horst Dieter Blume and Friedhelm Mann, Jahrbuch für Antike und Christentum Ergänzungsband 10 (Münster: Aschendorff, 1983), 58–63; L. Stephanie Cobb, "Polycarp's Cup: *The Martyrdom of Polycarp*," *JRH* 38 (2014) 224–40, who builds—in part—on the analysis in this chapter and extends it to the martyrdom of Polycarp; and Juraj Franek, "The Reception of Socrates in Tertullian," in *Brill's Companion to the Reception of Socrates*, ed. Christopher Moore, Brill's Companions to Classical Reception 18 (Leiden: Brill, 2019), 435–52, who notes that while Tertullian referred to Socrates 26 times, the most of any ante-Nicene writer, the portrait is largely negative—hardly a surprise for the North African.

trating gaze on the texts and second- and third-century Christians felt compelled to offer a response. I believe that it occurred as early as Luke's passion narrative. Like later Christians, the third evangelist made selective use of Socratic traditions to transform an embarrassment into an *exemplum*. While these traditions were not the only model at work in the Lukan passion narrative—anymore than they were the exclusive model for the later apologists—they serve a vital role in Luke's effort to explain the "foolishness" of the cross.

THE NOBLE DEATH

Deaths (τελευταί). Before I turn to the Lukan narrative it will be helpful to sketch the broad contours of the noble death tradition.[7] Ancient Greeks and Romans were as fascinated as moderns by the deaths of famous characters or persons, especially when their deaths were tragic. Quite predictably ancient authors satisfied their peers' curiosity by narrating the final moments of interesting figures. In the Hellenistic world a new tradition began in which individuals collected accounts of the deaths of significant individuals. These collections are appropriately known as "Deaths" (τελευταί). The first known collection occurs within the biographical tradition. Hermippus of Smyrna, whose floruit was in the third century BCE, was a Peripatetic philosopher who wrote a work on the lives of famous individuals, especially philosophers, in which he gave particular attention to their deaths.[8] The deaths were not necessarily noble, but were interesting. For example, Hermippus said that Chrysippus (ca. 280–207 BCE), the second founder of the Stoa, drank some unmixed wine at a party thrown by his students, slipped into a coma, and died five days later.[9] He similarly reported that Epicurus (341–270 BCE) "entered a bronze basin of warm water,

7. The most important works that address this tradition in whole or in part are: Herbert A. Musurillo, *The Acts of the Pagan Martyrs: Acta Alexandrinorum* (Oxford: Oxford University Press, 1954; repr., New York: Arno, 1979), 236–46; Allessandro Ronconi, "Exitus illustrium virorum," *RAC* 6 (1966): 1258–68; David Seeley, *The Noble Death: Graeco-Roman Martyrology and Paul's Concept of Salvation*, JSNTSup 28 (Sheffield: JSOT Press, 1990), 83–141; Arthur J. Droge and James D. Tabor, *A Noble Death: Suicide and Martyrdom among Christians and Jews in Antiquity* (San Francisco: Harper San Francisco, 1992); Adela Y. Collins, "The Genre of the Passion Narrative," *ST* 47 (1993): 3–28; and Ulrich Eigler, "Exitus illustrium virorum," *DNP* 4 (1998): 344–45.

8. On Hermippus see Fritz Wehrli, *Die Schule des Aristoteles: Texte und Kommentar, Supplementband 1: Hermippos der Kallimacheer* (Basel: Schwabe, 1974). I have used his edition.

9. Frag. 59 (Diogenes Laertius 7.184). Diogenes offered a second anonymous account in which Chrysippus is said to have expired during a fit of laughter (7.185).

asked for and gulped down unmixed wine, ordered his disciples to remember his teachings, and died."[10] In both cases the consumption of unmixed wine—often associated with barbarian habits—was their undoing.[11] Cicero (ca. 102–43 BCE) attests a similar literary practice in the Roman world. He said that he had collected examples of the deaths of Rome's most famous citizens in his now lost *On Consolation*, which he wrote after the death of his beloved Tullia.[12]

More relevant for our purposes are some of the accounts of the deaths of philosophers who perished resisting tyrants in the name of philosophy. Two of the most famous are Zeno of Elea (floruit fifth century BCE) and Anaxarchus of Abdera (floruit fourth century BCE) who were perceived as models of courageous defiance of tyrants. Zeno became involved in a plot against Nearchus, the tyrant of Elea (floruit fifth century BCE). According to one tradition, when the tyrant questioned him about his accomplices, the philosopher shrewdly accused Nearchus's own friends of involvement in the plot. Zeno then indicated that he wanted to communicate something privately to Nearchus. When Nearchus approached, Zeno bit his ear until the tyrant's guard stabbed the philosopher to death.[13] According to another version, Zeno implicated Nearchus's friends and then Nearchus himself. After rebuking the bystanders for submitting to the tyrant he bit off his own tongue and spat it out at Nearchus, presumably in an effort not to reveal any of the names of the real accomplices.[14] Hermippus added that he was executed by being thrown into a mortar trough and beaten to death. This led to the saying "He beat your body, but not you."[15] The fate of Anaxarchus was very similar. He was executed for his opposition to Nicocreon of Cyprus (floruit fourth century BCE) who ordered him to be pulverized with mortar pestles. He replied: "Beat Anaxarchus's sack, you are not beating Anaxarchus."[16]

10. Frag. 61 (Diogenes Laertius 10.15). Diogenes also cited a version attributed to Hermarchus that informs us that Epicurus died of renal calculus after a two-week illness (10.15).

11. Cf. the story of Brennus, the leader of the Gauls, who committed suicide in the same way (Pausanias 10.23.12; although see also Diodorus Siculus 22.9.2, who says that he drank unmixed wine and then slew himself). I owe this reference to Jan Willem van Henten.

12. Cicero, *Div.* 2.22.

13. Diodorus Siculus 10.18.2–6; Diogenes Laertius 9.26. Diogenes also preserved the tradition attributed to Demetrius that said that Zeno bit off Nearchus's nose rather than his ear (9.27).

14. So Antisthenes according to Diogenes Laertius 9.27. Cf. also Plutarch, *Garr.* 505d; *Stoic. rep.* 1051c; *Adv. Col.* 1126d; Clement of Alexandria, *Strom.* 4.57; Ammianus Marcellinus 14.9.6.

15. Frag. 28 (Diogenes Laertius 9.27–28). This thought became a commonplace, e.g., Epictetus 1.1.23–25.

16. Philo, *Prob.* 109, also cites this saying.

When Nicocreon commanded that his tongue be cut out, he bit it off and spat it out at the tyrant.[17]

The evident conflation in the traditions about the deaths of these two philosophers was due, in part, to the fact that their deaths became exemplars.[18] It was commonplace in later authors to use Zeno and Anaxarchus as models of how philosophers should respond to tyrants: Cicero, Philo of Alexandria, Tertullian, Valerius Maximus, and an anonymous commentator on Aristotle's *Nicomachean Ethics* all associate the two.[19] Philo expressed the typical function of the pairing when he contrasted the glory of these philosophers with that of epic heroes: the latter are famous as a result of an inherited nobility that is beyond their volition; the former are famous as a result of the virtues that are of their volition.[20]

Exitus illustrium virorum. Within the larger genre of *teleutai*, a subgenre developed among Latin authors that capitalized on the deaths of philosophers who resisted tyrants. The earliest attestation of it is Pliny (ca. 61–ca. 112 CE), who alluded to it in his correspondence. In a letter to Novius Maximus, he mentioned that he had just received word that Gaius Fannius died. The ever-informative Pliny tells us that Fannius "was writing about the departures of those who had been executed or exiled by Nero" (emperor 54–68 CE).[21] Later, in a letter to Cornelius Minicianus, Pliny indicated his plans to attend a reading by Titinius Capito, who "is writing about the deaths of famous people (*scribit exitus inlustrium virorum*)" under Domitian (emperor 81–96 CE).[22] The phrase that Pliny used has become the name of this specific subgenre since the end of the nineteenth century. Allessandro Ronconi defined *exitus illustrium virorum* literature as "those antimonarchical literary works with a Stoic stamp that attempt to glorify the sacrificial figures of the Caesars' tyranny."[23] Pliny and Tacitus (ca. 57–ca. 118 CE) both knew and used this material.[24]

17. Diogenes Laertius 9.59.

18. It is worth noting that Leaena, the famous Athenian courtesan, was also said to have bit off her tongue rather than reveal names under examination, e.g., Tertullian, *Apol.* 50.8. Cf. also Plutarch, *Garr.* 505d-e. The physical gesture became well enough known that Epictetus could allude to it without specifying its association (3.24.71).

19. Cicero, *Nat. d.* 3.82; *Tusc.* 2.51; Philo, *Det.* 176 and *Prob.* 106–109; Tertullian, *Apol.* 50.6–9; Valerius Maximus 3.3.2, ext. 2, 4; Anonymous Commentators to Aristotle, *Eth. nic.* 4.1 (ed. Gustav B. Heylbut; *Eustratii et Michaelis et anonyma in Ethica Nicomachea commentaria*, Commentaria in Aristotelem Graeca 20 [Berlin: Georg Reimer, 1892], 177 ll. 29–30).

20. Philo, *Prob.* 109.

21. Pliny, *Ep.* 5.5.3. Fannius had completed three volumes to date.

22. Pliny, *Ep.* 8.12.4. Cf. also 1.17.1–4, esp. 3–4.

23. Ronconi, "Exitus illustrium virorum," 1258.

24. On Tacitus see F. A. Marx, "Tacitus und die Literatur der Exitus Illustrium Virorum," *Philologus* 92 (1937–1938): 83–103.

Socrates as a Model. Spanning both the larger genre of *teleutai* and the more specific subgenre of *exitus illustrium virorum* is the tradition that developed around Socrates's death. Sometimes this was by association: Cicero and the anonymous commentator on Aristotle's *Nicomachean Ethics* both list Socrates with Zeno and Anaxarchus.[25] On other occasions, the death of Socrates became the lens by which the deaths of later philosophers were viewed. So, for example, the statements associated with the deaths of Zeno ("He beat your body, not you") and Anaxarchus ("Beat Anaxarchus's sack, you are not beating Anaxarchus") are based on the famous statement in Plato's *Apology*, "Note well, if you kill me, being the man that I say I am, you will hurt me less than yourselves. Neither Meletus nor Anytus can hurt me in any way."[26] The lines circulated as an aphorism: "Anytus and Miletus can kill me, but they cannot harm me."[27] The sayings associated with the deaths of Zeno and Anaxarchus took their inspiration from this famous line. It is the use of the story of Socrates for later deaths that interests us.

The basic sources for Socrates's death are Plato's four dialogues that have become one of the nine tetralogies in the Platonic corpus (the *Euthyphro* [preliminaries to the trial], the *Apology* [the trial], the *Crito* [Socrates in prison awaiting death], and the *Phaedo* [Socrates's final day]) and two of Xenophon's works (the *Apology* and the *Memorabilia* 1.1.1–2.64). Plato's dialogues, especially the *Phaedo*, exercised an enormous influence on the tradition that developed as different authors recast their heroes in the mold of Socrates.[28] Without

25. Cicero, *Nat. d.* 3.82 and Anonymous Commentators to Aristotle, *Eth. nic.* 4.1 (ed. Heylbut, *Eustratii et Michaelis*, 177 ll. 26–30).

26. Plato, *Apol.* 30c–d. The text goes on: "This is not possible. I do not think that God's law permits a better person to be hurt by a worse person. He may perhaps kill me or banish me or deprive me of my civil rights. But if he and some other as well thinks that these things are great evils, I do not. It is a far greater evil to do what he is now doing, to attempt to kill a person unjustly."

27. Plutarch, *Tranq. an.* 475e; Epictetus, *Diatr.* 1.29.18; 2.2.15; 3.23.21; *Ench.* 53.4. Cf. also Epictetus, *Diatr.* 4.152–155 in which he describes Diogenes in similar terms. Baumeister, "Anytos und Meletos können," 59, suggests that they knew a Stoic, or possibly Cynic, version of the famous saying.

28. The most important works tracing the influence of the traditions about Socrates are Klaus Döring, *Exemplum Socratis: Studien zur Sokratesnachwirkung in der kynisch-stoischen Popularphilosophie der frühen Kaiserzeit und im frühen Christentum*, Hermes 42 (Wiesbaden: Franz Steiner, 1979) and Moore, *Brill's Companion to the Reception of Socrates*. On the lasting influence of the *Phaedo* see Leendert G. Westerink, *The Greek Commentaries on Plato's Phaedo*, 2 vols., Verhandelingen der Koninklijke Nederlandse Akademie van Wetenschappen, Afd. Letterkunde, Nieuwe Reeks, deel 92 (Amsterdam: North Holland Publishing, 1976), 1:7–20. On the importance of Socrates for the thought of Hellenistic philosophy

making any pretense at being comprehensive, I will offer examples from three different authors to indicate some of the major motifs that emerged in the tradition: the first two are Greek authors and the third is a Roman.

Plutarch. The Middle Platonic philosopher Plutarch (ca. 50–ca. 120 CE) certainly knew and used the Socratic traditions. Interestingly, the parade example in his corpus is his version of Cato's death (234–149 BCE). He tells us that the famous Roman read through the *Phaedo* twice on the night of his execution—a straightforward signal to the reader that Plato's dialogue is the frame for the account of Cato.[29] As virtually all accounts that drew their inspiration from Socrates's death, Plutarch tells us that Cato calmed his friends.[30] He adds that he refused their efforts to save him, a detail that reminds us that Socrates had refused Crito.[31] While there are other possible echoes, the use of Socrates as a model for Plutarch's Cato is explicit.[32] This is hardly the occasion for surprise: Socrates and Cato were frequently associated in Roman authors (e.g., Cicero and Seneca linked the two).[33] Plutarch also used the Socratic tradition on other occasions as well, although not with the detail that we find here (e.g., Phocion).[34]

Lucian. The second-century CE satirist, Lucian, drew on the Socratic tradition on multiple occasions. When he related the trial of Demonax (floruit second century CE) he offered charges similar to those leveled against Socrates and permitted Demonax to make an explicit comparison between himself and Socrates in his defense speech.[35] Again, when he related the imprisonment of Peregrinus (floruit second century CE), he mentioned the fact that Christians called him "the new Socrates" (καινὸς Σωκράτης).[36] The decision to make

---

see Anthony A. Long, "Socrates in Hellenistic Philosophy," *CQ* 38 (1988): 150–71; repr. in *Stoic Studies* (Cambridge: Cambridge University Press, 1996), 1–34; Anthony A. Long, "The Socratic Legacy," in *The Cambridge History of Hellenistic Philosophy*, ed. Keimpre Algra, Jonathan Barnes, Jaap Mansfeld, and Malcolm Schofield (Cambridge: Cambridge University Press, 1999), 617–41; and the essays in Paul A. Vander Waerdt, ed., *The Socratic Movement* (Ithaca: Cornell University Press, 1994).

29. Plutarch, *Cat. Min.* 68.2; 70.1. Seneca also knew the tradition about Cato reading the *Phaedo*, which was apparently commonplace (*Ep.* 24.6–8).

30. Plutarch, *Cat. Min.* 67.2.

31. Plutarch, *Cat. Min.* 68.2–69.3 and Plato, *Crito*.

32. The full account is in Plutarch, *Cat. Min.* 66.4–70.6. Other possible echoes include a bath (66.4), a discourse after the meal (67.1–2), and the adieu to his family (68.1).

33. Cicero, *Tusc.* 1.74, who pointed out that like Socrates, Cato had a sign; and Seneca, *Ep.* 24.4, 6–8; 67.7; 71.17; 79.14; 98.12; 104.27–33.

34. Plutarch, *Phoc.* 38.2.

35. Lucian, *Demon.* 11.

36. Lucian, *Peregr.* 12. Cf. also §37.

the comparison explicit was a simple matter of preference since the tradition was ubiquitous in philosophical circles: Dio, Epictetus, Maximus of Tyre, and Philostratus all used it.[37]

Tacitus. We also have an example of a Roman author who combined the traditions about Socrates with the *exitus illustrium virorum* tradition to note Stoic opposition to the Caesars. Tacitus does so at least two times in the *Annals.* The first time is his narration of the death of Seneca (ca. 2 BCE–65 CE). A number of small details remind anyone familiar with the Platonic dialogues of the great Athenian: Seneca maintained a placid demeanor just as Socrates had throughout his ordeal. He consoled his friends and wife as Socrates had Xanthippe and his children.[38] The Stoic was an old man like Socrates, who was seventy.[39] He drank hemlock when he did not bleed quickly enough, just as Socrates had drained a cup of hemlock.[40] He offered a final libation to Jove the liberator as the Athenian offered a cock to Asclepius.[41] And, the Roman took a bath as had the Greek.[42] Some of these are part of a death scene—for example, the encouragement to family and friends and the bath. Others may be incidental—for example, the age—although this often appears in the tradition (see below). Others, however, appear to be direct echoes of the Socratic tradition—for example, the courage, the hemlock, and appropriate offering. However, the presence of so many parallels is more than accidental.

The second time is Tacitus's account of the death of Thrasea Paetus, another Stoic philosopher (died 66 CE). Again there are several echoes that create the feel of Socrates. The most impressive of these are: Thrasea spent his final hours discussing the nature of the soul and the separation of the spirit from the body just as Socrates had in the *Phaedo*; the Roman Stoic consoled his friends just as Socrates did throughout Plato's accounts; Thrasea remained calm like Socrates; and, like Seneca, he offered a libation to Jove the liberator in a manner reminiscent of Socrates's final request.[43]

---

37. Dio, *Charid.* 30 (esp. 11 [Plato, *Phaed.* 62b], 21 [*Phaed.* 60b–c], 24 [*Phaed.* 114b–c], 26 [*Phaed.* 62b]); Epictetus, *Diatr.* 1.1.21–25; 2.13.16–27, esp. 22–27; 4.7.25–32 (see F. Schweingruber, "Sokrates und Epiktet," *Hermes* 78 [1943]: 52–79); Maximus of Tyre (Döring, *Exemplum Socratis,* 130–38); and Philostratus, *Vit. Apoll.* 4.46; 7.11.13; 8.7.1 (see Döring, *Exemplum Socratis,* 138–39).

38. Tacitus, *Ann.* 15.62–63; Plato, *Phaed.* 60a, 116a–b.

39. Tacitus, *Ann.* 15.63; Plato, *Apol.* 17d.

40. Tacitus, *Ann.* 15.63–64; Plato, *Phaed.* 117a–c.

41. Tacitus, *Ann.* 15.64; Plato, *Phaed.* 118a.

42. Tacitus, *Ann.* 15.64; Plato, *Phaed.* 166a.

43. Tacitus, *Ann.* 16.34–35; Plato, *Phaed.* 118a. The text of Tacitus breaks off as Thrasea Paetus is dying.

In other works, Tacitus used the *exitus illustrium virorum* tradition without explicitly appealing to Socrates as a model. In his *Agricola*, he mentioned the death of Q. I. Arulenus Rusticus without making any reference to Socrates. Like Seneca and Thrasea Paetus, Arulenus Rusticus was a Stoic philosopher. His career spanned the period from Nero through Domitian. The latter executed him for his written account of Thrasea Paetus's death. The absence of any allusion to Socrates may be incidental since Tacitus only mentioned Arulenus Rusticus's execution—he did not narrate it.[44]

The use of the traditions about Socrates's death in these three authors is impressive. They demonstrate how different writers could appropriate the tradition in multiple ways. The three represent different literary genres: Tacitus was a historian, Plutarch was a philosopher, and Lucian was a litterateur who was influenced by philosophy. The two Greek authors made explicit reference to the traditions about Socrates's death whereas the Roman author only made implicit use of the traditions. This may be a result of their different orientations (philosophy vs. history) or a simple matter of stylistic preference. They drew on different literary traditions about deaths: the two Greek authors drew on the *teleutai* tradition while Tacitus used the *exitus illustrium virorum* tradition.

Jewish Martyrs

The Greeks and Romans were not the only authors intrigued by the deaths of famous individuals. Hebrew and Jewish authors related a large number of different types of deaths in the Hebrew Bible as well as in Second Temple and Rabbinic literature. The most significant accounts for our purposes are the stories of those who died for the Jewish faith during the Second Temple period.[45] In his polemic against Hellenistic historiography in *Against Apion*, Josephus claimed that Jewish loyalty to Torah was unconditional: "It is inborn in every Jew immediately from birth to consider these to be the teachings of God, to remain in them, and—if necessary—to die gladly for them."[46] He later added: "It should not occasion surprise if we face death for our laws more courageously than all others."[47] Such boasts were not uncommon. Philo made

---

44. Tacitus, *Agr.* 2.1; 45.1–2. Cf. also Suetonius, *Dom.* 10.3; Pliny, *Ep.* 1.5.2; Cassius Dio 67.13.2.

45. For later rabbinic stories see Gottfried Reeg, *Die Geschichte von den Zehn Märtyrern: Synoptische Edition mit Übersetzung und Einleitung*, TSAJ 10 (Tübingen: Mohr Siebeck, 1985).

46. Josephus, *Ag. Ap.* 1.42.

47. Josephus, *Ag. Ap.* 2.234; see also 232–35.

similar claims at an earlier date.[48] Nor were these claims without any basis: there were Jews who were willing to die for the law.

Jewish Martyrologies. Modern scholars have debated whether we should call such stories martyrdoms. The meaning appears to be a Christian invention.[49] Although ancient sources do not use *martys* (μάρτυς and its cognates) in the technical sense of martyr in reference to these accounts, the form and function of the texts are so similar to later Christian martyrologies that we should consider them to belong to the same genre.[50] A number of scholars have attempted to define a martyrdom by specifying its constituent features. A particularly detailed analysis is that of Ulrich Kellermann who identified eight characteristics of martyrdoms: a confrontation between Hellenism and Judaism, the religious policy of a foreign state toward devout Jews, the readiness of devout Jews to die for the Torah and their ancestral laws, the use of torture, the martyrs' explanation of their own deaths, a dialogue between the martyrs and their torturer, the death of the martyrs, and their postmortem

48. Philo, *Flacc.* 117; *Legat.* 210. Cf. also *Prob.* 22, 27, 88–91.

49. The first attested use is Mart. Pol. 1.1; 2.1; 14.2. For details see Gerd Buschmann, *Martyrium Polycarpi—Eine formkritische Studie: Beitrag zur Frage nach der Entstehung der Gattung Märtyerakte*, BZNW 70 (Berlin: de Gruyter, 1994), 136–41. See also the treatment of Candida Moss, *Ancient Christian Martyrdom: Diverse Practices, Theologies, and Traditions*, AYBRL (New Haven: Yale University Press, 2012), who has challenged the traditional understanding of martyrdom in the early centuries by arguing that it was more diverse.

50. One aspect of the debate is whether Jewish martyrologies influenced early Christian martyrologies. An important example of someone who denies the connection is Glen W. Bowersock, *Martyrdom and Rome* (Cambridge: Cambridge University Press, 1995), 1–21, esp. 9–13, and 77–81. Bowersock argues that the stories of the Maccabean martyrs arose in the second half of the first century CE, at the same time as the earliest Christian martyr stories. One of the most important representatives of the opposing view is Jan Willem van Henten, "The Martyrs as Heroes of the Christian People: Some Remarks on the Continuity of Jewish and Christian Martyrology, with Pagan Analogies," in *Martyrium in Multidisciplinary Perspective: Memorial Louis Reekmans*, ed. Mathijs Lamberigts and Peter van Deun (Leuven: Leuven University Press, 1995), 304–22, who provides an extensive bibliography. More recently Tessa Rajak, "The Fourth Book of Maccabees in a Multi-Cultural City," in *Jewish and Christian Communal Identities in the Roman World*, ed. Tessa Rajak, Ancient Judaism and Early Christianity 94 (Leiden: Brill 2016), 134–50, has argued that while there is no evidence for a Jewish cult that venerated the Maccabean martyrs, there was a Jewish tradition of honoring them as 4 Macc demonstrates. She dates 4 Macc to the late first century CE–mid-second century CE. There is no doubt about the Christian celebration of the Maccabean heroes. See Jennifer Wright Kunst, "'Who Were the Maccabees?': The Maccabean Martyrs and Performances on Christian Difference," in *Martyrdom: Canonisation, Contestation and Afterlives*, ed. Ihaab Saloul and Jan Willem van Henten (Amsterdam: Amsterdam University Press, 2020), 79–104.

acceptance by God.[51] Jan Willem van Henten and Friedrich Avemarie revised Kellermann's construct by collapsing it into five motifs: the enactment of oppressive measures by the authorities, the conflict that develops as a result of enforcement, the decision to die, the declaration of the decision during an examination that is sometimes accompanied by torture, and the execution. They distinguish among noble deaths in pagan contexts, stories of Jews and Christians who remain faithful to God when threatened but are delivered or commit heroic suicides in military contexts, and the violent deaths of prophets who are executed by their own people. I will follow van Henten's and Avemarie's construct of a martyr in what follows.[52] It has the merit of providing a narrow enough framework for careful analysis and yet is broad enough to include texts that share more similarities than dissimilarities.

The prototypes for Jewish martyrologies are the stories of Eleazar (2 Macc 6:18-31) and the seven brothers and their mother (2 Macc 7:1-42).[53] All five elements are present in each story in 2 Maccabees. Antiochus IV Epiphanes passed legislation that forbade Jewish observances (2 Macc 6:1-7). This set off a conflict (6:9) in which Eleazar (6:18-20) and the seven brothers and their mother resolved to maintain loyalty to the law (7:1-2). All made confessions during torture and were slain (6:21-31; 7:3-41). These stories with all of the same elements are expanded in the much later 4 Maccabees.

Socrates as a Model. Although these stories are ostensibly about the struggle of Judaism with Hellenism, they embrace Hellenism at various levels. Most importantly, they use Socrates as a model for the noble death. This is especially evident in the case of Eleazar in 2 Macc 6:18-31 and 4 Macc 5:1-7:23.[54]

51. Ulrich Kellermann, "Das Danielbuch und die Märtyrertheologie der Auferstehung," in *Die Entstehung der jüdischen Martyrologie*, ed. Jan Willem van Henten et al., StPB 38 (Leiden: Brill, 1989), 51-75, esp. 54-55. He lists fifty-one motifs on pp. 71-75. Cf. also the very helpful essay of Tessa Rajak, "Dying for the Law: The Martyr's Portrait in Jewish-Greek Literature," in *Portraits: Biographical Representation in the Greek and Latin Literature of the Roman Empire*, ed. Mark J. Edwards and Simon Swain (Oxford: Clarendon, 1997), 39-67, esp. 53-58, where she lists six archetypes.

52. Jan Willem van Henten and Friedrich Avemarie, *Martyrdom and Noble Death: Selected Texts from Graeco-Roman, Jewish and Christian Antiquity* (London: Routledge, 2002), 1-8, esp. 4-6.

53. Ulrich Kellermann, *Auferstanden in den Himmel: 2 Makkabäer 7 und die Auferstehung der Märtyrer* (Stuttgarter Bibelstudien 95; Stuttgart: Katholisches Bibelwerk, 1979), 35-53, esp. 38-40, argues that 2 Macc 7 is the "Urbild."

54. A similar case, though not as strong, could also be made for the mother and her seven sons (2 Macc 7:1-42 and 4 Macc 8:1-18:24). On the mother see Robin Darling Young, "The 'Woman with the Soul of Abraham': Traditions about the Mother of the Maccabean Martyrs,"

The epitomizer of Jason of Cyrene developed a number of parallels between Eleazar and Socrates.[55] So, for example, Eleazar refused to deliver himself by substituting his own meat for that of the king, just as Socrates refused to listen to his friends who tried to get him to go into exile.[56] In each case the suggestion of escape was a galling proposal since at their advanced ages it would have constituted a repudiation of their lives.[57] Throughout the ordeal, Eleazar displayed the same level of calm courage that Socrates had. Finally, the deaths of both served as examples to later generations.[58]

The author of 4 Maccabees expanded this narrative in numerous ways. The most important for our consideration is that the philosophical component received greater attention. Besides highlighting some of the same motifs that appear in 2 Maccabees—especially the advanced age of Eleazar, the possibility of escape, and the exemplary nature of his death—4 Maccabees openly describes Eleazar as a philosopher and his religion as a philosophy.[59] The point of the story is captured in the final editorial comment: "For who can practice philosophy according to the entire rule of philosophy, have faith in God, and know that it is a blessing to endure every distress for the sake of virtue, and not conquer the emotions as a result of piety? For only the wise and courageous person is master of human emotions" (4 Macc 7:21–23).[60]

---

in *"Women Like This": New Perspectives on Jewish Women in the Graeco-Roman World*, ed. Amy-Jill Levine, EJL 1 (Atlanta: Scholars Press, 1991), 67–81, who points out the indebtedness to philosophy but does not call attention to the tradition that we are considering.

55. Others who argue for Eleazar-Socrates parallels include Johannes Geffcken, "Die christlichen Martyrien," *Hermes* 45 (1910): 500–501; Kellermann, *Auferstanden in den Himmel*, 46–50, 51–52; H. S. Versnel, "'Quid Athenis et Hierosolymis?' Bemerkungen über die Herkunft von Aspekten des 'Effective Death,'" in *Die Entstehung der jüdischen Martyrologie*, 178–81, esp. 180–81; Jonathan A. Goldstein, *II Maccabees*, AB 41A (Garden City, NY: Doubleday, 1983), 285; Collins, "Genre of the Passion Narrative," 5–11; Jan Willem van Henten, *The Maccabean Martyrs as Saviours of the Jewish People: A Study of 2 and 4 Maccabees*, JSJSup 57 (Leiden: Brill, 1997), 270–94 and 301, esp. 272–78; and Rajak, "Dying for the Law," 178–81, esp. 181.

56. 2 Macc 6:21–23; Plato, *Crito*.

57. 2 Macc 6:24; Plato, *Apol.* 17d. Eleazar's age is given a prominence in 2 Maccabees that Socrates's age is not in the *Apology*. Rajak, "Dying for the Law," 181, astutely pointed out the connection between their refusals to accede to their friends' requests and their ages.

58. 2 Macc 6:31 and the tradition around Socrates.

59. 4 Macc uses several cognates: "to practice philosophy" (φιλοσοφεῖν in 5:7, 11; 7:21), "philosophy" (φιλοσοφία in 5:11, 22; 7:9, 21), and "philosopher" (φιλόσοφος in 5:35; 7:7).

60. In addition to the bibliography cited for 2 Maccabees, see Moses Hadas, *The Third and Fourth Books of Maccabees*, Jewish Apocryphal Literature (New York: Dropsie College for Hebrew and Cognate Learning, 1953; repr., New York: Ktav, 1976), 115–18 and Clara K.

Like Tacitus, the Jewish writers used the tradition, but not explicitly. They did not openly refer to Socrates or use Platonic language. They chose instead to sketch the picture of Jewish martyrs in shades that remind the reader of the portrait of Socrates. They wanted their readers to see that Jewish martyrs were people of principle just like the great Athenian who had died unjustly.

The Death of Jesus in the Third Gospel

We are now prepared to examine the portrait of Jesus in Luke's passion narrative. The passion narratives of the Gospels are complex literary units. Their origin, models, development, and interrelationships are all the subject of significant debates.[61] Several features of the Lukan passion narrative require preliminary comment.[62] First, the Lukan passion narrative is so different than Mark that the relationship between the two has been a point of extended discussion.[63] If we consider Luke's use of Q and Mark as a gauge, it is likely that he had access to ma-

---

Reggiani, *4 Maccabei*, Commentario, storico ed esegetico all' antico e al Nuovo Testamento, Supplementi 1 (Genova: Marietti, 1992), 39.

61. For a bibliography on the passion narratives see David E. Garland, *One Hundred Years of Study on the Passion Narratives*, National Association of Baptist Professors of Religion Bibliographic Series 3 (Macon, GA: Mercer University Press, 1989). Though dated, the most important work remains Raymond Brown, *The Death of the Messiah: From Gethsemane to the Grave (A Commentary on the Passion Narratives in the Four Gospels)*, 2 vols., ABRL (New York: Doubleday, 1994).

62. On the Lukan passion narrative see Garland, *One Hundred Years of Study on the Passion Narratives*, 27–30. See also John T. Carroll and Joel B. Green, *The Death of Jesus in Early Christianity* (Peabody: Hendrickson, 1995), 60–81; Dennis D. Sylva, ed., *Reimaging the Death of the Lukan Jesus*, BBB 73 (Frankfurt am Main: Anton Hain, 1990); and Benedetto Prete, *La passione e la morte di Gesù nel racconto di Luca*, 2 vols., Studi biblici 112 (Brescia: Paideia Editrice, 1996).

63. The four major views within the two source hypothesis and their most significant supporters are: Luke followed a different written source (Vincent Taylor, *The Passion Narrative of St. Luke: A Critical and Historical Examination*, SNTSMS 19 [Cambridge: Cambridge University Press, 1972] and Étienne Trocmé, *The Passion as Liturgy: A Study in the Origin of the Passion Narratives in the Four Gospels* [London: SCM, 1983]); Luke employed both Mark and another written source (Joel B. Green, *The Death of Jesus: Tradition and Interpretation in the Passion Narrative*, WUNT 2.33 [Tübingen: Mohr Siebeck, 1988] and François Bovon, "Le récit lucanien de la passion de Jésus (Lu 22–23)," in *The Synoptic Gospels: Source Criticism and the New Literary Criticism*, ed. Camille Focant, BETL 110 [Leuven: Leuven University Press, 1993], 393–423); Luke rewrote Mark on the basis of his own concerns and various oral traditions that he knew (Marion L. Soards, *The Passion according to Luke: The Special Material of Luke 22*, JSNTSup 14 [Sheffield: Sheffield Academic, 1987] and Brown, *Death of*

terial besides Mark. Fortunately, our purposes do not require the reconstruction of a source. It is enough to note the differences between Mark and Luke without speculating about the presence or absence of an additional source(s). Even if Luke had a different source for the sections that we will examine, his preference for that source over against Mark is still evidence of his understanding of Jesus's death.[64] Second, the third evangelist reshaped the traditions that he inherited by self-consciously situating them in the context of the larger Greco-Roman world. While this was for the benefit of insiders, it required a degree of acculturation that is not present in Mark. As we will see, the differences between the Markan and Lukan passion traditions are so stark that the specific model was different.[65] At minimum we can say that Luke was not satisfied with what he read in Mark. Third, as early as Karl Ludwig Schmidt and Martin Dibelius, scholars have suggested that Luke used the model of a Jewish martyr for his passion narrative.[66]

---

the Messiah, 1:64–67, 75); and Luke heavily redacted Mark (Frank J. Matera, "The Death of Jesus according to Luke: A Question of Sources," *CBQ* 47 [1985]: 469–85).

64. E.g., Bovon, "Le récit lucanien de la passion de Jésus," 413–15, argues that Luke had a different source for the scenes in Gethsemane and the cross.

65. Detlev Dormeyer, *Die Passion Jesu als Verhaltensmodell: Literarische und theologische Analyse der Traditions- und Redaktionsgeschichte der Markuspassion*, NTAbh 11 (Münster: Aschendorff, 1974), 238–58 and Detlev Dormeyer, *The New Testament among the Writings of Antiquity*, trans. Rosemarie Kossov (Sheffield: Sheffield Academic, 1998), 191–96, esp. 192, argued that the pre-Markan passion narrative was cast as "the acts of a Christian martyr." Adela Y. Collins, "From Noble Death to Crucified Messiah," *NTS* 40 (1994): 481–503, esp. 501, argued that both the pre-Markan and Markan passion narratives were sui generis and were the result of "the intractable and appalling facts of the end of Jesus' life . . . illuminated by a new use of Scripture." I am inclined to follow Collins.

66. Karl L. Schmidt, "Die literarische Eigenart der Leidensgeschichte Jesu," *Die Christliche Welt* 32 (1918): 114–16; repr. in *Redaktion und Theologie des Passionsberichtes nach den Synoptikern*, ed. M. Limbeck, Wege der Forschung 481 (Darmstadt: Wissenschaftliche Buchgesellschaft, 1981), 17–20; and Karl L. Schmidt, *Der Rahmen der Geschichte Jesu: Literarkritische Untersuchungen zur ältesten Jesusüberlieferung* (Berlin: Trowitsche und Sohn, 1919; repr., Darmstadt: Wissenschaftliche Buchgesellschaft, 1964), 303–6, only made a general comparison between the passion narrative and martyrologies; he did not compare the passion narrative of Luke-Acts to Jewish martyrologies. Martin Dibelius, *From Tradition to Gospel* (New York: Scribner's Sons, n.d.), 178–217, esp. 199–204, made the comparison explicit. His student, Hans-Werner Surkau, *Martyrien in jüdischer und frühchristlicher Zeit*, FRLANT 36 (Göttingen: Vandenhoeck & Ruprecht, 1938), esp. 90–100, attempted to work out this thesis in detail. For modern representatives see Klaus Berger, "Hellenistische Gattungen im Neuen Testament," *ANRW* 25.2:1248–59, who argued that the *exitus illustrium virorum* tradition stood closest to the passion narratives of the Gospels (pp. 1257–59); and Brian E. Beck, "'Imitatio Christi' and the Lucan Passion Narrative," in *Suffering and Martyrdom in the New Testament: Studies Presented to G. M. Styler by the Cambridge New Testament*

If we use van Henten's and Avemarie's model above, there is a great deal to be said for this view. The basic difference is that there were no decrees that forbade Jesus to practice his understanding of Judaism.[67] Whether this disqualifies the classification of the passion narrative as a martyrology depends on the extent to which one is willing to extend the genre or recognizes conceptual integration within the tradition. It is fair to say that Jewish martyrologies influenced the writing of the passion narrative, even if there are variations.

With these stipulations in mind, we can now ask whether the Socratic traditions that influenced *teleutai, exitus illustrium virorum,* and Jewish martyrological traditions also influenced the Lukan passion narrative. I am convinced that they did.[68] I would like to examine three major motifs.

The Calmness of Jesus. The first and most pronounced of these is the calmness with which Jesus faced death in the Third Gospel. The third evangelist consistently eliminated every hint of anxiety on the part of Jesus. This is most evident in the redaction of two major scenes: Gethsemane and the crucifixion.

The first scene in which Jesus demonstrated calmness is Gethsemane. The evangelist has so extensively rewritten the Markan Gethsemane scene that it has a new orientation.[69] The redaction is clear in several ways. The testing of Jesus in Mark has become the testing of the disciples in Luke (Mark 14:32–42 // Luke 22:39–46 [see synopsis 7.1 in the appendix]). Instead of Mark's "Stay here while I pray," Luke's Jesus tells the disciples: "Pray that you are not put to the test" (Mark 14:32 // Luke 22:40). This is picked up again when Luke transfers

---

Seminar, ed. William Horbury and Brian McNeil (Cambridge: Cambridge University Press, 1981), 28–47.

67. For a critique of the view that Jesus's death is presented as a martyr's death see Graham N. Stanton, *Jesus of Nazareth in New Testament Preaching,* SNTSMS 27 (Cambridge: Cambridge University Press, 1974), 32–36, and Brian J. Tabb, "Is the Lucan Jesus a 'Martyr'? A Critical Assessment of a Scholarly Consensus," *CBQ* 77 (2015): 280–301, who argues that Jesus's death is cast in the tradition of the persecuted "righteous one" of Wis 2–3 (based primarily on the use of δίκαιος) and the violent death of the prophets since—in Tabb's view—he was killed by his own people, a problematic assumption.

68. See also John S. Kloppenborg, "'Exitus clari viri': The Death of Jesus in Luke," *TJT* 8 (1992): 106–20, who argues the case on three grounds: the farewell discourse of Jesus, the presence of the disciples throughout the narrative, and the fearless demeanor of Jesus. For a more general assessment see Paul W. Gooch, *Reflections on Jesus and Socrates: Word and Silence* (New Haven: Yale University Press, 1996), esp. 109–60.

69. The most insightful analysis of this pericope is that of Jerome H. Neyrey, "The Absence of Jesus' Emotions: The Lucan Redaction of Lk. 22,39–46," *Bib* 61 (1980): 153–71 and Jerome H. Neyrey, *The Passion according to Luke: A Redaction Study of Luke's Soteriology* (New York: Paulist, 1985), 49–68.

the distress of the Markan Jesus to the disciples. The third evangelist did this by omitting the statement "My soul is deeply distressed (περίλυπος), even to the point of death" (Mark 14:34), and expanding the straightforward description "and he found them sleeping" (Mark 14:37) to incorporate the element of distress in the disciples: "He found them sleeping out of distress (ἀπὸ τῆς λύπης)" (Luke 22:45). What Mark attributes to Jesus, Luke ascribes to the disciples.

Luke has also dropped three Markan statements that suggest Jesus struggled: the editorial note "and he began to be disturbed and agitated" (Mark 14:33); the following statement that we have just cited, "My soul is distressed, even to the point of death" (Mark 14:34); and the first part of the prayer, "If it is possible, let this hour pass from me" (Mark 14:35). These omissions indicate that the evangelist was worried that someone might react as Celsus later did. The same concern probably governed the shift in Jesus's posture at prayer. Mark says: "He fell on the ground and prayed," which Luke rewrote: "He got down on his knees and prayed" (Mark 14:35 // Luke 22:41). Luke replaced what he feared some might consider a sign of collapse with a posture of piety.[70]

The only possible exception to this pattern is the famous textual *crux interpretum* of the angel strengthening Jesus in Luke 22:43-44. The manuscript evidence is divided: Western witnesses include the statement, while Alexandrian witnesses tend to exclude it. The decisive factor for me is that the statement runs counter to the distinct pattern that we have just observed. If the evangelist penned the episode, he undid what he had just so painstakingly accomplished. Jerry Neyrey has made the intriguing suggestion that the "agony" (ἀγωνία) is soteriological combat not fear.[71] However, the description of the extreme physical stress Jesus experienced runs counter to his otherwise placid composure in the narrative. It is worth noting that—as far as I can tell—early Christian authors all accepted the statement as a description of anxiety, even those who argued that Jesus did not fear death for himself. The best explanation is that a second-century scribe included it to accentuate Jesus's humanity over against those who might have used the absence of Jesus's emotions in this text to call his humanity into question.[72]

---

70. The phrase "he got down on his knees" (θεὶς τὰ γόνατα) occurs four times in Acts (7:60; 9:40; 20:36; 21:5).

71. Neyrey, *Passion according to Luke*, 55-65, 165-79. He takes it as "victorious struggle" (p. 58). He relates it to the "testing" (πειρασμός) of 4:1-13 on the basis of Adam-Christ typology. Following Conzelmann, he argues that 4:13 is picked up by 22:3, 31.

72. The best analysis is Bart D. Ehrman and Mark A. Plunkett, "The Angel and the Agony: The Textual Problem of Luke 22:43-44," *CBQ* 45 (1983): 401-16. For a defense of the text see Tabb, "Is the Lucan Jesus a 'Martyr'?," 286n34, with bibliography. In a significant forthcoming article, Claire Clivaz has argued that the text was authentic but omitted by

The second scene that the evangelist rewrote to underscore Jesus's calmness is the cross. The same motive that led to the rewriting of the Gethsemane scene led to the replacement of the Markan cry of dereliction on the cross with the affirmation of dedication in Luke (Mark 15:34-37 // Luke 23:44-46 [see synopsis 7.2 in the appendix]). The Second Gospel cites Ps 22:2: ελωι ελωι λεμα σαβαχθανι, which the evangelist translated as "My God, My God, why have you abandoned me?" (Mark 15:34). Luke omitted not only the citation but the entire episode it provoked. In place of Mark's plaintive cry, he substituted Ps 31:6: "Father, into your hands I entrust my spirit" (Luke 23:46). Why change psalms? One possibility is that Luke avoided Aramaic words and speculation about a future role for Elijah in his Gospel.[73] While this is true, it only explains the omission of the Aramaic not the substitution of a psalm of confidence for a lament. This is best explained by the consistent elision of any hint of an emotional struggle within Jesus.

Why did the Third Gospel omit the Markan struggle? There are several possibilities. Luke has removed emotional elements attributed to Jesus in Mark elsewhere in the gospel as well; this is part of a larger pattern.[74] There are, however, reasons for associating the elimination of the emotions in the passion narrative with the Socratic tradition. In the *Phaedo* Plato has Socrates say to Simmias of Thebes: "The true practitioners of philosophy practice dying and death is less fearful to them than for any others."[75] True to his own words, Socrates became the model of fearlessness in the face of death.[76] Seneca summarized the view of later generations when he wrote: "These (the imprisonment and the poison) changed Socrates's soul so little that they did not even change his expression."[77] For this reason the Stoic philosopher claimed that Socrates "will show you how to die if it is necessary."[78]

Jewish Christians in the early second century. See "Luke 22:43-44 and Judeo-Christian Memories," *REJ* (forthcoming).

73. E.g., Mark 9:11-13 is omitted. Luke consistently drops Mark's Aramaic terms: Mark 3:17 // Luke 6:14 (Βοανηργές); Mark 5:41 // Luke 8:54 (ταλιθα κουμ); Mark 7:11 (κορβᾶν) and 7:34 (εφφαθα) that are both part of the Big Omission of Mark 6:45–8:26 in Luke; Mark 11:9-10 // Luke 19:38 (ὡσαννά); Mark 14:36 // Luke 22:42 (αββα); Mark 15:22 // Luke 23:33 (Γολγοθᾶν); and Mark 15:34 // Luke 23:46 (discussed in the text). The author of Luke-Acts does add an Aramaic term in Acts 1:19 (᾿Ακελδαμάχ).

74. E.g., Mark 1:41, 43 // Luke 5:13, 14, where Luke omits Mark's "had compassion" (σπλαγχνισθείς) and "became stern" (ἐμβριμησάμενος).

75. Plato, *Phaed.* 67e.

76. E.g., Plato, *Apol.* 38d–e; *Phaed.* 68c–d, 117c; cf. also 83e–84b, 114d–115a; and Xenophon, *Apol.* 33.

77. Seneca, *Ep.* 104.28.

78. Seneca, *Ep.* 104.21.

The bases for Socrates's composure were his recognition that the time had come—he had his sign.[79] And, he had his belief in the immortality of the soul.[80] Similarly in Luke, Jesus knew that his time had come. This is obvious as early as 9:51 when he set out for Jerusalem. As was the case for Socrates, so for Jesus death was divinely determined.[81] Socrates told Crito: "If this is the gods' will, let it be."[82] Jesus prayed: "Do not let my will but your will be done."[83] As Socrates's belief in the immortality of the soul negated the sting of his verdict, so the resurrection of Jesus served as a vindication of his death sentence.[84] Although a belief in the immortality of the soul and a belief in the resurrection of a body are not identical, the way in which each belief functions in the texts is. The final words of each make this point strikingly clear. Socrates gave instructions to Crito: "We owe a cock to Asclepius. Pay it and do not forget."[85] By these instructions Socrates offered a thank offering to the god of healing just as any pious Greek who had recovered from an illness would have. He thus disproved the charges against him as he entered immortality. Jesus's words have a similar thrust: "Father, into your hands I commit my spirit" (Luke 23:46). As a pious Jew, he trusted God who would yet give him life. The final words show that both faced death serenely with the confidence that it was not the end.[86]

An Innocent Man. Their piety suggests another important aspect of their deaths: they were both innocent of the crimes that led to their executions. Luke made his point by altering the centurion's confession from "Truly this man was God's Son" (Mark 15:39) to "Certainly this man was innocent (δίκαιος)" (Luke 23:47; see synopsis 7.3). While it is possible to debate whether δίκαιος means "just" as this is understood against the background of the suffering of

---

79. Plato, *Apol.* 40a–c, 41d; *Phaed.* 62c; Xenophon, *Apol.* 49, cf. 22. Plato emphasized that it was God's will for Socrates to die, *Crito* 43b, 54e. On the importance of the sign in early Christian martyrologies, see Droge and Tabor, *Noble Death*, 156.

80. E.g., Plato, *Phaed.* 63b–c, 63e–64a, 69d–e, 91b, 95b–c.

81. E.g., Luke 24:25–26, 45–46; Acts 2:23; 3:18; 4:26; 13:27–29; 17:3; 26:23.

82. Plato, *Crito* 43d. Epictetus cited this in *Diatr.* 1.4.24.

83. Luke 22:42.

84. Acts 2:23–24; 3:14–15; 4:10; 5:30; 10:39–40; 13:27–31.

85. Plato, *Phaed.* 118.

86. Doohee Lee, *Luke-Acts and "Tragic History": Communicating Gospel with the World*, WUNT 2.346 (Tübingen: Mohr Siebeck, 2013), argues that Luke-Acts incorporates a tragic style that was common among some historians, an argument that I find difficult to accept. More particularly, he notes the presence of strong emotional expression as a constituent feature of this style and, just as correctly, does not include the death of Jesus as an example.

the innocent just person in Jewish tradition,[87] or has specific Christological significance,[88] or simply means "innocent," it is hard to deny that it includes the concept of "innocence."[89] Several contextual signals require this. Luke expanded Mark's account of Jesus's trial before Pilate to include three declarations of Jesus's innocence (Luke 23:4, 14–15, 22). The second of these includes a confirmation by Herod Antipas who concurred in Jesus's innocence (Luke 23:15). Luke also expanded the Markan allusion to the taunting of Jesus by those who were crucified with him (Mark 15:32) by supplying the exchange between the criminals and Jesus: one repeated the taunts hurled by the high priests and soldiers; the other rebuked him, "Do you not fear God since you are suffering the same penalty? We suffer this justly (δικαίως), for we are receiving what our actions deserve. But he has done nothing out of place" (Luke 23:40–41). The repeated emphasis on Jesus's innocence and the use of the adverb "justly" (δικαίως) by the criminal makes it difficult to avoid the conclusion that the centurion declared Jesus innocent.

Why? Clearly, the Third Gospel is concerned with the political implications of Jesus's execution. There may, however, be another factor at work. The *Phaedo* ends with these words: "Such was the end, O Echechrates, of our companion who was, as we may say, of all those with whom we have had experience, the best and also the wisest and most upright (δικαιότατος)."[90] The final word of the *Phaedo* played a pivotal role in one of the most famous *chreiai* that circulated about Socrates's death. In the version that Xenophon preserved, Apollodorus exclaimed that it hurt him to see Socrates executed unjustly (ἀδίκως). Socrates responded: "Dearest Apollodorus, would you prefer to see me die justly or unjustly (δικαίως ἢ ἀδίκως)?"[91] This *chreia* became a standard *topos* in rhetorical exercises: it is, for example part of the *Progymnasmata* of

---

87. So Beck, "'*Imitatio Christi*' and the Lucan Passion Narrative," 40–46; Robert J. Karris, *Luke: Artist and Theologian. Luke's Passion Account as Literature*, Theological Inquiries (New York: Paulist, 1985), 16–18, 79–119; and Tabb, "Is the Lucan Jesus a 'Martyr'?" 295–98, who associate this with Wis 1–5. I find the associations between the death of the just person in Wisdom of Solomon with Jesus to be greater in the Fourth Gospel than they are in the third. Death is the moment of glorification in both Wisdom of Solomon and John; it is an embarrassment in Luke.

88. Cf. Acts 3:14; 7:52; 22:14. Matera, "Death of Jesus according to Luke," 479–84, argues for a Christological reading of the text on the basis of the usage of δίκαιος elsewhere in Luke-Acts. He does not exclude the political reading of "innocent."

89. So also Carroll and Green, *Death of Jesus in Early Christianity*, 72–74, who provide additional bibliography.

90. Plato, *Phaed.* 118; cf. also *Apol.* 17c.

91. Xenophon, *Apol.* 28.

Theon.[92] It was widely known in two different forms. Seneca, Theon, and John Chrysostom all attest a form in which a student of Socrates makes the initial statement.[93] Valerius Maximus, Diogenes Laertius, and Tertullian attest a form in which Xanthippe, Socrates's wife, provokes the aphorism.[94] The extent of this attestation suggests that it was a story that any educated person in antiquity would have known.[95] Intriguingly, it played a role in a later Christian martyrology that pointed out the similarity of the unjust sentences of Socrates and of Jesus.[96] For these reasons I think that many first-century Christians would have heard an echo of Socrates's death in the confession of the centurion.

A Paradigm. How did these allusions function? We have seen that in the Greco-Roman and Jewish traditions, the deaths of Socrates and those who imitated him took on a paradigmatic quality. Does Jesus's death function similarly? The first hint comes in the passion story. As Luke retold the story of Simon carrying Jesus's cross, he added an interesting detail: he tells us that Simon was "behind Jesus" (ὄπισθεν τοῦ ᾽Ιησοῦ).[97] While this could be a matter of narrative color, it fits well with the Lukan view of discipleship: "If anyone wants to come after me (ὀπίσω μου), let him deny himself and take up his cross daily and follow me;" and again, "Whoever does not carry his own cross and come after me (ὀπίσω μου), cannot be my disciple."[98] Simon is Jesus's disciple who followed the Lord with a cross.

This is not the only suggestion that Jesus's death is a model. It is well known that the third evangelist used architectonic parallels between the Gospel and Acts. In particular, virtually all recognize the similarities between Jesus and Stephen.[99] The relationship is evident in both the transfer of a number of elements from the passion of Jesus in Mark to the martyrdom of Stephen in Acts

---

92. Ronald F. Hock and Edward N. O'Neil, *The Chreia in Ancient Rhetoric*, vol. 1: *The Progymnasmata*, SBLTT 27 (Atlanta: Scholars Press, 1986), 90–91, 337.

93. Seneca, *Constant.* 7.3; Theon (Hock and O'Neil, *Chreia*, 90–91, 337); John Chrysostom, *Hom. Act.* 14 (PG 60:119–20).

94. Valerius Maximus 7.2 Ext. 1; Diogenes Laertius 2.35; Tertullian, *An.* 1. Cf. also Leo Sternbach, *Gnomologium Vaticanum (e codice Vaticano graeco 743)*, Texte und Kommentare 2 (Berlin: de Gruyter, 1963), 177n478.

95. Cf. also Teles 3.93–96; Aulus Gellius 12.9.6; and Arnobius, *Against the Heathen* 40.

96. The Martyrdom of Apollonius 41 (Musurillo, *Acts of the Christian Martyrs*, 100–101).

97. Mark 15:21 // Luke 23:26.

98. Luke 9:23; 14:27. Surkau, *Martyrien in jüdischer und frühchristlicher Zeit*, 95–96, pointed this out years ago.

99. One of the more important treatments of these parallels that supplies a bibliography is David P. Moessner, "'The Christ Must Suffer': New Light on the Jesus, Stephen, Paul Parallels in Luke-Acts," *NovT* 28 (1986): 220–56.

(see chapter 5) and in the adaptation of Jesus's final words as Stephen's last cry, "Lord Jesus, receive my spirit."[100] The use of gospel material in the account of Stephen suggests that Jesus's death was paradigmatic for early Christians.

There is one other significant twist to this line of argumentation. On two different occasions, those who followed Jesus explicitly remind us of the Socratic tradition. The first occurrence takes place when the apostles were arrested in Jerusalem. They defied the Sanhedrin with a statement that reminds us of Socrates: "We must obey God rather than humans (πειθαρχεῖν δεῖ θεῷ μᾶλλον ἢ ἀνθρώποις)."[101] According to Plato, Socrates said to the Athenians: "I will be obedient to god rather than to you (πείσομαι δὲ μᾶλλον τῷ ὑμῖν)." The second occurrence happens—appropriately enough—when Paul came to Athens. The Athenians charged: "He seems to be a proclaimer of strange divinities (ξένων δαιμονίων)" (Acts 17:18). I find it impossible not to think of one of the two charges that the Athenians leveled against Socrates. According to Plato's formulation of the charge, Socrates was accused of introducing "new and different divinities" (ἕτερα δὲ δαιμόνια καινά)."[102] If the apostles who followed Jesus were cast in the mold of Socrates, should we be surprised to discover that their paradigm had been as well? The evangelist was more direct in the allusions in Acts than in the Gospel, but the allusions are present in both.

CONCLUSIONS

How did the third evangelist come to know the traditions about Socrates's death? There are numerous possibilities. He could have known them directly since he paraphrased the *Apology*. On the other hand, he could have learned about the tradition through basic rhetorical training since the *chreia* about whether Socrates died justly or unjustly was in the handbooks. Or he could have known it indirectly through Jewish martyrologies. The widespread nature of the

---

100. For the final cry see Luke 23:46 and Acts 7:59.

101. Plato, *Apol.* 29d and Acts 5:29. Cf. also Acts 4:19-20: "If it is just before God to listen to you rather than God, you must judge; for we are not able to refrain from saying what we have seen and heard" (εἰ δίκαιόν ἐστιν ἐνώπιον τοῦ θεοῦ ὑμῶν ἀκούειν μᾶλλον ἢ τοῦ θεοῦ, κρίνατε· οὐ δυνάμεθα γὰρ ἡμεῖς ἃ εἴδαμεν καὶ ἠκούσαμεν μὴ λαλεῖν).

102. Plato, *Euthyphr.* 3b; *Apol.* 24b, 26b. Cf. also Xenophon, *Mem.* 1.1.1; Diogenes Laertius 2.40. For the influence of Socrates as a paradigm for Paul see Loveday C. A. Alexander, "Acts and Ancient Intellectual Biography," in *The Book of Acts in Its Ancient Literary Setting*, ed. Bruce W. Winter and Andrew C. Clarke; vol. 1 of *The Book of Acts in Its First Century Setting*, ed. Bruce W. Winter (Grand Rapids: Eerdmans; Paternoster: Carlisle, 1993), 56-63.

tradition makes it both impossible and unnecessary to pinpoint the source of knowledge for the evangelist. The allusions in the text suggest that he knew what most moderately well-educated people in the Greco-Roman world knew.

It is more interesting to ask why he used the tradition. We can answer by illustrating how the process worked in reverse. Later generations told the story of Socrates's life and death in ways that echoed the accounts of Jesus in the Gospels. One of the most famous examples is Erasmus's use of Gethsemane for Socrates's Athenian prison cell in his *Convivium religiosum*. After discussing the views of Cato (in Cicero) and Socrates (in Plato) on death, Erasmus has Chrysoglottus say: "I do not think that I have ever read among the pagans what is more fitting for a true Christian than what Socrates said to Crito shortly after drinking the hemlock." Erasmus then paraphrased Socrates's words in *Phaedo* 69d rather than his final statement in *Phaedo* 118: "Whether God will approve our works, I do not know. We have certainly tried very hard to please him. Nevertheless, I am hopeful that he will be pleased with our efforts." Why cite this earlier statement rather than the later one? Chrysoglottus explained: "He admittedly lacks confidence in his deeds, nevertheless because the will of his soul was eager to submit to the divine will he conceived a good hope. . . ." The words of Socrates's prayer echo those of Jesus in Gethsemane, who prayed: "Not my will, but let yours be done" (Luke 22:42).[103] Erasmus has used Jesus's prayer as a model for Socrates. Nephalius was so moved that he said: "Saint Socrates, pray for us" (*sancte Socratis, ora pro nobis*).[104] With this statement Erasmus has christened Socrates. Why? Christianity had become the dominant culture: the best way to win acceptance of an ancient Greek was to associate him with Christianity. The *imitatio Socratis* of the Greco-Roman world has become the *imitatio Christi* of the Christian world. This is what Erasmus did, and did so well that the line *sancte Socratis, ora pro nobis* is justly famous.[105]

I suggest that the author of the Third Gospel used the same procedure but with the roles reversed: the evangelist carefully reworked the death of Jesus

103. Cf. also Matt 26:42 // Mark 14:36.

104. Erasmus, *Convivium religiosum* verses 700–710 (*Opera omnia Desiderii Erasmi Roterodami*, ed. Jan H. Waszink et al. [Amsterdam: North Holland Publishing, 1972], 1.3:254). On the place of Socrates among the humanists see R. Marcel, "'Saint' Socrate Patron de l'Humanisme," *Revue internationale de philosophie* 5 (1951): 135–43.

105. On the figure of Socrates in Erasmus see Linda Gregorian Christian, "The Figure of Socrates in Erasmus' Works," *Sixteenth Century Journal* 3 (1972): 1–10 and Katy O'Brien Weintraub, "O Sancte Socrate, Ora pro Nobis: Erasmus on the Problem of Athens and Jerusalem," in *Cultural Visions: Essays in the History of Culture*, ed. Penny Schine Gold and Benjamin C. Sax, Internationale Forschungen zur Allgemeinen und Vergleichenden Literaturwissenschaft 41 (Amsterdam: Rodopi, 2000), 259–70.

at critical places to remind the hearer/reader of the paradigmatic martyr of his society, Socrates. Like the author of 2 Maccabees and Tacitus, the evangelist made the comparison implicitly not explicitly. Why? Several explanations are possible. It could have been a simple literary decision: the use of implicit allusion is more effective in some contexts than an explicit comparison; for example, Erasmus used it to good effect above. On the other hand, an explicit comparison would not have been consistent with the earlier explicit comparisons of Jesus to a prophet.[106] Again, the author, like Justin Martyr who qualified the comparison carefully a half a century later, may have been reticent because he wanted to claim more for Jesus than he would have been willing to claim for Socrates.[107] Finally, it is important to remember that the use of Socratic traditions is not exclusive; that is, the use of some allusions to Socrates does not exclude the use of other models as well. I think that Luke is closest to 2 Maccabees in his combination of a martyr who died like Socrates than to any of the other sources that we have canvassed. At the same time, there are other models that we have not considered, such as the just one (Acts 7:52). It would be a mistake to reduce the Lukan passion narrative to a single set of allusions. The text has several. I have only tried to point out one of the more important but neglected sets.

The allusions are important because they were made at critical points in the narrative. The echoes they reverberated softened the hard reality of the cross by associating it with a death that was viewed positively, the *mors Socratis*. I think that Celsus would have found it difficult to fault Luke's depiction. Had the critic only had Luke, he instead of Origen would have been reduced to silence on this point. This illustrates the *ars narrandi* of apologetic historians who used the traditions of the Greco-Roman world to make their story intelligible and acceptable within the the the framework of that larger culture.

APPENDIX

The Death of Jesus in Luke

Synopsis 7.1: Gethsemane

Mark 14:32–42
³²Καὶ ἔρχονται εἰς χωρίον

Luke 22:40–46
⁴⁰γενόμενος δὲ ἐπὶ τοῦ τόπου

106. E.g., Luke 4:24–27; 7:16; 9:8, 19; 24:19.
107. Justin Martyr, 2 *Apol.* 10 and 1 *Apol.* 5.

οὗ τὸ ὄνομα Γεθσημανὶ
καὶ λέγει τοῖς μαθηταῖς αὐτοῦ·
καθίσατε ὧδε ἕως προσεύξωμαι.

εἶπεν αὐτοῖς·
προσεύχεσθε
μὴ εἰσελθεῖν εἰς πειρασμόν.

³³καὶ παραλαμβάνει τὸν Πέτρον
καὶ [τὸν] Ἰάκωβον
καὶ [τὸν] Ἰωάννην μετ᾽ αὐτοῦ
καὶ ἤρξατο ἐκθαμβεῖσθαι
καὶ ἀδημονεῖν
³⁴καὶ λέγει αὐτοῖς·
περίλυπός ἐστιν ἡ ψυχή μου
ἕως θανάτου·
μείνατε ὧδε καὶ γρηγορεῖτε.

³⁵καὶ προελθὼν
μικρὸν
ἔπιπτεν ἐπὶ τῆς γῆς
καὶ προσηύχετο
ἵνα εἰ δυνατόν ἐστιν
παρέλθῃ
ἀπ᾽ αὐτοῦ ἡ ὥρα,
³⁶καὶ ἔλεγεν·
αββα ὁ πατήρ
πάντα δυνατά σοι·
παρένεγκε
τὸ ποτήρον τοῦτο ἀπ᾽ ἐμοῦ·
ἀλλ᾽ οὐ τί ἐγὼ θέλω
ἀλλὰ τί σύ.

⁴¹καὶ αὐτὸς ἀπεσπάσθη ἀπ᾽ αὐτῶν
ὡσεὶ λίθου βολὴν
καὶ θεὶς τὰ γόνατα
προσηύχετο ⁴²λέγων·

πάτερ,
εἰ βούλει
παρένεγκε
τοῦτο τὸ ποτήριον ἀπ᾽ ἐμοῦ·
πλὴν μὴ τὸ θέλημά μου
ἀλλὰ τὸ σὸν γινέσθω.¹⁰⁸

³⁷καὶ ἔρχεται
καὶ εὑρίσκει αὐτοὺς καθεύδοντας,

καὶ λέγει τῷ Πέτρῳ·
Σίμων, καθεύδεις;
οὐκ ἴσχυσας μίαν ὥραν γρηγορῆσαι;

⁴⁵καὶ ἀναστὰς ἀπὸ τῆς προσευχῆς
ἐλθὼν πρὸς τοὺς μαθητὰς
εὗρεν κοιμωμένους αὐτοὺς
ἀπὸ τῆς λύπης,
⁴⁶καὶ εἶπεν αὐτοῖς·
τί καθεύδετε;

108. I consider vv. 43–44 to be a second-century addition (see the discussion in the chapter): ⁴³ὤφθη δὲ αὐτῷ ἄγγελος ἀπ᾽ οὐρανοῦ ἐνισχύων αὐτόν. ⁴⁴καὶ γενόμενος ἐν ἀγωνίᾳ ἐκτενέστερον προσηύχετο· καὶ ἐγένετο ὁ ἱδρὼς αὐτοῦ ὡσεὶ θρόμβοι αἵματος καταβαίνοντες ἐπὶ τὴν γῆν.

³⁸γρηγορεῖτε καὶ προσεύχεσθε,
ἵνα μὴ ἔλθητε εἰς πειρασμόν·
τὸ μὲν πνεῦμα πρόθυμον
ἡ δὲ σάρξ ἀσθενής.
³⁹Καὶ πάλιν ἀπελθὼν
προσηύξατο τὸν αὐτὸν λόγον εἰπών.
⁴⁰καὶ πάλιν ἐλθὼν εὗρεν
αὐτοὺς καθεύδοντας,
ἦσαν γὰρ αὐτῶν
οἱ ὀφθλαμοὶ καταβαρυνόμενοι,
καὶ οὐκ ᾔδεισαν
τί ἀποκριθῶσιν αὐτῷ.
⁴¹Καὶ ἔρχεται τὸ τρίτον
καὶ λέγει αὐτοῖς·
καθεύδετε τὸ λοιπὸν
καὶ ἀναπαύεσθε·
ἀπέχει· ἦλθεν ἡ ὥρα,
ἰδοὺ παραδίδοται
ὁ υἱὸς τοῦ ἀνθρώπου
εἰς τὰς χεῖρας τῶν ἁμαρτωλῶν.
⁴²ἐγείρεσθε ἄγωμεν·
ἰδοὺ ὁ παραδιδούς με ἤγγικεν.

ἀναστάντες προσεύχεσθε,
ἵνα μὴ ἔλθητε εἰς πειρασμόν·

Synopsis 7.2: The Cross

Mark 15:33-37
³³Καὶ γενομένης ὥρας ἕκτης
σκότος ἐγένετο
ἐφ᾽ ὅλην τὴν γῆν
ἕως ὥρας ἐνάτης.
³⁴καὶ τῇ ἐνάτῃ ὥρᾳ

ἐβόησεν ὁ Ἰησοῦς φωνῇ μεγάλῃ·

ελωι ελωι λεμα σαβαχθανι;
ὅ ἐστιν μεθερμηνευόμενον·
ὁ θεός μου ὁ θεός μου,
εἰς τί ἐγκατέλιπές με;

Luke 23:44-46
⁴⁴Καὶ ἦν ἤδη ὡσεὶ ὥρα ἕκτη
καὶ σκότος ἐγένετο
ἐφ᾽ ὅλην τὴν γῆν
ἕως ὥρας ἐνάτης.
⁴⁵τοῦ ἡλίου ἐκλιπόντος,
ἐσχίσθη δὲ τὸ καταπέτασμα
τοῦ ναοῦ μέσον.
⁴⁶καὶ φωνήσας φωνῇ μεγάλῃ
ὁ Ἰησοῦς εἶπεν·

πάτερ, εἰς χεῖράς σου
παρατίθεμαι τὸ πνεῦμά μου.

³⁵καί τινες τῶν παρεστηκότων
ἀκούσαντες ἔλεγον·
ἴδε Ἠλίαν φωνεῖ.
³⁶δραμὼν δέ τις
[καὶ] γεμίσας σπόγγον ὄξους
περιθεὶς καλάμῳ
ἐπότιζεν αὐτὸν λέγων·
ἄφετε ἴδωμεν εἰ ἔρχεται Ἠλίας
καθελεῖν αὐτόν.
³⁷ὁ δὲ Ἰησοῆς ἀφεὶς φωνὴν μεγάλην   τοῦτο δὲ εἰπὼν
ἐξέπνευσεν.   ἐξέπνευσεν.

Synopsis 7.3: The Centurion's Confession

Mark 15:39   **Luke 23:47**
Ἰδὼν δὲ ὁ κεντυρίων ὁ παρεστηκὼς   Ἰδὼν δὲ ὁ ἑκατοντάρχης
ἐξ ἐναντίας αὐτοῦ
ὅτι οὕτως ἐξέπνευσεν   τὸ γενόμενον
εἶπεν·   ἐδόξαζεν τὸν θεὸν λέγων·
ἀληθῶς οὗτος ὁ ἄνθρωπος   ὄντως ὁ ἄνθρωπος οὗτος
υἱὸς θεοῦ ἦν.   δίκαιος ἦν.

8

"Athletes of Virtue"

The Major Summaries of the Jersualem Community in Acts

This is then their life, so highly prized that not only private persons but even great kings admiring the men are amazed and make their worthiness of respect even more respectable through favors and honors.

Philo, *Hypoth.* 8.11.18[1]

The only New Testament author who attempted to narrate the story of Christianity was the author of Acts. The only community that the author of Acts chose to describe *in extenso* was the early Jerusalem community. The presentation of the earliest Christian community appears in two forms: five extended narratives (2:1–40; 3:1–4:31; 4:36–5:11; 5:12–42; 6:1–8:3)[2] and three summaries (Acts 2:41–47; 4:32–35; and 5:12–16).[3]

---

1. This is the conclusion of Philo's description of the Essenes in *Hypoth.* The fragment is preserved in Eusebius, *Praep. ev.* 8.11.18.

2. These are the largest connected literary units in this section of Acts; there are smaller literary units within these larger narratives that are also connected.

3. There is some question about where the summary in Acts 2 begins: is it with v. 41, v. 42, or v. 43? Three reasons lead me to place it at v. 41. First, the οἱ μὲν οὖν in v. 41 is a favorite formula in Acts denoting a new unit in continuity with what precedes. For example: 1:6; 5:41; 8:4, 25; 9:31 [ἡ μὲν οὖν]; 11:19; 13:4 [αὐτοὶ μὲν οὖν]; 15:3, 30; 16:5 [αἱ μὲν οὖν]; 23:31. For other examples of μὲν οὖν in Acts see 1:18; 12:5; 14:3; 17:12, 17, 30; 19:32, 38; 23:18, 22; 25:4, 11; 26:4, 9; 28:5. Second, v. 42 begins with an understood subject that must be supplied from v. 41. Third, v. 41b ("and there were added in that day about three thousand people" [καὶ προσετέθησαν ἐν τῇ ἡμέρᾳ ἐκείνῃ ψυχαὶ ὡσεὶ τρισχίλιαι]) forms an inclusio with v. 47 ("the Lord was adding to them daily those who were saved" [ὁ δὲ κύριος προσετίθει τοὺς σῳζομένους καθ᾽ ἡμέραν ἐπὶ τὸ αὐτό]). In her study, Maria Co argues the summary does not begin until v. 42 on the basis of the connections of v. 41 with vv. 1–40, the shift in the temporal setting (i.e., the shift in tense from the aorist in v. 41 to the imperfect periphrastic in v. 42), and the corresponding change of subject from entrance into the community to a description of community life (Ma-

Since Martin Dibelius first suggested and Henry Cadbury argued that the summaries are generalizations of typical incidents that serve as connectors within the narrative, New Testament scholars have debated three related questions.[4] One, do these summaries preserve independent traditions that the author has redacted or are they authorial compositions? Two, what ideological constructs or literary models have influenced the shape of the summaries? Three, how do these summaries function within the text of Acts; that is, are they idealistic or hortatory? In this chapter, I will offer answers to the three questions by arguing that the summaries are authorial compositions based primarily on traditions embedded in the surrounding narratives that the author has generalized by means of a specific literary model, the description of religious-philosophical groups. Since the author's techniques in composition have a bearing on our assessment of possible literary models, I will begin with them.

THE COMPOSITION OF THE SUMMARIES

In recent work, there have been three views regarding the composition of the summaries.[5] The first is that they preserve independent traditions that the author has redacted. Adherents of this view appeal to the inconcinnities, repetitions, and hapax legomena within the summaries. While this is the minority view, it still has a number of significant representatives.[6] The second is the view of Pierre Benoit

---

ria Anicia Co, "The Major Summaries in Acts: [Acts 2,42–47; 4,32–35; 5,12–16] Linguistic and Literary Relationship," *ETL* 68 [1992]: 49–85, esp. 58–61). However, these are not decisive: the connection of the beginning of the summary with the preceding context is a feature of each of the three summaries and entrance into the community is a regular feature of the summary form (see the discussion in the next section). Co fails to address the use of οἱ μὲν οὖν and discounts the inclusio of 2:41b and 47 by pointing to common vocabulary in 2:47 and 2:39, 40, as well as 2:41. The presence of God (θεός), Lord (κύριος), and save (σώζω) in these verses hardly offsets the force of the much more obvious inclusio, especially when the uses of this common vocabulary are not identical. She does provide convincing cases for considering 4:32–35 and 5:12–16 as integral literary units (Co, "Major Summaries in Acts," 61–63).

4. Martin Dibelius, "Style Criticism of the Book of Acts," in *Studies in the Acts of the Apostles*, 9–10; Henry J. Cadbury, "The Summaries in Acts," in *The Beginnings of Christianity, I: The Acts of the Apostles*, 5 vols., ed. Frederick J. Foakes Jackson and Kirsopp Lake (London: Macmillan, 1920–1933; repr., Grand Rapids: Baker, 1979), 5:392–402; and Cadbury, *Making of Luke-Acts*, 58–59, 324–25, 329–30.

5. For a refutation of the older source theories see Jacques Dupont, *The Sources of the Acts* (New York: Herder & Herder, 1964), esp. 17–61.

6. Major representatives include Lucien Cerfaux, "La composition de la première partie du Livre des Actes," *ETL* 13 (1936): 667–91; Lucien Cerfaux, "La première communauté chrétienne à Jérusalem (Act., II, 41–V, 42)," *ETL* 16 (1939): 5–31, repr. in *Recueil Lucien Cerfaux*,

who argued that Luke was responsible for the earliest level of the summaries, but that a later editor consistently made insertions into the middle of the summaries.[7] The third view is that the author composed the summaries—a view that need not exclude the use of traditions altogether, but accentuates the role of the author.[8]

There are two major lines of evidence to support the third position. First, the language and themes of all three summaries reflect the concerns of Acts. This is clear from the similarity of the language to the surrounding narratives as well as the repetitions within the summaries themselves. Virtually every phrase has a parallel—often multiple parallels (see chart 8.1 in the appendix). The language is thoroughly Lukan. The combination of Lukan vocabulary with the repetition of linguistic formulations within the three summaries has led Maria Anicia Co to describe the relationship among the summaries accurately as "parallel composition with motif-rearrangement."[9]

This is substantiated by a second line of reasoning. The author has verbally connected the summaries to the surrounding narratives. Each summary has a Janus-like quality looking both backward to the preceding narrative and forward to the succeeding. In Acts 2:41–47 the opening statement, "Those who accepted his message were baptized" (2:41), recalls the closing admonition of Peter's sermon, "Repent and let each one of you be baptized . . ." (2:38). The reference to the miracles in 2:43 and to the temple in 2:46 set up the healing of the lame man in the temple precincts in 3:1–10.[10] Similarly, the miraculous power that accompanied the apostles' testimony of the resurrection in 4:33 answers the prayer of the church to speak with boldness in 4:29 (cf. also 4:31).

---

2 vols., BETL 6–7 (Louvain: J. Duculot, 1954), 2:63–91 and 125–56, respectively; Joachim Jeremias, "Untersuchungen zum Quellenproblem der Apostelgeschichte," *ZNW* 36 (1937): 205–21, repr. in *Abba: Studien zur neutestamentlichen Theologie und Zeitgeschichte* (Göttingen: Vandenhoeck & Ruprecht, 1966), 238–55, esp. 240–41; Heinrich Zimmerman, "Die Sammelberichte der Apostlegeschichte," *BZ* 5 (1961): 71–82; Hans-Joachim Degenhardt, *Lukas Evangelist der Armen: Besitz und Besitzverzicht in den lukanischen Schriften (Eine traditions- und redaktionsgeschichtliche Untersuchung)* (Stuttgart: Katholisches Bibelwerk, 1964), 160–72; Rudolf Pesch, *Die Apostelgeschichte*, EKKNT 5.1–2 (Köln: Benziger; Neukirchen-Vluyn: Neukirchener Verlag, 1986), 1:129–30; and Gerd Lüdemann, *Early Christianity according to the Traditions in Acts: A Commentary*, trans. John Bowden (Minneapolis: Fortress, 1989), 48.

7. Pierre Benoit, *Jesus and the Gospel*, 2 vols. (New York: Seabury, 1974), 2:94–103, esp. 96.

8. Clearly and forcefully argued by Haenchen, *Acts of the Apostles*, 190–96, 230–35, 242–46, esp. 195–96 and 244–45, where he does allow for a tradition about Peter's healing shadow. An important subsequent treatment is that of Co, who provides a more detailed survey of research up until that time ("Major Summaries in Acts," 49–55).

9. Co, "Major Summaries in Acts," 63–81, esp. 81.

10. The "many wonders and signs" (πολλὰ τέρατα καὶ σημεῖα) in 2:43 also recall the "wonders and signs" (τέρατα καὶ σημεῖα) in 2:19.

The verbal similarities of 4:34–35; 4:37; and 5:1–2 (set in italics) demonstrate that 4:32–35 is designed as a lead-in to the two specific examples that follow.

4:34–35
they *sold* (πωλοῦντες) and *brought* (ἔφερον) the proceeds of what was sold and *laid* (ἐτίθουν) them *at the feet of the apostles* (παρὰ τοὺς πόδας τῶν ἀποστόλων)

4:37
he *sold* (πωλήσας) and *brought* (ἤνεγκεν) the funds and *laid* (ἔθηκεν) them at *the feet of the apostles* (πρὸς τοὺς πόδας τῶν ἀποστόλων)

5:1–2
he *sold* (ἐπώλησεν) a piece of property . . . and *brought* (ἐνέγκας) part of it and *laid* (ἔθηκεν) it *at the feet of the apostles* (παρὰ τοὺς πόδας τῶν ἀποστόλων)

The repetition of the verbs "sold," "brought," "laid," and the phrase "at the feet of the apostles" ties the summary directly to the stories of Barnabas (4:36–37) and Ananias and Sapphira (5:1–11) that follow. Finally, 5:12–16 looks back (5:13) to the *mysterium tremendum* generated by the deaths of Ananias and Sapphira (5:11) and forward to the arrest of the apostles as a result of the great popularity they enjoyed (5:16 in anticipation of 5:17–42, especially v. 17).

These two lines of evidence, the common vocabulary and the explicit connections of the summaries to the surrounding narratives, suggest that the author composed the summaries as generalizations of the traditions contained in the narratives.[11] This is most easily seen in 4:32–35. The evidence cited above makes it clear that the author composed v. 33 ("the apostles were giving their witness to the resurrection of the Lord Jesus with great power") with 4:23–31 in mind (the prayer of the community to speak boldly) and vv. 32, 34–35 in anticipation of two examples of early community members selling their property in 4:36–5:11. This is confirmed by the difference between the summary and the narratives. According to the summary, the believers had everything in common (4:32); according to the stories, each member of the community maintained their own possessions and had the right to sell or to retain them.[12] The use of

11. I am not making any claims about the historicity of the traditions; I am only arguing that the author knew these as traditions and did not invent them. I base this conclusion largely on the way in which the author worked in Luke.

12. See esp. 5:4. Alan C. Mitchell, "The Social Function of Friendship in Acts 2:44–47 and 4:32–37," *JBL* 111 (1992): 262–64, points out that in the friendship tradition, individuals may own private property but put it at the disposal of the larger group. The distinction is thus

the famous aphorism in the summary, "all things in common," to characterize particular events in the narratives suggests that the summary generalizes the narratives. There is no reason to think that the summary preserves traditions independent of those preserved in the narratives. On the contrary, the traditions it generalizes from the surrounding narratives are fairly obvious: the specific traditions about Barnabas[13] and Ananias and Sapphira[14] for the sharing of goods; and the healing of the lame man (3:1–10) for the miraculous nature of the apostles' ministry.[15] It thus appears that the author composed 4:32–35 on the basis of these traditions and the exigencies of the surrounding narratives.

With the exception of the tradition about Peter's healing shadow (see discussion in the next section), it would be easy to provide a similar analysis for the third summary. The first summary, however, is different: it goes beyond the bounds of the growth of the community and the miraculous apostolic ministry in the surrounding narratives to present a picture of the life and practices of a unified body of believers. This picture of community life demands that we look beyond the immediate narratives for an adequate means to explain the summaries.

LITERARY MODELS

Did the author have any literary precedents for this procedure? Previous researchers have suggested two major possibilities.

---

between ownership and use. Catherine M. Murphy, *Wealth in the Dead Sea Scrolls and in the Qumran Community*, STDJ 40 (Leiden: Brill, 2002), has convincingly argued that this was also the case at Qumran. The practice appears to have been true for different groups in various locales. This may explain how the author of Acts set the summaries side by side with the individual traditions in the final text. However, the juxtaposition of two different views that are connected to two distinct literary forms (one to the narrative and one to the summary) still forces us to ask about the literary relationship between the narratives and the summaries.

13. There is some evidence for traditions in the story about Barnabas. Certainly the association of Barnabas with Cyprus appears in multiple places. Barnabas and Paul evangelize Cyprus (13:4–12) and then Barnabas and John Mark sailed there (15:39). The selling of the field is also probably traditional. The placement of the tradition into the framework of Acts is more questionable; e.g., was it as early as the text suggests or later, when Barnabas was active in missionary efforts?

14. The similarities between Josh 7 and Acts 5 are well known (cf. esp. the verbal echo of Josh 7:1 ["appropriated" (ἐνοσφίσαντο)] in Acts 5:2 ["appropriated" (ἐνοσφίσατο)]). The differences between the two accounts, however, lead me to conclude that the author of Acts has shaped a tradition on the basis of Josh 7 and not composed a new story.

15. Acts 3:1–10 appears to be an independent miracle story that the author has taken over from tradition.

Mark. Henry Cadbury argued that the summaries in Acts could be understood vis-à-vis the summaries in Luke where the evangelist demonstrates dependence on the summaries in Mark.[16] Luke certainly knew and drew on Mark's summaries in the Third Gospel. Of the eight summaries in Mark 1:14–6:33, Luke drew on all of them except the minor summary in Mark 6:6b.[17] However, the relationship between the two gospels is not as straightforward as the parallels might suggest. In some instances, there are notable variations between the two accounts. This is especially true with regard to Mark 1:14–15, which appears to have inspired Luke 4:14–15, but is significantly different in wording.[18]

What role did the Markan summaries play in the writing of Luke-Acts? First, it is clear that the author knew and incorporated the Markan summaries. While the author had presumably encountered summaries in other literary documents, Mark at least has a claim as a precedent.

Second, in one instance there is the possibility that a summary in Acts reflects Markan language:

Mark 6:55–56	Acts 5:15–16
[55]They ran around	
through that entire region	
and began to carry the ill on pallets	[15] . . . so that they carried the ill
to the place they heard he was.	into the streets

16. Cadbury, *Beginnings of Christianity*, 5:392–94; Henry J. Cadbury, *The Style and Literary Method of Luke*, HTS 6 (Cambridge: Harvard University Press, 1920; repr., New York: Krauss, 1969), 105–15, esp. 108–11.

17. Mark 1:14–15 // Luke 4:14–15; Mark 1:21–22 // Luke 4:31–32; Mark 1:32–34 // Luke 4:40–41; Mark 3:7–12 // Luke 6:17–19; Mark 6:12–13 // Luke 9:6; and Mark 6:30–33 // Luke 9:10–11. Luke omitted Mark 6:53–56 as part of the Big Omission (see chapter 3). Minor summaries include Mark 1:28 // Luke 4:37; Mark 1:45 // Luke 5:15–16; Mark 11:18 // Luke 19:47. These are not all of the texts that have been identified in Mark as summaries. Cf. also Mark 1:5, 39; 2:1–2, 13, 15; 4:33–34; 5:21; 6:1; 9:30–32; 10:1, 32. Luke also has summaries that are not part of Mark: Luke 1:80; 2:40; 2:52; 8:1–3. Other texts in the Third Gospel that some consider to be summaries include Luke 1:65; 2:18; 3:18; 4:22, 44; 7:1, 17; 9:43, 51; 11:53–54; 13:17, 22; 19:48; 21:37–38; 23:48; 24:52. For discussions and bibliography of the Markan texts see Wilhelm Egger, *Frohbotschaft und Lehre: Die Sammelberichte des Wirkens Jesu im Markusevangelium*, Frankfurter Theologische Studien 19 (Frankfurt am Main: Josef Knecht, 1976) and Charles W. Hedrick, "The Role of 'Summary Statements' in the Composition of the Gospel of Mark: A Dialog with Kark Schmidt and Norman Perrin," *NovT* 26 (1984): 289–311. For the summaries in Luke-Acts see Johannes De Zwaan, "Was the Book of Acts a Posthumous Edition?" *HTR* 17 (1924): 101–10, esp. 102–4. On the relationship between Markan and Lukan summaries see Co, "Major Summaries in Acts," 57, for a brief discussion and bibliography.

18. Other examples could also be cited; e.g., Mark 15:40–41 may have influenced Luke 8:2–3.

[56]Wherever he entered—
villages or cities or fields,
they set the sick in marketplaces, and set them on cots and pallets
and urged him so that as Peter passed by,
to let them touch even his shadow
the fringe of his garment; might fall on some of them.
[16]The crowd from the cities
around Jerusalem came together
bringing their sick
and those disturbed by unclean spirits,

and as many as touched him,
were made whole. who were all healed.

While the two texts are far from identical, there are several factors that suggest that this Markan summary warrants consideration as a possible source for Acts.[19] Mark 6:55–56 belongs to Luke's Big Omission of Mark 6:45–8:26 at Luke 9:17 (see chapter 3). It is possible that the author of Luke-Acts decided to employ a text he had earlier omitted. There is at least one solid example of such a delayed use of a Markan text, the temple charge that appears in Mark 14:58 and Acts 6:14 but not in Luke (see chapter 3). The strongest piece of textual evidence for dependence is the presence of "pallet" (κράβαττος), which Luke consistently dropped in the gospel.[20] The presence of "pallet" (κράβαττος) here, however, cannot be pushed too far since it also appears in Acts 9:33. The most that can be said is that it is possible that Mark 6:55–56 served as a basis for Acts 5:15–16. Even if it did, it only served as a source for part of one summary and not as a model for the summary as a whole.

The third possible influence of the Markan summaries on Luke-Acts is their function as structural markers. Norman Perrin argued that the summaries in Mark serve as indicators of the narrative's structure.[21] There is no doubt that

19. So Alfred M. Loisy, *Les Actes des Apôtres* (Paris: F. Rieder, 1920), 274, cited by Haenchen, *Acts of the Apostles*, 243; and Co, "Major Summaries in Acts," 66, who thinks the author of Acts may have drawn from both Mark 3:10 and 6:55–56.

20. Cf. Mark 2:4, 9, 11, 12 // Luke 5:19, 23, 24, 25. The term "cot" (κλινάριον) in Acts 5:15 is a hapax legomenon.

21. Norman Perrin, "Towards an Interpretation of the Gospel of Mark," in *Christology and a Modern Pilgrimage: A Discussion with Norman Perrin*, ed. Hans Dieter Betz (Claremont: Society of Biblical Literature, 1971), 1–78. Following the lead of Perrin and John R. Donahue, "Mark," in *Harper's Bible Commentary*, ed. James L. Mays (San Francisco: Harper & Row, 1988), 986, 991, I suggest that the summaries help to mark out the structure of the

the author of Luke-Acts used summaries in this way. The infancy narrative of the Gospel of Luke has three clear structural markers: 1:80 marks the termination of the section on John; 2:40 notes the end of Jesus's infancy; and 2:52 rounds off the independent tradition about Jesus as a *Wunderkind*. The same is true for the three major summaries in Acts. Each marks a transition from one major narrative strand to another: 2:41–47 marks the end of the Pentecost narrative in 2:1–40 and sets us up for the second extended narrative in 3:1–4:31; 4:32–35 winds up 3:1–4:31 and introduces us to 4:36–5:11; and 5:12–16 serves the same function for 4:36–5:11 and 5:17–42. The summaries thus serve to mark the termini of the major narrative strands. Did the author learn this from Mark? While this is a possible deduction, it is problematic since the structure set up by the Markan summaries is not carried over into Luke: the third evangelist either did not recognize their function as structural markers or chose to ignore the structure they set up. Whichever alternative is correct, we cannot conclude with assurance that the author learned this from Mark. Besides, the use of summaries as structural markers is not limited to Mark in the ancient world.[22] The author of Acts could have learned this from a number of sources.

Did Mark influence the summaries in Acts? It is clear that Mark serves both as a precedent for the author of Luke-Acts and as a source for some of the summaries in Luke and possibly in Acts. However, the Markan summaries are insufficient as models for the longer summaries in Acts.

Philosophical Traditions. In more recent years, investigators have examined Greek philosophical traditions as a possible background. Eckhard Plümacher argued that a number of expressions come from the repertoire "of the descriptions of the earliest times and utopian states in Greek philosophy."[23] The author of Acts employed them as a means of presenting early Christianity as an "Idealpolis."[24] It is important to recognize that the parallels Plümacher cites come from the philosophical tradition of the ideal state (e.g., Plato's *Re-*

---

first half of Mark (1:14–8:21) into three major units each beginning with a summary (1:14–15; 3:7–12; 6:6b), immediately followed by a discipleship story (1:16–20; 3:13–19; 6:7–13), and ending in a note of opposition (3:6; 6:1–6a; 8:11–19).

22. For example, Philo offered summary statements as conclusions to books in his treatment of Moses: *Mos.* 1.334 and 2.292. Both Philo and Josephus used summaries and transition statements to mark the structures of their works. This is especially true for Josephus in *Ag. Ap.*

23. Plümacher, *Lukas als hellenistischer Schriftsteller*, 16–18, esp. 16. So also Conzelmann, *Acts of the Apostles*, 24; David L. Mealand, "Community of Goods and Utopian Allusions in Acts II–IV," *JTS* 28 (1977): 96–99; Luke Timothy Johnson, *Sharing Possessions: Mandate and Symbol of Faith*, OBT 9 (Philadelphia: Fortress, 1981), 21–23, 119–32; and Schneider, *Die Apostelgeschichte*, 1:106.

24. Plümacher, *Lukas als hellenistischer Schriftsteller*, 18.

public).[25] He apparently has in mind either political philosophical tractates or idealized philosophical descriptions of original communities, such as Plato's presentation of primitive Athens in the *Critias* or Iamblichus's description of Pythagoras's original principles.[26] These philosophical traditions should be kept distinct from the utopias they influenced (i.e., works describing distant peoples living on remote islands). We know of at least four of the latter.[27] These, however, are not parallel to the summaries in Acts since they describe fictitious peoples living in fictitious places.[28]

There is another possibility within the philosophical tradition: the maxims stem from the Hellenic understanding of friendship. Johann Jakob Wettstein made this connection as early as 1752.[29] Alan Mitchell donned Wettstein's mantle and argued against the ideal or early state tradition and in favor of the friendship tradition, especially for the two aphorisms "all things in common" (ἄπαντα κοινά in 2:42; 4:32) and "one soul" (ψυχὴ μία in 4:32). Mitchell maintains that the author cites these proverbs in an attempt to reshape the community's understanding of friendship: by overturning the principle of reciprocity

25. Cf. Acts 4:32 and Plato, *Resp.* 462c; 416d; 457cd; *Leg.* 739bcd.

26. Iamblichus, *Vit. Pyth.* 167–68, which anachronistically elevates the status of Pythagoras. The standard text is Ludwig Deubner and Ulrich Klein, eds., *Iamblichus: De vita Pythagorica liber*, Teubner (Stuttgart: Teubner, 1975). There is now an English translation of this text: John Dillon and Jackson Hershbell, eds., *Iamblichus: On the Pythagorean Way of Life (Text, Translation, and Notes)*, SBLTT 29 (Atlanta: Scholars Press, 1991).

27. Theopompus (b. 378 BCE) described a large and remote continent (*FGH* 115 frag. 75c); Euhemerus (floruit 311–298 BCE) portrayed Panchaia, an island in the East in *The Sacred Inscription* (*FGH* 63); Iambulus (250–225 BCE) set his utopia on an island (Diodorus Siculus 2.55–60); and Dionysius Scytobrachion (second–first centuries BCE) wrote about the islands of Hespera in the West and Mysa in the Triton River (*FGH* 32). For a treatment of utopias in antiquity see John Ferguson, *Utopias of the Classical World* (Ithaca: Cornell University Press, 1975).

28. I would make the same criticism of Troels Engberg-Pedersen, "Philo's *De vita contemplative* as a Philosopher's Dream," *JSJ* 30 (1999): 40–74, who argued that the Therapeutae in Philo's *Contempl.* were an utopian community, not a real community. See the critiques of Mary-Ann Beavis, "Philo's Therapeutai: Philosopher's Dream or Utopian Construction?," *JSP* 14 (2004): 30–42; Mary-Ann Beavis, *Jesus and Utopia: Looking for the Kingdom of God in the Roman World* (Minneapolis: Fortress, 2006), esp. 60; and Joan E. Taylor and David M. Hay, *Philo of Alexandria "On the Contemplative Life": Introduction, Translation, and Commentary*, PACS 7 (Leiden: Brill, 2021), 25–31.

29. Johann J. Wettstein, *Novum Testamentum Graecum* (Amsterdam: Dommerian, 1752), 2:470 (non vidi). He is followed by Jacques Dupont, "La communauté des biens aux premiers jours de l'église (Actes 2,42.44–45; 4,32.34–35)," in *Études sur les Actes des Apôtres*, LD 45 (Paris: Les Éditions du Cerf, 1967), 503–19; Jacques Dupont, "L'union entre les premiers chrétiens dans les Actes des Apôtres," in *Nouvelles Études sur les Actes des Apôtres*, LD 118 (Paris: Les Éditions du Cerf, 1984), 296–318, esp. 301–3; and Luke Timothy Johnson, *The Literary Function of Possessions in Luke-Acts*, SBLDS 39 (Atlanta: Scholars Press, 1977), 2–3, 5, 199, 221.

in friendship he challenges the members of the community who enjoy higher status to share their possessions with those who have lower status.[30]

Plümacher and Mitchell are both correct in pointing out the connections between the Acts accounts of the unity of the early Jerusalem community, especially the sharing of goods, and the Greek philosophical tradition. Where they differ is in the determination of the specific source for the maxims and in the function they assign to the material: for Plümacher the parallels with philosophical descriptions of original communities suggest that the statements are ideal; for Mitchell the parallels with friendship traditions suggest they are hortatory. The location of thematic ties between limited parts of the summaries and the Greek philosophical tradition does not, however, solve our larger literary question. Nor can such limited connections enable us to determine the function of the summaries satisfactorily. Is there a literary tradition that does? I am convinced there is.

Religious-Philosophical Groups in the Hellenistic World

One of the literary traditions that emerged in the Hellenistic world was the description of religious or philosophical groups.[31] These descriptions stem from the ethnographic practice of describing the society and customs of a particular *ethnos* or people.[32] Early ethnographers often singled out specific groups that were either important or unusual.[33] This practice was carried over into historical, geographical, and apologetic works in the Hellenistic and Roman worlds, especially for religious or philosophical groups. In some cases, authors devoted entire works to specific groups (e.g., Philo's description of the Therapeutae in *De vita contemplativa*).[34] In other instances, descriptions were

30. Mitchell, "Social Function of Friendship," 255-72 and Alan C. Mitchell, "'Greet the Friends by Name': New Testament Evidence for the Greco-Roman Topos on Friendship," in *Greco-Roman Perspectives on Friendship*, ed. John Fitzgerald; RBS 34 (Atlanta: Scholars Press, 1997), 225-62.

31. On the literary tradition see A. J. Festugière, "Sur une nouvelle Edition du 'De Vita Pythagorica' de Iamblique," *Revue des Études Grecques* 50 (1937): 476-78; and H. Strathmann, "Chairemon," *RAC* 2 (1954): 991.

32. Arrian's description of Indian society is a clear example of this dependence on the older ethnographic tradition. Arrian's basic sources were Nearchus and Megasthenes. Even a figure as late as Philostratus reflects ethnographic concerns in his description of the Indian Brahmans. The topics of *Vit. Pyth.* 3.45-49 are standard ethnographic topoi. On Greek ethnography see chapter 1 and the bibliography cited there.

33. E.g., Herodotus's description of the Egyptian marsh people in *Hist.* 2.92.1-95.2.

34. For the literary and apologetic associations of this tractate see Hans Conzelmann,

incorporated within a larger narrative (e.g., the numerous descriptions of the Essenes).[35] I have called this a literary tradition since it can assume the status of a genre (when the entire work is devoted to such a description) or a literary form (when a description is a constituent element in a larger narrative).[36]

I suggest that the summaries presenting the Jerusalem community use this literary tradition as a model. I will compare the content, form, and function of the summaries of Acts with two groups. The first set consists of religious-philosophical groups as described by Greco-Roman authors: the Egyptian priests in Chaeremon (first century CE);[37] the Essenes in Pliny (23/24–79 CE),[38] the Indian sages in Arrian (second century CE),[39] and Philostratus (ca. 170–244/49 CE);[40] the naked Egyptian sages in Philostratus;[41] and the Pythagoreans in Iamblichus (ca. 250–325 CE).[42] The second set is the Essenes described by Jewish authors:

Gentiles-Jews-Christians: Polemics and Apologetics in the Greco-Roman Era, trans. Eugene Boring (Minneapolis: Fortress, 1992), 189–92; David Hay, "Things Philo Said and Did Not Say about the Therapeutae," SBLSP 31 (1992): 673–83; and Taylor and Hay, *Philo of Alexandria "On the Contemplative Life,"* 1–31.

35. For collections of the classical accounts of the Essenes see Alfred Adam, *Antike Berichte über die Essener*, 2nd ed., KlT 182 (Berlin: de Gruyter, 1972); and Geza Vermes and Martin D. Goodman, *The Essenes according to the Classical Sources*, Oxford Centre Textbooks 1 (Sheffield: JSOT Press, 1989).

36. This is by no means the only example of such a "tradition"; e.g., a symposium can be an entire work (e.g., Plato, Xenophon, Aristotle, etc.) or a subunit within a larger work (e.g., Let. Arist. 172–300).

37. *Apud* Porphyry, *Abst.* 4.6–8. I have used the edition of van der Horst, *Chaeremon*, frag. 10. Cf. also frag. 11. We do not know from which work of Chaeremon Porphyry excerpted this fragment.

38. Pliny, *Nat.* 5.73.

39. Arrian, *Indica* 11.1–8. These are the first of the seven castes in India that Arrian describes (11.1–12.9). Cf. also his *Anab.* 7.1–2. Arrian is probably dependent on Megasthenes for his general description as the agreement with Diodorus Siculus 2.40.1–41.5 and Strabo 15.1.39–41, 46–49, suggests. He apparently supplemented Megasthenes with material from Nearchus as the explicit reference to the latter attests (11.7). On Nearchus see *FGH* 133 frags. 6, 23. Aristobulus of Cassandreia (*FGH* 139 frag. 41) also has an account.

40. Philostratus, *Vit. Apoll.* 3.10–51, esp. 10–18. In order to maintain consistency in comparisons I have only included the material from 10–18 in the chart; there are other elements that appear in 19–51 that are not listed in the chart.

41. Philostratus, *Vit. Apoll.* 6.6.

42. Iamblichus, *Vit. Pyth.* 96–100. This may be from Aristoxenus's *Pythagorean Sayings*, which Iamblichus knew through Nicomachus. So Erwin Rhode, "Die Quellen des Jamblichus in seiner Biographie des Pythagoras," *RhM* 27 (1872): 35–37; followed by Dillon and Hershbell, *Iamblichus: On the Pythagorean Way of Life*, 121n1, 123n3, 125n6.

Philo (20 BCE–50 CE)[43] and Josephus (37/38–ca. 100 CE).[44] While there are other texts that also fall into this category, these are from a broad enough chronological and geographical spread to establish the connections of the Acts summaries with a well-known tradition.[45] I have set the descriptions of the Jerusalem community into a final chart (8.1) in the appendix to make comparisons easy.

Content. There are several impressive agreements between the contents of the Acts summaries and the descriptions of religious-philosophical groups in other texts. First, they all describe the community life of a select subgroup that is either a religious or philosophical community. Second, there is a remarkable degree of similarity between the topoi in the summaries of Acts and the accounts of religious-philosophical groups. I have tabulated the agreements in the following three charts. I began by noting common topoi in the descriptions. It became apparent that some of the topoi naturally fall into general categories. I created a general category when there were two or more topoi that dealt with a common theme; I placed the general category above the topoi in bold font and placed the topoi directly beneath them. I have only noted the presence of the topoi, not the general categories. I have marked texts that include a specific topos with an X. The purpose of the general categories is to indicate the broad areas addressed by the texts; these are only for the sake of analysis. It should be noted that an author may reverse the position of the other texts. In such cases, I have placed an R in the column rather than an X. For example, Josephus mentions the Essenes exclusion from the temple and Acts includes rather than excludes women. I have listed the total number of characteristics or topoi for each text at bottom of the column.

43. Philo, *Prob.* 75–91 and *Hypoth.* 8.11.1–18 (*apud* Eusebius, *Praep. ev.* 8.11.1–18). Philo probably devoted an entire scroll to the Essenes that has been lost (see *Contempl.* 1).

44. Josephus, *J.W.* 2.120–161 and *Ant.* 18.18–22. On Josephus's accounts of the Essenes see Todd S. Beall, *Josephus' Description of the Essenes Illustrated by the Dead Sea Scrolls*, SNTSMS 58 (Cambridge: Cambridge University Press, 1988) and Roland Bergmeier, *Die Essener-Berichte des Flavius Josephus: Quellenstudien zu den Essenertexten im Werk des jüdischen Historiographen* (Kampden: Kok Pharos, 1993). Beall compares the Josephan texts to the relevant texts from Qumran and concludes that Josephus is basically reliable, but issues two caveats: one, Josephus has a tendency to exaggerate; two, he tends to cast his material in Hellenic forms. Bergmeier isolates four sources for the traditions about the Essenes: a collection of anecdotes collected from the history of Nicolaus of Damascus, a doxographical source listing the three Jewish schools of philosophy, a Hellenistic Jewish source, and a "pythagoraisierende Essener-Quelle." If his analysis proves to be convincing, it simply pushes the question of the literary form back to the sources. Bergmeier recognizes the common literary nature of his sources with the descriptions, which I refer to here (e.g., pp. 80–81).

45. I have not included the Therapeutae in Philo's *Contempl.* since this is an entire tractate devoted to the group rather than a unit within a larger text.

GRECO-ROMAN AUTHORS ON RELIGIOUS-PHILOSOPHICAL GROUPS

	Chaere-mon	Pliny	Arrian	Philostratus, *Vit. Apoll.* 3	Philostratus, *Vit. Apoll.* 6	Iambli-chus
Characteristic/topos						
Places of residence						
Geographical locale		X		X	X	
Domiciles	X		X	X	X	
Time in temple	X					R
Customs						
Description of clothing		X		X	X	X
Description of food	X		X			X
Daily routine/behavior	X			X		X
Occupations	X					
Community organization						
Community structure	X					
Initiation		X				
Expulsion	X					
Absence of women		X				
Absence of en-slaved persons						
Common life						
Common treasury		X		X		
Common meals						X
Common clothing						

	Chaere-mon	Pliny	Arrian	Philostratus, *Vit. Apoll.* 3	Philostratus, *Vit. Apoll.* 6	Iambli-chus
Care for needy						
Religion						
Rites	X		X	X	X	X
Miraculous powers			X	X		
Meaning of name/character						
Beliefs						
Instruction/ learning	X					X
Distinctive beliefs				X	X	X
Explicit association with philosophy	X		X	X		X
Influence						
Numbers			X			
Reputation	X	X	X	X	X	
Separation from larger community	X					
Number of characteristics/ topoi	*12*	*5*	*8*	*10*	*6*	*9*

JEWISH AUTHORS ON THE ESSENES

	Philo, *Prob.*	Philo, *Hypoth.*	Josephus, *J.W.*	Josephus, *Ant.*
Characteristic/topos				
Places of residence				
Geographical locale	X	X		
Domiciles	X	X	X	
Time in temple				R

	Philo, *Prob.*	Philo, *Hypoth.*	Josephus, *J.W.*	Josephus, *Ant.*
Customs				
Description of clothing		X	X	
Description of food			X	
Daily routine/behavior	X		X	
Occupations	X	X	X	X
Community organization				
Community structure	X	X	X	X
Initiation		X	X	
Expulsion			X	
Absence of women		X	X	X
Absence of enslaved persons	X			X
Common life				
Common treasury	X	X	X	X
Common meals	X	X	X	X
Common clothing	X	X		
Care for needy	X	X	X	
Religion				
Religious rites	X		X	X
Miraculous powers			X	
Meaning of name/character	X	X		
Beliefs				
Instruction/learning	X		X	
Distinctive beliefs	X		X	X
Explicit association with philosophy	X	X	X	X
Influence				
Numbers	X			X
Reputation	X	X	X	X
Separation from larger community	X			
Number of characteristics/topoi	*18*	*14*	*18*	*12*

The Early Jerusalem Community according to Acts

Characteristic/topos	Acts 2	Acts 4	Acts 5
Places of residence			
Geographical locale			
Domiciles	X		
Time in temple	X		X
Customs			
Description of clothing			
Description of food			
Daily routine/behavior			
Occupations			
Community organization			
Community structure	X	X	
Initiation	X		X
Expulsion			
Absence of women	R		R
Absence of enslaved persons			
Common life			
Common treasury	X	X	
Common meals			
Common clothing			
Care for needy	X	X	
Religion			
Religious rites	X		
Miraculous powers	X	X	X
Meaning of name/character			
Beliefs			
Instruction/learning	X		
Distinctive beliefs			
Explicit association with philosophy	X	X	
Influence			
Numbers	X		

	Acts 2	Acts 4	Acts 5
Reputation	X	X	X
Separation from larger community			X
Number of characteristics/topoi	*13*	*6*	*6*

While there are variations in individual presentations, a basic pattern does emerge. All of the texts use the same general categories to describe their respective groups. The only lacuna in the summaries of Acts is the absence of any description of customs. The reason for this omission is that unlike most of the other texts that are addressed *ad extra*—whether they are written by an outsider or insider—Luke-Acts is addressed *ad intra*. There is no need for any description.[46]

If we examine the specific topoi, we find a correlation between the length of the description and the number of topoi. So, for example, the longer descriptions of the Essenes in Philo's *Prob.* and Josephus's *J.W.* have more topoi than any other description—yet even these have only 72 percent of the total number of topoi attested in all the texts represented here. The shorter accounts have fewer topoi; for example, the description of the Essenes in Pliny, the summaries of the Jerusalem community in Acts, and the portrayal of the naked Egyptian sages in Philostratus (*Vita Apoll.* 6.6). The first summary in Acts is, however, a noteworthy exception among these shorter accounts: it contains approximately the same number of topoi as several of the longer descriptions such as Chaeremon's account of the Egyptian priests, Philo's presentation of the Essenes in *Hypoth.*, or Josephus's description of the Essenes in *Ant.* It is clear that Acts 2:41–47 sketches a general picture of community life. While the second and the third summaries are shorter and have fewer topoi, they reinforce the image created by this earlier and longer description by repeating the same topoi.

While such quantitative observations are important, the realization that every point in the three summaries of Acts is part of the common pattern is even more impressive. This cannot be coincidental since the agreements are extensive. For example, if we compare the topoi in Acts 2:41–47 with the other ten texts (excluding Acts 4:32–35 and 5:12–16), we find that each Acts topos is

46. We can readily see the difference the addressees make by contrasting the implied audiences of Josephus's *Ant.* and Luke-Acts. Josephus must explain even basic Jewish customs (e.g., *Ant.* 17.200, 213; 20.106, 216). The author of Luke-Acts does not offer any explanations for Christian practices such as baptism or the breaking of bread; the implied reader is expected to know what they are in advance. There is, therefore, no need for treatment of customs in the summaries.

well attested. The specific topoi and the number of other texts that have the same topos are as follows: domiciles (7), time in temple (4), community structure (5), initiation (3), common treasury (6), common meals (5), care for needy (3), religious rites (8), miraculous powers (3), instruction/learning (4), explicit association with philosophy (8), numbers (3), and reputation (9). Thus of the thirteen topoi in Acts 2:41–47, four are attested in 30 percent of the other texts, two in 40 percent, two in 50 percent, one in 60 percent, one in 70 percent, two in 80 percent, and one in 90 percent. These numbers compare very favorably to Josephus's description of the Essenes in *Ant*. Using the same set of texts but exchanging the roles of *Ant*. and Acts 2, we find that of the topoi in *Ant*., one has a parallel in 10 percent of the other texts, three in 30 percent, four in 50 percent, one in 60 percent, two in 80 percent, and one in 90 percent. There is, therefore, no significant difference between the use of common topoi in the first summary of Acts and Josephus's summary of the Essenes in *Ant*.

The presence of these common topoi suggests that the author had a literary model in mind when composing the summaries, a model that had a direct bearing on the selection of the specific topoi in the summaries. A classic example of this is the debate over the possible literary relationship between Chaeremon's description of the Egyptian priests and Philo's description of the Therapeutae. There are a significant number of striking similarities between the two accounts. While it was once fashionable to argue that Philo based his portrait of the Therapeutae on Chaeremon's description of the Egyptian priests, it is much more likely that both drew from a common literary tradition that set a common agenda.[47]

This general impression is strengthened when we realize that the similarities extend even to the point of similar phraseology:

Acts 2:44; 4:32[48]
and they had all things in common
but they held all things in common

---

47. See van der Horst, *Chaeremon*, 56, for bibliography and details. To the bibliography that he cites add Johannes Leipoldt, *Griechische Philosophie und frühchristliche Askese*, Berichte über die Verhandlungen der sächsischen Akademie der Wissenschaften zu Leipzig, philologische-historische Klasse 106.4 (Berlin: Akademie-Verlag, 1961), 25–27, who thinks that Philo made use of Chaeremon, but acknowledges the differences between the two accounts, and Taylor and Hay, *Philo of Alexandria "On the Contemplative Life,"* 8–19, who think that Philo responded to Chaeremon, e.g., p. 18: "Therefore, we may imagine the speakers from two sides of the dispute between the Hellenes and the Jews in Rome—Chaeremon and Philo—as making presentations of philosophical excellence on their own behalf, and deriding the examples put forward by the other, in a rhetorical battle. . . ." I think that this is possible, but it is important to note that they drew on a common literary tradition.

48. For a summary of traditions that have this motif, see Keener, *Acts*, 1:1012–26.

Philo, *Prob.* 86
there is one treasury for all, <common> distributions,
common clothes, common food since they eat together

Josephus, *Ant.* 18.20
their possessions are held in common by them

Acts 2:45; 4:35
and they were distributing these to all, as any had need
they were distributed to each, as any had need

Josephus, *J. W.* 2.127
but each gives what is theirs to the one in need
and receives something helpful from that person in exchange

Acts 4:32
and no one claimed that any possession was private property

Philo, *Prob.* 85, 86, and *Hypoth.* 11.4
first, no house is private property
they do not treat wages as private property
no one holds that he possesses private property at all

While these all relate to the single category of the common life of each group, they still make it very clear that these texts use well known topoi to present their groups.

Form. The literary shape of each of these texts is an eclectic résumé. There is no discernible pattern or consistent order in the descriptions. The specific shape that each assumes depends on a number of factors including the sources of information and the requirements of the larger narrative. There is, however, one distinct trend that consistently appears in the case of non-Hellenic groups: the description of the practices of the group are hellenized through the ideals of Greek philosophy. The authors are not shy about making this clear: Chaeremon began his presentation of the Egyptian priests with the claim that they were considered philosophers by the Egyptians (frag. 10 [*apud* Porphyry, *Abst.* 4.6]); Josephus presented the Jewish sects as philosophical schools (*J. W.* 2.119; *Ant.* 18.11); and Philostratus repeatedly introduces philosophical concerns into his long descriptions (e.g., *Vit. Apoll.* 3.13, 18).

The summaries of Acts follow the tradition of providing an eclectic résumé of a specific community. In keeping with this tradition, the author of Luke-

Acts hellenizes the Jerusalem community through appeals to the philosophical tradition. In this instance the appeals come in the form of the two friendship aphorisms cited by the author in the first and second summaries: "all things in common" (ἅπαντα κοινά) and "one soul" (ψυχὴ μία).[49] The presence of these proverbs suggests that readers should think of the community in philosophical terms. Two other considerations support this deduction. First, as noted above, this language is common to Acts, Philo, and Josephus. I suggest that the language evokes the same impression in all three—that is, a philosophical community. Second, this is not the only time the author of Acts appeals to the philosophical tradition.[50] There is nothing unusual about such an appeal here: it is part of a literary tradition.[51]

There are, however, several differences between the Acts summaries and some of these group descriptions. First, the summaries in Acts are relatively short: Acts 2:41–47 has 117 words; 4:32–35 contains 80 words; and 5:12–16 includes 87 words. Their lengths, however, are similar to the lengths of Pliny's depiction of the Essenes (65 words), Josephus's presentations of the Jewish philosophical schools in *Ant.* 18 (the Pharisees, 154 words; the Sadducees, 73 words; and the Essenes, 177 words), and Philostratus's portrait of the naked Egyptian sages (128 words).[52] Their relative brevity is not, therefore, as unusual as an initial impression might suggest. A second and more substantial difference is the triplicate form of the summaries in Acts. This is a result of the author's use of summaries as structural markers. Just as there are three parallel summaries in the infancy narrative of the Gospel, so there are three parallel summaries in the early chapters of Acts. The author of Acts is not the only one who opted to modify the general tendency: Philostratus scatters his descrip-

49. On the proverbial nature of these cf. Aristotle, *Eth. nic.* 9.8.2 (1168b): "All the proverbs concur like 'one soul,' and 'the possessions of friends are common' and 'friendship is equality' and 'the knee is closer than the shin.'" It is worth pointing out that Epicurus did not concur with this statement. Cf. Diogenes Laertius 10.11.

50. The most obvious example elsewhere is the appeal to Socrates. Compare Acts 4:19 and 5:29 with Plato, *Apol.* 29d; and Acts 17:18, 20 with Xenophon, *Mem.* 1.1.1. See chapter 7 for details.

51. We should also point out that the text does much the same thing for the biblical tradition in citing Deuteronomic legislation. Compare Acts 4:34, "for there was no needy person among them" with Deut 15:4, "there will be no needy among you." The combination of biblical and Hellenic elements is deliberate. Cf. my treatment in *Historiography and Self-Definition*, 350–74.

52. See Pliny, *Nat.* 5.65; Josephus, *Ant.* 18.12–15, on the Pharisees; 18.16–17, on the Sadducees; 18.18–22, on the Essenes; and Philostratus, *Vit. Apoll.* 6.6.

tions of the Indian sages and the naked Egyptian sages in a diffuse narrative.[53] In each case the author adapted a specific literary tradition to a literary strategy—examples of blending on a small scale. This means that we cannot isolate the three early summaries in Acts from the author's larger use of summaries. At the same time, these differ from the other summaries in Luke-Acts in several aspects: they are longer than any of the other summaries and all concentrate on a single community within one major section of the narrative.[54] These factors suggest that these summaries are drawing from a different literary model than the other summaries in Acts. Why, however, should the descriptions of religious-philosophical groups serve as a model for only three of the numerous summaries in Luke-Acts?

Function. In order to answer this question, it is necessary first to determine how descriptions of religious-philosophical groups function. If the author is a Hellene describing a non-Hellenic group, the description functions ethnographically—that is, the author singles out a group whom he or she admires or finds exceptionally interesting and describes them for the audience. So, for example, Philostratus has Apollonius explain to Iarchas why he traveled to India to visit the sages: "I consider your understanding wiser and far more divine."[55] Philostratus has simply placed the *raison d'être* for the description in the mouth of his hero. If, on the other hand, the group is a subgroup of the author's own *ethnos* or group, then the summary functions apologetically. So Chaeremon claims that the Egyptians honored the priests "as if they were certain sacred animals."[56] The purpose of this honor is made explicit in the accounts of the Essenes by Philo and Josephus. Philo prefaced his account in *Prob.* by observing that just as Persia has the Magi and India the gymnosophists, so Palestine-Syria has the Essenes.[57] He concludes with a panegyric in which he calls them "athletes of virtue" (ἀθληταὶ ἀρετῆς).[58] A similar refrain concludes the account in *Hypoth.*, where he claims that commoners and kings alike have

---

53. Philostratus, *Vit. Apoll.* 3.10–51, where he expands the description with exchanges and narratives; and 6.6–22, which includes some comparative material on the Brahmans in India.

54. The longest summaries in Luke are 6:17–19 (sixty-three words) and 8:1–3 (sixty-two words). Other summaries in Acts are brief; e.g., the summary statements reflecting the growth of Christianity (6:7; 9:31; 12:24; 16:5; 19:20). There is nothing comparable to the three summaries of the early Jerusalem community, which together total 284 words.

55. Philostratus, *Vit. Apoll.* 3.16.

56. Chaeremon, frag. 10 (Porphyry, *Abst.* 4.6).

57. Philo, *Prob.* 74–75.

58. Philo, *Prob.* 88–91, esp. 88. It is worth noting that Philo goes on to describe Calanus, the gymnosophist (92–97).

stood in admiration and amazement at the Essene way of life.[59] Why does Philo make such a claim? In this explicitly apologetic work, which Philo probably wrote during the crisis following the pogrom in Alexandria, he selected and described a single group of Jews. He is holding them out to the outside world as the living embodiment of the highest ideals of Judaism, ideals that align with the highest ideals of Hellenic philosophy.[60] Josephus does the same. He has a similar flourish of rhetorical hyperbole that makes the apologetic nature of the description patent: "They are worthy of admiration unlike all who claim virtue because there was never any such standard of virtue for any of the Greeks or barbarians—not even for a short time—as has been true of them in the past and has not ceased."[61] Thus both Philo and Josephus offer their descriptions of the Essenes as responses to real or potential detractors: the Jews are not at all inferior to any other *ethnos* or group as their "athletes of virtue" demonstrate.[62]

I suggest that the summaries in Acts share this apologetic function. Three reasons lead to this conclusion. First, like the texts cited above, Acts repeatedly tells us that outsiders held the earliest community in honor.[63] The point of this claim is straightforward: this was an extraordinary community that elicited praise then and—by extension—should now. Second, this is the only Christian community for whom the author makes such a claim.[64] Just as the Essenes could exemplify the principles of Judaism or the Egyptian priests the values of Egyptians, so the early Jerusalem community is presented as the embodi-

---

59. *Apud* Eusebius, *Praep. ev.* 8.11.18. See the citation of this text to open the chapter.

60. For details see Gregory E. Sterling, "Philo and the Logic of Apologetics: An Analysis of the *Hypothetica*," *Society of Biblical Literature 1990 Seminar Papers*, SBLSP 29 (Atlanta: Scholars Press, 1990), 412–30 and Gregory E. Sterling, "Philosophical Treatises of Philo: *Hypothetica*," in *Outside the Bible*, 2501–22.

61. Josephus, *Ant.* 18.20. Cf. also 22 where he compares them to the Ktistae of the Dacians.

62. So also Mason, *Josephus and the New Testament*, 132–35, 219, who argues that the Essenes represent part of Josephus's ideal portrait of Judaism.

63. Acts 2:47; 4:33; 5:13, 15–16. Some have challenged this interpretation of "having favor with all the people" in 2:47 on linguistic grounds by arguing that it means "having goodwill toward all the people," e.g., T. D. Andersen, "The Meaning of ΕΧΟΝΤΕΣ ΧΑΡΙΝ ΠΡΟΣ in Acts 2.47," *NTS* 34 (1988): 604–10. There are, however, two factors that lead me to maintain the traditional translation: the three summaries appear to make the same point that is unambiguous in 5:13; and the early chapters of Acts stress the esteem that the early Christians—especially the apostles—enjoyed among the populace (4:21; 5:26). I, therefore, prefer to follow the traditional understanding. So also Co, "Major Summaries in Acts," 75–77, who provides additional bibliography.

64. So, for example, the author never claims that any other community "had all things common." In fact the opposite is the case: Mary later owns a house in Jerusalem (12:12) and Paul offers his practice of self-support as a model to the Ephesian elders (20:33–35).

ment of Christian values. Third, the use of the common life was a widespread apologetic device for early Christians. This is an example of the anticipation of later Christian apologetic in the early church.[65]

There is, however, a significant difference between the claims of the Acts summaries and those of someone like Philo or Josephus. Acts is addressed to Christians. Why make such a claim? I suggest that it is an example of an indirect rather than direct apology; that is, the text addresses insiders who will have to deal with the outside world. The summaries help them formulate an understanding of themselves as Christians. The question it addresses is whether Christians are at all comparable to other people. The answer is yes: Christianity has also had its "athletes of virtue."

This is, again, an example of how the author brought the narrative into alignment with the values of the larger culture. In this instance, the summaries assured the early Christian communities that they had moral exemplars just as the Jews or other groups had. They should not feel like they were a backwater movement that could not hold their own against other established groups. They could: the early Jerusalem community was the proof.

APPENDIX

Chart 8.1: The Common Language of the Summaries[66]

Acts 2:41–47	Parallels in Acts
41a	8:12; 16:14–15; 18:8; 19:5
41b	*2:47b*; *5:14*; 11:24b (cf. also 6:7; 9:31; 12:24)
42	1:14; 2:46; 6:4 (cf. also Luke 24:35)
43a	5:5b, 11; 19:17 (cf. also Luke 1:65)
43b	*5:12a*
44a	1:15b; 2:16, *47c*
44b	*4:32c*
45a	*4:34b*
45b	*4:35b*

65. Louis William Countryman, *The Rich Christian in the Church of the Early Empire: Contradictions and Accommodations*, Texts and Studies in Religion 7 (New York: Edwin Mellen, 1980), 76–81, esp. 78–80, recognized the apologetic nature of the presentation of communal property in Acts based on the use of the same claim in patristic sources.

66. When the parallel occurs within the summaries, I have set the reference in italics.

46a	1:14; *5:12b*, 42 (cf. also Luke 24:53)
46b	2:42; 20:7, 11
46c	14:17
47a	*4:33b; 5:13b* (cf. also Luke 2:52)
47b	*2:41b; 5:14*; 11:24b (cf. also 6:7; 9:31; 12:24)
Acts 4:32–35	**Parallels in Acts**
32a	*2:46c*
32b	*2:44b*
33a	1:22b
33b	*2:47b; 5:13b* (cf. also Luke 2:52)
34a	
34b	4:37; 5:4
34c	4:37; 5:1–2
35a	4:37; 5:2
35b	*2:45b*
Acts 5:12–16	**Parallels in Acts**
12a	*2:43b*; 6:8
12b	1:14; *2:46a*; 3:11b; 5:42 (cf. also Luke 24:53)
13a	2:43; 5:5b, 11; 19:17b
13b	*2:47b; 4:33b*; 19:17c
14	*2:41b, 47c*; 11:24b (cf. also 6:7; 11:21; 12:24; 16:5; 18:8; 19:10)
15	(cf. Mark 6:55–56)
16	(cf. Luke 6:18)

9

"Customs That Are Not Lawful"

The Social Apology of Luke-Acts

> *Is it not lamentable that people of a despicable, illicit, and hopeless sect should attack the gods? They collect ignoramuses from the lowest dregs and women gullible because of the defective nature of their sex, and form a mob of vulgar conspiracy, a mob bound together by nocturnal assemblies and solemn fasts and inhuman foods, not by any sacred rite but by sacrilege.*

Minucius Felix, *Octavius* 8.3–4[1]

THE EARLIEST OBSERVATIONS about Christians from Greco-Roman authors are far from flattering.[2] We have a trio of early second-century authors who shared a common opinion. Tacitus, the Silver Age historian who wrote two long histories narrating imperial history from 14 to 96 CE, includes a brief mention of Christians in connection with the infamous fire of 64 CE. Like the fires that later ravaged San Francisco following the 1906 earthquake, this fire decimated large sections of Rome. Rumors that Nero, who wanted to rebuild sections of the city on a lavish scale, was the culprit soon began to fly. Tacitus

---

1. Some ancient—and unfortunately some modern—authors were not shy about expressing outrageous prejudices (in this case, prejudices particularly against women). It is worth remembering that Minucius Felix has placed the current gossip about Christians into the speech of his pagan opponent, Caecilius.

2. For a collection of the early Greco-Roman comments about Christians see Molly Whittaker, *Jews and Christians: Graeco-Roman Views*, Cambridge Commentaries on Writings of the Jewish and Christian World 200 BC to AD 200 (Cambridge: Cambridge University Press, 1984). For analyses of pagan perceptions of Christians during the early Christian period see Stephen Benko, "Pagan Criticism of Christianity During the First Two Centuries A.D.," *ANRW* 23.2:1055–118; Stephen Benko, *Pagan Rome and the Early Christians* (Bloomington: Indiana University Press, 1984); and Wilken, *Christians as Romans Saw Them*.

wrote: "Therefore in order to abolish the rumor, Nero substituted culprits and imposed the most torturous punishments on those viewed askance because of their scandalous conduct whom the populace called Christians." He then provided some background on Christianity that he may have collected from Pilate's official records: "The author of that name, Christus, had been executed by the procurator Pontius Pilate during Tiberius's principate." This did not, however, achieve the desired effect: "Suppressed for the moment, that deadly superstition (*exitiabilis superstitio*) began breaking out again not only through-out Judea, the source of the evil, but also throughout the city where all that is hideous and shameful flows from everywhere else and is practiced."[3]

A friend of Tacitus, Pliny the Younger, served as the governor of Bithynia under Trajan (ca. 111–113 CE). During his tenure as governor, Pliny found it necessary to write to the emperor for advice on various matters including on how to deal with Christians. He explained to the emperor that he was unaware of a precedent established by formal proceedings for dealing with them and wanted to make sure that he was following proper procedure. Although he knew nothing about Christians, he had decided to punish those who would not renounce their Christianity on the grounds of obstinacy. Once he began, the number of accusations mushroomed. He then made an effort to discover what the movement was all about. He says that he investigated two women deacons, but "found nothing other than a perverse and unrestrained super-stition (*superstitio prava et immodica*)."[4]

A traveling companion of Pliny also mentioned the new movement.[5] Sueto-nius referred to them as he described Nero's reform efforts to clamp down on asocial groups. These included not only the chariot drivers who, like modern athletes, often acted with impudent immunity, pantomimes whose actions fre-quently resulted in brawls, but also "the Christians, a group of people devoted to a new and wicked superstition (*superstitio nova et malefica*)"—a superstition that Nero deemed worthy of punishment.[6]

We might dismiss the fact that all three characterize early Christianity as a despised cult or "superstition" (*superstitio*) rather than a formally recognized religion (*religio*) by pointing out that they were elite Romans commenting on a movement popular among those of lower status, except we have a good deal of evidence that supports the view that the contempt for Christians was

---

3. Tacitus, *Ann.* 15.44.
4. Pliny, *Ep.* 10.96.8. Cf. 10.97 for Trajan's reply.
5. See Pliny, *Ep.* 10.94.1.
6. Suetonius, *Nero* 16.2.

common across a wide range of social groups. The evidence comes both from detractors and from Christians who were anxious to rebut such charges. The exchanges began in earnest in the second century when, on the one hand, Christians began writing defenses of their beliefs and practices,[7] and when, on the other hand, Christianity became significant enough that outsiders could not ignore it.[8] There are, however, earlier works that offer evidence of concern for outsiders' perceptions of Christianity.

One of the earliest is the two-scroll work we know as Luke-Acts. It has been common to explore the political agenda of these texts. The result has been a debate whether the two narratives offer an *apologia pro Paulo*,[9] an *apologia pro ecclesia*,[10] an *apologia pro imperio*,[11] or no apology at all.[12] I am arguing that Luke-Acts was an attempt to provide early Christians with a sense of identity

7. Early Christian apologies fall into a couple of literary groups. During the second century, Eusebius mentioned a number of Christians who wrote apologies that were ostensibly addressed to the Roman emperor or senate. This convention went through the reign of Marcus Aurelius (121–180 CE, ruled 161–180 CE). These include Quadratus (ca. 125 CE with fragment in Eusebius, *Hist. eccl.* 4.3.1–2); Aristides (floruit ca. 140 CE), *Apol.* (Eusebius, *Hist. eccl.* 4.3.3); Justin Martyr (died 165 CE), *1 Apol., 2 Apol.* (Eusebius, *Hist. eccl.* 4.8.3–9.3; 4.11.8–12.1; 4.17.1–18.2); Melito (ca. 161–180 CE), *Apol.* (Eusebius, *Hist. eccl.* 4.26.1–14, esp. 2, 5–11); Apollinarius of Hierapolis (floruit ca. 161–180 CE), *Apol.* (Eusebius, *Hist. eccl.* 4.26.1); Miltiades (floruit ca. 161–180 CE), *Apol.* (Eusebius, *Hist. eccl.* 5.17.5); Athenagoras (floruit 161–180 CE), *Legatio* (work not mentioned by Eusebius); and Tertullian (born ca. 165 and died after 220 CE), *Apol.* (Eusebius, *Hist. eccl.* 5.5.5). Other Christians used various genres and attempted to engage the larger culture, especially after Marcus Aurelius. Authors who did so prior to Constantine include Tatian (ca. 120–ca. 180 CE), *Or. Graec.*; Theophilus of Antioch (floruit ca. 180 CE), *Autol.*; Clement of Alexandria (ca. 150–215 CE), *Protr.*; Origen (ca. 185–ca. 254 CE), *Cels.*; and Minucius Felix (floruit third century CE), *Oct.*

8. See the critiques of Celsus, *True Discourse* (known via Origen's rebuttal, *Cels.*); Lucian, *Peregr.*; and Porphyry, *Christ.* and *Philos. orac.*

9. E.g., William Ramsay, *St. Paul the Traveler and the Roman Citizen* (New York: Putnam, 1896), 307–8. He argued that Paul served as a precedent for later Christians.

10. One of the first advocates of this view was Johannes Weiss, *Über die Absicht und den literarischen Character der Apostelgeschichte* (Göttingen: Vandenhoeck & Ruprecht, 1897), 54–59. This became the dominant view in the middle of the twentieth century. The most important advocates were Haenchen, *Acts of the Apostles*, 630–31 and Conzelmann, *Theology of St. Luke*, 138–44.

11. Walasky, *"And So We Came to Rome,"* and Klaus Wengst, *Pax Romana and the Peace of Jesus Christ* (Philadelphia: Fortress, 1987).

12. The two most important representatives are Jacob Jervell, *Luke and the People of God: A New Look at Luke-Acts* (Minneapolis: Augsburg, 1972); Jacob Jervell, *The Theology of the Acts of the Apostles* (Cambridge: Cambridge University Press, 1996), 15–16; and Eric Franklin, *Christ the Lord: A Study in the Purpose and Theology of Luke-Acts* (Philadelphia: Fortress, 1975).

in the larger world.[13] While I think that it was concerned with the political standing of "the Way" in the Roman Empire, it had a broader concern. It was concerned with the way that Christians were perceived, much as Josephus was concerned about the social standing of Jews in the Roman Empire in the *Jewish Antiquities*. The *Antiquities* were written to win respect for the Jewish people.[14] While Luke-Acts was not addressed to outsiders, I suggest that it shares the concern for the standing of Christians in the Roman Empire: it attempted to help them understand their place in the larger world.

This dimension of Luke-Acts has not been studied with the thoroughness that it deserves. One of the first studies to explore this was an essay by Abraham J. Malherbe in *Second Century*.[15] There have been several efforts since his essay to develop this perspective, including a monograph by Kavin Rowe, but there is still more that can be done.[16] In this chapter, I propose to explore the social apology by taking three of the most common criticisms leveled against early Christians by later authors and then asking whether the author of Luke-Acts betrays sensitivity to these charges. In each case, I will first summarize the evidence for the criticism and then explore whether the author of Luke-Acts indicates an awareness of it.

ILLITERATE COUNTRY BUMPKINS

The Pagan Critique. The first charge that we will consider is that Greek and Roman authors often portrayed Christians as illiterate country bumpkins. The specific charge could take several forms. Lucian of Samosata, the second-century CE satirist, ridiculed Christians for their naivete in his account of the Cynic philosopher Peregrinus (ca. 100–165 CE). According to Lucian, Peregrinus was an unprincipled character who was forced to flee his home. Although he had managed to escape the consequences of several notorious affairs, he could not extricate himself from the charge of patricide and was forced into exile. In his travels he became associated with Christians in Palestine. Lucian wrote, "In no time he made them appear to be children, being himself

13. See also Sterling, *Historiography and Self-Definition*, 311–89.

14. See Sterling, *Historiography and Self-Definition*, 297–308.

15. Abraham J. Malherbe, "'Not in a Corner': Early Christian Apologetic in Acts 26:26," *SecCent* 5 (1985–1986): 193–210.

16. C. Kavin Rowe, *World Upside Down: Reading Acts in the Graeco-Roman Age* (Oxford: Oxford University Press, 2009).

the prophet, ruler of the cult, synagogue leader, and everything."[17] His new status as a Christian, however, led to his arrest. Christians began supplying him lavishly in prison. Lucian was almost beside himself as he described the gullibility of the Christians in their care for the imposter: "They despise all things equally and consider them common [property], having received such views without any reliable evidence." This credulity made them easy prey: "If any cheat or flimflam person comes to them who is capable of taking advantage of the circumstances, he immediately becomes wealthy by despising simple people (ἰδιώταις ἀνθρώποις)."[18] Peregrinus made the most out of Christian naivete.

Such bemused amazement at the simplicity of early Christians took on a more sinister tone when it came to the evangelistic methods of Christians. Celsus was caustic in his critique: "We see in private houses wool-workers, shoemakers, launderers, and the most illiterate country bumpkins who dare not say anything in front of the older and wiser masters." The situation changed, however, when the masters were not present: "But when they get ahold of their children in private and some unintelligent women with them, they make outlandish statements that it is not necessary to pay attention to their father and teachers but to obey them."[19] Celsus turned the naivete that Lucian lampooned into a charge of manipulation of the gullible.

The same critique surfaced in the West as well as the East. The Latin-speaking Minucius Felix (floruit first half of the third century CE) whose apologetic dialogue, *Octavius*, offers a debate among the author, Octavius (a Christian), and Caecilius (a pagan who may represent the perspective of Fronto, the teacher of Marcus Aurelius). In the course of the exchange, Caecilius characterized Christians as people "who by means of ignoramuses collected from the lowest dregs and credulous women, who are defective as a result of the heedlessness of their sex, form a motley crew of an impious conspiracy. . . ."[20] Caecilius linked credulity and social status.

These three examples do not exhaust witnesses to the charge of low social status, but illustrate the diverse forms that it could take and its geographical spread.[21] The fact that our knowledge of this charge comes from the efforts of early Christians to rebut it indicates their concern. It is difficult to imagine

17. Lucian, *Peregr.* 11.
18. Lucian, *Peregr.* 13.
19. Celsus, *True Doctrine* in Origen, *Cels.* 3.55. Cf. also 3.44.
20. Minucius Felix, *Oct.* 8.4. Cf. also 5.4.
21. Cf. also Tatian, *Or. Graec.* 32.

how they could avoid taking it seriously. The sociological work of the twentieth century all points in the same direction: Christians probably came from a range of social positions but they were largely from the middle to lower social levels of the Roman Empire.[22]

22. The most extensive discussions have dealt with communities founded by Paul. The *point d'appui* for the discussion was Adolf Deissmann, *Light from the Ancient East: The New Testament Illustrated by Recently Discovered Texts of the Graeco-Roman World*, trans. Lionel R. M. Strachan (New York: Harper & Brothers, 1927), esp. 246–47, 290–91, 328–29, 338, 394–97, and Adolf Deissmann, *Paul: A Study in Social and Religious History*, trans. William E. Wilson (New York: Harper & Brothers, 1957), 241–43, who argued that Christians were from among the lower strata of society, a distinction based largely on class—a category made explicit in the fourth edition of *Licht vom Osten* (1923), which was the basis for the English translation above. The first edition of *Licht vom Osten* appeared in 1908 and the first ET in 1910. The first German edition of *Paulus* appeared in 1911 and the second edition in 1925. In the second half of the twentieth century, several scholars corrected this by pointing out that we should use social status rather than class as a means for assessing the standing of early Christians: Abraham J. Malherbe, *Social Aspects of Early Christianity*, 2nd ed. (Philadelphia: Fortress, 1983), 29–59, and—more pointedly—Wayne Meeks, *The First Urban Christians: The Social World of the Apostle Paul*, 2nd ed. (New Haven: Yale University Press, 1983, 2003), 51–73. Two other critically important voices in the assessment of the social level of Pauline Christians during this same period were E. A. Judge, *The Social Patterns of the Christian Groups in the First Century: Some Prolegomena to the Study of New Testament Ideas of Social Obligation* (London: Tyndale, 1960); E. A. Judge, *Social Distinctives of the Christians in the First Century. Pivotal Essays by E. A. Judge*, ed. David M. Scholer (Peabody, MA: Hendrickson, 2008); and Gerd Theissen, *The Social Setting of Pauline Christianity*, trans. John H. Schütz (Philadelphia: Fortress, 1982). More recently Justin J. Meggitt, *Paul, Poverty, and Survival*, Studies of the New Testament and Its World (Edinburgh: T&T Clark, 1998); Steven J. Friesen, "Poverty in Pauline Studies: Beyond the So-Called New Consensus," *JSNT* 26 (2004): 323–61; and Steven J. Friesen, "Prospects for a Demography of the Pauline Mission: Corinth among the Churches," in *Urban Religion in Roman Corinth: Interdisciplinary Approaches*, ed. Daniel N. Schowalter and Steven J. Friesen, HTS 53 (Cambridge: Harvard University Press, 2005), 351–70, have applied Moses I. Finley's understanding of the ancient economy (*The Ancient Economy* [Berkeley: University of California Press, 1973]) to Pauline churches. While Meggitt used a binary model, Friesen more helpfully constructed a seven-stage scale of wealth and poverty for the Roman urban settings based on economic resources. He divided the population of major cities as follows: imperial elites (0.04 percent), regional elites (1 percent), municipal elites (1.76 percent), people with moderate surplus (7 percent), people with stable near subsistence levels of existence (22 percent), people at subsistence (40 percent), and individuals below subsistence (25 percent). His work has been reviewed by John Barclay, "Poverty in Pauline Studies: A Response to Steve Friesen," *JSNT* 26 (2004): 363–66; Peter Oakes, "Constructing Poverty Scales for Graeco-Roman Society: A Response to Steven Friesen's 'Poverty in Pauline Studies,'" *JSNT* 26 (2004): 367–71; and notably by Bruce W. Longenecker, *Remember the Poor: Paul, Poverty, and the Greco-Roman World* (Grand Rapids: Eerdmans, 2010). The most significant recent treatment is John S.

Luke-Acts. Was this reality and the criticism that it provoked a concern for the author of Luke-Acts? On at least one occasion, the author reflected the criticism in a direct way. Following Peter's second sermon and the healing of a lame cripple, the Sanhedrin arrested Peter and John. When they brought them into court, they noted that Peter and John "were uneducated and simple men (ἄνθρωποι ἀγράμματοί εἰσιν καὶ ἰδιῶται)" (Acts 4:13).[23] It is hard not to hear an anticipation of later criticisms.[24] This is especially the case since the charge appears hollow in the context. Readers have just heard Peter deliver two coherent and effective speeches. Why say that he is uneducated and a simpleton? The author went on to note that the members of the Sanhedrin "were amazed and took note that they had been with Jesus." This is a fulfillment of the promise of Jesus that they need not worry about what they should say when they were arrested: he would provide them with what they needed (Luke 21:12–15).[25] While this explains the source of their eloquence, it also confirms the later criticism: Galilean fishermen were not among the elite. Is the author merely anticipating what later pagan critics said or does the reversal signal sensitivity to the charge of outsiders? I think that the latter is more likely. Justin Martyr made the same argument in his *First Apology.* He recognized that the twelve were "simple men" (ἰδιῶται), yet became powerful speakers by divine power.[26] In both Acts and in Justin, low social status could be overturned by God. What appears to be a basis for criticism became evidence for divine empowerment.

The author of Luke-Acts was not, however, content to overturn the criticism; he went out of his way to note the higher social status of select members of "the Way."[27] It is not necessary to argue for the historicity of each identification or individual. It is important to recognize that the social standing of individuals who became Christians was a point of concern to the author of Acts. The author makes the point consistently: it is true of those who were Jews, provincials, and Romans. Among Jews, two individuals had a direct connection to the court of Herod Antipas: Joanna, the wife of Herod Antipas's manager (Luke 8:3), and Manean, a prophet or teacher in the church at Antioch and the tetrarch's

---

Kloppenborg, *Christ's Associations: Connecting and Belonging in the Ancient City* (New Haven: Yale University Press, 2019), 162–208.

23. Cf. Pseudo-Clement, *Rec.* 1.62.2, where this is rehearsed again. MS D omits καὶ ἰδιῶται.

24. This is rarely recognized by commentators.

25. Compare Justin Martyr, *1 Apol.* 60.11; *2 Apol.* 10.8.

26. Justin Martyr, *1 Apol.* 39.

27. On the status of converts in Acts see David W. J. Gill, "Acts and the Urban Élites," in *The Book of Acts in Its First Century Setting,* vol. 2: *Graeco-Roman Setting,* ed. David W. J. Gill and Conrad Gempf (Grand Rapids: Eerdmans, 1994), 105–18.

childhood companion (Acts 13:1). Among Jewish converts the author points out the social standing of Barnabas, a Levite with property in Cyprus (Acts 4:36), a sizeable number of priests (Acts 6:7) and Crispus, the leader of the synagogue in Corinth (Acts 18:8).[28] There were also provincials with significant social standing including: an Ethiopian official (Acts 8:26–40); Lydia, a reasonably well-to-do business woman (Acts 16:14–15);[29] the official in charge of the prison at Philippi (Acts 16:27–34); some of the most prominent women of Thessalonica (Acts 17:4) and Berea (Acts 17:12); and Dionysius, a member of the Athenian council (Acts 17:34).[30] There were even some Romans of note: Cornelius, a Roman centurion (Acts 10:1–11:18) and Sergius Paulus, the proconsul of Cyprus (Acts 13:6–12). Besides those directly involved in the movement, there were well-placed supporters such as the Asiarchs who befriended Paul (Acts 19:31).

Does the identification of a person's position indicate a concern of the author to identify the social position of early Christians, or is it merely a means to identify and differentiate individuals in the narrative?[31] The most telling case is Sergius Paulus, the proconsul of Cyprus (Acts 13:6–12).[32] If the Sergius Paulus of

---

28. See also 1 Cor 1:14, where he is not identified as a Jew. Later in the story, the crowd seized and beat Sosthenes, the leader of the synagogue (Acts 18:17). On Sosthenes see also 1 Cor 1:1. Scholars debate whether Crispus and Sosthenes are different names for the same individual. Barrett, *Acts of the Apostles*, 2:875; Fitzmyer, *Acts of the Apostles*, 630–31; and Pervo, *Acts*, 448–49, think they are two individuals. Richard G. Fellows, "Renaming in Paul's Churches: The Case of Crispus-Sosthenes Revisited," *TynBul* 56 (2005): 111–30, argues that they are one. I see no compelling reason why they must be identified as the same individual; the synagogue may have had more than one leader or Sosthenes may have succeeded Crispus. Even if one agrees with Pervo (*Acts*, 448–49) that the author of Acts has made Crispus a Jew and elevated him to a prominent position based on Pauline traditions, it only serves to reinforce the point that the author wanted to give social prominence to the converts.

29. She was an artisan much like Simon (Acts 9:43) and Priscilla and Aquila (Acts 18:3).

30. Eusebius, *Hist. eccl.* 3.4.10, claims that he was later the head of the church in Corinth. Acts 17:34 also mentions Damaris, but does not make any claim about her status; MSS D and E embellish her status, but these are clearly additions.

31. Padilla, *Speeches of Outsiders in Acts*, 234–35, noted that the speeches given by outsiders in both Hellenistic Jewish literature and in Acts were typically given by individuals of high social status. In Acts these were Gamaliel (5:35–39), Gallio (18:14–15), Demetrius the silversmith (19:24–27), the Ephesian town clerk (19:35–40), Claudius Lysias (23:26–30, a letter), Tertullus (24:2–8), and Festus (25:24–27). Their generally positive statements—Demetrius and Tertullus offer accusations—were designed to give Jews and Christians confidence in their standing. Kucicki, *Function of the Speeches in the Acts of the Apostles*, treats the speeches of Gamaliel (pp. 82–87, 309–10), Gallio (pp. 277–80, 321–22), Demetrius the silversmith (pp. 280–84, 322–23), the Ephesian town clerk (pp. 284–90, 323–24), Claudius Lysias (pp. 186–91, 332–33), Tertullus (pp. 191–97, 333–34), and Festus (pp. 296–301, 38), but he is focused on the narrative functions of the speeches and does not address the social concern that Padilla does.

32. Most think that there is a tradition behind this story, although it is structurally sim-

Acts is the same as the Sergius in several inscriptions, he had praetorian rank.[33] What is the significance of the reference to his status? Arthur Darby Nock famously wrote, "The proconsul's conversion, which would have been an event of the first importance, is just stated as though it were that of a washerwoman."[34] Nock is correct that the author does not elaborate on his position; however, the author never noted the occupation of washerwomen when they were converted! The author only noted the social standing of those who had more elevated status, a point that Nock's student, Abraham Malherbe, recognized in his essay.[35] I cannot imagine the author of Acts writing the words of the narrative's protagonist when describing the social position of converts: "not many wise by human standards, not many powerful, not many born to noble families" (1 Cor 1:26). On the contrary, the author of Acts made the most out of the little that there was.[36]

DISTURBERS OF THE SOCIAL ORDER

The Pagan Critique. One of the most delicate issues that surfaced in the early centuries of Christianity was the impact of the distinctive social values of early Christians. These became the occasion for the *Second Apology* of Justin Martyr. A female convert to Christianity found herself in a difficult position. Her conversion to Christianity convinced her that she had to alter her lifestyle. She was, however, unable to persuade her husband to give up his accustomed mode of living. His refusal began to erode her affection. Things became tense enough that while he was away in Alexandria, she divorced him.[37] When he returned, he denounced her as a Christian. When she won a reprieve to set her affairs in order, her husband turned on her teacher, Ptolemaeus. As a result,

---

ilar to the account of Felix and Drusilla in Josephus, *Ant.* 20.141–143. In Josephus's account Felix, a Roman governor, persuades Drusilla to marry him through the agency of a Jew from Cyprus who pretended to be a magician.

33. There is an inscription from Cyprus and one from Rome that are relevant. *IGR* 3.935, from Chytri (modern Kytheria), mentions a Quintus Sergius who appears to have been the proconsul. The emperor's name immediately follows, but it is not clear whether it is Gaius or Claudius. *CIL* 6.4.2, p. 3116 no. 31545 mentions an L. Sergius Paullus as the third of five curators of the Tiber at the time of Claudius.

34. Arthur Darby Nock, "Paul and the Magus," in *The Beginnings of Christianity, Part I: The Acts of the Apostles*, 5 vols., ed. Frederick J. Foakes Jackson and Kirsopp Lake (London: Macmillan, n.d.), 5:187.

35. Malherbe, "'Not in a Corner,'" 196.

36. For a balanced assessment see Pervo, *Profit with Delight*, 77–81.

37. This is a classic example of the situation envisioned in 1 Cor 7:12–16.

Ptolemaeus and two other Christians were executed.³⁸ To many Hellenes the woman's behavior would have been outrageous: a wife should follow the religious practices of her husband, not the reverse.³⁹ Christianity called this into question with results that were often disruptive.

Pagans reacted. Aelius Aristides, the second-century CE author whose health forced him to leave a public career, bitterly denounced Christians for their practices in a telling contrast, "They are the most useless of all people in joining to accomplish anything advantageous." Yet, "They are the cleverest of all people at ruining a house, at upsetting and setting those within at odds with one another, and claiming that they can manage everything."⁴⁰ Early Christians were not known for their "family values," at least not positively.

Luke-Acts. The author of Luke-Acts appears to have been aware of this perception. He made it a formal charge on five occasions. The first is the trial of Jesus in Luke. When Jesus was brought before Pilate, three charges were leveled against him: he misled the people (διαστρέφειν τὸ ἔθνος), obstructed the payment of taxes, and claimed to be a king (Luke 23:2). Mark and Matthew do not have these charges, although Mark did note that the high priests accused Jesus of "many things" (Mark 15:3), which may have inspired the specification of the charges in Luke. Interestingly, it is the first charge that is repeated in the Lukan narrative. After Pilate asked Jesus whether he was a king and announced his innocence for the first time, the people insisted that "he had been stirring up the people" (ἀνασείειν τὸν λαόν) (Luke 23:5). After Pilate sent Jesus to Herod and Herod returned him, Pilate announced to the leaders and people that they had brought "this man as someone who was subverting the people (ἀναστρέφειν τὸν λαόν)" (Luke 23:14). The main charge in the Lukan trial did not deal with the obstruction of taxes or even a claim to kingship, but with social discord among the Jewish people.⁴¹

The charge is echoed four more times in Acts. The first time occurs in the account of Paul exorcising a Pythian spirit from a mantic prophet at Philippi. The sudden loss of her power enraged her owners who hauled Paul and Silas before the city magistrates and charged: "These men are creating havoc (ἐκταράσσειν) in our city; they are Jews and are proclaiming customs which are not lawful for

---

38. Justin Martyr, *2 Apol.* 2.1–20.

39. E.g., see the advice Plutarch offers to a bride in *Conj. praec.* 140b.

40. Aelius Aristides, *On Behalf of the Four,* 672. Cf. also Celsus, *True Doctrine* in Origen, *Cels.* 3.55 (cited above) and Apuleius, *Metam.* 9.14.

41. It is possible to understand the first charge of Luke 23:2 as the main charge and the next two charges as specific examples of it; i.e., Jesus misled the people by obstructing the payment of taxes and making a royal claim. So Fitzmyer, *Gospel according to Luke,* 2:1473.

us to adopt or practice since we are Romans" (Acts 16:20–21).[42] Like Jesus, Paul was accused of being a troublemaker. The ground for the trouble was that Paul and his companions were trying to persuade Romans to accept Jewish customs. While it was an ancient principle that Romans did not adopt the cults of other people unless they had been sanctioned by the Senate, this had long ago been relaxed.[43] It is highly unlikely that the author or the readers would have known the fine points of Roman law. Nor is there any clear evidence that prohibited Jews from proselytism at this period. There was, however, a clear sense that national traditions should be treasured and a pronounced bias against Jewish proselytizing among Roman elites.[44] The author is reflecting popular prejudices captured in the memorable phrase of Juvenal who said that Romans were tired of the dumping of the flotsam of the Orontes into the rivers of the West.[45]

The charge is echoed again in the next city when a Jewish-led mob substituted Jason and some others when they could not lay their hands on Paul and company, hauled them before the magistrates, and charged: "These who have turned the world upside down (ἀναστατοῦν) have come here, whom Jason has received. These behave contrary to the decrees of Caesar claiming another king, Jesus" (Acts 17:6–7).[46] The two charges echo the first and the third charge in Luke, only the obstruction of the payment of taxes is missing. The "decrees of Caesar" are ambiguous in this text, perhaps deliberately so.[47] The real point is to emphasize that the promotion of an alternate king was subversive.

Paul does not fare any better in Corinth where the Jews hauled him to the *bema* of Gallio, the proconsul of Achaia, and charged: "This man persuades people to worship God contrary to the law" (Acts 18:13). Scholars have debated the identity of the law: was it Roman law or Jewish law? The key appears to lie in the response of Gallio who pointed out that if were a matter of a "crime" (ἀδίκημα) or a "serious

---

42. For a detailed treatment of the charges see Willem C. van Unnik, "Die Anklange gegen die Apostel in Philippi (Apostelgeschichte xvi 20f)," Publicazioni della Società italiana per la ricerca dei papiri greci e latini in Egitto, in *Sparsa Collecta: The Collected Essays of Willem C. van Unnik*, 4 vols., NovTSup 29, 30, 31, 156 (Leiden: Brill, 1973–2014), 1:374–85.

43. A. N. Sherwin-White, *Roman Society and Roman Law in the New Testament* (Oxford: Clarendon, 1963), 80–82.

44. Cassius Dio 57.18.5, indicated that the Jews were banished from Rome in 19 CE for their efforts to convert Romans to their "customs" (ἔθη).

45. Juvenal, *Sat.* 3.62–65: "The Syrian Orontes has for too long polluted the Tiber and brought with it its language, customs, oblique strings along with flute-players, not to mention its foreign tambourines, and the girls who are ordered to sell themselves at the Circus."

46. For a detailed discussion of the charges see Rowe, *World Upside Down*, 95–102.

47. Barrett, *Acts of the Apostles*, 2:815–16, offers a helpful summary of recent efforts to identify these decrees.

misdeed" (ῥᾳδιούργημα)—in other words, a matter that would bring Roman law into play—he would entertain their charge. However, "since it is a matter of debates about words, names, and your own law," he rejected it (18:15). Gallio called the hand of the accusers: he rejected the implication that it was about Roman law (18:14), and stated plainly that it was about Jewish law (18:15).[48] In other words, the charge was deliberately ambiguous: the accusers wanted Gallio to take it as Roman law, but he saw through their subterfuge, rejected it, and gave a clear and decisive answer.[49] The author has skillfully made the case that Christianity is not a threat to the social order; it is a movement within Judaism.

The final occurrence—the fourth in Acts and the fifth in Luke-Acts—of the charge occurs when Paul is tried before Felix. Tertullus, the hired attorney/rhetor who spoke for the prosecution, laid out a series of charges against Paul: he was a plague or a disease (λοιμός) that troubled the world, he promoted rebellions (κινεῖν στάσεις) among all of the Jews throughout the world—a serious accusation if στάσις is understood as rebellion (seditio) rather than disturbance since rebellion (seditio) was treason (maiestas)[50]—he was a ringleader of the Nazarenes, and he desecrated the temple (Acts 24:5-6).[51] There are four charges, although the first two are related and can be collapsed into one: Paul was a pestilent troublemaker, a leader of a dissident sect, and a desecrator of the temple. The charges are an echo of the statements made by the Jews from Asia.[52] The Asian visitors to Jerusalem had earlier stirred the populace against Paul by declaring: "This is the man who teaches everyone everywhere against our people, our law, and this place; in addition, he brought Greeks into the temple and defiled this holy place" (21:28).[53] The author explained the reference to the temple charge by noting that the Jews from Asia had seen Paul in Jerusalem with Trophimus and had concluded that he had brought him into the temple (21:29). The Romans had given the Jews the extraordinary privilege of executing a person who violated the temple.[54] Tertullus explained the reason that this had not

48. Compare Acts 23:29.

49. Commentators often fail to see this; however, some have, e.g., Conzelmann, *Acts of the Apostles*, 153 and Schneider, *Die Apostelgeschichte*, 2:252n54. Contra Rowe, *World Upside Down*, 58.

50. Tacitus, *Ann.* 1.72.

51. For a full discussion of the charges see Rowe, *World Upside Down*, 72–78.

52. On this group see also Acts 24:19.

53. Balch, *Contested Ethnicities and Images*, 102–17, has addressed the issue of violating ancestral customs. He recognizes the close association of this concern in Luke-Acts and the same concern in Josephus.

54. See Josephus, *J.W.* 6.124–128. According to Josephus, the temple had a stone balustrade that separated off the inner courts. The balustrade had slabs with warnings in Greek

occurred was that the Jews had seized Paul and prevented him from entering the inner courts of the temple (24:6). The charge is thus an illustration of how Paul provoked trouble everywhere that he went—even in Jerusalem.

What can we make of these five accounts? The accusation of troublemaking was relatively easy to make and could be effective—at least temporarily. It was frequently leveled against Jews in the Roman Empire.[55] As is the case with most of the charges directed against Christians, this had a basis in fact. Acts narrates the trouble that befell Paul in virtually every city he visited. The trouble is not, however, restricted to Acts. We need only think of the famous "anti-family" sayings of Q—the reconstructed source of the sayings of Jesus preserved in Matthew and Luke but not in Mark—to recall how the kingdom of God can disrupt the accepted values of family life.[56] While the author of Luke-Acts does not omit these or tone them down, they are offset by the examples of household conversions in Acts.[57]

A flash point in this critique as well as in the first critique that we considered is the role of women. They have an ambivalent role within Luke-Acts. On the one hand, the historian appears to go out of his way to include references to women. He regularly pairs men and women in an attempt to demonstrate the important place of women.[58] He singles out the conversion of women as worthy of notice.[59] He also specifies the roles of women: they are patrons of Jesus (Luke 8:1-3) and early churches (Acts 12:12; 16:15), missionaries (Acts 18:1-4), and prophetesses

---

and Latin that announced that any non-Jew who passed beyond this point would suffer capital punishment (Josephus, *J.W.* 5.193-194; *Ant.* 15.417). Two copies of the inscriptions have been found (*CIJ* 1400 // *OGIS* 598). For bibliography on the inscriptions see Fitzmyer, *Acts of the Apostles*, 698.

55. See the letter of Claudius to the Jewish community in Alexandria that threatens any who disregard the strictures of the letter by promising requital on them as fomenters of a plague (*CPJ* 153 2:36-55). See also Josephus, *Ant.* 19.285. Suetonius, *Claud.* 25.4, indicates that Claudius expelled Jews from Rome because of trouble caused by Chrestus, probably an allusion to conflicts in synagogues arising from Christian missionaries. For other examples of the charge see *Pap. London* 1912:96-100; *Acts of Isidore* 8877:22-24.

56. Matt 8:18-22 // Luke 9:57-60; Matt 10:34-36 // Luke 12:51-53; Matt 10:37-38 // Luke 14:26-27; Matt 24:40-41 // Luke 17:34-35.

57. Cornelius (Acts 11:14), Lydia (Acts 16:15), the jailor (Acts 16:31), and Crispus (Acts 18:8).

58. In Luke there are a series of twin stories that juxtapose a woman and a man, one in each of the two stories: there are two annunciations (1:5-23, 28-38), two songs (1:46-56, 67-79), two prophets (2:25-35, 36-38), two precedents (4:25-26, 27), two miracles (4:31-37, 38-39), two miracles (7:1-10, 11-17), two accusers (11:29-32), two miracles (13:10-17; 14:1-6), two parables (13:18-19, 20-21), two parables again (15:1-7, 8-10), and two taken at the parousia (17:34, 35); in Acts there are two miracles (9:32-35, 36-43).

59. Acts 5:14; 8:12; 13:50; 17:4, 12, 34.

(Luke 2:36–38; Acts 21:8–9). On the other hand, they do not step across the boundaries of acceptable behavior in the Greco-Roman world. The point becomes obvious if we compare the presentation of women in the canonical Acts with that of Thecla in the *Acts of Paul and Thecla*. The latter is a sometimes independent unit of the larger second-century biographical romance known as the *Acts of Paul*. In the *Acts of Paul and Thecla*, Thecla does everything Paul does including preaching. This stands in sharp contrast to the portrait of women in the canonical Acts: Lydia, Priscilla, and Philip's daughters are all active, but do not violate the accepted values of the larger society by preaching in public. This balancing of both recognition and restriction points to the author's sensitivity to the role of women in early Christianity: he is aware of the price of violating basic social values.[60]

Obscene Rituals: Thyestean Banquets and Oedipean Intercourse

The Pagan Critique. The prominence of women within Christianity also fueled another set of charges, charges compounded by the fact that early Christians often met in secret. Just as secretive meetings are an occasion for the wagging of tongues today, so they inspired gossip in antiquity. Minucius Felix has Caecilius put it this way: "Certainly suspicion goes hand in hand with hidden and nocturnal rites."[61] The common gossip was that Christians ate children and engaged in sexual orgies. Minucius Felix realized he had to face both charges and so placed them on the lips of Caecilius. The first is associated with an initiation rite. An infant covered with meal was set before the initiates who were encouraged to kill it unwittingly through what appear to be harmless blows: "Eagerly they drink its blood, they compete with one another to divide its limbs; they are allied together by means of this victim, they are bound to mutual silence by this private knowledge of crime."[62] While the details vary in other accounts, the same invidious charge is made.[63]

Caecilius makes the second charge by describing the feasts of Christians: "On an appointed day they assemble for a feast with all of their children, wives,

---

60. For a detailed analysis see Mary Rose D'Angelo, "Women in Luke-Acts: A Redactional View," *JBL* 109 (1990): 441–61.
61. Minucius Felix, *Oct.* 9.4.
62. Minucius Felix, *Oct.* 9.5.
63. The earliest is Pliny, *Ep.* 10.96.7.

and mothers—people of both sexes and all ages." It is "thereafter a good deal of feasting, when the dinner party warms up and the intoxicating heat of incestuous lust flares up, that a dog which is tied to the candlestick is provoked to lunge and leap by the toss of a morsel beyond the reach of the cord with which he is bound." Now the unspeakable—or the greatly rumored—occurs: "Thus with the light which would be witness overturned and extinguished, in shameless darkness they entwine themselves in embraces of shocking passion according to the uncertainties of chance."[64]

This scurrilous gossip enjoyed wide circulation in the second century.[65] There is evidence that it was present at the beginning of the second century. Pliny, whose report to Trajan we mentioned above, also included some details about early Christian meetings. In particular he noted that their meals involved "common and harmless food" (*cibum promiscuum . . . innoxium*).[66] Why did the legate inform the emperor about the nature of the food? The specification is best understood as a response to the suspicion or the rumor that the food was of a different variety. Thus at around or shortly after the time of the writing of Luke-Acts, there is evidence that rumors of cannibalism were circulating—at least in Bithynia.

The rumor of Thyestean banquets and unbridled orgies involving Oedipean intercourse were attempts at labeling Christians a threat to society.[67] In all fairness, we should note that there were probably some bases for such accusations. It is not difficult to imagine how someone on the outside could move from statements like John 6:52–59 to a charge of cannibalism. Similarly, there may have been some Christian groups such as the Carpocratians or Borborites with libertine practices who helped to fuel the rumors of orgies.[68] These were, however, later developments. What about the first century? Is there any evidence that such slander was already circulating?

Luke-Acts. Several passages in Luke-Acts hint at this. On two occasions, the author described the eucharistic meal. The first is the Lukan version of the Last Supper where only Jesus is explicitly linked with verbs of eating and

64. Minucius Felix, *Oct.* 9.6.

65. E.g., Apuleius, *Metam.* 9.14; Celsus, *True Doctrine* in Origen, *Cels.* 5.63 and the widespread concern among Christian authors to renounce it.

66. Pliny, *Ep.* 10.96.7.

67. Andrew McGowan, "Eating People: Accusations of Cannibalism Against Christians in the Second Century," *JECS* 2 (1994): 413–42.

68. On the Carpocratians see Clement of Alexandria, *Strom.* 3.25; Irenaeus, *Haer.* 1.25.1–6; Eusebius, *Hist. eccl.* 4.7.10. On the Borborites see Epiphanius, *Pan.* 26.3.3–5.8.

drinking (Luke 22:15–20). So Jesus said, "I have fervently desired to eat this Passover with you before I suffer" (22:15). He continued, "I will by no means eat it until it is fulfilled in the kingdom of God" (22:16) and "I will by no means drink from this point on from the fruit of the vine until the kingdom of God comes" (22:18). The evangelist then shifts to the third person in narration and quotes Jesus's instructions to the disciples (22:19–20) but dropped Mark's "and they all drank from it" (Mark 14:23 // Luke 22:20). This means that only Jesus is explicitly said to eat or drink at the Lukan Last Supper (22:16, 18). While it would be foolish to put too much emphasis on this point—especially since the disciples were expected to eat and drink the meal (Luke 22:17, 19) and the textual tradition underlying these verses is problematic—it is worth noting that the third evangelist showed some reluctance to follow Mark fully.[69]

The second occasion is the nocturnal worship assembly in Troas (Acts 20:7–12). The author frames the story of the resuscitation of Eutychus, who dozed off during a long discourse of Paul and fell several stories to his death, by telling us that there was a "large number of lamps" in the upper room (Acts 20:8). Why set the stage by referring to the well-lit nature of the room? Are we supposed to understand that Eutychus fell asleep because of the heat and smoke from the lamps, as many commentators suggest?[70] If we are to imagine these are standard oil lamps, it is hard to see how they could have generated enough heat to make a difference. They may have produced a good deal of smoke. Perhaps we are to imagine that Eutychus fell asleep in spite of the lamps: he slumbered even though the room was well lit.[71] Another explanation is that the well-lit room where Paul preached stood in contrast to the darkness outside.[72]

There is yet another possibility, one that is not necessarily exclusive of the possibilities already noted. The author may have mentioned the large number of lamps to counter the standard rumor that Christian only used a single lamp. Since the text was addressed to Christians, there was no need to explain the reference. Christians who heard this would have immediately known why

69. There are two basic forms for Luke 22:15–20 in the MSS tradition: most MSS have vv. 15–20 and preserve the sequence of cup-bread-cup; however, the Western tradition omits vv. 19b–20 and has the sequence of bread-cup (there are variations within these). I think that the longer form is preferable both on the basis of the MSS tradition and the transmission probabilities; i.e., it is easy to understand why a scribe would excise vv. 19b–20 (although it would have made more sense to excise v. 17). For details on the MSS, see Metzger, *Textual Commentary on the Greek New Testament*, 148–50. Bovon, *Luke*, 3:154–56, suggests that Luke combined two sources (vv. 15–18 and vv. 19–20).

70. E.g., Barrett, *Acts of the Apostles*, 2:953; Fitzmyer, *Acts of the Apostles*, 669; Pervo, *Acts*, 510.

71. So Conzelmann, *Acts of the Apostles*, 169.

72. Schneider, *Die Apostelgeschichte*, 2:286.

the reference to "a large number of lamps" was there. While this explanation is only a possibility, it is strengthened by the description of the worship that follows. The activities of the assembly are specified (Acts 20:7, 11). It may well be that the author is telling Christian readers to let outsiders know what takes place in a Christian assembly. Justin Martyr would later throw open the doors of a Christian assembly in his *First Apology* to dispel any gossip about Christian gatherings.[73] It is possible that Acts has done the same.

While the nature and the extent of these references are more opaque and less numerous than the references to the social status or the politically innocent behavior of early Christians, there is enough to raise one's eyebrows. The description of the eucharist and the narration of a Christian assembly that we have in Luke and in Acts appear to have been written with sensitivity to the rumors that were circulating about early Christians. The author does not offer a rebuttal—this would make the text a direct apology—but composes the narratives so that they avoid providing any substance to the validity of the rumors. The concern is handled in much the same way that Josephus attempted to win respect for Jews in his *Jewish Antiquities*. For example, when Josephus narrated the story of Moses putting his hand into his bosom and then drawing it out, he avoided giving any credibility to the charge that Moses and the Israelites were lepers. The MT of Exod 4:6 said that when Moses drew his hand out it was "leprous like snow" (מצרעת כשלג). Josephus followed the LXX ("his hand became like snow") in dropping the reference to leprosy, but altered the specifics: he said that his hand was "white, like a color similar to chalk."[74] Josephus was well aware of the charges that the Jews were lepers who escaped Egypt.[75] He did not note the charge or rebut it in the *Antiquities* as he did in *Against Apion*, but wrote the narrative in a way that avoided giving it any credence. The author of Acts has used the same technique.

CONCLUSIONS

The evidence that we have considered suggests that Luke-Acts was concerned about the social standing of Christians at the end of the first century or beginning of the second. We should remember that the work opens with a literary preface, the only work in the New Testament to do so. The preface is a claim that the

73. Justin Martyr, *1 Apol.* 67.1–8.
74. Josephus, *Ant.* 2.273.
75. E.g., Josephus, *Ag. Ap.* 1.229.

work will situate the movement in the larger Greco-Roman world.[76] This made the author sensitive to the ways that the larger world perceived Christians.

The effort to provide a sense of identification in the larger world meant that the author had to develop a dialectical relationship with it. On the one hand, the author had to engage the larger culture. This required a degree of acceptance of the values of that culture, such as that learning and refinement are important and the social order may be valuable—at least it should be respected, and the ethics of the larger world may have merit. Our author is thus far removed from the mindset of the Essenes who withdrew to the northwest shore of the Dead Sea and relegated themselves to the archaeologist's spade.[77] On the other hand, the author did not equate the values of Christianity with the values of the larger world uncritically. Excessive acculturation would have resulted in a loss of self-identity. This was the fate of the majority of people and traditions that became part of the Roman Empire. Luke-Acts attempted to avoid this danger by providing early Christians with a self-identity through a historical narrative. The author realized that we must know who we are before we can relate to the larger world or we run the risk of losing the qualities that would permit us to influence that world.

Luke-Acts thus set up a dialectical relationship between allegiance to the values of Christianity and the need to take a place in the world. It was not a question of either/or but of both/and. This meant living with the tension of criticizing and accepting the values of the larger world. Luke-Acts is an attempt to provide a basis for this dialectic by offering an understanding of what it meant to be a part of the movement that had taken its place in the larger world.

76. Rudolf Bultmann, *Theology of the New Testament*, 2 vols., trans. Kendrick Grobel (New York: Scribner's Sons, 1951–1955), 2:116, astutely recognized that the author of Luke-Acts made Christianity "an entity of world history."

77. This is where I have a significant difference with Rowe, *World Upside Down*, who emphasizes the countercultural stance of Christians as a result of their loyalty to Christ. While I agree that loyalty to Christ is the priority, the author of Acts did accept some of the values of the larger culture. For example, the concern with social status and the role of women only make sense if the author has accepted the values—at least in part—of the larger world.

Conclusions

LUKE-ACTS CONSTITUTES nearly one-fourth of the New Testament. How should we approach it? How should we think of it as a narrative? If we were intimately familiar with ancient Hellenistic Jewish sources, I imagine that we would associate it most closely with Hellenistic Jewish historians whose works are now, unfortunately, only preserved in fragments. While these works are known only to specialists today, they would have been important to Jewish communities in the diaspora. They were well enough known in the ancient world that a Roman polymath named Alexander Polyhistor (ca. 105–ca. 35 BCE) collected them and included them in a work that he entitled *Concerning the Jews*.[1] Unfortunately, Polyhistor's works, including *Concerning the Jews*, have been lost. Fortunately, Eusebius (and Clement of Alexandria) had access to a copy and included a large number of excerpts in book 9 of his *Preparation for the Gospel*.

In *Historiography and Self-Definition*, I argued that these works stood in the same historiographical tradition as Josephus's *Jewish Antiquities*. While there are differences between the smaller and less sophisticated fragmentary historians and the Jewish historian who wrote in a villa formerly occupied by the emperor of Rome, they appear to align with the prototype. They told the story of a people (the Jewish people) by using their ancestral Scriptures as a basic source along with other traditions from the larger world or within their own communities. Such conceptual integrations are to be expected. These historians related their traditions in extended Greek prose that literarily moved their communities into the larger world by hellenizing the traditions. In each case they wrote for Jewish audiences in an effort to give their community/ies a self-understanding based on their history. While they varied in specifics, they are enough like the prototype instantiated in Josephus's *Jewish Antiquities* that I made the case that they represented the historiographical tradition.

1. *FGH* 273 frags. 19, 101, 102, 117?, 121.

In this work I have tried to make this case for Luke-Acts in a far more extended way than I did in *Historiography and Self-Definition*. We began with a comparative treatment of Josephus, Luke-Acts, and Eusebius as a means of introducing the broad contours of the tradition. I then explored the presence of the tradition in the ancient world by examining Josephus's claim in *Against Apion* that Easterners wrote their histories in ways that were different than their Hellenic counterparts. While our evidence is fragmentary, it is substantial enough to posit a tradition of historical writing among Egyptian, Babylonian, and Phoenician authors. Josephus's claim should thus be taken with more seriousness than a rhetorical move. It is against the background of this tradition that I have evaluated Luke-Acts.

While scholars will undoubtedly continue to argue about the relationship between Luke and Acts, it appears to me that the basic contours and substance of Acts were planned when Luke was written. It was common for an ancient author to sketch a plan of a work or to make notes in advance of composing a work. So, for example, Josephus tells us that while he was in the Roman camp outside the walls of Jerusalem, "I wrote a careful record, noticing what took place in the Roman camp and was the only one to understand the things related by the deserters. Then, when I had the leisure in Rome and everything for the account was ready and I had access to some assistants for the Greek, I wrote my narrative of those events."[2] I suggest that the author of Luke-Acts also prepared materials for his two scrolls, wrote and released the first, and then wrote the second and released it after a period of time. I do not believe that Acts was ever intended to stand apart from Luke. The key piece of evidence—which I will someday address—is the presence of the secondary preface in Acts. This brief secondary preface suggests that the work cannot stand on its own. Authors wrote relatively brief prefaces that summarized the preceding scroll and introduced the current scroll. This was a common practice among those who wrote multiple scrolls for a larger work: Diodorus Siculus,[3] Josephus,[4] and Philo[5] all regularly used secondary prefaces to connect

2. Josephus, *Ag. Ap.* 1.49–50.

3. All of the extant books of Diodorus except for 2, 3, and 11 have secondary prefaces. Even a number of the partially preserved books have them. See Kenneth S. Sacks, "The Lesser Proemiums of Diodorus Siculus," *Hermes* 110 (1982): 434–43 and Kenneth S. Sacks, *Diodorus Siculus and the History of the First Century* (Princeton: Princeton University Press, 1990), 9–22.

4. Josephus, *Ant.* 8.1; 13.1; 14.1; 15.1; 20.1; *Ag. Ap.* 2.1–7.

5. Philo used them in the Allegorical Commentary in *Plant.* 1; *Ebr.* 1; *Sobr.* 1; *Her.* 1; *Fug.* 1–2; and *Somn.* 1.1. Every treatise in the Exposition of the Law has a secondary preface except

scrolls that were part of larger works they wrote. This means that we have a history of the Way from John through Paul. It is the story of a people, related biographically through different figures much like Herodotus's *Histories*, but it is about a larger unit.

Historical narratives in apologetic historiography have hybrid characters: they are heavily indebted to their own traditions and at the same time deliberately situate these traditions in the framework of the larger culture. We examined the former in part two and the latter in part three.

The author indicates that the work is a continuation of the incomplete LXX. He does so by following the practice of continuators or historians who pick up where their predecessor left off and continue the story. This is why the author begins with John (Luke 16:16), who is the transitional figure between Israel and Jesus. Thus, unlike Josephus, who offered his *Jewish Antiquities* as a replacement of the LXX to the larger Greco-Roman world, the author of Luke-Acts offered his work as a continuation of the LXX to communities that accepted the LXX as Scripture. The author laid out his understanding of history in the speech of Paul in Pisidia of Antioch (Acts 13:16b–41) in which he aligns his understanding of history with the literary works of the LXX and his own narrative. While the story of Jesus has changed the way that the author read the LXX, it is clear that the author knew the ways in which Hellenistic Jewish historians retold their stories. The speech of Stephen in Acts 7:2–50 makes this clear. The story of Luke-Acts is thus deeply rooted in understandings of Israel, although it offers a fresh understanding.

Apologetic historians also felt compelled to move their traditions into the culture of the larger world by incorporating literary forms and values of the larger culture. This orientation is immediately evident: the work opens with a literary preface (Luke 1:1–4) and is the only work in the NT to do so; a fact that should tell us something about the importance of situating the Way within the larger world. I have tried to illustrate how the author did this in three ways. These by no means exhaust the ways in which the author has hellenized the traditions, but they illustrate the phenomenon. Two of the three illustrations are linked to philosophy, the death of Jesus, and the summaries that describe the Jerusalem community: the former was modeled on the death of Socrates;

---

for the introductory *Mos.* and the opening treatise, *Opif.*: *Abr.* 1–6; *Ios.* 1; *Decal.* 1; *Spec.* 1.1; 2.1; 3.7; 4.1; 4.133–134, for the opening of the treatment of the virtues; and *Praem.* 1–3. See also *Mos.* 2.1–7. On the use of these secondary prefaces see Gregory E. Sterling, "'Prolific in Expression and Broad in Thought': Internal References to Philo's Allegorical Commentary and Exposition of the Law," *Euphrosyne* 40 (2012): 56–76, esp. 60–63, 69–72.

the latter on the tradition of depicting select religious/philosophical communities as "athletes of virtue." While Luke-Acts does not betray any awareness of the nuances of Hellenistic philosophy, it does use it in a popular way to win social respectability for the fledgling movement it narrates. The larger social apology that moves well beyond philosophy is built into the structure of the narrative in much the same way that Josephus built his social apology for the Jewish people into the fabric of the *Jewish Antiquities*. Both authors deflect criticisms deftly and adroitly, not directly and brutishly. Both insist on the antiquity of their people, but in different ways. Josephus can rattle the chain back five thousand years; Luke must connect the people he describes with Israel—a conceptual integration.

The author has done this in an attempt to let members of the Way understand who they are. Telling them their story was a means of providing a self-understanding.[6] It was how the author wanted the disciples to understand and make sense of the world they inhabited and their place in it. It is important to acknowledge that not all early followers of Jesus would have agreed with this account, but it became influential enough that it became part of the canon of texts held sacred by Christians. In this way the argument that it was a continuation of the LXX was brought to fruition.

When *Historiography and Self-Definition* was first released in 1992, David L. Balch kindly arranged to devote a session at the International Meeting of the Society of Biblical Literature to review it and Richard Burridge's *What Are the Gospels?*, both of which had appeared in the same year.[7] My respondent was the famous German classicist Albrecht Dihle (Loveday Alexander responded to Richard). Dihle had fought in the Second World War and lost an arm when he was seriously wounded. The contrast between an established German professor nearing the end of a long and distinguished career and a young American who was just beginning his own was not lost on me—and I am sure was not lost on the audience. There was a point in our exchange when the tone of the conversation changed. When Professor Dihle realized that I had read the ancient texts that we were discussing—histories, biographies, and novels—and

6. Margaret R. Somers, "The Narrative Constitution of Identity: A Relational and Network Approach," *Theory and Society* 23 (1994): 605–49, has made a case for "narrative identity" that combines the social construction of identity with narrative analysis. She points out that most of the work on identity comes out of a concern to recontextualize groups from the margins. She understands narrative as social ontology and social epistemology and not simply representation. More could be done along these lines.

7. Richard A. Burridge, *What Are the Gospels? A Comparison with Greco-Roman Biography*, SNTSMS 70 (Cambridge: Cambridge University Press, 1992).

was not dependent upon modern summaries, his facial expression changed as did the tone of the conversation. I do not know that I convinced him of my thesis, but we both appreciated the need to ground our theses in close readings of ancient sources. And so I now leave this sequel with readers, hoping that you will appreciate that I have made this case on the basis of my reading of the ancient texts. While I hope that the arguments of this book convince you of my thesis, it is more important that they send you back to the texts—*ad fontes.*

Bibliography

Adam, Alfred. *Antike Berichte über die Essener*. 2nd ed. KlT 182. Berlin: de Gruyter, 1972.

Adams, Sean A. *The Genre of Acts and Collected Biography*. SNTSMS 156. Cambridge: Cambridge University Press, 2013.

Adler, William. *Time Immemorial: Archaic History and Its Sources in Christian Chronography from Julius Africanus to George Syncellus*. Dumbarton Oaks Studies 26. Washington, DC: Dumbarton Oaks, 1989.

Alexander, Loveday C. A. "Acts and Ancient Intellectual Biography." Pages 56–63 in *The Book of Acts in Its Ancient Literary Setting*. Edited by Bruce W. Winter and Andrew C. Clarke. Vol. 1 of *The Book of Acts in Its First Century Setting*. Edited by Bruce W. Winter. Grand Rapids: Eerdmans, 1993.

———. "Formal Elements and Genre: Which Greco-Roman Prologues Most Closely Parallel the Lukan Prologues?" Pages 9–26 in *Jesus and the Heritage of Israel: Luke's Narrative Claims upon Israel's Legacy*. Edited by David P. Moessner. Harrisburg, PA: Trinity, 1999.

———. *The Preface to Luke's Gospel: Literary Convention and Social Context in Luke 1.1–4 and Acts 1.1*. SNTSMS 78. Cambridge: Cambridge University Press, 1993.

Andersen, T. D. "The Meaning of ΕΧΟΝΤΕΣ ΧΑΡΙΝ ΠΡΟΣ in Acts 2.47." *NTS* 34 (1988): 604–10.

Argyle, Aubrey W. "The Greek of Luke and Acts." *NTS* 20 (1973–1974): 441–45.

Armstrong, Sharon L., Lila R. Gleitman, and Henry Gleitman. "What Some Concepts Might Not Be." *Cognition* 12 (1983): 263–308.

Attridge, Harold W., ed. *Nag Hammadi Codex I (the Jung Codex)*. 2 vols. NHS 22–23. Leiden: Brill, 1985.

Attridge, Harold W., and Robert A. Oden Jr. *Philo of Byblos, "The Phoenician History": Introduction, Critical Text, Translation, Notes*. CBQMS 9. Washington, DC: Catholic Biblical Association, 1981.

Backhaus, Knut. *Das Lukanische Doppelwerk: Zur literarischen Basis frühchristlicher Geschichtsdeutung*. BZNW 240. Berlin: de Gruyter, 2022.

Bacon, Benjamin W. *An Introduction to the New Testament*. London: Macmillan, 1907.

———. "Stephen's Speech: Its Argument and Doctrinal Relationship." Pages 213–76 in *Biblical and Semitic Studies: Critical and Historical Essays by the Members of the Semitic and Biblical Faculty of Yale University*. New York: Scribner's Sons, 1901.

Baden, Hans. "Untersuchungen zur Einheit der *Hellenika* Xenophons." Diss., Universität Hamburg, 1966.

Balch, David L. *Contested Ethnicities and Images: Studies in Luke-Acts*. WUNT 345. Tübingen: Mohr Siebeck, 2015.

Barber, Godfrey L. *The Historian Ephorus*. Cambridge: Cambridge University Press, 1935. Repr., Chicago: Ares, 1993.

Barclay, John. *Against Apion: Translation and Commentary*. FJTC 10. Leiden: Brill, 2007.

———. "Poverty in Pauline Studies: A Response to Steve Friesen." *JSNT* 26 (2004): 363–66.

Bar-Kochva, Bezalel. *Pseudo-Hecataeus: Legitimizing the Jewish Diaspora*. HCS 21. Berkeley: University of California Press, 1996.

Barnard, Leslie W. "Saint Stephen and Early Alexandrian Christianity." *NTS* 7 (1960–1961): 31–45.

Barnes, Timothy D. "The Editions of Eusebius' *Ecclesiastical History*." *GRBS* 21 (1980): 191–201.

Barreto, Eric. *Ethnic Negotiations: The Function of Race and Ethnicity in Acts 16*. WUNT 2.294. Tübingen: Mohr Siebeck, 2010.

Barrett, Charles K. *A Critical and Exegetical Commentary on the Acts of the Apostles*. 2 vols. ICC. Edinburgh: T&T Clark, 1994–98.

———. "Old Testament History according to Stephen and Paul." Pages 57–69 in *Studien zum Text und zur Ethik des Neuen Testaments: Festschrift zum 80. Geburtstag von Heinrich Greeven*. Edited by Wolfgang Schrage. BZNW 47. Berlin: de Gruyter, 1986.

———. "The Third Gospel as a Preface to Acts." Pages 1451–66 in *The Four Gospels: Festschrift. Frans Neirynck*. Edited by F. van Segbroek et al. 3 vols. BETL 100. Leuven: Leuven University Press, 1992.

Baumeister, Theofried. "Anytos und Meletos können mich zwar töten, schaden jedoch können sie mir nicht." Pages 58–63 in *Platonismus und Christentum: Festschrift für H. Dörrie*. Edited by Horst Dieter Blume and Friedhelm Mann. Jahrbuch für Antike und Christentum Ergänzungsband 10. Münster: Aschendorff, 1983.

Baumgarten, Albert I. "Philo of Byblos." *ABD* 5:342–44.

———. *"The Phoenician History" of Philo of Byblos: A Commentary.* EPRO 89. Leiden: Brill, 1981.

Beall, Todd S. *Josephus' Description of the Essenes Illustrated by the Dead Sea Scrolls.* SNTSMS 58. Cambridge: Cambridge University Press, 1988.

Beavis, Mary-Ann. *Jesus and Utopia: Looking for the Kingdom of God in the Roman World.* Minneapolis: Fortress, 2006.

———. "Philo's Therapeutai: Philosopher's Dream or Utopian Construction?" *JSP* 14 (2004): 30–42.

Beck, Brian E. "'Imitatio Christi' and the Lucan Passion Narrative." Pages 28–47 in *Suffering and Martyrdom in the New Testament: Studies Presented to G. M. Styler by the Cambridge New Testament Seminar.* Edited by W. Horbury and B. McNeil. Cambridge: Cambridge University Press, 1981.

Begg, Christopher T. *Flavius Josephus, Judean Antiquities 5–7.* FTJC 4. Leiden: Brill, 2005.

Beggs, Mike. "From Kingdom to *Ethnos*: The Transformation of a Metaphor in Eusebius' *Historia Ecclesiastica.*" PhD diss., University of Notre Dame, 1999.

Benko, Stephen. "Pagan Criticism of Christianity during the First Two Centuries A.D." *ANRW* 23.2:1055–118. Part 2, *Principat,* 23.2. Edited by Hildegard Temporini and Wolfgang Haase. New York: de Gruyter, 1980.

———. *Pagan Rome and the Early Christians.* Bloomington: Indiana University Press, 1984.

Benoit, Pierre. *Jesus and the Gospel.* 2 vols. New York: Seabury, 1974.

Benz, Ernst. "Christus und Sokrates in der alten Kirche (Ein Beitrag zum altkirchlichen Verständnis des Märtyers und des Martyriums)." *ZNW* 43 (1951): 195–244.

Berger, Klaus. "Hellenistische Gattungen im Neuen Testament." *ANRW* 25.2:1031–432, 1831–35. Part 2, *Principat,* 25.2. Edited by Hildegard Temporini and Wolfgang Haase. New York: de Gruyter, 1984.

Bergmeier, Roland. *Die Essener-Berichte des Flavius Josephus: Quellenstudien zu den Essenertexten im Werk des jüdischen Historiographen.* Kampden: Kok Pharos, 1993.

Bertelli, Lucio. "Hecataeus: From Genealogy to Historiography." Pages 67–94 in *The Historian's Craft in the Age of Herodotus.* Edited by Nino Luraghi. Oxford: Oxford University Press, 2001.

Biblia Patristica: Index des citations et allusions bibliques dans la littérature patristique. Vol. 4 of *Eusèbe de Césarée, Cyrille de Jérusalem, Épiphane de Salamine.* Paris: Éditions du Centre National de le Recherche Scientifique, 1987.

Bickerman, Elias J. "Origines Gentium." *CP* 47 (1952): 65–81.

Bidez, Joseph, ed. *Philostorgius, Kirchengeschichte: Mit dem Leben des Lucian von*

Antiochien und den Fragmenten eines arianischen Historiographen. 3rd ed. GCS n. F. Berlin: Akademie-Verlag, 1981.

———. *Sozomenus, Kirchengeschichte.* 2nd ed. GCS n. F. 4. Berlin: Akademie-Verlag, 1995.

Bihler, Johannes. *Die Stephanusgeschichte in Zusammenhang der Apostelgeschichte.* Münchener Theologische Studien 1.16. Munich: Max Hueber, 1963.

Billerbeck, Paul. "Ein Synagogen-gottesdienst in Jesu Tagen?" *ZNW* 55 (1964): 143–61.

Birnbaum, Ellen, and John Dillon. *Philo of Alexandria "On the Life of Abraham": Introduction, Translation, and Commentary.* PACS 6. Leiden: Brill, 2021.

Bodnar, Istvan. "Anaximander." *BNP* 1:660–61. Edited by Hubert Cancik and Helmuth Schneider. Leiden: Brill, 2002.

Bovon, François. "Le récit lucanien de la passion de Jésus (Lu 22–23)." Pages 393–423 in *The Synoptic Gospels: Source Criticism and the New Literary Criticism.* Edited by Camille Focant. BETL 110. Leuven: Leuven University Press, 1993.

———. *Luke.* 3 vols. Translated by Christine M. Thomas (vol. 1), Donald S. Deer (vol. 2), and James Crouch (vol. 3). Hermeneia. Minneapolis: Fortress, 2002–2013.

Bowersock, Glen W. *Martyrdom and Rome.* Cambridge: Cambridge University Press, 1995.

Bowker, John W. "Speeches in Acts. A Study in Proem and Yellammedenu Form." *NTS* 14 (1967): 96–111.

Braumann, Georg, ed. *Das Lukas-Evangelium: Die redaktions- und kompositionsgeschichtliche Forschung.* Wege der Forschung 280. Darmsttadt: Wissenschaftliche Buchgesellschaft, 1974.

Braun, Herbert. *Qumran und das Neue Testament.* 2 vols. Tübingen: Mohr Siebeck, 1966.

Brooke, George J. *Exegesis at Qumran: 4QFlorilegium in Its Jewish Context.* JSOTSup 29. Sheffield: JSOT Press, 1985.

Brown, Dee. *Bury My Heart at Wounded Knee: An Indian History of the American West.* New York: Bantam, 1971.

Brown, Raymond E. *The Birth of the Messiah: A Commentary on the Infancy Narrative in the Gospels of Matthew and Luke.* Rev. ed. New York: Doubleday, 1993.

———. *The Death of the Messiah: From Gethsemane to the Grave (A Commentary on the Passion Narratives in the Four Gospels).* 2 vols. AYBRL. New York: Doubleday, 1994.

Brubaker, Rogers. *Ethnicity without Groups.* Cambridge: Harvard University Press, 2004.

Bruce, Frederick F. "Paul's Use of the Old Testament in Acts." Pages 71–79 in *Tra-*

dition and Interpretation in the New Testament: Essays in Honor of E. Earle Ellis. Edited by Gerald F. Hawthorne and Otto Betz. Tübingen: Mohr Siebeck; Grand Rapids: Eerdmans, 1987.

———. "Stephen's Apologia." Pages 37–50 in *Scripture: Meaning and Method; Essays Presented to Anthony Tyrell Hanson for His Seventieth Birthday.* Pickering: Hull University Press, 1987.

Buell, Denise. *Why This New Race: Ethnic Reasoning in Early Christianity.* New York: Columbia University Press, 2005.

Bultmann, Rudolf. "Ist voraussetzungslose Exegese möglich?" *TZ* 13 (1957): 409–17. Repr. pages 289–96, 314–15 in Rudolf Bultmann, *Existence and Faith: Shorter Writings of Rudolf Bultmann.* Edited and translated by Schubert Ogden. Cleveland: World Publishing Books, 1960.

———. *Theology of the New Testament.* Translated by Kendrick Grobel. 2 vols. New York: Scribner's Sons, 1951–1955.

Burgess, Richard W. "The Dates and Editions of Eusebius' *Chronici Canones* and *Historia Ecclesiastica.*" *JTS* 48 (1997): 471–504.

Burridge, Richard A. *What Are the Gospels? A Comparison with Greco-Roman Biography.* SNTSMS 70. Cambridge: Cambridge University Press, 1992.

Buschmann, Gerd. *Martyrium Polycarpi—Eine formkritische Studie: Beitrag zur Frage nach der Entstehung der Gattung Märtyerakte.* BZNW 70. Berlin: de Gruyter, 1994.

Buss, Matthäus F.-J. *Die Missionspredigt des Apostels Paulus im pisidischen Antiochien: Analyse von Apg 13,16–41 im Hinblick auf die literarische und thematische Einheit der Paulusrede.* Stuttgart: Katholisches Bibelwerk, 1980.

Cadbury, Henry J. *The Making of Luke-Acts.* New York: Macmillan, 1927. Repr., London: SPCK, 1961.

———. *The Style and Literary Method of Luke.* HTS 6. Cambridge: Harvard University Press, 1920. Repr., New York: Krauss, 1969.

———. "The Summaries in Acts." Pages 392–402 in *The Beginnings of Christianity, Part I: The Acts of the Apostles.* Edited by Frederick J. Foakes Jackson and Kirsopp Lake. 5 vols. London: Macmillan, 1920–1933. Repr., Grand Rapids: Baker, 1979.

Cagnat, R., and G. LaFaye, eds. *Inscriptiones Graecae ad res Romanas pertinentes.* 4 vols. Paris: Ernest Leroux, 1901–1927.

Campbell, Anthony F. "Psalm 78." *CBQ* 41 (1979): 51–79.

Canfora, Luciano. "Il ciclo storico." *Belfagor* 26 (1971): 653–70.

Carriker, Andrew J. *The Library of Eusebius of Caesarea.* VCSup 67. Leiden: Brill, 2003.

Carroll, John T., and Joel B. Green. *The Death of Jesus in Early Christianity.* Peabody, MA: Hendrickson, 1995.

Cerfaux, Lucien. "La composition de la première partie du Livre des Actes." *ETL* 13 (1936): 667–91. Repr. pages 63–91 in vol. 2 of *Recueil Lucien Cerfaux*. 2 vols. BETL 6–7. Louvain: J. Duculot, 1954.

———. "La première communauté chrétienne à Jérusalem (Act., II, 41-V, 42)." *ETL* 16 (1939): 5–31. Repr. pages 125–56 in vol. 2 of *Recueil Lucien Cerfaux*. 2 vols. BETL 6–7. Louvain: J. Duculot, 1954.

Chestnut, Glenn F. "Eusebius, Augustine, Orosius, and the Later Patristic and Medieval Christian Historians." Pages 687–713 in *Eusebius, Christianity and Judaism*. Edited by Harold W. Attridge and Gohei Hata. Detroit: Wayne State University Press, 1992.

———. *The First Christian Histories: Eusebius, Socrates, Sozomen, Theodoret, and Evagrius*. 2nd ed. Macon, GA: Mercer University Press, 1986.

Christian, Linda Gregorian. "The Figure of Socrates in Erasmus' Work." *Sixteenth Century Journal* 3 (1972): 1–10.

Clark, Albert C. *The Acts of the Apostles*. Oxford: Clarendon, 1933.

Clifford, Richard J. "In Zion and David a New Beginning: An Interpretation of Psalm 78." Pages 121–41 in *Traditions in Transformation*. Edited by Baruch Halpern and Jon D. Levinson. Winona Lake, IN: Eisenbrauns, 1981.

Clivaz, Claire. "Luke 22:43–44 and Judeo-Christian Memories." *REJ* (forthcoming).

Co, Maria Anicia. "The Major Summaries in Acts: (Acts 2,42–47; 4,32–35; 5,12–16) Linguistic and Literary Relationship." *ETL* 68 (1992): 49–85.

Cobb, L. Stephanie. "Polycarp's Cup: *The Martyrdom of Polycarp*." *JRH* 38 (2013): 224–40.

Cohen, Shaye J. D. "History and Historiography in the *Against Apion* of Josephus." *History and Theory* 27 (1988): 1–11. Repr. pages 1–11 in *Essays in Jewish Historiography*. SFSHJ 15. Atlanta: Scholars Press, 1991.

———. "Respect for Judaism by Gentiles according to Josephus." *HTR* 80 (1987): 409–30.

Collins, Adela Y. "From Noble Death to Crucified Messiah." *NTS* 40 (1994): 481–503.

———. "The Genre of the Passion Narrative." *ST* 47 (1993): 3–28.

———. "Introduction." *Semeia* 15 (1986): 1–11.

Collins, John J. *Between Athens and Jerusalem: Jewish Identity in the Hellenistic Diaspora*. New York: Crossroad, 1992.

———. "Introduction: Morphology of a Genre." *Semeia* 14 (1979): 1–20.

Conzelmann, Hans. *Acts of the Apostles*. Translated by James Limburg, A. Thomas Kraabel, and Donald H. Juel. Hermeneia. Philadelphia: Fortress, 1987.

———. *Gentiles-Jews-Christians: Polemics and Apologetics in the Greco-Roman Era*. Translated by Eugene Boring. Minneapolis: Fortress, 1992.

———. *The Theology of St. Luke*. Translated by Geoffrey Buswell. New York: Harper & Row, 1966.

Countryman, Louis William. *The Rich Christian in the Church of the Early Empire: Contradictions and Accommodations*. Texts and Studies in Religion 7. New York: Edwin Mellen, 1980.

Cowan, J. Andrew. *The Writings of Luke and the Jewish Roots of the Christian Way: An Examination of the Aims of the First Christian Historian in the Light of Ancient Politics, Ethnography, and Historiography*. LNTS 599. London: T&T Clark, 2019.

Crockett, Larrimore C. "Luke 4:25–27 and Jewish-Gentile Relations in Luke-Acts." *JBL* 88 (1969): 177–83.

Croke, Brian, and Alanna M. Emmett. "Historiography in Late Antiquity: An Overview." Pages 1–13 in *History and Historians in Late Antiquity*. Edited by Brian Croke and Alanna M. Emmett. Sydney: Pergamon, 1983.

Cullmann, Oscar. *The Johannine Circle*. Translated by John Bowden. Philadelphia: Westminster, 1975.

———. "The Significance of the Qumran Texts for Research into the Beginnings of Christianity." *JBL* 74 (1955): 213–26.

Damschen, Gregor. "Lysimachus [6]." *DNP* 7:608. Edited by Hubert Cancik and Helmuth Schneider. Stuttgart: Metzler, 1997.

D'Angelo, Mary Rose. "Women in Luke-Acts: A Redactional View." *JBL* 109 (1990): 441–61.

Davies, William D. *The Gospel and the Land: Early Christianity and Jewish Territorial Doctrine*. Berkeley: University of California Press, 1974. Repr., Sheffield: JSOT Press, 1994.

Defosse, P. "A propos du début insolite des 'Helléniques.'" *Revue Belge* 46 (1968): 1–24.

Degenhardt, Hans-Joachim. *Lukas–Evangelist der Armen: Besitz und Besitzverzicht in den lukanischen Schriften (Eine traditions- und redaktionsgeschichtliche Untersuchung)*. Stuttgart: Katholisches Bibelwerk, 1964.

Deissmann, Adolf. *Light from the Ancient East: The New Testament Illustrated by Recently Discovered Texts of the Graeco-Roman World*. Translated by Lionel R. M. Strachan. New York: Harper & Brothers, 1927.

———. *Paul: A Study in Social and Religious History*. Translated by William E. Wilson. New York: Harper & Brothers, 1957.

Delling, Gerhard. "Israels Geschichte und Jesusgeschehen nach Acta. " Pages 187–97 in *Neues Testament und Geschichte: Historisches Geschehen und Deutung im Neuen Testament: Oscar Cullmann zum 70 Geburtstag*. Edited by Heinrich Baltensweiler and Bo Reicke. Zurich: Theologischer Verlag; Tübingen: Mohr Siebeck, 1972.

Dench, Emma. "Ethnography and History." Pages 493–503 in *A Companion to Greek and Roman Historiography*. Edited by John Marincola. 2 vols. Oxford: Blackwell, 2007. Repr., Chichester: Wiley-Blackwell, 2011.

DeSilva, David A. "Paul's Sermon in Antioch of Pisidia." *BSac* 154 (1994): 32–49.

Deubner, Ludwig, and Ulrich Klein, eds. *Iamblichus: De vita Pythagorica liber.* Stuttgart: Teubner, 1975.

De Zwaan, Johannes. "Was the Book of Acts a Posthumous Edition?" *HTR* 17 (1924): 95–153.

Dibelius, Martin. *From Tradition to Gospel.* New York: Scribner, n.d.

———. *Studies in the Acts of the Apostles.* Edited by Heinrich Greeven. New York: Scribner's Sons, 1956.

Dillery, John. *Clio's Other Sons: Berossus and Manetho, with an Afterword on Demetrius.* Ann Arbor: University of Michigan Press, 2015.

———. "Greek Historians of the Near East: Clio's 'Other' Sons." Pages 221–30 in *A Companion to Greek and Roman Historiography*. Edited by John Marincola. 2 vols. Oxford: Blackwell, 2007. Repr., Chichester: Wiley-Blackwell, 2011.

Dillon, John, and Jackson Hershbell, eds. *Iamblichus: On the Pythagorean Way of Life (Text, Translation, and Notes).* SBLTT 29. Atlanta: Scholars Press, 1991.

Dinkler, Michal Beth. *Literary Theory and the New Testament.* AYBRL. New Haven: Yale University Press, 2019.

———. "The Politics of Stephen's Storytelling: Narrative Rhetoric and Reflexivity in Acts 7:2–53." *ZNW* 111 (2020): 33–64.

Dodd, Charles H. *According to the Scriptures.* London: Collins, 1952.

Donahue, John R. "Mark." Pages 983–1009 in *Harper's Bible Commentary*. Edited by James L. Mays. San Francisco: Harper & Row, 1988.

Donaldson, Terence L. "Moses Typology and the Sectarian Nature of Early Christian Anti-Judaism: A Study in Acts 7." *JSNT* 12 (1981): 27–52. Repr. pages 230–52 in *New Testament Backgrounds: A Sheffield Reader*. Edited by Craig A. Evans and Stanley Porter. Sheffield: Sheffield Academic, 1997.

Doran, Robert. "The Jewish Hellenistic Historians before Josephus." *ANRW* 20.1:246–97. Part 2, *Principat*, 20.1. Edited by Hildegard Temporini and Wolfgang Haase. New York: de Gruyter, 1987.

Döring, Klaus. *Exemplum Socratis: Studien zur Sokratesnachwirkung in der kynisch-stoischen Popularphilosophie der frühen Kaiserzeit und im frühen Christentum.* Hermes 42. Wiesbaden: Franz Steiner, 1979.

Dorival, Gilles, Marguerit Harl, and Olivier Munnich. *La Bible grecque des Septante: du judaïsme hellénistique au christianisme ancien.* Initiations au christianisme ancien. Paris: Éditions du C.N.R.S., 1988.

Dormeyer, Detlev. *Die Passion Jesu als Verhaltensmodell: Literarische und theolo-*

gische Analyse der Traditions- und Redaktionsgeschichte der Markuspassion. NTAbh 11. Münster: Aschendorff, 1974.

———. *The New Testament among the Writings of Antiquity.* Translated by Rosemarie Kossov. Sheffield: Sheffield Academic, 1998.

Drews, Robert. *The Greek Accounts of Eastern History.* Washington, DC: The Center for Hellenic Studies. Cambridge: Harvard University Press, 1973.

Droge, Arthur. "The Apologetic Dimensions of the *Ecclesiastical History.*" Pages 495–98 in *Eusebius, Christianity, and Judaism.* Edited by Harold W. Attridge and Gohei Hata. Detroit: Wayne State University Press, 1992.

———. *Homer or Moses? Early Christian Interpretations of the History of Culture.* HUT 26. Tübingen: Mohr Siebeck, 1989.

Droge, Arthur J., and James D. Tabor. *A Noble Death: Suicide and Martyrdom among Christians and Jews in Antiquity.* San Francisco: Harper San Francisco, 1992.

Dumais, Marcel. *Le langage de l'évangélisation: L'Announce missionaire en milieu juif (Actes 13, 16–41).* Coll. 'Théologie. Recherches' 16. Tournai: Desclé; Montreal: Belarmin, 1976.

Dunn, James D. G. *The Parting of the Ways between Christianity and Judaism and Their Significance for the Character of Christianity.* 2nd ed. London: SCMS, 2006.

Dupont, Jacques. "La communauté des biens aux premiers jours de l'église (Actes 2,42.44–45; 4,32.34–35)." Pages 503–19 in *Études sur les Actes des Apôtres.* LD 45. Paris: Cerf, 1967.

———. "L'interprétation des psaumes dans les Actes des Apôtres." Pages 357–88 in *Le Psautier: Ses origenes. Ses problèmes littéraires. Son influence.* Orientalia et biblica lovaniensia 4. Louvain: Publications universitaires, 1962.

———. *The Sources of the Acts.* New York: Herder & Herder, 1964.

———. "L'union entre les premiers chrétiens dans les Actes des Apôtres." Pages 296–318 in *Nouvelles Études sur les Actes des Apôtres.* LD 118. Paris: Cerf, 1984.

———. "Vin veux, vin nouveau (Lu 5,39)." *CBQ* 25 (1963): 286–304.

Egger, Wilhelm. *Frohbotschaft und Lehre: Die Sammelberichte des Wirkens Jesu im Markusevangelium.* Frankfurter Theologische Studien 19. Frankfurt am Main: Josef Knecht, 1976.

Ehrman, Bart D. *The Apostolic Fathers.* 2 vols. LCL 24–25. Cambridge, MA: Harvard University Press, 2003.

Ehrman, Bart D., and Mark A. Plunkett. "The Angel and the Agony: The Textual Problem of Luke 22:43–44." *CBQ* 45 (1983): 401–16.

Eigler, Ulrich. "Exitus illustrium virorum." *DNP* 4:344–45. Edited by Hubert Cancik and Helmuth Schneider. Stuttgart: Metzler, 1998.

Ek, Sven. *Herodotismen in der Archäologie des Dionys von Halikarnass: Ein Beitrag zur Beleuchtung des beginnenden Klassizismus.* Lund: Gleerupska Univ.-bokhandeln, 1942.

Eliot, George. *Daniel Deronda.* Edited by Graham Handley. Oxford: Clarendon, 1984.

Engberg-Pederson, Troels. "Philo's *De vita contemplativa* as a Philosopher's Dream." *JSJ* 30 (1999): 40–64.

Erasmus, Desiderius. *Opera Omnia Desiderii Erasmi Roterodami.* Edited by Jan H. Waszink et al. 9 ordines in 55 vols. Amsterdam: North-Holland, 1969–.

Fascher, Erich. "Sokrates und Christus: Eine Studie 'zur aktuellen Aufgabe der Religionsphänomenologie' dem Andenken Heinrich Fricks († 31.12.52)." *ZNW* 45 (1954): 1–41.

Feldman, Louis H. *Jew and Gentile in the Ancient World.* Princeton: Princeton University Press, 1993.

———. *Judean Antiquities Books 1–4.* FJTC 3. Leiden: Brill, 1999.

Feldman, Louis H., and John R. Levison. *Josephus' "Contra Apionem": Studies in Its Character and Context with a Latin Concordance to the Portion Missing in Greek.* AGJU 34. Leiden: Brill, 1996.

Fellows, Richard G. "Renaming in Paul's Churches: The Case of Crispus-Sosthenes Revisited." *TynBul* 56 (2005): 111–30.

Ferguson, John. *Utopias of the Classical World.* Ithaca: Cornell University Press, 1975.

Festugière, A. J. "Sur une nouvelle Edition du 'De Vita Pythagorica' de Iamblique." *Revue des Etudes Grecques* 50 (1937): 476–78.

Finley, Moses I. *The Ancient Economy.* Berkeley: University of California Press, 1973.

Fitzmyer, Joseph A. "'4QTestimonia' and the New Testament." *TS* 18 (1957): 513–37.

———. *The Acts of the Apostles.* AB 31. New York: Doubleday, 1998.

———. *The Gospel according to Luke.* AB 28 and 28A. 2 vols. Garden City, NY: Doubleday, 1981–1984.

———. *Luke the Theologian: Aspects of His Teaching.* New York: Paulist, 1989.

Foakes Jackson, Frederick J., and Kirsopp Lake, eds. *The Beginnings of Christianity: The Acts of the Apostles.* 5 vols. London: Macmillan, 1920–1933. Repr., Grand Rapids: Baker, 1979.

Fornara, Charles W. *Herodotus: An Interpretative Essay.* Oxford: Oxford University Press, 1971.

———. *The Nature of History in Ancient Greece and Rome.* Eidos: Studies in Classical Kinds. Berkeley: University of California Press, 1983.

Fornaro, Sotera. "Herennios Philon." *DNP* 5:410–11. Edited by Hubert Cancik and Helmuth Schneider. Stuttgart: Metzler, 1998.

Franek, Juraj. "The Reception of Socrates in Tertullian." Pages 435–52 in *Brill's Companion to the Reception of Socrates*. Edited by Christopher Moore. Brill's Companions to Classical Reception 18. Leiden: Brill, 2019.

Franklin, Eric. *Christ the Lord: A Study in the Purpose and Theology of Luke-Acts*. Philadelphia: Fortress, 1975.

Fraser, Peter M. *Ptolemaic Alexandria*. 3 vols. Oxford: Clarendon, 1972.

Frede, Michael. "Chaeremon der Stoiker." *ANRW* 36.3:2067–103. Part 2, *Principat*, 36.3. Edited by Hildegard Temporini and Wolfgang Haase. New York: de Gruyter, 1989.

Friesen, Steven J. "Poverty in Pauline Studies: Beyond the So-Called New Consensus." *JSNT* 26 (2004): 323–61.

———. "Prospects for a Demography of the Pauline Mission: Corinth among the Churches." Pages 351–70 in *Urban Religion in Roman Corinth: Interdisciplinary Approaches*. Edited by Daniel N. Schowalter and Steven J. Friesen. HTS 53. Cambridge: Harvard University Press, 2005.

Gabba, Emilio. *Dionysius and "The History of Archaic Rome."* Sather Classical Lectures 56. Berkeley: University of California Press, 1991.

Garland, David E. *One Hundred Years of Study on the Passion Narratives*. National Association of Baptist Professors of Religion Bibliographic Series 3. Macon, GA: Mercer University Press, 1989.

Gaston, Lloyd. *No Stone on Another: Studies in the Significance of the Fall of Jerusalem in the Synoptic Gospels*. NovTSup 23. Leiden: Brill, 1970.

Geffcken, Johannes. "Die christlichen Martyrien." *Hermes* 45 (1910): 481–505.

———. *Zwei Griechische Apologeten*. Sammlung wissenschaftlicher Kommentare zu griechischen und römischen Schrifstellern. Leipzig: Teubner, 1907.

Gerber, Christine. *Ein Bild des Judentums für Nichtjuden von Flavius Josephus: Untersuchungen zu seiner Schrift "Contra Apionem."* AGAJU 40. Leiden: Brill, 1997.

Gill, David W. J. "Acts and the Urban Élites." Pages 105–118 in *Graeco-Roman Setting*. Edited by David W. J. Gill and Conrad Gempf. Vol. 2. of *The Book of Acts in Its First Century Setting*. Edited by Bruce M. Winter. Grand Rapids: Eerdmans, 1994.

Glombitza, Otto. "Akta xiii.15–41: Analyse einer lukanischen Predigt vor Juden: Ein Beitrag zum Problem der Reden in Akta." *NTS* 5 (1958–59): 306–17.

Goldingay, John. *Psalms*. 3 vols. Grand Rapids: Baker Academic, 2007–2008.

Goldstein, Jonathan A. *II Maccabees*. AB 41A. Garden City, NY: Doubleday, 1983.

Gomme, Arnold W., Antony Andrewes, and Kenneth J. Dover, eds. *A Historical Commentary on Thucydides*. 5 vols. Oxford: Clarendon, 1945–1981.

Gooch, Paul W. *Reflections on Jesus and Socrates: Word and Silence*. New Haven: Yale University Press, 1996.

Good, R. S. "Jesus, Protagonist of the Old in Lk 5:33–39." *NovT* 25 (1983): 19–36.

Grant, Robert M. *Eusebius as Church Historian*. Oxford: Clarendon, 1980.

Gray, Vivienne. *The Character of Xenophon's "Hellenica."* Baltimore: Johns Hopkins University Press, 1989.

———. "Mimesis in Greek Historical Writing." *AJP* 108 (1987): 467–86.

Green, Joel B. *The Death of Jesus: Tradition and Interpretation in the Passion Narrative*. WUNT 2.33. Tübingen: Mohr Siebeck, 1988.

Gregory, Andrew F., and C. Kavin Rowe, eds., *Rethinking the Unity and Reception of Luke and Acts*. Columbia: University of South Carolina Press, 2010.

Gruen, Erich. *Ethnicity in the Ancient World—Did It Matter?* Berlin: de Gruyter, 2020.

———. *Heritage and Hellenism: The Reinvention of Jewish Tradition*. HCS 30. Berkeley: University of California Press, 1998.

Gruenstein, E. L. "Mixing Memory and Design: Reading Psalm 78." *Proof* 10 (1990): 197–208.

Grünstäudl, Wolfgang. "Luke's Doublets and the Synoptic Problem." *NTS* 68 (2022): 13–25.

Haacker, Klaus. "Die Stellung des Stephanus in der Geschichte des Urchristentums." ANRW 26.2:1515–53. Part 2, *Principat*, 26.2. Edited by Hildegard Temporini and Wolfgang Haase. New York: de Gruyter, 1995.

Hadas, Moses. *The Third and Fourth Books of Maccabees*. Jewish Apocryphal Literature. New York: Dropsie College for Hebrew and Cognate Learning, 1953. Repr., New York: Ktav, 1976.

Haenchen, Ernst. *The Acts of the Apostles: A Commentary*. Translated by Bernard Noble and Gerald Shinn. Revised by Robert McL. Wilson. Philadelphia: Westminster, 1971.

Halpern-Amaru, Betsy. "Land Theology in Josephus' *Jewish Antiquities*." *JQR* 71 (1980): 201–29.

———. *Rewriting the Bible: Land and Covenant in Post-Biblical Jewish Literature*. Valley Forge, PA: Trinity, 1994.

Hansen, Günther C., ed. *Sokrates, Kirchengeschichte*. GCS n. F. 1. Berlin: Akademie-Verlag, 1995.

———, ed. *Theodoret, Kirchengeschichte*. 3rd ed. GCS n. F. 5. Berlin: Akademie-Verlag, 1996.

Hardwick, Michael E. *Josephus as an Historical Source in Patristic Literature through Eusebius*. BJS 128. Atlanta: Scholars Press, 1989.

Harnack, Adolf von. "Sokrates und die alte Kirche." Pages 29–48 of vol. 1.1 in *Reden und Aufsätze*. 7 vols. Gießen: A. Töpelmann, 1903.

Hartman, Lars. "David's Son: Apropa Acta 13, 16–41." *Svensk Exegetisk Arsbok* 28–29 (1963–1964): 117–34.

Hay, David. "Things Philo Said and Did Not Say about the Therapeutae." *SBLSP* 31 (1992): 673–84.

Heath, Michael J. "A Short Debate Concerning the Distress, Alarm, and Sorrow of Jesus." Pages 1–67 in vol. 70 of *Collected Works of Erasmus*. Toronto: University of Toronto Press, 1998.

Hedrick, Charles W. "The Role of 'Summary Statements' in the Composition of the Gospel of Mark: A Dialog with Kark Schmidt and Norman Perrin." *NovT* 26 (1984): 289–311.

Hengel, Martin. *Between Jesus and Paul: Studies in the Earliest History of Christianity*. Translated by John Bowden. Philadelphia: Fortress, 1987.

Hengel, Martin, and Roland Deines, eds. *The Septuagint as Christian Scripture: Its Prehistory and the Problem of Its Canon*. Edinburgh: T&T Clark, 2002.

Henry, William P. *Greek Historical Writing: A Historiographical Essay Based on Xenophon's Hellenica*. Chicago: Argonaut, 1967.

Heylbut, Gustav B., ed. *Eustratii et Michaelis et anonyma in Ethica Nicomachea commentaria*. Vol. 20 of *Commentaria in Aristotelem Graeca*. Berlin: Georg Reimer Berolini, 1892.

Hill, Craig C. *Hellenists and Hebrews: Reappraising Divisions within the Earliest Church*. Minneapolis: Fortress, 1992.

Hock, Ronald F., and Edward N. O'Neil. *The Progymnasmata*. Vol. 1 of *The Chreia in Ancient Rhetoric*. SBLTT 27. Atlanta: Scholars Press, 1986.

Hofstadter, Richard. *The Progressive Historians: Turner, Beard, Parrington*. New York: Knopf, 1968.

Högemann, Peter. "Xanthos [3]." *DNP* 12.2:604–5. Edited by Hubert Cancik and Helmuth Schneider. Stuttgart: Metzler, 1996.

Hogg, Michael A., and Dominic Abrams. *Social Identificaitons: A Social Psychology of Intergroup Relations and Group Processes*. London and New York: Routledge, 1998.

Holladay, Carl R. *Fragments from Hellenistic Jewish Authors*. 4 vols. SBLTT 20, 30, 39, 40. Chico, CA: Scholars Press, 1983–2003.

Holleaux, Maurice. *Études d'epigraphie et d'histoire grecques*. Edited by L. Robert. 6 vols. Paris: Adrien-Maisonneuve, 1938–1968.

Horrell, David G. *Ethnicity and Inclusion: Religion, Race, and Whiteness in Constructions of Jewish and Christian Identities*. Grand Rapids: Eerdmans, 2020.

Horst, Pieter W. van der. *Chaeremon: Egyptian Priest and Stoic Philosopher*. The

Fragments Collected and Translated with Explanatory Notes. EPRO 101. Leiden: Brill, 1984.

Inwood, Brad. "Chaeremon [2]." *DNP* 2:1082. Edited by Hubert Cancik and Helmuth Schneider. Stuttgart: Metzler, 1997.

Jacobson, Howard. *A Commentary on Pseudo-Philo's* Liber Antiquitatum Biblicarum. 2 vols. Leiden: Brill, 1996.

Jacoby, Felix. *Die Fragmente der griechischen Historiker.* 4 vols. Leiden: Brill, 1923–2021.

———. "Über die Entwicklung der griechischen Historiographie." *Klio* 9 (1909): 80–123.

James, Montague R. *The Biblical Antiquities of Philo.* Translations of Early Documents Series 1: Palestinian Jewish Texts (Pre-Rabbinic). London: SPCK, 1917. Repr., New York: Ktav, 1971.

Jellicoe, Sidney. "The Occasion and Purpose of the Letter of Aristeas: A Re-Examination." *NTS* 12 (1965–1966): 144–50.

Jennings, Willie James. *Acts.* Belief: A Theological Commentary on the Bible. Louisville: Westminster John Knox, 2017.

Jeremias, Joachim. *Heiligengräber in Jesu Umwelt (Mt. 23,29; Lk. 11,47): Eine Untersuchung zur Volksreligion der Zeit Jesu.* Göttingen: Vandenhoeck & Ruprecht, 1958.

———. *Die Sprache des Lukasevangeliums: Redaktion und Tradition im Nicht-Markusstoff des dritten Evangeliums.* Göttingen: Vandenhoeck & Ruprecht, 1980.

———. "Untersuchungen zum Quellenproblem der Apostelgeschichte." *ZNW* 36 (1937): 205–21. Repr. pages 238–55 in *Abba: Studien zur neutestamentlichen Theologie und Zeitgeschichte.* Göttingen: Vandenhoeck & Ruprecht, 1966.

Jervell, Jacob. *Luke and the People of God: A New Look at Luke-Acts.* Minneapolis: Augsburg, 1972.

———. *The Theology of the Acts of the Apostles.* Cambridge: Cambridge University Press, 1996.

Johnson, Luke Timothy. *The Literary Function of Possessions in Luke-Acts.* SBLDS 39. Atlanta: Scholars Press, 1977.

———. *Sharing Possessions: Mandate and Symbol of Faith.* OBT 9. Philadelphia: Fortress, 1981.

Josephus. Translated by Henry St. J. Thackeray et al. 10 vols. LCL. Cambridge: Harvard University Press, 1926–1965.

Judge, E. A. *Social Distinctives of the Christians in the First Century. Pivotal Essays by E. A. Judge.* Edited by David M. Scholer. Peabody, MA: Hendrickson, 2008.

————. *The Social Patterns of the Christian Groups in the First Century: Some Prolegomena to the Study of New Testament Ideas of Social Obligation.* London: Tyndale, 1960.

Kaiser, Walter C., Jr. "The Promise to David in Psalm 16 and Its Application in Acts 2:25–33 and 13:32–37." *JETS* 23 (1990): 219–29.

Karris, Robert J. *Luke: Artist and Theologian. Luke's Passion Account as Literature.* Theological Inquiries. New York: Paulist, 1985.

Kasher, Aryeh. *Neged "Apyon."* 2 vols. Jerusalem: Merkaz Zalman, 1996.

Keener, Craig S. *Acts: An Exegetical Commentary.* 4 vols. Grand Rapids: Baker Academic, 2012–2015.

Kellermann, Ulrich. *Auferstanden in den Himmel: 2 Makkabäer 7 und die Auferstehung der Märtyrer.* SBS 95. Stuttgart: Katholisches Bibelwerk, 1979.

————. "Das Danielbuch und die Märtyrertheologie der Auferstehung." Pages 51–75 in *Die Entstehung der jüdischen Martyrologie.* Edited by Jan Willem van Henten, B. A. G. M. Dehandshutter, and H. J. W. van der Klaauw. StPB 38. Leiden: Brill, 1989.

Kenyon, F. G., et al. *Greek Papyri in the British Museum.* 7 vols. London: British Museum, 1893–1974.

Kilgallen, John J. "The Function of Stephen's Speech (Acts 7, 2–53)." *Bib* 70 (1989): 173–93.

————. *The Stephen Speech: A Literary and Redactional Study of Acts 7,2–53.* AnBib 67. Rome: Biblical Institute Press, 1976.

Kirk, Geoffrey S., John E. Raven, and Malcolm Schofield. *The Presocratic Philosophers.* 2nd ed. Cambridge: Cambridge University Press, 1983.

Klauck, Hans-J. "Die heilige Stadt: Jerusalem bei Philo und Lukas." *KAIROS* 28 (1986): 129–51.

Klijn, Albertus F. J. "The Letter of Aristeas and the Greek Translation of the Pentateuch in Egypt." *NTS* 11.2 (1965): 154–58.

————. "Stephen's Speech–Acts vii 2–53," *NTS* 4.1 (1957): 25–31.

Kloppenborg, John S. *Christ's Associations: Connecting and Belonging in the Ancient City.* New Haven: Yale University Press, 2019.

————. "'Exitus clari viri': The Death of Jesus in Luke." *TJT* 8 (1992): 106–20.

Knust, Jennifer Wright. "'Who Were the Maccabees?': The Maccabean Martyrs and Performances on Christian Difference." Pages 79–104 in *Martyrdom: Canonisation, Contestation and Afterlives.* Edited by Ihaab Saloul and Jan Willem van Henten. Amsterdam: Amsterdam University Press, 2020.

Koester, Helmut. *Ancient Christian Gospels: Their History and Development.* Philadelphia: Trinity, 1990.

Koetschau, Paul, ed. *Die Schrift vom Martyrium, Buch I-IV, Gegen Celsus.* Vol. 1 of *Origenes Werke.* GCS 2. Leipzig: Hinrichs, 1899.

Krauss, Rolf. "Manethon." *DNP* 7:804–5. Edited by Hubert Cancik and Helmuth Schneider. Stuttgart: Metzler, 1997.

Kucicki, Janusz. *The Function of the Speeches in the Acts of the Apostles: A Key to Interpretation of Luke's Use of Speeches in Acts.* BibInt 158. Leiden: Brill, 2018.

Lakoff, George. *Women, Fire, and Dangerous Things: What Categories Reveal about the Mind.* Chicago: University of Chicago Press, 1987.

Laqueur, Richard. *Eusebius als Historiker seiner Zeit.* Berlin: de Gruyter, 1929.

Larsson, Edvin. "Temple Criticism and the Jewish Heritage: Some Reflections on Acts 6–7." *NTS* 39 (1993): 379–95.

Lee, Doohee. *Luke-Acts and "Tragic History": Communicating Gospel with the World.* WUNT 2.346. Tübingen: Mohr Siebeck, 2013.

Légasse, Simon. *Stephanos: Histoire et discours d'Étienne dans les Actes des Apôtres.* LD 147. Paris: Cerf, 1992.

Leipoldt, Johannes. *Griechische Philosophie und frühchristliche Askese.* Berichte über die Verhandlungen der sächsischen Akademie der Wissenschaften zu Leipzig, philologische-historische Klasse 106.4. Berlin: Akademie-Verlag, 1961.

Levine, Amy-Jill. *The Misunderstood Jew: The Church and the Scandal of the Jewish Jesus.* New York: HarperOne, 2006.

Lindars, Barnabas. *New Testament Apologetic: The Doctrinal Significance of the Old Testament Quotations.* Philadelphia: Westminster, 1961.

Litke, Wayne. "Acts 7:3 and Samaritan Chronology." *NTS* 42 (1996): 156–60.

Lloyd, Alan B. "Egypt." Pages 415–35 in *Brill's Companion to Herodotus.* Edited by Egbert J. Bakker, Irene J. F. de Jong, and Hans van Wees. Leiden: Brill, 2002.

Loeschcke, Gerhard, ed. *Gelasius Kirchengeschichte.* GCS 28. Leipzig: Hinrichs, 1918.

Lohmeyer, Ernst. *Galiläa und Jerusalem bei Lukas.* FRLANT n. F. 34. Göttingen: Vandenhoeck & Ruprecht, 1936.

Loisy, Alfred M. *Les Actes des Apôtres.* Paris: F. Rieder, 1920.

Long, Anthony A. "Socrates in Hellenistic Philosophy." *CQ* 38 (1988): 150–71. Repr. pages 1–34 in *Stoic Studies.* Cambridge: Cambridge University Press, 1996.

———. "The Socratic Legacy." Pages 617–41 in *The Cambridge History of Hellenistic Philosophy.* Edited by Keimpe Algra, Jonathan Barnes, Jaap Mansfeld, and Malcolm Schofield. Cambridge: Cambridge University Press, 1999.

Longenecker, Bruce W. *Remember the Poor: Paul, Poverty, and the Greco-Roman World.* Grand Rapids: Eerdmans, 2010.

Lord, Albert B. *A Singer of Tales.* Harvard Studies in Comparative Literature 24. Cambridge: Harvard University Press, 1960.

—. *The Singer Resumes the Tale*. Edited by Mary L. Lord. Ithaca: Cornell University Press, 1995.

Louth, Andrew. "The Date of Eusebius' *Historia Ecclesiastica*." *JTS* 41 (1990): 111–23.

Lüdemann, Gerd. *Early Christianity according to the Traditions in Acts: A Commentary*. Translated by John Bowden. Minneapolis: Fortress, 1989.

Machen, John Gresham. *The Virgin Birth of Christ*. New York: Harper & Row, 1930. Repr., Grand Rapids: Baker, 1965.

Malherbe, Abraham J. "'Not in a Corner': Early Christian Apologetic in Acts 26:26." *SecCent* 5 (1985–1986): 193–210.

—. *Social Aspects of Early Christianity*. 2nd ed. Philadelphia: Fortress, 1983.

Marcel, R. "'Saint' Socrate Patron de l'Humanisme." *Revue internationale de philosophie* 5 (1951): 135–43.

Marchant, Edgar C. *Xenophontis opera omnia*. 5 vols. OCT. Oxford: Clarendon, 1900–1920.

Marchant, Edgar C., and George E. Underhill, eds. *Xenophon's* Hellenica. 2 vols. Oxford: Clarendon, 1900–1906. Repr., Salem, NH: Ayer, 1984.

Marcus, Joel. *Mark 1–8*. AB 27. New York: Doubleday, 2000.

Marguerat, Daniel. *The First Christian Historian: Writing the Acts of the Apostles*. SNTSMS 131. Cambridge: Cambridge University Press, 2002.

Marincola, John. *Authority and Tradition in Ancient Historiography*. Cambridge: Cambridge University Press, 1997.

—. "Universal History from Ephorus to Diodorus." Pages 171–79 in *A Companion to Greek and Roman Historiography*. Edited by John Marincola. 2 vols. Oxford: Blackwell, 2007. Repr., Chichester: Wiley-Blackwell, 2011.

Markus, Robert A. "Church History and the Early Church Historians." SCH 11 (1975): 1–17.

Marshall, I. Howard. "Acts and the 'Former Treatise.'" Pages 174–75 in *Ancient Literary Setting*. Edited by Bruce W. Winter and Andrew D. Clarke. Vol. 1 of *The Book of Acts in Its First Century Setting*. Edited by Bruce W. Winter. Grand Rapids: Eerdmans, 1993.

—. *The Gospel of Luke: A Commentary on the Greek Text*. NIGTC 3. Grand Rapids: Eerdmans, 1978.

Marx, F. A. "Tacitus und die Literatur der Exitus Illustrium Virorum." *Philologus* 92 (1937–1938): 83–103.

Mason, Steve. "Jews, Judaeans, Judaizing, Judaism: Problems of Categorization in Ancient History." *JSJ* 38 (2007): 457–512.

—. *Josephus and the New Testament*. Peabody, MA: Hendrickson, 1992.

Mason, Steve, and Philip Esler. "Judean and Christ-Follower Identities: Grounds for a Distinction." *NTS* 63 (2017): 493–515.

Matera, Frank J. "The Death of Jesus according to Luke: A Question of Sources." *CBQ* 47 (1985): 469–85.

McCown, Chester C. "The Geography of Luke's Central Section." *JBL* 57 (1938): 51–66.

———. "Gospel Geography: Fiction, Fact, and Truth." *JBL* 60 (1941): 1–25.

McGowan, Andrew. "Eating People: Accusations of Cannibalism Against Christians in the Second Century." *JECS* 2 (1994): 413–42.

McKechnie, Paul R., and Stephen J. Kern, eds. *Hellenica Oxyrhynchia*. Warminster, Wiltshire: Aris & Phillips, 1989.

McLaren, Malcolm. "A Supposed Lacuna at the Beginning of Xenophon's *Hellenica*." *AJP* 100 (1979): 228–38.

McNicol, Allan J. "Rebuilding the House of David: The Function of the Benedictus in Luke-Acts." *ResQ* 40 (1998): 25–38.

Mead, A. H. "Old and New Wine St. Luke 5:39." *ExpTim* 99 (1987–1988): 234–35.

Mealand, David L. "Community of Goods and Utopian Allusions in Acts II–IV." *JTS* 28 (1977): 96–99.

Meggitt, Justin J. *Paul, Poverty, and Survival*. Studies of the New Testament and Its World. Edinburgh: T&T Clark, 1998.

Meister, Klaus. "Charon [3]." *BNP* 3:203–4. Edited by Hubert Cancik and Helmuth Schneider. Leiden: Brill, 2003.

———. *Die griechische Geschichtsschreibung: Von den Anfängen bis zum Ende des Hellenismus*. Stuttgart: W. Kohlhammer, 1990.

———. "Ephorus." *BNP* 4:1035–36. Edited by Hubert Cancik and Helmuth Schneider. Leiden: Brill, 2004.

———. "Hecataeus of Miletus." *BNP* 6:35–37. Edited by Hubert Cancik and Helmuth Schneider. Leiden: Brill, 2005.

———. "Hellanicus [1]." *BNP* 6:79–80. Edited by Hubert Cancik and Helmuth Schneider. Leiden: Brill, 2005.

Mendels, Doron. "'Creative History' in the Hellenistic Near East in the Third and Second Centuries BCE: The Jewish Case." *JSP* 2 (1988): 13–20.

Merkelbach, Reinhold. *Isis regina – Zeus Sarapis: Die griechisch-ägyptische Religion nach den Quellen dargestellt*. Stuttgart: Teubner, 1995.

Merrill, E. H. "Paul's Use of 'About 450 Years' in Acts 13:20." *BSac* 138 (1981): 246–57.

Metzger, Bruce M. *A Textual Commentary on the New Testament*. 2nd ed. Stuttgart: Deutsche Bibelgesellschaft/United Bible Societies, 1994.

Mitchell, Alan C. "'Greet the Friends by Name:' New Testament Evidence for the Greco-Roman Topos on Friendship." Pages 225–62 in *Greco-Roman Perspectives on Friendship*. Edited by John Fitzgerald. RBS 34. Atlanta: Scholars Press, 1997.

———. "The Social Function of Friendship in Acts 2:44–47 and 4:32–37." *JBL* 111 (1992): 255–72.

Moessner, David P. "The Appeal and Power of Poetics (Luke 1:1–4): Luke's Superior Credentials (παρηκολουθηκότι), Narrative Sequence (καθεξῆς), and Firmness of Understanding (ἀσφάλεια) for the Reader." Pages 84–123 in *Jesus and the Heritage of Israel: Luke's Narrative Claim upon Israel's Legacy*. Edited by David P. Moessner. Harrisburg, PA: Trinity, 1999.

———. "'The Christ Must Suffer': New Light on the Jesus, Stephen, Paul Parallels in Luke-Acts." *NovT* 28 (1986): 220–56.

Momigliano, Arnaldo. *Alien Wisdom: The Limits of Hellenization*. Cambridge: Cambridge University Press, 1975.

———. *The Classical Foundations of Modern Historiography*. Sather Classical Lectures 54. Berkeley: University of California Press, 1990.

Montanari, Franco. "Apion." *DNP* 1:845–47. Edited by Hubert Cancik and Helmuth Schneider. Stuttgart: Metzler, 1996.

Moss, Candida. *Ancient Christian Martyrdom: Diverse Practices, Theologies, and Traditions*. AYBRL. New Haven: Yale University Press, 2012.

Moulton, James H., Wilbert F. Howard, and Nigel Turner. *A Grammar of New Testament Greek*. 4 vols. Edinburgh: T&T Clark, 1906–1976.

Moyer, Ian S. "Luculentissima fragmenta: Manetho's *Aegyptiaca* and the Limits of Hellenism." Pages 84–141 in *Egypt and the Limits of Hellenism*. Cambridge: Cambridge University Press, 2011.

Müller, Johann G. *Des Flavius Josephus Schrift gegen den Apion: Text und Erklärung*. Basel: Bahnmaier [C. Detloff], 1877. Repr., Hildesheim: Georg Olm, 1969.

Munck, Johannes. *The Acts of the Apostles*. Rev. ed. AB 31. Garden City: Doubleday, 1967.

Murphy, Catherine M. *Wealth in the Dead Sea Scrolls and in the Qumran Community*. STDJ 40. Leiden: Brill, 2002.

Murphy, Frederick J. *Pseudo-Philo: Rewriting the Bible*. New York: Oxford University Press, 1993.

Musurillo, Herbert A. *The Acts of the Pagan Martyrs: Acta Alexandrinorum*. Oxford: Oxford University Press, 1954. Repr., New York: Arno, 1979.

Neibuhr, Barthold G. "Über Xenophons *Hellenika*." *Das Rheinische Museum für Philologie* 1 (1828): 194–98.

Nenci, Giuseppe. *Hecataei Milesii Fragmenta*. Biblioteca di Studi Superiori, Filol. Greca, 22. Florence: La Nuova Italia, 1954.

The New Testament in Greek, The Gospel according to Luke, Part One: Chapters 1–12. Edited by the American and British Committees of the International Greek New Testament Project. Oxford: Clarendon, 1984.

Newsom, Carol A. "Pairing Research Questions and Theories of Genre: A Case Study of the Hodayot." *DSD* 17 (2010): 241–59.

———. "Spying out the Land: A Report from Genology." Pages 19–30 in *Bakhtin and Genre Theory in Biblical Studies*. Edited by Roland Boer. SemeiaSt 63. Atlanta: Society of Biblical Literature, 2007.

Neyrey, Jerome H. "The Absence of Jesus' Emotions: The Lucan Redaction of Lk. 22,39–46." *Bib* 61 (1980): 153–71.

———. *The Passion according to Luke: A Redaction Study of Luke's Soteriology*. New York: Paulist, 1985.

Nikiprowetzky, Valentin. "La spiritualisation des sacrifices et le culte sacrificiel au Temple de Jérusalem chez Philon d'Alexandrie." *Semitica* 17 (1967): 97–116. Repr. pages 79–96 in *Études philoniennes*. Patrimoines Judaïsme. Paris: Cerf, 1996.

Nobbs, Alanna. "Acts and Subsequent Ecclesiastical Histories." Pages 153–63 in *Ancient Literary Setting*. Edited by Bruce W. Winter and Andrew D. Clarke. Vol. 1 of *The Book of Acts in Its First Century Setting*. Edited by Bruce W. Winter. Grand Rapids: Eerdmans, 1993.

Nock, Arthur Darby. "Paul and the Magus." Pages 164–88 in *The Beginnings of Christianity, Part I: The Acts of the Apostles*. Edited by Frederick J. Foakes Jackson and Kirsopp Lake. 5 vols. London: Macmillan, 1920–1933. Repr., Grand Rapids: Baker, 1979.

Nolland, John. *Luke*. 3 vols. WBC 35A, 35B, 35C. Dallas: Word, 1989–1993.

Nongbri, Brent. *Before Religion: A History of a Modern Concept*. New Haven: Yale University Press, 2013.

Novum Testamentum Graece. Edited by Barbara and Kurt Aland, Johannes Karavidopoulos, Carlo Martini, and Bruce Metzger. 27th ed. Stuttgart: Deutsche Bibelgesellschaft, 1993.

Novum Testamentum Graece. Edited by Barbara and Kurt Aland, Johannes Karavidopoulos, Carlo Martini, and Bruce Metzger. 28th ed. Stuttgart: Deutsche Bibelgesellschaft, 2012.

Oakes, Peter. "Constructing Poverty Scales for Graeco-Roman Society: A Response to Steven Friesen's 'Poverty in Pauline Studies.'" *JSNT* 26 (2004): 367–71.

Oden, Robert A., Jr. "Philo of Byblos and Hellenistic Historiography." *PEQ* 110 (1978): 115–26.

Ó Fearghail, Fearghus. "The Imitation of the Septuagint in Luke's Infancy Narrative." *Proceedings of the Irish Biblical Association* 2 (1989): 57–78.

Papiri greci e latini. Publicazioni della Società italiana per la ricerca dei papiri greci e latini in Egitto. 15 vols. Firenze: Felice le Monnier, 1912–1979.

Parsons, Mikeal C., and Richard I. Pervo. *Rethinking the Unity of Luke and Acts*. Minneapolis: Fortress, 1993.

Pearson, Lionel. *The Early Ionian Historians*. Oxford: Clarendon, 1939.

Pelletier, Andre. *Flavius Josèphe, adaptateur de la Lettre d'Aristée: Une réaction atticisante contre la Koinè*. Limoges: A. Bontemps, 1962.

Penner, Todd. *In Praise of Christian Origins: Stephen and the Hellenists in Lukan Apologetic Historiography*. Emory Studies in Early Christianity 10. New York: T&T Clark, 2004.

Penner, Todd, and Caroline Vander Stichele, eds. *Contextualizing Acts: Lukan Narrative and Greco-Roman Discourse*. SBLSS 20. Atlanta: Society of Biblical Literature, 2003.

Pennington, James W. C. *A Text Book of the Origin and History of the Colored People*. Hartford: L. Skinner, 1841.

Perrin, Norman. "Towards an Interpretation of the Gospel of Mark." Pages 1–78 in *Christology and a Modern Pilgrimage: A Discussion with Norman Perrin*. Edited by Hans Dieter Betz. Claremont: Society of Biblical Literature, 1971.

Pervo, Richard. *Acts: A Commentary*. Hermeneia. Minneapolis: Fortress, 2009.

———. *Profit with Delight: The Literary Genre of the Acts of the Apostles*. Philadelphia: Fortress, 1987.

Pesch, Rudolf. *Die Apostelgeschichte*. EKKNT 5.1–2. Köln: Benziger; Neukirchen-Vluyn: Neukirchener Verlag, 1986.

Pfättisch, Joannes M. "Christus und Sokrates bei Justin." *TQ* 90 (1908): 503–23.

Pilhofer, Peter. *Presbyteron Kreitton: Der Altersbeweis der jüdischen und christlichen Apologeten und seine Vorgeschichte*. WUNT 2.39. Tübingen: Mohr Siebeck, 1990.

Pillai, C. A. Joachim. *Apostolic Interpretation of History: A Commentary on Acts 13:16–41*. Hicksville, NY: Exposition, 1980.

———. *Early Missionary Preaching: A Study of Luke's Report in Acts 13*. Hicksville, NY: Exposition, 1979.

Plümacher, Eckhard. *Lukas als hellenistischer Schriftsteller: Studien zur Apostelgeschichte*. SUNT 9. Göttingen: Vandenhoeck & Ruprecht, 1972.

Plummer, Reinhard. "The Samaritan Pentateuch and the New Testament." *NTS* 22 (1976): 441–43.

Pongratz-Leisten, Beate. "Beros(s)os." *DNP* 2:579–80. Edited by Hubert Cancik and Helmuth Schneider. Stuttgart: Metzler, 1997.

Prete, Benedetto. *La passione e la morte di Gesù nel racconto di Luca*. 2 vols. Studi biblici 112. Brescia: Paideia Editrice, 1996.

Rajak, Tessa. "Dying for the Law: The Martyr's Portrait in Jewish-Greek Literature." Pages 39–67 in *Portraits: Biographical Representation in the Greek and Latin Literature of the Roman Empire*. Edited by Mark J. Edwards and Simon Swain. Oxford: Clarendon, 1997.

———. "The Fourth Book of Maccabees in a Multi-Cultural City." Pages 134–50 in

Jewish and Christian Communal Identities in the Roman World. Edited by Tessa Rajak. Ancient Judaism and Early Christianity 94. Leiden: Brill 2016.

———. "Josephus and the 'Archaeology' of the Jews." *JJS* 33 (1982): 465–77.

Ramsay, William. *St. Paul the Traveler and the Roman Citizen*. New York: Putnam, 1896.

Reeg, Gottfried. *Die Geschichte von den Zehn Märtyrern: Synoptische Edition mit Übersetzung und Einleitung*. TSAJ 10. Tübingen: Mohr Siebeck, 1985.

Reggiani, Clara K. *4 Maccabei*. Commentario, storico ed esegetico all' antico e al Nuovo Testamento, Supplementi 1. Genova: Marietti, 1992.

Reinmuth, Eckart. *Pseudo-Philo und Luka: Studien zum Liber Antiquitatum Biblicarum und seiner Bedeutung für die Interpretation des lukanischen Doppelwerks*. WUNT 74. Tübingen: Mohr Siebeck, 1994.

Rese, Martin. "Die Funktion der alttestamentlichen Zitate und Anspielungen in den Reden der Apostelgeschichte." Pages 61–79 in *Les Actes des Apôtres: Traditions, rédaction, théologie*. Edited by Jacob Kremer. BETL 48. Leuven: Leuven University Press, 1979.

Rhode, Erwin. "Die Quellen des Jamblichus in seiner Biographie des Pythagoras." *Rheinisches Museum für Philologie* 26–27 (1871–1872): 554–76 and 23–61.

Richard, Earl. *Acts 6:1–8:4: The Author's Method of Composition*. SBLDS 41. Missoula, MT: Scholars Press, 1978.

———. "Acts vii: An Investigation of the Samaritan Evidence." *CBQ* 39 (1977): 190–208.

———. "The Polemical Character of the Joseph Episode in Acts 7." *JBL* 98 (1979): 255–67.

Richards, Herbert. "The Hellenica of Xenophon." *The Classical Review* 15 (1901): 197–203.

Riley, Gregory J. "Influence of Thomas Christianity on Luke 12:14 and 5:39." *HTR* 88 (1995): 229–35.

Ringgren, Helmer. "Luke's Use of the Old Testament." *HTR* 79 (1986): 227–35.

Robinson, James M., Paul Hoffmann, and John S. Kloppenborg, eds. *The Critical Edition of Q*. Hermeneia. Minneapolis: Fortress, 2000.

Ronconi, Allessandro. "Exitus illustrium virorum." *RAC* 6 (1966): 1258–68.

Rothschild, Clare K. *Luke-Acts and the Rhetoric of History: An Investigation of Early Christian Historiography*. WUNT 2.175. Tübingen: Mohr Siebeck, 2004.

Rowe, C. Kavin. *World Upside Down: Reading Acts in the Graeco-Roman Age*. Oxford: Oxford University Press, 2009.

Runia, David T. *Philo in Early Christian Literature: A Survey*. CRINT 3.3. Assen: Van Gorcum; Minneapolis: Fortress, 1993.

———. "Polis and Megapolis: Philo and the Founding of Alexandria." *Mnemosyne* 42 (1989): 398–412.

Rusam, Dietrich. *Das Alte Testament bei Lukas.* BZNW 112. Berlin: de Gruyter, 2003.

Russell, Donald A. "*De Imitatione.*" Pages 1–16 in *Creative Imitation and Latin Literature.* Edited by David West and Anthony Woodman. Cambridge: Cambridge University Press, 1979.

Sabbe, Maurita. "The Son of Man Saying in Acts 7,56." Pages 245–49 in *Les Actes des Apôtres: Traditions, rédaction, théologie.* Edited by Jacob Kremer. BETL 48. Leuven: University Press, 1979.

Sacks, Kenneth S. *Diodorus Siculus and the History of the First Century.* Princeton: Princeton University Press, 1990.

———. "The Lesser Proemiums of Diodorus Siculus." *Hermes* 110 (1982): 434–43.

Sandt, Huub van de. "The Quotations in Acts 13,32–52 as a Reflection of Luke's LXX Interpretation." *Bib* 75 (1994): 26–58.

Sawaki, Tomoko. *Analysing Structure in Academic Writing.* Postdisciplinary Studies in Discourse. London: Palgrave Macmillan, 2016.

Scharlemann, Martin H. *Stephen: A Singular Saint.* AnBib 34. Rome: Pontifical Biblical Institute, 1968.

Schäublin, Christoph. "Josephus und die Griechen." *Hermes* 110 (1982): 316–41.

Schmidt, Karl L. "Die literarische Eigenart der Leidensgeschichte Jesu." *Die Christliche Welt* 32 (1918): 114–16. Repr. pages 17–20 in *Redaktion und Theologie des Passionsberichtes nach den Synoptikern.* Edited by M. Limbeck. Wege der Forschung 481. Darmstadt: Wissenschaftliche Buchgesellschaft, 1981.

———. *Der Rahmen der Geschichte Jesu: Literarkritische Untersuchungen zur ältesten Jesusüberlieferung.* Berlin: Trowitsche und Sohn, 1919. Repr., Darmstadt: Wissenschaftliche Buchgesellschaft, 1964.

Schmitt, J. "Kerygma pascal et lecture scripturaire dans l'instruction d'Antioche (Act. 13,22–37)." Pages 155–67 in *Les Actes des Apôtres: Traditions, rédaction, théologie.* Edited by Jacob Kremer. BETL 48. Leuven: Leuven University Press, 1979.

Schneider, Gerhard. *Die Apostelgeschichte.* 2 vols. HThKNT 5.1–2. Freiburg: Herder, 1980–1982.

———. "Stephanus, die Hellenisten und Samaria." Pages 215–40 in *Les Actes des Apôtres: Traditions, rédaction, théologie.* Edited by Jacob Kremer. BETL 48. Leuven: Leuven University Press, 1979.

Schreckenberg, Heinz. *Die christlichen Adversus-Judaeos-Texte und ihr literarisches und historisches Umfeld (1.-11. Jh.).* Europäische Hochschulschriften 23.172. Frankfurt am Main: Peter Lang, 1990.

————. *Die Flavius-Josephus-Tradition in Antike und Mittelalter.* ALGHJ 5. Leiden: Brill, 1972.

————. "Josephus und die christliche Wirkungsgeschichte seines 'Bellum Judaicum.'" *ANRW* 21.2:1106–217. Part 2, *Principat*, 21.2. Edited by Hildegard Temporini and Wolfgang Haase. New York: de Gruyter, 1984.

Schreckenberg, Heinz, and Kurt Schubert. *Jewish Historiography and Iconography in Early and Medieval Christianity.* CRINT 3.2. Minneapolis: Fortress, 1992.

Schröter, Jens, Benjamin A. Edsall, and Joseph Verheyden, eds. *Jews and Christians—Parting Ways in the First Two Centuries CE? Reflections on the Gains and Losses of a Model.* BZNW 253. Berlin: de Gruyter, 2021.

Schürmann, Heinz. *Das Lukasevangelium.* HThKNT 3. Freiburg: Herder, 1969.

————. "Die Dubletten im Lukasevangelium: Ein Beitrag zur Verdeutlichung des lukanischen Redaktionsverfahrens." *ZKT* 75 (1953): 338–45. Repr. pages 272–78 in *Traditionsgeschichtliche Untersuchungen zu den synoptischen Evangelien: Beiträge.* Düsseldorf: Patmos, 1968.

————. "Die Dublettenvermeidungen im Lukasevangelium: Ein Beitrag zur Verdeutlichung des lukanischen Redaktionsverfahrens." *ZKT* 76 (1954): 83–93. Repr. pages 279–89 in *Traditionsgeschichtliche Untersuchungen zu den synoptischen Evangelien: Beiträge.* Düsseldorf: Patmos, 1968.

Schweingruber, F. "Sokrates und Epiktet." *Hermes* 78 (1943): 52–79.

Scobie, Charles H. H. "The Origins and Development of Samaritan Christianity." *NTS* 19 (1973): 390–414.

————. "The Use of Source Material in the Speeches of Acts iii and vii." *NTS* 25 (1978–1979): 399–421.

Scroggs, Robin. "The Earliest Hellenistic Christianity." Pages 176–206 in *Religions in Antiquity: Essays in Memory of Erwin Ramsdell Goodenough.* Edited by Jacob Neusner. SHR 14. Leiden: Brill, 1968.

Seeley, David. *The Noble Death: Graeco-Roman Martyrology and Paul's Concept of Salvation.* JSNTSup 28. Sheffield: JSOT Press, 1990.

Sherwin-White, A. N. *Roman Society and Roman Law in the New Testament.* Oxford: Clarendon, 1963.

Shrimpton, Gordon S. *Theopompus the Historian.* Montreal & Kingston: McGill-Queen's University Press, 1991.

Simon, Marcel. *St. Stephen and the Hellenists in the Primitive Church.* London: Longmans, Green and Co., 1958.

Sinding, Michael. "After Definitions: Genre, Categories, and Cognitive Science." *Genre* 35 (2002): 181–220.

Skinner, Joseph E. *The Invention of Greek Ethnography from Homer to Herodotus.* Oxford: Oxford University Press, 2012.

Sleeman, Matthew. *Geography and the Ascension Narrative in Acts.* SNTSMS 146. Cambridge: Cambridge University Press, 2009.

Soards, Marion L. *The Passion according to Luke: The Special Material of Luke 22.* JSNTSup 14. Sheffield: Sheffield Academic, 1987.

———. *The Speeches in Acts: Their Content, Context, and Concerns.* Louisville: Westminster John Knox, 1994.

Soltau, Wilhelm. "Die Herkunft der Reden in der Apostelgeschichte." *ZNW* 4 (1903): 128–54.

Somers, Margaret R. "The Narrative Constitution of Identity: A Relational and Network Approach." *Theory and Society* 23 (1994): 605–49.

Sordi, Marta. "I caratteri dell'opera storiografica di Senofonte nelle *Elleniche.*" *Athenaeum* 28 (1950): 3–53 and 29 (1951): 273–348.

Spencer, F. Scott. *The Portrait of Philip in Acts: A Study of Roles and Relations.* JSNTSup 67. Sheffield: Sheffield Academic, 1992.

Spilsbury, Paul. "*Contra Apionem* and *Antiquitates Judaicae*: Points of Contact." Pages 348–68 in in *Josephus' "Contra Apionem": Studies in Its Character and Context with a Latin Concordance to the Portion Missing in Greek.* Edited by Louis H. Feldman and John R. Levison. AGJU 34. Leiden: Brill, 1996.

Stanton, Graham N. *Jesus of Nazareth in New Testament Preaching.* SNTSMS 27. Cambridge: Cambridge University Press, 1974.

Steck, Odil H. *Israel und das gewaltsame Geschick der Propheten: Untersuchungen zur Überlieferung des deuteronomistischen Geschichtsbildes im Alten Testament, Spätjudentum und Urchristentum.* WMANT 23. Neukirchen-Vluyn: Neukirchener Verlag, 1967.

Sterling, Gregory E. "The Account of the Jewish Constitution in Josephus's "Contra Apionem": Afterthought or Addition?" Forthcoming.

———. "Explaining Defeat: Polybius and Josephus on the Wars with Rome." Pages 135–51 in *Internationales Josephus-Kolloquium Aarhus 1999.* Edited by J. U. Kalms. Münsteraner Judaistische Studien 6. Münster: LIT, 2000.

———. *Historiography and Self-Definition: Josephos, Luke-Acts and Apologetic Historiography.* NovTSup 64. Leiden: Brill, 1992. Repr., Atlanta: Society of Biblical Literature, 2006.

———. "A Human *Sui Generis*: The Structure and Composition of Philo's *De vita Moysis.*" *JJS* (forthcoming).

———. "Hypothetica." Pages 2501–22 in *Outside the Bible.* Edited by Louis Feldman, James Kugel, and Lawrence H. Schiffman. 3 vols. Lincoln: University of Nebraska Press; Philadelphia: Jewish Publication Societyof America, 2013.

———. "Monotheism as an Identity Norm: Philo of Alexandria on Community Identity." Pages 245–64 in *A Question of Identity: Formation, Transition,*

Negotiation. Edited by Noah Hachem and Lilach Sagiv. Berlin: de Gruyter, 2019.

———. "'The Most Ancient and Reliable Record of the Past': The Jewish Appropriation of Hellenistic Historiography." Pages 231–43 in *Companion to Greek and Roman Historiography*. Edited by John Marincola. Oxford: Blackwell, 2007.

———. "'Opening the Scriptures': The Legitimation of the Jewish Diaspora and the Early Christian Mission." Pages 199–225 in *Jesus and the Heritage of Israel: Luke's Narrative Claim upon Israel's Legacy*. Edited by David P. Moessner. Harrisburg, PA: Trinity, 1999.

———. "Philo and the Logic of Apologetics: An Analysis of the *Hypothetica*." Pages 412–30 in *Society of Biblical Literature 1990 Seminar Papers*. SBLSP 29. Atlanta: Scholars Press, 1990.

———. "Philo of Alexandria." Pages 299–316 in *A Guide to Early Jewish Texts and Traditions in Christian Transmission*. Edited by Alexander Kulik et al. Oxford: Oxford University Press, 2019.

———. "'Prolific in Expression and Broad in Thought': Internal References to Philo's Allegorical Commentary and Exposition of the Law." *Euphrosyne* 40 (2012): 56–76.

———. "Pseudo-Eupolemus." Pages 705–13 in *Outside the Bible*. Edited by Louis Feldman, James Kugel, and Lawrence H. Schiffman. 3 vols. Lincoln: University of Nebraska Press; Philadelphia: Jewish Publication Society of America, 2013.

———. "Recherché or Representative? What Is the Relationship between Philo's Treatises and Greek-Speaking Judaism?" *SPhiloA* 11 (1999): 1–30.

Stern, Menahem. *Greek and Latin Authors on Jews and Judaism*. 3 vols. Jerusalem: The Israel Academy of Sciences and Humanities, 1974.

Sternbach, Leo. *Gnomologium Vaticanum (e codice Vaticano graeco 743)*. Texte und Kommentare 2. Berlin: de Gruyter, 1963.

Strathmann, H. "Chairemon." *RAC* 2 (1954): 990–93. Edited by Theodor Klausner, Franz Joseph Dölger, Hans Leitzmann, Jan Hendrik Wasznik, and Leopold Wenger. Stuttgart: A. Hiersemann, 1950–2019.

Streeter, Burnett H. *The Four Gospels: A Study in Origins, Treating of the Manuscript Tradition, Sources, Authorship and Dates*. London: Macmillan, 1956.

Stuart Jones, H., and J. E. Powell. *Thucydidis Historiae*. 2 vols. Rev. ed. Oxford: Oxford University Press, 1963.

Surkau, Hans-Werner. *Martyrien in jüdischer und frühchristlicher Zeit*. FRLANT 36. Göttingen: Vandenhoeck & Ruprecht, 1938.

Swales, John M. *Genre Analysis: English in Academic and Research Settings*. Cambridge: Cambridge University Press, 1990.

Sylva, Dennis D. "The Meaning and Function of Acts 7.46–50." *JBL* 106 (1987): 261–75.

———, ed. *Reimaging the Death of the Lukan Jesus.* BBB 73. Frankfurt am Main: Anton Hain, 1990.

Tabb, Brian J. "Is the Lucan Jesus a 'Martyr'? A Critical Assessment of a Scholarly Consensus." *CBQ* 77 (2015): 280–301.

Talbert, Charles H. *Literary Patterns, Theological Themes and the Genre of Luke-Acts.* SBLMS 20. Missoula, MT: Scholars Press, 1974.

———. *Reading Luke: A Literary and Theological Commentary on the Third Gospel.* New York: Crossroad, 1982.

Tannehill, Robert C. "Israel in Luke-Acts: A Tragic Story." *JBL* 104 (1985): 69–85.

Taylor, Joan E. *Jewish Women Philosophers of First-Century Alexandria: Philo's Therapeutae Reconsidered.* Oxford: Oxford University Press, 2003.

Taylor, Joan E., and David M. Hay. *Philo of Alexandria "On the Contemplative Life": Introduction, Translation and Commentary.* PACS 7. Leiden: Brill, 2021.

Taylor, Vincent. *The Passion Narrative of St. Luke: A Critical and Historical Examination.* SNTSMS 19. Cambridge: Cambridge University Press, 1972.

Tcherikover, Victor A., et al. *Corpus Papyrorum Judaicarum.* 4 vols. Turnhout: Brepols, 1957–2020.

Thackeray, Henry St. J. *Josephus: The Man and the Historian.* New York: Jewish Institute of Religion, 1929. Repr., New York: Ktav, 1969.

Thapar, Romila. *A History of India.* Vol. 1. Harmondsworth: Penguin Books, 1966.

Theissen, Gerd. *The Social Setting of Pauline Christianity.* Translated by John H. Schütz. Philadelphia: Fortress, 1982.

Tobin, Thomas, ed. *Timaeus of Locri: On the Nature of the World and the Soul.* SBLTT 26. Chico, CA: Scholars Press, 1985.

Trebilco, Paul. *Self-Designations and Group Identity in the New Testament.* Cambridge: Cambridge University Press, 2012.

Trocmé, Étienne. *The Passion as Liturgy: A Study in the Origin of the Passion Narratives in the Four Gospels.* London: SCM, 1983.

Troiani, Lucio. *Commento storico al "Contro Apione" di Giuseppe.* Biblioteca degli studi classici e orientali 9. Pisa: Giardini, 1977.

Tuplin, Christopher. *The Failings of Empire: A Reading of Xenophon Hellenica 2.3.11–7.5.27.* Historia 76. Stuttgart: Franz Steiner, 1993.

Turner, Mark, and Gilles Fauconnier. "A Mechanism of Creativity." *Poetics Today* 20 (1999): 397–418.

Unnik, Willem C. van. "Die Anklange gegen die Apostel in Philippi (Apostelgeschichte xvi 20f)." Pages 374–85 in *Sparsa Collecta: The Collected Essays of*

Willem C. van Unnik. 4 vols. NovTSup 29, 30, 31, 156. Leiden: Brill, 1973–2014.

———. *Tarsus or Jerusalem: The City of Paul's Youth.* London: Epworth, 1962.

Usener, Hermann, ed. *Dionysii Halicarnassensis quae fertur Ars rhetorica.* Leipzig: Teubner, 1895.

Usher, Stephen. "The Style of Dionysius of Halicarnassus in the 'Antiquitates Romanae.'" *ANRW* 30.1:817–38. Part 2, *Principat*, 30.1. Edited by Hildegard Temporini and Wolfgang Haase. New York: de Gruyter, 1987.

Uytanlet, Samson. *Luke-Acts and Jewish Historiography: A Study on the Theology, Literature, and Ideology of Luke-Acts.* WUNT 2.366. Tübingen: Mohr Siebeck, 2014.

VanderKam, James C. *From Joshua to Caiaphas: High Priests after the Exile.* Minneapolis: Fortress; Assen: Van Gorcum, 2004.

Vander Waerdt, Paul A., ed. *The Socratic Movement.* Ithaca: Cornell University Press, 1994.

van Henten, Jan Willem. *The Maccabean Martyrs as Saviours of the Jewish People: A Study of 2 and 4 Maccabees.* JSJSup 57. Leiden: Brill, 1997.

———. "The Martyrs as Heroes of the Christian People: Some Remarks on the Continuity of Jewish and Christian Martyrology, with Pagan Analogies." Pages 304–22 in *Martyrium in Multidisciplinary Perspective: Memorial Louis Reekmans.* Edited by M. Lamberigts and P. van Deun. Leuven: Leuven University Press, 1995.

van Henten, Jan Willem, and Friedrich Avemarie. *Martyrdom and Noble Death: Selected Texts from Graceo-Roman, Jewish and Christian Antiquity.* London: Routledge, 2002.

van Henten, Jan Willem, B. A. G. M. Dehandshutter, and H. J. W. van der Klaauw, eds. *Die Entstehung der jüdischen Martyrologie.* StPB 38. Leiden: Brill, 1989.

Vannicelli, Pietro. "Herodotus' Egypt and the Foundations of Universal History." Pages 211–40 in *The Historian's Craft in the Age of Herodotus.* Edited by N. Luraghi. Oxford: Oxford University Press, 2001.

Verheyden, Joseph, ed. *The Unity of Luke-Acts.* BETL 142. Leuven: Leuven University Press, 1999.

———. "The Unity of Luke-Acts—One Work, One Author, One Purpose?" Paper presented at the Annual Meeting of the Society for New Testament Studies. Pretoria, South Africa, August 2017.

Vermes, Geza, and Martin D. Goodman. *The Essenes according to the Classical Sources.* Oxford Centre Textbooks 1. Sheffield: JSOT Press, 1989.

Versnel, H. S. "'Quid Athenis et Hierosolymis?' Bemerkungen über die Herkunft von Aspekten des 'Effective Death.'" Pages 162–96 in *Die Entstehung der jüdischen Martyrologie*. Edited by Jan Willem van Henten, B. A. G. M. De-handshutter, and H. J. W. van der Klaauw. StPB 38. Leiden: Brill, 1989.

Vielhauer, Philipp. "On the 'Paulinism' of Acts." Pages 33–50 in *Studies in Luke-Acts*. Edited by Leander E. Keck and Louis Martyn. Philadelphia: Fortress, 1966.

Vonder Bruegge, John M. *Mapping Galilee in Josephus, Luke, and John: Critical Geography and the Construction of an Ancient Space*. AGJU 93. Leiden: Brill, 2016.

Wacholder, Ben Z. "Biblical Chronology in the Hellenistic World Chronicles." *HTR* 61 (1968): 451–81.

Walasky, Paul W. *"And So We Came to Rome": The Political Perspective of St. Luke*. SNTSMS 49. Cambridge: Cambridge University Press, 1983.

Walbank, Frank W. *A Historical Commentary on Polybius*. 3 vols. Oxford: Oxford University Press, 1956–1979.

———. *Polybius*. The Sather Classical Lectures 42. Berkeley: University of California Press, 1972.

Walter, Nikolaus. *Fragmente jüdisch-hellenistischer Historiker*. 2nd ed. JSHRZ 1.2. Gütersloh: Gerd Mohn, 1980.

———. "Jüdisch-hellenistische Literatur vor Philo von Alexandrien (unter Ausschluß der Historiker)." *ANRW* 20.1:67–120. Part 2, *Principat*, 20.1. Edited by Hildegard Temporini and Wolfgang Haase. New York: de Gruyter, 1987.

Walters, Patricia. *The Assumed Authorial Unity of Luke and Acts: A Reassessment of the Evidence*. SNTSMS 145. Cambridge: Cambridge University Press, 2009.

Weber, Beat. "Psalm 78: Geschichte mit Geschichte deuten." *TZ* 56 (2000): 193–214.

Wehrli, Fritz. *Die Schule des Aristoteles: Texte und Kommentar, Supplementband 1: Hermippos der Kallimacheer*. Basel: Schwabe, 1974.

Weinert, Francis D. "Luke, Stephen, and the Temple in Luke-Acts." *BTB* 17 (1987): 88–90.

Weintraub, Katy O'Brien. "O Sancte Socrate, Ora pro Nobis: Erasmsus on the Problem of Athens and Jerusalem." Pages 259–70 in *Cultural Visions: Essays in the History of Culture*. Edited by Penny Schine Gold and Benjamin C. Sax. Internationale Forschungen zur Allgemeinen und Vergleichenden Literaturwissenschaft 41. Amsterdam: Rodopi, 2000.

Weiss, Johannes. *Über die Absicht und den literarischen Character der Apostelgeschichte*. Göttingen: Vandenhoeck & Ruprecht, 1897.

Wengst, Klaus. *Pax Romana and the Peace of Jesus Christ*. Philadelphia: Fortress, 1987.

Westerink, Leendert G. *The Greek Commentaries on Plato's Phaedo*. 2 vols. Verhandelingen der Koninklijke Nederlandse Akademie van Wetenschappen,

Afd. Letterkunde, Nieuwe Reeks, deel 92. Amsterdam: North Holland Publishing, 1976.

Wettstein, Johann J. *Novum Testamentum Graecum*. 2 vols. Amsterdam: Dommerian, 1751–1752.

Whittaker, Molly. *Jews and Christians: Graeco-Roman Views*. Cambridge Commentaries on Writings of the Jewish and Christian World 200 BC to AD 200. Cambridge: Cambridge University Press, 1984.

Wilken, Robert L. *The Christians as Romans Saw Them*. New Haven: Yale University Press, 1984.

———. *The Myth of Christian Beginnings*. Notre Dame: University of Notre Dame Press, 1971.

Wilckens, Ulrich. *Die Missionsreden der Apostelgeschichte: Form- und traditionsgeschichtliche Untersuchungen*. 3rd ed. WMANT 5. Neukirchen-Vluyn: Neukirchener Verlag, 1974.

Wilson, N. G. *Herodoti Historiae*. 2 vols. OCT. Oxford: Clarendon, 2015.

Wolf, Friedrich A. *Prolegomena ad Homerum, sive, De operum Homericorum: Prisca et genuine forma variisque mutationibus et probabilii ratione emendandi*. Halis Saxonum: E. Libraria Orphaotrophei, 1795. Repr., *Prolegomena to Homer*. Princeton: Princeton University Press, 1985.

Wolfson, Henry A. *Philo: Foundations of Religious Philosophy in Judaism, Christianity, and Islam*. 2 vols. Cambridge: Harvard University Press, 1947.

Wright, Benjamin G., III. "Joining the Club: A Suggestion about Genre in Early Jewish Texts." *DSD* 17 (2010): 289–314.

Young, Robin Darling. "The 'Woman with the Soul of Abraham': Traditions about the Mother of the Maccabean Martyrs." Pages 67–81 in *"Women Like This": New Perspectives on Jewish Women in the Graeco-Roman World*. Edited by Amy-Jill Levine. EJL 1. Atlanta: Scholars Press, 1991.

Zimmerman, Heinrich. "Die Sammelberichte der Apostlegeschichte." *BZ* 5 (1961): 71–82.

Index of Authors

Index of Subjects

Abraham, 28, 35, 75, 109, 113–18, 120–23, 125, 128
Acts: in relation to Luke, 64–66, 68, 72–76, 99, 111, 192–94, 206–7, 217, 223, 230; in Scripture, 23–24, 72–73, 75, 108, 112, 119–23, 125–27, 129, 138–39, 143, 145, 147–53, 181, 183, 187, 189, 193, 203–4, 206, 217–18, 221–22, 224, 226–27, 231; structure and style of, 23, 38, 63, 65–66, 68, 73–75, 99, 102, 108–9, 111, 120–21, 123–24, 126–28, 138, 143, 148, 150, 154, 180, 187–89, 195–98, 203, 205–9, 219–20, 223
Aegyptiaca, 18, 50–51, 56, 58, 62
Alexander the Great, 18, 95
Anaxarchus of Abdera, 164–66
Apuleius, 220, 225
Aristides, Aelius, 220
Arrian, 196–97, 199–200
Artapanus, 29, 117–19, 123–24, 139
audience, 36, 38–39, 96, 105, 119, 138–39, 142, 207, 229, 232

Babylon, 20, 48, 52, 54–56, 58, 230
Babyloniaca, 52–53, 62
Berrosus, 44, 45, 49, 52, 53, 55, 56, 57, 58, 90

Celsus, 161, 213, 215, 220, 225
Chaeremon, 50, 55, 197, 199–200, 204, 207

Christian Antiquities, 33, 35, 105
Christianity: in relation to Judaism, 21, 33, 36, 40, 104–5, 128, 153, 222 (*see also* Judaism); movement of, 21, 23, 26–27, 30, 32–38, 64–65, 78, 104–5, 108, 126, 128, 153, 161, 182, 187, 194, 209, 212–13, 219–20, 222, 223; terms and values within, 24, 228
Christians: authors, 15–16, 21, 25, 33, 38, 62–63, 90, 96, 139, 162, 176, 227; Jewish-Christian, 21, 96, 110 (*see also* Judaism); mission of, 124, 126–29; as a people, 17, 23–27, 34–36, 38–40, 66–67, 73–75, 99, 104–5, 126, 145, 153, 161, 163, 167, 170–71, 180–82, 187, 208–9, 211–20, 223–26, 228, 232
Clement of Alexandria, 15, 26, 229
Clement of Rome, 15
Cleodemus Malchus, 113, 117–18, 139

David, 24, 141–45, 147–48, 153
diaspora, 91, 108, 112–13, 119, 122, 124, 129, 138, 229
Dionysius of Athens, 218

Egypt, 18, 20, 28–29, 44–45, 48–52, 55–56, 58, 63, 108, 116–19, 121–25, 128–29, 138, 197, 203–8, 227, 230
Epiphanius, 225
Erasmus of Rotterdam, 162, 182
Eupolemus, 29, 115–16

Index of Scripture and Other Ancient Sources